D1325251

Death Valley to Yosemite:

Frontier Mining Camps & Ghost Towns

THE MEN, THE WOMEN, THEIR MINES & STORIES

The Greenwater and Death Valley Mining Company, Greenwater, Death Valley.
(Photograph by Larson, Nevada Historical Society)

Death Valley to Yosemite:

Frontier Mining Camps & Ghost Towns

THE MEN, THE WOMEN, THEIR MINES & STORIES

BY L. BURR BELDEN & MARY DEDECKER
EDITED BY WYNNE BENTI

Spotted Dog Press, Inc. • Bishop, California

Death Valley to Yosemite: Frontier Mining Camps &
Ghost Towns –
The Men, The Women, Their Mines & Stories
By L. Burr Belden & Mary DeDecker
Comprising the books:
Mines of Death Valley & Mines of the Eastern Sierra

SPOTTED
DOG PRESS®

© 2005 Spotted Dog Press, Inc.
All rights reserved.
Published exclusively by Spotted Dog Press, Inc.
Bishop, California

Spotted Dog Press, Inc.
ISBN-13: 978-0-9647530-8-1
ISBN-10: 0-9647530-8-1
  3 4 5 6 7 8

Cover photographs: A rare photograph of a woman in a turn of the century
mining camp, north of Death Valley (Nevada Historical Society). Background
photograph of the Reward Mine (Eastern California Museum).

"Panamint Annie" & "Dangers In and Around Mines" ©1998 by Wynne Benti
Maps, book design, and layout by Spotted Dog Press, Inc.

Library of Congress Cataloging-in-Publication Data
Belden, L. Burr.
    Death Valley to Yosemite: Frontier Mining Camps & Ghost Towns –
The Men, The Women, Their Mines & Stories / by L. Burr Belden & Mary DeDecker:
edited by Wynne Benti. — 1st ed.
    p. cm.
    "Comprising the books Mines of Death Valley [by L. Burr Belden, 1966] & Mines
of the Eastern Sierra [by Mary DeDecker, 1966]" — T.p. version.
    New chapters have been added to both works.
    Includes bibliographical references and index.
    ISBN 0-9647530-8-1 (alk. paper)
    1. Gold mines and mining — California — Mono County — History.
    2. Gold mines and mining — California — Inyo County — History. 3. Mono
County (Calif.) — Gold discoveries. 4. Inyo County (Calif.) — Gold discoveries.
I. DeDecker, Mary. II. Benti, Wynne. III. Belden, L. Burr. Mines of Death Valley.
IV. DeDecker, Mary. Mines of the Eastern Sierra. V. Title.
    TN423.C2B45 1998
    979. 4'87 — dc21   98-37278
                                                            CIP

Printed in the United States of America

Acknowledgments

Many years ago, when asked who could write a book about the mines of the eastern Sierra, L. Burr Belden, Death Valley historian and editor for the San Bernardino Sun-Telegram newspaper suggested Mary DeDecker, longtime resident of Independence, California. So it seems only fitting that their independently written books, *Mines of Death Valley* and *Mines of the Eastern Sierra*, should be combined together in one complete work that covers both Inyo and Mono Counties, from Death Valley to Dogtown, just north of Yosemite.

Spotted Dog Press, Inc. would like to thank author Mary DeDecker for her insights into Inyo County life and history, and: Corky Hays, Chief of Interpretation, Death Valley National Park; Lee Brumbaugh, Curator of Photography, Nevada Historical Society; Blair Davenport, Museum Curator, Death Valley National Park; Bill Michael, Director of the Eastern California Museum, Inyo County; and Kari Coughlin, Interpretive Ranger at Manzanar National Historic Site; Ella Power Wheelock; and geologist and mining historian, Andy Zdon.

Spotted Dog Press, Inc. would like to acknowledge the late Walt Wheelock, our friend and the original publisher of *Mines of Death Valley* and *Mines of the Eastern Sierra*. It was his wish before he passed away in 1997, that Spotted Dog Press, Inc. carry on the tradition of La Siesta Press. We wish Walt was here today. We know he would be proud.

Borax Smith's famous mule team. Smith was a pioneer in western borax mining. The rock ruins of his first store still stand on the north side of Teel's Salt Marsh in what is now the Marietta Wild Burro Range, Nevada. (Nevada Historical Society)

CONTENTS

13   FOREWORD

16   IT STARTED IN 1849

19   PANAMINT ANNIE
THE WOMEN STAKED THEIR CLAIMS

22   SALT SPRING
THE FIRST MINE

27   THE GUNSIGHT
AND GUNSIGHTERS

31   PANAMINT
SENATORS RESCUE BANDITS

37   VISITING PANAMINT CITY TODAY

41   BREYFOGLE
INDIAN CAPTIVE

46   CHLORIDE CLIFF
THE FIRST ROAD

50   WINGATE PASS
SCOTTY FOOLS THEM ALL

57   GREENWATER
AND DIAMOND LIL

64   BULLFROG
SHORTY LIKED TO TALK

73   SKIDOO
HE WAS HANGED TWICE

78   ASHFORD MILL
THE FORT

83   JEAN LE MOIGNE
AND HIS BANK

87   HANAUPAH
THE BURRO WORE A BATHROBE

94   AGUERREBERRY
AND HARRISBURG

97 GREATER VIEW
WOODEN LEG MONUMENT

101 LATER DAYS
TALC, LEAD, EPSOM SALTS

111 THE HIGH SIERRA RUSH

117 COSO
ANCIENT HOT SPRINGS

122 CERRO GORDO
LAWLESS COMSTOCK EAST OF THE SIERRA

135 RUSS & INYO DISTRICTS
PIONEERING THE OWENS RIVER VALLEY

145 BEVERIDGE
HIGH IN THE INYO MOUNTAINS

149 KEARSARGE
NAMED FOR A CIVIL WAR BATTLESHIP

154 HOMER DISTRICT
MINING AT 12,000 FEET

159 TIOGA
A SHEPHERD FINDS GOLD

162 PRESCOTT
ALONG THE MONO TRAIL

165 BENTON
BLIND SPRING, WHITE PEAK,
INDIAN & CLOVER PATCH DISTRICTS

170 LAKE DISTRICT
MAMMOTH LAKES

176 DOGTOWN & MONOVILLE
LIQUOR STORES OUTNUMBERED HOMES

178 DANGERS IN AND AROUND MINES
TRAVELING SAFELY • EXPLOSIVES • SHAFTS, CAVE-INS,
& TIMBER • WATER & "BAD AIR" • FLASH FLOODS &
WASH OUTS • RATTLESNAKES, SCORPIONS & OTHER
CREATURES • A WORD ABOUT ARTIFACTS

185 SUGGESTED READING & REFERENCES

188 INDEX

Death Valley

Through the eerie silence of Death Valley,
a treasure seeker leads a couple of burros past
corrugated tawny hills and undulating dunes
toward the sandy plain…
From the Arctic Circle to the Mexican border,
the prospector's world is a remote wilderness,
and the prospector an insignificant speck
dwarfed by its immensity.

A Mine of Her Own
Women Prospectors in the American West, 1850-1950
Sally Zanjani

Mrs. Bennett and Mrs. Arcan were in

heart-rending distress.

The four children were crying for water

but there was not a drop to give them, and none could be

reached before some time next day.

The mothers were nearly crazy, for they expected

the children would choke with thirst

and die in their arms...

For the love of gold they had left their homes

where hunger had never come...

Death Valley in '49
William Manly

MILLIONS
== ARE BURIED IN THE ==
FUNERAL RANGE

DEATH VALLEY
== IS A GREAT ==
TREASURE TROVE

TOMBSTONES are not very numerous in this deathlike country, but monuments marking the greatest prospective **copper mines** in the world are scattered over these **desert mountains** for a distance of **fifty miles.** We have secured the exclusive right to sell the only RELIEF MAP of the great GREENWATER MINING DISTRICT made, showing a panoramic view of the entire district, and giving the relative locations of all the incorporated mining properties. The map is worth a fortune to any investor who wishes to become acquainted with the district, and cannot visit Greenwater. It is the best guide that a visitor to the district can secure. We will send the map to any address for **$2.00.**

The Mining Advertising Agency
Greenwater, California

The Death Valley Chuck-Walla (Zdon Collection)

FOREWORD
BY WYNNE BENTI

A raven flies from the mountains of blue-gray granite and delicate alpine flowers across the valley, to the magnificent desert of creosote and alkali, where the color of sage, pale indigo and purple swirl together as the land meets the sky. From the highest point in the contiguous United States (14,496') to the lowest point (-282') in the Western Hemisphere, the raven flies in a matter of hours.

A miner sits in the shade of a tunnel scratched from the side of a steep ridge. He eats his lunch — a tin of meat with a bottle of water to wash it down. He wipes his fingers on his pants which haven't seen soap since he bought them. He wonders — how does a man live in this place during the summer? Water must be carried in on the back of a burro. The temperatures, which stay well above 100°, no doubt can burn the shirt right off a man's back. The miner looks up, and sees the raven with wings outstretched, riding a current of air on the warm wind above.

When Death Valley was first set aside as a National Monument in 1933, "for the preservation of the unusual features of scenic, scientific, and educational interest," an exception was made to allow prospecting and mining to continue within its borders. There is no doubt that the National Park Service, Congress, and President Herbert Hoover had in mind the "single blanket jackass miner" who prowled and prospected. He dug with pick and shovel, and *his or her* "gopher holes" had little impact upon the land.

His or hers you ask? When the railroads had not yet been built and grizzlies still foraged in the Sierra Nevada, a woman traveled to the western territories one of three ways — she came by wagon with

her family and friends; she made the treacherous, long trip by boat
around Cape Horn of South America; or she rode her horse across
the prairie and mountains. Women went west as wives, teachers,
missionaries, housekeepers, and prostitutes. There were not many
occupations which society considered suitable for a woman. In
fact, before the 20th century, it was very difficult for a woman to
live independently or raise children on her own once her husband
died. Proper "ladies" married and subsequently, were dependent
upon their husbands, their fathers, or their sons for support.

Movement west to the new territories dramatically changed
this. Survival demanded that the laws of the east and the dictates
of polite society be cast aside. With survival, came independence.
With the discovery of gold on the west side of California's Sierra
Nevada in 1849, the stories spread like wildfire across the continent while the prospectors staked their claims across the mountain
range, east to the deserts of the Great Basin and Mojave. The idea
that nuggets of gold could be picked up off the ground was inspiration enough for people to bid farewell to the green rolling farm-
lands and warm hearths of home to head west. The California gold
rush, followed fifty years later by its Canadian counterpart in the
Yukon Territory, saw both men and women head for the goldfields.

When sodium borate, with its ease of processing, was discovered
near the town of Mojave, it marked the end for Death Valley borax,
which was the last mineral of import mined in the valley.

However, with the development of fiberglass, colemanite was again in demand. Soon, vast tailings piles appeared on the hillsides, and claim markers were scattered across Zabriskie Point, one of Death Valley's most scenic overlooks, while a huge open-pit mine began operating in Furnace Creek Wash near Ryan. The mining company responsible requested another permit to mine a short distance from Dante's view. When the California Desert Protection Act was signed into law in 1994, future mining activity was stopped, while the new Death Valley National Park boundaries were drawn specifically to exclude current large-scale mining operations. All that remained of recent projects within park boundaries, were a few small to medium size sites in the process of reclamation.

Not even a hundred miles to the west, miners toiled on the steep inclines of the eastern Sierra Nevada, at elevations of 10,000 feet or more. These mining towns had their own brand of stories, which have been recorded in this work by longtime Inyo County resident, historian, and native plant botanist, Mary DeDecker.

In stark contrast to the rigors of life in Death Valley, water and food sources were a constant during Sierra summers. Winters were long, harsh, and brought deep snow, which drifted above rooftops. With plenty of wood, stored supplies, a winter could be survived quite comfortably within the confines of one's cabin. The biggest threat to life in the camps during winter were the thunderous avalanches, which rolled off the steep slopes without warning.

The old mining camps are quiet now. When the gold vanished, so did the people, leaving behind empty towns. Some places were so remote and isolated that one wonders how people lived there at all. Magnificent brick and wood buildings were knocked down, their materials carted off to build other towns. Nature may have reclaimed their old camps, but the pioneers won't be forgotten — a deed recorded on a county ledger, or a photograph in a museum archive, the towns that died, and those that lived — their mark was indelibly left on the last great frontier.

IT STARTED IN 1849

Gold!

A paying vein of gold that continued to yield for some 115 years was found in California's Mojave Desert in 1849, nearly 450 miles from the celebrated Coloma discovery made by John Marshall. Simultaneously, in the same region, a piece of silver float triggered the initial prospector rush to Death Valley — the land with the forbidding name.

Between the Argonauts of 1849 and the final years of mining claim filings during World War II, thousands of single-blanket jackass prospectors and their burros picked and kicked the uncounted rock formations from Cave Springs north to Oriental Wash and from Ash Meadows west to Panamint Valley.

Some struck it rich. More failed. All gave their bit to the writing of one of the West's most fabulous chapters of history. Today, ruins of mills, rusted dump cars and sagging headframes faithfully mark the spots of yesteryear's bonanzas.

It is not our purpose to chronicle the troy weight of bullion recovered from the World Beater, the Tizzie or the Dublin Colleen. Rather, the writer seeks to reveal the human side of this ever-optimistic breed of rainbow chasers, and preserve for today and tomorrow a bit of the "you were there" feeling that must come from learning of the doings and adventures of these all-but-forgotten men.

This might be rightly termed a story that has take 43 years to compile, for the writer's first Death Valley trip was back in 1923 when he heard some of the "impossible but true" accounts of how the area's mines and boom camps originated. A burro strays — its owner finds the critter chomping grass over a rich outcropping of gold. A weary traveler beds down but can't sleep because a rock keeps punching his back. Morning discloses a fine gold vein. Stage robbers hide out from the law in a remote canyon, and find themselves millionaires when pecking at rocks for amusement. A prospector picks up a likely looking piece of float and then spends half a day squinting around to find correctly its true source. Another becomes intrigued with an abandoned Indian camp only to find a rich silver-lead vein. Green-stained rocks around a mountain spring lead to the discovery of copper ore. A party of travelers gets lost when clouds drop so low they obliterate a mountain trail. Dawn reveals scores of gold-bearing rocks bordering their blankets.

Such oddities are true stories that tell the start of famous strikes in the Death Valley region, stories recounted over the years by members of the dwindling fraternity of pack-and-pick men who grubbed at Skidoo, sank shafts at Harrisburg, and lived it up in Ballarat.

L. Burr Belden

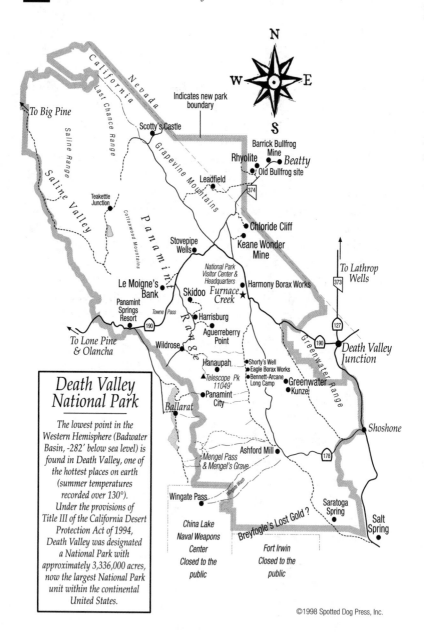

N
W E
S

Indicates new park boundary

To Big Pine

California
Nevada
Last Chance Range
Saline Range
Saline Valley
Grapevine Mountains
Cottonwood Mountains
Panamint
Range

Scotty's Castle

Barrick Bullfrog Mine
Rhyolite • • *Beatty*
• Old Bullfrog site
Leadfield
374

Teakettle Junction

Chloride Cliff
Keane Wonder Mine

Stovepipe Wells •

National Park Visitor Center & Headquarters
Harmony Borax Works
To Lathrop Wells
373

Le Moigne's Bank •
Skidoo •
Furnace Creek ★

Panamint Springs Resort •
Towne Pass
190
Harrisburg •
Aguerreberry Point •

To Lone Pine & Olancha
Wildrose •
127
Hanaupah •
Shorty's Well •
Eagle Borax Works •
Bennett-Arcane •
Long Camp •
Greenwater •
Kunze •
▲ Telescope Pk 11049'
• Panamint City
Greenwater Range
190
Death Valley Junction

Ballarat

Shoshone

Mengel Pass & Mengel's Grave
Ashford Mill •
178

Wingate Wash

Wingate Pass
Saratoga Spring
Salt Spring

Breyfogle's Lost Gold?

China Lake
Naval Weapons
Center
Closed to the
public

Fort Irwin
Closed to the
public

Death Valley National Park

The lowest point in the Western Hemisphere (Badwater Basin, -282' below sea level) is found in Death Valley, one of the hottest places on earth (summer temperatures recorded over 130°). Under the provisions of Title III of the California Desert Protection Act of 1994, Death Valley was designated a National Park with approximately 3,336,000 acres, now the largest National Park unit within the continental United States.

PANAMINT ANNIE
THE WOMEN STAKED THEIR CLAIMS

IN 1838, MARY RICHARDSON was one of the first women of European descent to go west, not as a miner, but as a missionary, riding nearly 2,300 miles across the continent on a horse, side-saddle. Nearly twenty years after Mary Richardson crossed the Rocky Mountains, the first mining claims were recorded in women's names, perhaps by relatives, or very possibly, by themselves.

However, it wasn't until the mid-1870's when the first women, Nellie Cashman and Ferminia Sarras, emerged from the history records, making a name for themselves, and a living, as miners. They staked their claims and traveled across the west looking for the strike that would make them rich. Nellie Cashman prospected from Pioche, Nevada to the Klondike while Ferminia Sarras' home base was located in Metallic City, in the Candaleria Hills of western Nevada (as a result of the "second" Nevada mining boom, Metallic City was mined out by the Kinross-Candaleria Mining Company during the 1980's, and no longer exists).

Following the Klondike discovery, the number of women who went to the goldfields steadily increased. From Death Valley to the Arctic Circle, they were staking their claims. They worked alongside or partnered with men, many of whom were either impressed with, or curious as to why, a woman would leave behind the comforts of home and marriage to engage in such a rough profession. The fact was, that mining made it possible for women to be independent. They could support themselves financially by operating their own business without having to resort to prostitution or housekeeping — far away from a society that still denied them the right to vote.

Mining camp northeast of Death Valley. (Nevada Historical Society)

Many women miners found that it was more comfortable to wear men's clothes while working their prospects than the restrictive high-heeled boots and ankle-length dresses of the time. A woman found that by dressing as a man she was usually mistaken for a man by men, which had its advantages in the rough and violent days of the old mining camps. During the latter part of the nineteenth century, on either coast, a woman could be arrested for wearing pants, which were considered strictly men's clothing — to be worn only by men.

In the late 1890's, bored by life as an actress on Broadway, one Lillian Malcolm decided to leave New York behind, for the gold-fields of Dawson Creek in the Yukon Territory. By her own account, she went to the Yukon, singlehandedly crossed the Chilkoot Trail with the required 1,000 pounds of provisions, and made it 500 miles down the Yukon River to the Klondike goldfields. Soon after, she went south to California, where she roamed the hills of Death Valley with Shorty Harris. Later, she hooked up with Bill Keys, and the two were rumored to be more than just friends. When he was arrested for ambushing two investors at Wingate Wash during a sensational scheme devised by Death Valley Scotty (described later in the chapter "Wingate Wash"), it was Lillian who put up the money for Keys' legal defense.

Mary White first came to Death Valley in 1931 at the age of twenty, hoping to find a cure for her tuberculosis. She stayed at the southern end of the valley at Shoshone where the hot springs and dry desert air did her young lungs good. She recovered and attempted to find work. Before coming west, she had cooked on dude ranches, but with few restaurants or ranches in that lonesome expanse of big country, she decided to try her hand at mining. She staked her claims from the south end of the valley, to the high ridges of the Panamint Mountains to the west. She lived on the land with a group of prospectors — her "family," who shared camp chores and living arrangements, on a purely platonic basis.

Mary reminded the old-timers of another Death Valley woman prospector, who they had affectionately nicknamed "Panamint Annie." Soon, they started calling Mary by her vanished predecessor's nickname, a name which stayed with her for the rest of her life.

One of Annie's daughters recalled living with her mother and her mining family on the high ridges of the Panamints, in an oral history given to Death Valley National Park Ranger Kari Coughlin. It was the height of the depression and mining in the Panamints was as good a way to make a living as any other. Annie made quite a few good strikes, but the money was usually spent quickly paying off debts and boarding school tuition (she didn't want her children growing up around the mining camps, so she sent them away to school).

Panamint Annie became quite a legendary figure in Death Valley while she was alive. She spent her entire life there, prospecting her claims, raising her children and living the life of a hard rock miner, determined and independent. When she died in 1979, she was buried in a small cemetery at the long-abandoned ghost town of Rhyolite, beneath the vast blue sky in the desert she loved so much.

SALT SPRING
THE FIRST MINE

THE OLD SPANISH TRAIL, a pack route connecting northern Mexican outposts of Santa Fe and Los Angeles, was opened in the 1830's. Based in part on the earlier explorations of Father Garcés at the west, and Escalante at the east, this route described a vast irregular arc with an apex far up in Utah. A more direct westerly extension of the famed Santa Fe Trail was desired, but blocked temporarily by Indian hostility in northern Arizona. Simultaneously, with Mexican War of 1846 which saw the United States taking what approximates the present states of New Mexico, Arizona, California, Nevada and Utah, the Latter Day Saints — followers of the teachings of Joseph Smith — were driven from their "Zion" at Nauvoo, Illinois. Under the leadership of Brigham Young, they headed west for an undecided location remote enough to escape religious persecution.

While en route to the west, this deeply religious migration was visited by United States Army representatives who sought to enlist a battalion of volunteers for war service. President Young of the Mormon Church saw the occasion as an opportunity both to achieve an informal armistice with the government and to relieve the great financial burden of the migration. The battalion was formed and headed toward Santa Fe. Then it was divided, with the less physically fit turning to join the church's migration while the others, under the command of Lieutenant Colonel Philip St. George Cooke headed for California and broke out a crude wagon road in the process. When the Mormon battalion arrived in Los Angeles, they erected Fort Moore, guarded the Cajon Pass against Walkara's horse raiders, and even aided Colonel Isaac Williams' crop harvesting at Santa Ana del Chino.

When the Mormon soldiers were paid, they dutifully turned a tenth, or "tithe," of pay over to the church and forwarded much of the remainder to their families who had ended their westward trek to found "Deseret" in the valley of the Great Salt Lake. The church messengers utilized the Old Spanish Trail, and its new branch to Salt Lake, for repeated trips back and forth between Deseret and southern California. As battalion enlistments were nearing their expiration, the Army proposed second hitches for those desiring. Captain Jefferson Hunt was placed in command of the battalion. He went to Salt Lake City to confer with President Young, and returned with word that the church needed young men to help build the "new Zion." As a result, the battalion was mustered out of service.

The returning soldiers filled a wagon with grape cuttings, seed, fruit, grain and other supplies. They brought the wagon through Cajon Pass and over the desert, thus proving that the Spanish Trail was adaptable to wheeled vehicles.

The year of 1849 witnessed what must have seemed to settlers in pioneer Salt Lake City as the migration of "half the world" — all bound for the California gold fields. So heavy was the traffic, that there were those who worried that food supplies might give out in Deseret before the 1850 harvest. When some 500 Argonauts arrived too late in the season to chance a crossing of the Sierra Nevada before the deep snows of winter, the Mormon leaders proposed that these groups continue their journey by the longer route, the Spanish Trail, which was safe in winter. Captain Hunt had made three trips over the trail, and was available as a guide. The Sand Walking Company was organized and started southwestward.

The dissension within and ultimate division of this caravan near Enterprise, Utah is recounted in the next chapter. The dissenters formed the famous ill-fated Death Valley party. The others, who remained with Captain Hunt, continued over the regular trail and arrived in southern California in time for their Christmas dinner at Santa Ana del Chino.

The old trail entered California from Pahrump Valley with a stop at Resting Spring where there was pure water in sufficient abundance to fill casks for the desert ahead. After Resting Spring, the trail struck west toward today's Tecopa, then descended the valley of the Amargosa River to its big bend at the southern end of Death Valley. Close to this bend is another oasis with a little pond of brackish water which is named Salt Spring. Beyond this oasis, the trail headed through a rough, waterless stretch that terminated only when the Mojave River was reached — downstream from today's Daggett. The journada was only broken by one hole of vile water called Bitter Spring. Hunt's caravan halted at Salt Spring to check on equipment. Some of the members looked around and found some gold-bearing rock on the hill beside the little lake. The caravan moved onward.

In Los Angeles, the gold samples were exhibited and plans were made for some of the men to go back and start mining. That was January 1850. The Salt Spring gold deposit and other gold veins in the Avawatz Mountains nearby were referred to as "Mormon Diggings" in early maps. Later writers, as is so often the case when remote areas are concerned, changed "Mormon Diggings" to "Lost Mormon Diggins." There is nothing lost about the gold at Salt Spring. It has been mined almost continuously for 115 years. One of the most famous Sublette brothers, Andrew, served as foreman of this mine in the 1850's following an earlier career in the fur trade and the Oregon Battalion.

The original finder of the Salt Spring gold was a Mr. Roan, according to Sublette, who went to the mine in 1851 to represent the Los Angeles Mining Company, of which Benjamin D. Wilson was a founder along with Colonel Williams. The ore was rich but the location was too remote to be attractive. A second mining company, having a claim nearby, was the Desert Mining Company with James F. Hibbard as president. Operating costs were high because of the long hauls. The company was forced to the wall late that summer.

In November of the same year, Benjamin D. Wilson formed the

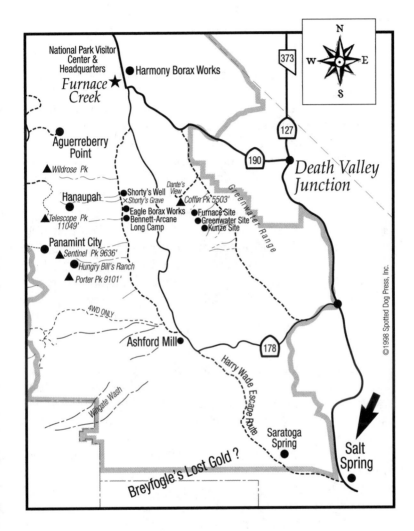

Salt Spring Mining Company, taking over the claims of the two rival companies. It became an on and off again operation. Records indicate they were frequently visited by Indians asking for food.

In the early days of the Civil War, Major James H. Carleton established redoubts at both Bitter Spring and Resting Spring. Things became more peaceful. Then the California volunteers ceased patrolling the trail with the war's end. Paiute Indians filtered down from the north to prey on the trail. The Army sent regulars to patrol the Old Government Road to the south but forgot about the outposts along the Salt Lake Trail. A year after Appomattox, seven miners were at Salt Spring. Indians who were camping at Sheep Spring, overlooking the oasis, began to threaten the miners. One of the miners slipped out and rode 45 miles to the Army's post at Marl Spring, near today's Kelso, to get help. The soldiers arrived too late to save the miners who had in the meantime been killed by the Indians. They dug six graves and laid the miners to rest.

In the 1880's, new machinery was set up by another group of owners, and much gold recovered. It was not until 1902 however, that Salt Spring became a bonanza under the ownership of J.B. Osborn of Daggett. Osborn also operated the Gunsight at Resting Spring, another venerable operation dating back to the 1870's. He also owned the Noonday Mine near Tecopa.

At Salt Spring, Osborn hit a pocket of high grade so rich that he recovered $60,000 in a single week. Thus, in 1907 when the Tonapah & Tidewater built north from Ludlow, Osborn conceived the idea of reaching the Gunsight and the Noonday by rail. He had a route surveyed up the hill from the T&T which wound around like a snake over gullies and ridges. Osborn ordered the road built in a near straight line, reasoning that the ore hauling would be all downhill. On the first trip, it was necessary to lock the brakes. This procedure was repeated on each subsequent trip, thus giving the Tecopa Railroad flat-wheeled cars. W.W. "Wash" Cahill of the T&T, ordered all Tecopa ore reloaded and forbid the use of flat-wheeled cars on T&T rails.

The Tecopa stopped running. In 1942, when Sharpe & Fellows dismantled the T&T to supply scrap-metal for World War II, they tore up the Tecopa as well.

Not even World War II stopped Salt Springs for keeps. In 1960, four miners were working there. Orville Massey, one of the miners, pointed out to the writer the old shafts of the 1850's, the grave sites of the six miners, the workings where Osborn got his $60,000 bonanza, and then displayed some of the rich ore currently being mined from other veins.

THE GUNSIGHT
AND GUNSIGHTERS
— ✳ —

THE PARTY OF ARGONAUTS who headed down the Old Spanish Trail late in 1849 included a sizable group of dissenters who seceded from Captain Jefferson Hunt's guidance near Enterprise, Utah and struck almost due west. En route from Salt Lake to Enterprise, a pack train had temporarily joined in with the Sand Walking Company. This train of traders was headed by a man known to '49ers as Captain O.K. Smith. Captain Smith carried a map which purported to show a short cut to the California mines. It was a Fremont map of the period on which "an old mountain man" had traced a short cut as told to him by the Ute chief Walkara. Walkara was the most celebrated raider among horse thieves who preyed on California's Mexican rancheros prior to the Mexican War. Walkara had driven off horse herds from ranchos as far north as San Luis Obispo and in so doing had blazed a trail from the Cojo District of Tulare County, through Walker Pass, and across the upper Mojave Desert. Walkara had described landmarks as he recalled them. His descriptions had been interpreted as heading west from about Enterprise. In reality, Walkara's turnoff appears to have been far south in the Pahrump Valley near Resting Springs.

The Hunt party split, with the majority of the 50 wagons and some 400 men electing to follow the horsethief's map rather than continue under the leadership of their guide who was making what was at least his third trip over the route. Gold fever does strange things to mens' reason. The Walkara short cut was neither a road nor a trail. Captain Hunt declared it would lead "straight to hell."

He was quite right. It led into the middle of Death Valley. Long before Death Valley was reached, the seceding party started to fall apart at the seams. On the banks of Beaver Dam Wash, several turned south to rejoin the Hunt leadership. Captain Smith promptly forgot his "followers" who were at a loss to get their wagons across the wash, and he nonchalantly disappeared into the west.

As they were able, the stranded Argonauts followed the Smith tracks. After days of rough going, the lost gold seekers emerged from Forty Mile Canyon on the desert north of Ash Meadows. They split into clans. These clans, or platoons, were the Jayhawkers, the Bennett-Arcan families, the Mississippians, the Georgians or the "Bug-Smashers," and the Earhart-Nusbaumer group. The Reverend J.W. Brier was traveling with his wife and three small sons. He was chaplain of the Mississippians. At the end of Forty Mile Canyon, the Brier wagon broke down. Valuables were buried and the Briers struggled ahead on foot. In the Amargosa Desert, probably south of Big Dune, the Georgians camped and abandoned wagons — backpacking west. At the head of Furnace Creek Canyon, only a mile or two from Death Valley Junction, the Mississippians left their wagons. At this juncture, along came the Briers on foot. Ahead were the Bennett-Arcan, the Jayhawker and the Earhart-Nusbaumer parties.

Going down to Furnace Creek, Wash the Jayhawkers had turned north to camp on the valley floor south of present Stovepipe Wells Hotel. The Bennett-Arcan party, with the family of Harry Wade, turned south down the valley and camped at what historians later identified as Tule Spring. The Earhart-Nusbaumer group looked at the desolate valley expanse and pushed south, veering somewhat to the east, then rejoined the Spanish Trail somewhere around today's Tecopa. The Georgians tramped past the Jayhawker camp and continued on their compass course over Tucki Mountain, one of the hardest routes imaginable. The Briers camped with the Jayhawkers. The Mississippians also came but did not tarry. They noted that the Jayhawkers were burning their wagons and using the wood to dry meat of the oxen they butchered.

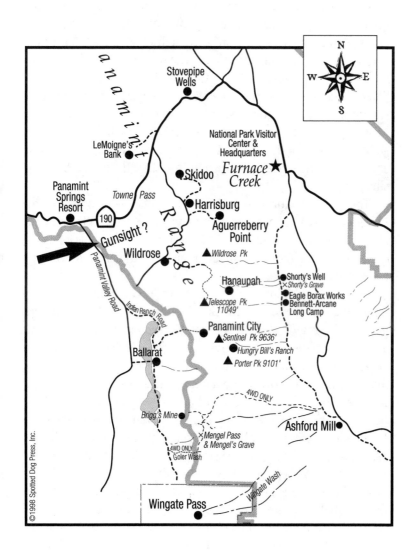

©1998 Spotted Dog Press, Inc.

From the Jayhawkers camp, now identified as Burned Wagons Point, the Mississippians cut around the head of the Funeral Range and up Emigrant Wash toward distant Towne Pass. Their group was in charge of Captain Martin — who deserves to rank as co-discoverer of the pass, along with Captain Towne of the Georgians. Somewhere along the wash between where the Stovepipe Wells resort and the Emigrant Ranger Station now stand, a young Mississippian picked up a piece of silver float. He had lost the front sight of his gun and was able to replace it that night, by whittling and hammering out a reproduction from that float from the wide silver vein.

The next day or two, one of the Jayhawkers overtook the Mississippians and heard about the silver gunsight. By the time the exhausted parties reached Los Angeles six weeks later, this lone gunsight had grown into a "mountain of silver" and thereby touched off Death Valley's first boom.

Down in Panamint Valley below Wildrose Canyon, the two platoons of Jayhawkers, with the Brier family, and the Mississippians got together briefly at what they call Horsebones Camp. There the Mississippian displayed his silver gunsight, which by this time had attracted quite a bit of attention. Who was this enterprising young man? None of the diaries or reminiscences of the '49ers say. He may have been one of the Turner brothers who are known to have been close friends of the Briers. The Briers went to Los Angeles. Dr. E. French Darwin told of having talked with the Turner brothers at Tejon Ranch. Most of the Mississippians left Horsebones Camp and headed up Shepherd Canyon over the Argus Range to Walker Pass. That the gunsight-maker went to Los Angeles is known from the fact that a gunsmith named John Goler replaced it there, and promptly closed shop to head for Death Valley. The Turners are also believed to have gone back for a second helping as well.

PANAMINT CITY
SENATORS RESCUE BANDITS

EARLY IN 1873, a group of four or five bandits hauled some bullion they had taken from a Wells Fargo express box into Surprise Canyon in the Panamint Range. They were certain of pursuit, but reasoned rightly that neither a sense of duty nor the posted rewards would bring venturesome law officers up the steep, winding canyon where an ambush was possible at every turn. The highway men had a supply of provisions. They were sure that the hot breath of pursuit would cool after a bit, or be diverted to some fresher crime.

Needless to say, there was not much in the way of diversion in Surprise Canyon. The first settlers amused themselves by more or less aimlessly pecking at the rock walls. Imagine their feelings when these aimless peckings revealed a ledge of almost pure silver, "wide enough to drive a wagon through." They had found a second Virginia City, they thought. But what good did it do to own a million if they were unable to go outside and spend it? The only answer was to pay off Wells Fargo. Such a plan would require a go-between, and a good one.

Neighboring Nevada had a spectacular senator, one William M. Stewart, who was known throughout the West both as fighter and a great silver backer. By chance, one of the robbers knew the Stewart family and fortunately, he seemed to have been unknown to the express company. At least his name had not appeared on the reward posters. Taking several samples of ore in his saddlebags, this robber-turned-mine-owner, rode north to the Comstock Lode where he contacted the senator. The senator agreed, and would find out what the express company wanted as a settlement of the whole affair. The senator's price would be an interest in the mines,

The Surprise Valley Mill at Panamint City in its heyday. Its ruins are located high
in the pinyons and junipers of the Panamint Mountains at 6,800 feet.
The road up Surprise Canyon was washed out by a flash flood in 1984 and
is considered impassable by most four-wheel drive vehicles.
(L. Burr Belden, courtesy U.S. Borax Company).

plus an interest for his colleague, Senator John P. Jones. Jones, incidentally, had been attracted by the Panamint ore when some of it had been displayed a few weeks earlier by a promoter known as Colonel Raines, who had tried without success, to do just what Senator Stewart had agreed to do. The shares of the two senators meant quite a bite in the prospective fortune, but from the bandits' viewpoint, it was still a bargain.

Senator Stewart arranged to pay off Wells Fargo. By April, Panamint claims were being filed. Original locators were W.L. Kennedy, R.B. Stewart, and R.C. Jacobs. The publisher at Bishop, W.A. Chalfant, who dug up the location notices had no idea whether or not the trio were members of the hiding banditti. In fact, he surmised that assumed names might have been used, names the men adopted at the time of their "reformation." Senator Stewart himself was silent on the point in his autobiography, published more than thirty years later.

Road-making and milling machinery followed the filing of the claims. Additional prospecting brought other strikes with several more claims recorded in June. Indians were hired as woodcutters and charcoal kilns were erected (not the famous kilns in Wildrose Canyon). Not even the two senators could induce Wells Fargo to run a single stage line into Panamint. The express company wanted to keep the boom camp's first citizens safe from temptation.

A stage mail service was a necessity, however. Senator Stewart went to San Bernardino where, with a down payment of bullion as heavy as he could lift to the counter, he obtained the promise of Caesar Myerstein to run the line. The Myerstein Brothers were general merchants and did considerable desert freighting, running wagons as far as Salt Lake City. It was agreed that the stage would make weekly trips. When it was found that the sandy route took two weeks to traverse, it meant using extra rigs. The stage left San Bernardino, crossed Cajon Pass over Brown's Toll Road, followed the Mojave River from the Verde Ranch down to present Helendale, then cut north to Harper Lake, where Black's Ranch served as a supply point and depot. With fresh horses, the route went north up

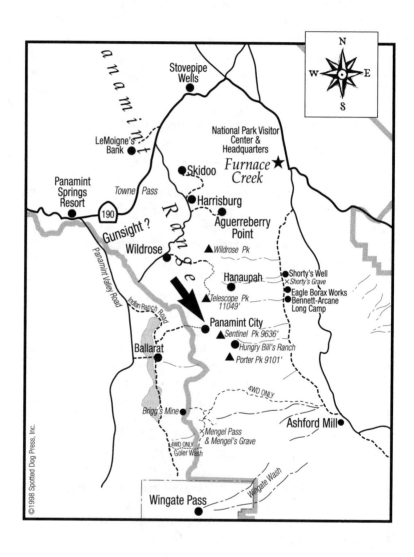

Black Canyon, past Granite Wells, through lower Panamint Valley and on to a spring near the site of Ballarat. From the spring the line turned east for the last leg up Surprise Canyon.

Not all of Panamint's residents appear to have made peace with the law, or there may well have been some new arrivals. At any rate, the spring in north Panamint Valley, the one near the site of Ballarat, received the name "Postoffice Spring," and for good reason. When the stage driver received a letter addressed to John Doe at Postoffice Spring, he simply dropped it off and hung a rag on a nearby creosote bush. The spring was out on the flat with no secret approaches. A hiding bandit could thus get his mail in safety.

Panamint boomed. The mine owners envisioned a bonanza that held values with depth. Senator Stewart became so optimistic that he promoted the Los Angeles and Independence Railroad, by way of Panamint, of course. The road was actually built and operated between Santa Monica and Los Angeles. It was surveyed to San Bernardino and on up over Cajon Pass. Atop the West Cajon, competition was encountered in the form of surveyors for the Southern Pacific which was then planning its line east to run from the Tehachapi to the Cajon, effectively relegating Los Angeles to the sidelines. The rival survey crews exchanged shots, but the SP men didn't know that the LA&I had a big grading crew at work only a mile or so away. The firing brought the LA&I reinforcements on the run, a roaring blast answered the few scattered SP shots. The Southern Pacific surveyors wisely retreated.

After the Cajon Pass repulse, the SP listened to a subsidy offered by Los Angeles County and built over their present route. The LA&I never did build east beyond Los Angeles. Years later, the line was bought by the Southern Pacific, the assets of course, included the right-of-way over west Cajon. Ninety years later, the Southern Pacific built a line between Colton and Palmdale paralleling the Santa Fe through east Cajon, rather than following the old right-of-way — and for good reason. The east Cajon summit is more than 1,000 feet lower.

Stores, saloons, boarding houses, the Bank of Panamint, and a newspaper all blossomed in Surprise Canyon, a canyon so narrow that there could be no back streets. The main one was over a mile long. The town was destroyed by flash floods several times, which also wiped out the road. T.S. Harris moved his *Panamint News* to Darwin shortly after the great July 4, 1875 celebration. United States Senator George Hearst was developing Modoc across the Panamint Valley in the Argus Range. Nearby, the towns of Lookout and Darwin were booming. Panamint values held, but its rock became harder with depth and blunted the miners' tools. Gradually, the camp creaked to a close. High silver prices have brought brief subsequent revivals, one of the latest having been foiled when the newly rebuilt road washed out once again.

Panamint mill owners just didn't trust bandits. When the mill boss was tipped off that a bunch was waiting to hijack the monthly cleanup he had the silver cast in cannonballs weighing some 700 ponds apiece. The holdup came off as scheduled. The bandits tried in vain to heft a cannon ball. They rode off cussing the "dirty mine owners who wouldn't let a honest highwayman make a living."

VISITING
PANAMINT CITY TODAY

A two or three day backpack up Surprise Canyon from the west side of the Panamint Range is the most interesting, and perhaps the easiest way to see Panamint City today. During the winter of 1984, a flash flood wiped out the one road to the townsite at the mouth of the canyon, making access by foot a challenge, and for four-wheel drive vehicles, a virtual impossibility. According to backcountry road expert, Roger Mitchell, author of "Death Valley Jeep Trails," once a year, an experienced four-wheel-drive group, with permission of the Park Service, use winches, ramps and other accessories, to pull their vehicles over the "crux" maneuver at the mouth of the canyon. With this one exception, no vehicles travel the road and very few people actually visit this historic site. Those who do visit, do so on foot. If you have the time to plan an overnight desert backpack, this is a wonderful trip. Beginning on the alluvial fan above Panamint Dry Lake, the route winds up Surprise Canyon, to the now quiet remains of this historic mining camp, which once had a population of 10,000.

The best time of the year to make this trip is in spring just after the snow melt (depending on the year, the snow pack may be very heavy) or in late autumn, just before the snow falls. Summer, of course, is too hot. The summit of Sentinel Peak, one of the range highpoints, at 9,634', (Telescope Peak is the highpoint of the Panamints at 11,048') is a 1.5 mile southeasterly walk uphill from Panamint City.

From the Panamint Springs resort (hotel, restaurant, and campground) on Highway 190, now located inside the Death Valley

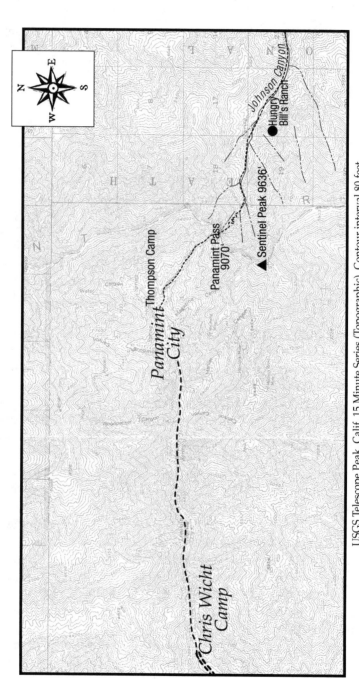

USGS Telescope Peak, Calif. 15 Minute Series (Topographic). Contour interval 80 feet

National Park boundary, drive east about 2.4 miles on Hwy 190 and turn right (south) on Panamint Valley Road. At 7.5 miles turn right again on the Trona-Wildrose Road. At 0.4 miles, turn left on Indian Ranch Road, good graded dirt. Follow this south approximately 10 miles. Turn left on the road to Surprise Canyon, marked by a white boulder and a green sign. Drive another 3.5 miles east to the end and Chris Wicht Camp (inhabited).

Surprise Canyon can also be approached from the south via the historic ghost town of Ballarat, a collection of antiquated shacks, inhabited by a few stalwart residents. From the center of Ballarat, turn left (north) on Wingate Road. Drive approximately 1.9 miles, then turn right, on the road to Surprise Canyon. Drive 3.5 miles to the end of the road, and Chris Wicht's Camp. The mouth of Surprise Canyon is a boulder-hop across the wash to the north of the parking area. When I first hiked to Panamint City, the boundary of the national park ended on the east at the crest of range. My hiking partners and I brought fresh fruit and beer to "George" who was living at the camp at the time, so he would keep an eye on our cars. The camp still remains outside the new national park boundary.

The one-way walk to Panamint City is a strenuous 4.5 miles and 4,200 feet of gain along a good dirt road. The only obstacle is at the mouth of Surprise Canyon, where the 1984 floodwaters lifted years of silt and gravel deposits up like a bedcover, exposing the light-colored craggy rock beneath. This short rocky section can be carefully crossed with a full pack, using hands for stability. Not far past this, the visitor is greeted by a few cars and trucks standing on end, imbedded in the wash gravels and sand — a colorful reminder of the unpredictable power of a desert thunderstorm.

We carried our own water for the entire two day trip — about 2.5 gallons per person. There are two water sources at the mining camp which some people trust enough to drink — a water faucet just to the east of the modern welder's shop and a water tank with spring just a short distance up the road from the welder's shop. Remnants of the last mining operation in the early 1980's, pepper the canyon. New buildings stand near the remaining miner's shacks. Take your chances sleeping in them. There are a lot of mice (and biting fleas).

When we first did this trip in 1986, we discovered a cache of dynamite left by the last residents of Panamint City. From all appearances, their retreat during that fateful winter storm was swift, and once the road was washed out, there was no returning to retrieve their possessions, except by foot. As soon as we got back to Panamint Valley, we called the Inyo County Sheriff's Department and reported our find.

Another interesting route to Panamint City, though even longer and more strenuous (13.5 miles one way, approximately 5,000' of gain) is from the east side, over the crest of the range, via Johnson Canyon and Hungry Bill's Ranch. This is a waterless backpack route with a stopover the first night at the old ranch ruins, home in the early 1800's to its namesake, Hungry Bill, a Timbisha Shoshone. The site also served as an autumn camp for the annual Timbisha Shoshone pine nut harvest. The camp was eventually abandoned before the gold rush of the late 1800's. During the Panamint mining boom of the 1870's, an entrepreneurial desert rat named William Johnson took up residence at Hungry Bill's. He grew assorted fruit and vegetables which he sold to the miners just over the crest at Panamint City. Even today, the old grape vines and some of the old fruit trees bear fruit.

Panamint City is one of the great Death Valley historic sites and is protected by the Antiquities Act of 1906 and the Archaeological Resources Protection Act of 1979. Enjoy its solitude and the remains of its historic past.

Wynne Benti

BREYFOGLE
INDIAN CAPTIVE

WHEN THE GUNSIGHT SILVER started the first prospector stampede into the Death Valley region, it all but started a precedent — the wave of silver hunters who followed were dubbed "Gunsighters." The Gunsighter who made the biggest splash was a former treasurer of Alameda County, California, who found and lost — an outcropping of high grade gold to the east of Death Valley. He was Charles Breyfogle.

Breyfogle's find touched off a surge of "lost mine" hunting that made the earlier Gunsight stampede look like kindergarten stuff. Incidentally, it brought the coining of the word "Breyfogle" which was applied to those seeking his treasure source.

It happened in 1863. More than a century has passed, and as many versions of the story have appeared in print as there have been intervening years. Breyfogle has been called "Jake," "Bill," and "Sam." Stories told about the scene of his find have it located between Goldfield and Las Vegas.

Here, in a capsule, are the known facts based primarily on the 1863 files of the *Reese River Reveille* newspaper published in Austin, Nevada. Breyfogle was keeping a hotel at Genoa, a town south of Austin. One night three men with heavy camping outfits stopped. They kept to themselves, and engaged in earnest conversation. Now and then they consulted a map. Early the next morning, they were gone.

It didn't take long for Breyfogle to convince himself that his guests were hot on the trail of the Lost Gunsight. Breyfogle hastily assembled an outfit, and started out along the trail of the three men which pointed south down the Great Smoky Valley toward the present

Tonopah. He really covered ground. At dark he saw a campfire ahead. Sure enough, his ex-guests were there. Entering the fireside circle Breyfogle asked, if because of Indian danger, would they let him join the prospecting trip instead of hunting alone. He had guessed wrong. His mysterious guests of the night before were not prospectors — they were Confederate sympathizers who were following the back trails to reach Southern armies in Texas. However, they agreed to let Breyfogle go along with them until they reached the Salt Lake Trail where he could throw in with a passing caravan for protection.

Two or three days later they camped in the Amargosa Valley at a site approximating Shoshone. Breyfogle rolled in his blankets, a bit to one side. In the pre-dawn gray he awoke to see and hear Indians smashing the heads of his three companions. Quietly he rolled out into the shadows — just in time — as the savages threw fresh fuel on the fire embers to offer light for the looting then under way. After hiding in a bush or grass clump, Breyfogle got to his feet and ran. There was no time to get either gun or supplies, and no time to put his boots on — he ran with them clutched in his hands. He wandered for hours on the desert, and stopped only when his cut and bleeding feet could stand no more, and then rested behind a rocky ledge.

The next morning it was impossible for him to put his boots on his swollen feet. He found a little spring, and filled his boots as an improvised canteen. The next day and the next Breyfogle wandered over the desert without a vague idea where he was. There were hours and hours of delirium for the starving man. At one point — he knew not where — he found an outcropping of rich gold ore. Realizing its value he filled his pockets and then resumed his wandering. Finally, he found another spring, and sank down in deep sleep. He was wakened at day by a party of Indians who took him to their camp as a captive. There he was made a slave to collect wood and water for the squaws. Between chores the children took command. They had him get down on all fours and mounted him as a horse. They jabbed his ribs with sticks to make "horsey"

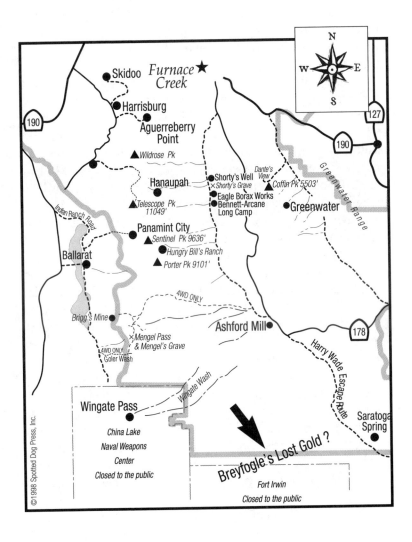

buck.   Tiring of this pastime, one older delinquent smashed Breyfogle alongside the head with a length of tree limb.   The blow injured both the equilibrium and memory of the prisoner.   The Indians reasoned he would die, and gladly sold him to a passing wagon train.

Members of the emigrant train, noting Breyfogle's weakened condition, stopped at the Manse Ranch, a few miles north of Stump Spring, in Pahrump Valley. There, Mrs. Yount, wife of the owner, and her daughter, Mrs. Harsha White, nursed Breyfogle back to health. His payment for their kindness was a handful of his rich nuggets. He could not, however, give any clear idea where he had found the ore. The Yount boys drove him around to what they thought might be likely spots — without success.

With returning strength Breyfogle was able to join another passing caravan and eventually returned to the Reese River area in Central Nevada — where he showed his remaining nuggets. Other groups fitted up outfits and back they went with Breyfogle trying to guide the way. He could remember — up to a point. On one trip, the searchers believed they found the massacre site, and so they reasoned that Breyfogle's escape route had been through Chicago Canyon which connects the Amargosa Valley with Pahrump Valley near the Pahrump Ranch. That was as close to the treasure as anybody got.   For 26 years Breyfogle sought his lost bonanza — in vain. He headed dozens of search parties that combed the deserts around Goldfield, Lida, Horn Silver, Bullfrog, Leeland, Keane Wonder, Saratoga, Salt Spring, and even down to Sandy and Ivanpah.   At least once, his companions thought he was bluffing, and left Breyfogle stranded near Bonnie Claire. He wasn't bluffing. The Indian youths' savage treatment had permanently impaired his memory.

The Breyfogle lost bonanza story has appeared in many places; yet no two versions agree. In 1957, the writer was shown a piece of the original Breyfogle ore by a Mrs. Stella White Fisk, daughter of Mrs. Harsha White, and granddaughter of Mrs. Joseph Yount who had nursed Charles Breyfogle back to health after his ransom and release from the Stump Spring band of Paiute-Shoshone. The Yount boys, Mrs. White's brothers, made prospecting something of a vocation in between jobs with the Atlantic and Pacific railroad builders at Fenner. One day they found some ore that, matched the Breyfogle samples. It was at Johnnie, at the northern end of Pahrump Valley. The Johnnie Mine proved to be a rich producer. It was worked for a time, and then sold. It had a turbulent subsequent history which included a gunfight when some persons attempted to jump the claim.

The story of Breyfogle's experience and release from Indian captivity appeared as a Sunday historical page in the *Sun Telegram* of San Bernardino. A month afterwards, a letter came from Richard Dillon, director of the Sutro Library in San Francisco, who furnished the names and addresses of relatives of Breyfogle. Among the latter were Lewis Breyfogle of Chanute, Kansas, and Mrs. Eva Breyfogle Lovelace, of Lakewood, Colorado, who had copied the diary of Breyfogle's 1849 overland trek with his brother, Joshua. Charles settled on the East Bay and became treasurer of Alameda County. A grand jury discovered a fund shortage in the department; Breyfogle was indicted and convicted — though protesting his innocence. A year later his successor noted a couple of unusual bookkeeping entries, both in the same handwriting; he trapped a clerk who confessed, and cleared the convicted former treasurer. Then came an unusual chapter in legal history; the district attorney who had prosecuted Breyfogle, and the judge who had pronounced sentence, asked California's governor to correct an error in justice. Breyfogle was finally pardoned.

Charles Breyfogle then tried to pick up the broken pieces of his interrupted career by buying and running a hotel in Genoa. Later, in between lost bonanza hunts, he helped organize the rich Eureka, Nevada Mining District in 1889.

This is the story of the Argonaut who found and lost one of the West's most fabled mines, a very human person who now comes down through the years in a clear three-dimensional portrait.

CHLORIDE CLIFF
THE FIRST ROAD

PERCHED HIGH IN THE FUNERAL MOUNTAINS, about five miles south of Daylight Pass and near the east boundary of the Death Valley National Park, is a ghost town of picturesquely sagging roofs, a long deserted stone mill foundation, and piles of rubble long since grown over with weeds.

Few visitors to Death Valley National Park know about Chloride Cliff — and it would be a banner day if more than a single party should visit the site. The only passable roads, rough and rocky, either lead directly across the Amargosa Desert from the ghost town of Carrera, or head south from Daylight Pass, a short distance east of the California – Nevada boundary.

Despite its isolation and the fact it has received little notice for some 90 years, Chloride Cliff is important. The old camp is even older than Panamint. In fact, it marks the site of one of the first commercially operated mines in the entire Death Valley region. Claims were filed in 1873 and operation is said to have started the following year at that remote location 250 miles from the nearest grocery store. Chloride Cliff gave forth rich ore assaying enough to make profitable that distant operation which in the 1870's was surrounded by parties of Paiute Indians bent on waylaying travelers. Chloride Cliff must have kept a force big enough and armed well enough to discourage attack. The J. L. Yount family which first settled Pahrump Valley and the famous "Lost Breyfogle" mine party were each attacked in this same general area within the same decade.

With the rush of Anglo settlers to California goldfields, subsequent raids and skirmishes between settlers and bands of the

Chloride Cliff (Death Valley National Park Museum)

Paiute-Shoshone followed, particularly in the Owens Valley and outlying areas to the east along Death Valley's western perimeter. To stop the skirmishes and attacks, the federal government sent the United States Army to the Owens Valley where the isolated outpost, Camp Independence, was established. Many of the Paiute and Shoshone people were rounded up and forced to walk south nearly 250 miles to a reservation at Fort Tejon.

Chloride Cliff's principal claim to fame lies in the fact these pioneer miners of the 1870's built the first road connecting Death Valley with civilization. It was, incidentally, the road used afterward by the Eagle Borax Works in 1882, and by Harmony Borax the following year until Harmony's superintendent J.W.S. Perry hired Charley Bennett to construct the famous Wingate Pass road from Furnace Creek to Mojave, the greatly publicized route of the Twenty-Mule Teams.

The Chloride Cliff road left what is now the Barstow area and went north. Actually, in its southern reaches it was much the same

as the route of the San Bernardino–Panamint Stage Line. At Pilot
Knob, or Granite Wells, the Chloride Cliff road went east of the
peak — a pass where the bandit Tuburcio Vasquez once kept a rock-
walled hideout. Near Goldstone, the route went more truly north,
past Hidden Springs and Myrick Spring to enter Long Valley about
opposite the junction of the Needle Peak lateral. From Long Valley
it descended Wingate Wash, went up the west side of Death Valley,
then crossed south of Furnace Creek, ascended Death Valley's eastern side to Beatty Junction. Where the old Keane Wonder Mine
road leaves the present highway the original Chloride Cliff trace
followed, a similar pattern but, of course, continued on to the pioneer mining camp.

It is impossible to follow the old route today. The upper end
shows faintly, but has not felt a tire for decades. From the head of
Wingate Wash south, the old route goes through China Lake Naval
Weapons Center, and is therefore, off-limits.

For years, students of Death Valley history wondered how
Chloride Cliff ever obtained supplies back in the 1870's. Then
someone recalled the old *Elliot History* of San Bernardino County,
published in 1883. Sure enough the road is mentioned — even with
mileage to landmarks — some of which are a bit confusing. In the
1950's researchers for the National Park found a long, forgotten
crossing of the middle valley — Devil's Golf Course. They surmised
it might antedate the Harmony Borax road. Sure enough, it does.

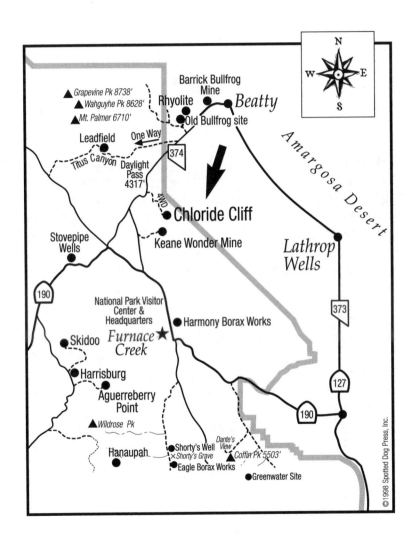

▲ Grapevine Pk 8738'
▲ Wahguyhe Pk 8628'
▲ Mt. Palmer 6710'

Barrick Bullfrog Mine
Rhyolite
Beatty
Old Bullfrog site

Leadfield
One Way
Titus Canyon
374
Daylight Pass 4317'

Amargosa Desert

400
Chloride Cliff

Keane Wonder Mine

Stovepipe Wells

Lathrop Wells

190

National Park Visitor Center & Headquarters

Harmony Borax Works

Skidoo
Furnace Creek ★

Harrisburg

Aguerreberry Point

373

▲ Wildrose Pk

Dante's View
Shorty's Well
✕ Shorty's Grave
▲ Coffin Pk 5503'
Eagle Borax Works

190

127

Hanaupah

Greenwater Site

© 1998 Spotted Dog Press, Inc.

WINGATE PASS
SCOTTY FOOLS THEM ALL
— ❧❧ —

DEATH VALLEY SCOTTY became a household word following the record-shattering Los Angeles to Chicago trip of his chartered "Coyote Special" train in July 1905. Born "Walter Scott" — the publicity loving extrovert had come west as a youth to join his older brother Warner, in the Virginia City area. He then drifted south across the desert. He made various claims to fame — including making a single trip on a twenty-mule team borax wagon from Harmony to Mojave as a swamper, touring with Buffalo Bill's Wild West Show, and picking up a bit of coin running an assay office of sorts at Goldfield.

Scotty's special train east was one of the world's greatest publicity stunts. To one and all Scotty had told stories of his famous mine in Death Valley. The Santa Fe was eager to publicize its route as the fastest one east. After the Coyote Special run, the railroad put out an advertising booklet replete with pictures of Scotty, his wife Josephine, and of course, the rolling equipment. In the railroad pamphlet it was related that the desert Midas asked about the train possibility, and its price, at Santa Fe's general offices in Los Angeles. When Scotty was told the price would be $10,000, the railroad booklet went on to say that Scott reached into one boot and pulled out $5,000 then extracted an equal amount from the other boot. It made good reading, but it didn't happen that way. Nearly 35 years later, an author named C. B. Glasscock, who had been publisher of the local paper at Greenwater in 1906, located the Santa Fe receipt that had been issued to Scotty. It was for $5,500 — not $10,000. Payment was by check written by Burdon Gaylord, eastern

Death Valley Scotty (L. Burr Belden Collection)

mining promoter. The Coyote Special with Scotty tossing out silver and gold en route was a publicity gag that surpassed all others. After his return from the amazing trip Scotty received top-billing as the star in a San Francisco melodrama titled "Scotty, King of the Desert Mine." It played only one night. The second day found Scotty in jail, arrested on a telegraphed warrant from Sheriff John C. Ralphs of San Bernardino. The warrant was a sequel to a skirmish, or holdup, in Wingate Wash at the southwest end of Death Valley — a skirmish that became known as "The Battle of Wingate Pass." During the "holdup," Scotty and his eastern capitalist companions were accosted by two men that Scotty had sent ahead for just that purpose.

The holdup pair had instructions to shoot one of Scotty's mules. Instead, a wild bullet hit and seriously wounded Scotty's brother, Warner. In the excitement, Scotty forgot his assumed role, spurred ahead, and shouted, "Stop shooting, you hit one of my men." The easterners, disgusted with the apparent deception, shed their role of "suckers" and began prosecution.

One of the men who agreed to ambush Scotty's party, and probably the only survivor of the skirmish, was Bill Keys, miner and longtime companion of Scotty. In 1966, the retired Keys, lived on his ranch in Joshua Tree National Monument, where his beautiful desert reservoirs are a favorite camping spot for the youth groups he loves.

In 1954, nearly 50 years after the Wingate incident, Keys broke his silence and told of the battle. One morning, this writer's telephone rang. The caller was the editor of *Westways Magazine*. He asked, "Can you run out to Bill Keys' ranch and get him to tell the true story of the Wingate Pass battle?" Knowing Keys, this seemed a doubtful assignment, for no one had heard him allude to the battle — after which, incidentally, he had been arrested.

Out at the desert ranch, sitting under a sprawling grape arbor, the question was posed. "Bill, would you be willing to tell about that Wingate Pass battle in which Indian Bob Belt shot Warner Scott?"

Keys, who had been describing a new lead he had recently uncovered in his Desert Queen mine, became silent. Then, a smile spread over his face and, he said, "Well, I guess the statute of limitations has run out by now, so it won't hurt."

This is the way Bill Keys remembers the battle. When Scotty was in New York he had interested a broker in his mine and obtained a grubstake from Julian Gerard of the Knickerbocker Trust Company. The $1,500 grubstake was to provide Gerard with a half-interest in the new and very rich prospect Scotty was developing. After Scotty had made his famous train ride to Chicago, Gerard started writing about the mine. Scotty appeared in Riverside with a heavy chain-bound bundle he said contained gold amalgam. Riversiders scarcely raised an eye-brow. Next, he went to

Discrimination persisted in many of the mining camps in the west, including
Rhyolite. After they were refused service in every restaurant in town,
Death Valley Scotty and this Asian American businessman (who loaned Scotty
money), had to eat a takeout lunch and enjoy their cigars on a Rhyolite street.
(Nevada Historical Society)

Philadelphia where he claimed he was robbed while en route to show Gerard the gold. The newspapers quoted Scotty as saying he had lots more, and Gerard seemed satisfied for a time. But then, the Gotham banker began to write to get a report on the mine's progress. He wanted a big operation to show people, and probably float stock. Replies from Scotty continued to be optimistic, but patience was wearing thin on Wall Street.

Gerard wrote Scotty that he was coming out to see the mine with his own eyes. Scotty had a camp in Desert Hound Canyon, northeast of where Ashford Mill now stands in Death Valley. On the canyon side he had a prospect hole that showed a fair vein of gold, but Scotty had never taken the time to open the vein beyond the 10-foot level. A half-mile down the canyon, Keys had a mine, a good one, which he later sold to some Boston investors. There was a road up Desert Hound, now renamed Scotty Canyon. It ended at the Keys Mine. There was just a mule trail from there up to Scotty's camp.

When Scotty received word that Julian Gerard was coming to Death Valley to see the mine, he was perplexed — but ever the showman, Scotty evolved a plan to give Gerard a taste of the traditional wild west, and in so doing — he hoped — cause the banker to lose all taste for Death Valley and its secluded mines. Scotty conferred with Keys, and they planned to fake a holdup and turn around before reaching Death Valley. Keys interposed, "Suppose this Gerard doesn't scare and demands to go ahead?" It was agreed that if that were the case Scotty would show them Keys' mine — passing it off as his own.

In preparation for the Gerard party, Scotty polished up a four-mule rig. Harness buckles were nickeled, and the buckboard freshly varnished. Warner Scott and Albert M. Johnson, Chicago insurance magnate whom Scotty introduced as a doctor, went along on horseback.

Keys and an Indian named Bob Belt, started out a day ahead. They were to ride up the old Wingate route to the east end of Long Valley, wait there for the Scott-Gerard party, and then shoot a lead

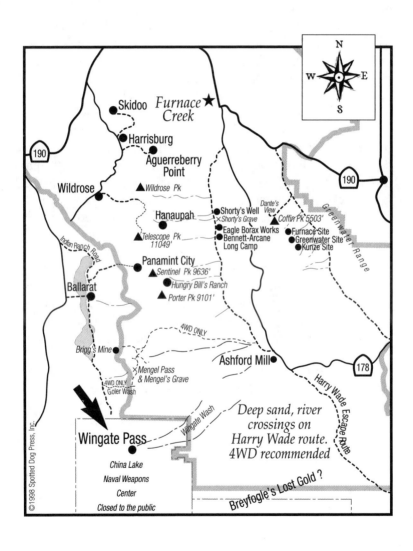

N
W   E
S

Skidoo   *Furnace* ★
          Creek

Harrisburg

190

Aguerreberry
Point

Wildrose   ▲ *Wildrose Pk*

Hanaupah   ● Shorty's Well   *Dante's*
            ✕ *Shorty's Grave*   *View*   ▲ *Coffin Pk 5503'*
            ● Eagle Borax Works   ● Furnace Site
▲ *Telescope Pk* ● Bennett-Arcane   ● Greenwater Site
  11049'   Long Camp   ● Kunze Site

190

Indian Ranch Road

Panamint City
▲ *Sentinel Pk 9636'*
  ✕ *Hungry Bill's Ranch*
Ballarat   ▲ *Porter Pk 9101'*

4WD ONLY

Brigg's Mine ●   Ashford Mill ●   178

✕ *Mengel Pass*
  & Mengel's Grave
4WD ONLY
Goler Wash

Harry Wade Escape Route

Wingate Wash

Deep sand, river
crossings on
Harry Wade route.
4WD recommended

Wingate Pass
●

China Lake
Naval Weapons
Center
Closed to the public

Breyfogle's Lost Gold ?

©1998 Spotted Dog Press, Inc.

mule of Scotty's team of four. Plans started according to the book, but unknown to Keys, Belt carried whiskey rather than water in one canteen. It was hot up in the rocks bordering Wingate Pass. To complicate matters, Scotty's caravan was late. By the time it was within gunshot of the "highwaymen," Belt was so drunk his gun barrel described an arc of 20 degrees. He shot just the same — his bullet hit Warner Scott in the groin. It was then that Scotty panicked and in so doing, unfortunately, tipped off the easterners.

San Bernardino County Sheriff Ralphs was not a lawman to be trifled with. When the news of the fake holdup reached San Bernardino, Ralphs headed north. He wanted Walter Scott, but Scotty had caught a train for San Francisco. Warner was taken to a Los Angeles hospital by Johnson, while the Gerard party chased Keys, who surrendered after first eluding the Sheriff. S. W. McNabb, Ralphs' undersheriff and later U. S. District Attorney, went to Los Angeles where he brushed aside guards to personally inspect Warner Scott's wound.

Trial was set in San Bernardino superior court with both the district attorney and sheriff professing an air-tight case. As the trial opened however, the defense introduced a surveyor who testified that the battle scene was actually 440 yards north of the San Bernardino-Inyo County boundary.

That threw the case to Independence, more than 200 miles north in Owens Valley. Inyo's superior court was not to convene for another three months. Gerard and his friends decided they were suckers after all, and went back to New York. It seemed that there were more important things for the vice president of the Knickerbocker Trust Company to do than to prosecute Death Valley Scotty.

So ends the saga of the Battle of Wingate Pass.

GREENWATER
AND DIAMOND TOOTH LIL

EAST OF THE BLACK MOUNTAINS, between the Shoshone-Ashford Mill road to the south and the Ryan borax areas to the north, there is an upland mesa bearing the name of Greenwater Valley. The name comes from a highly publicized copper camp which boomed nearly a century ago, only to fade after the panic of 1907. Greenwater copper stocks were widely sold and eagerly bought on the mining exchanges, much of the eagerness being due to the magic name of Charles M. Schwab, mining and steel tycoon, who was a backer of Greenwater's largest company.

The early 1900's saw the fabulous mining boom in southern Nevada. It started with Tonopah, moved south to Goldfield, branched west to the Lida district, and continued south to Bullfrog,

Rhyolite, and Gold Center. The Bullfrog discovery came in 1904 and set forth a boom that spawned Rhyolite, one of the most fabulous mining towns in the region. Boomers continued to move on south, bringing life to the almost forgotten Chloride Cliff again, and on to Greenwater Valley, where some copper ore deposits gave substance to many dreams and stock sales.

Greenwater was rough and tough. The desperadoes who were escorted out of camps farther north landed at Greenwater at the end of the line. Some of these gunmen were so tough that even Greenwater's constable quit. Miners and merchants who wanted a decent chance to survive, got together and chose a huge youngster from Alabama with nerves of steel as the new constable. His name was Charles A. Brown. After facing down a dozen or so bad men, Brown earned a reputation that caused the lawless tribe to shun the copper camp. It was no surprise to those who knew Charley Brown that he went on to become highway commissioner, county supervisor, and then a powerful senior member of the California Senate.

The camp which became Greenwater was not, ironically, the start of the brief boom. The start was at a nearby site named Furnace —for the Furnace Creek Copper Company.

Before the arrival of the Tonopah & Tidewater Railroad, the bustling copper camp was reached by stage from the Las Vegas & Tonopah over at Ash Meadows. In between the railroad and Salsberry Pass was a way spot known as Fairbanks Ranch. It was a desert station where the traveler bought meals, drink, and feed. The owner was Ralph J. Fairbanks who became the founder of Shoshone and Baker successively. One of the best loved desert men, "Dad" Fairbanks was a prospector — but above all, a humanitarian who rescued dozens of hapless men, from the region's searing heat.

The Fairbanks Ranch is a good place to introduce another Greenwater resident whose name invariably comes up when old timers reminisce. The chug line, as the stage was called, halted one day at the ranch for lunch. Fairbank's daughter Stella ran to her mother and exclaimed, "Mama, a lady got off the stage and started drinking in the saloon with the men. She is smoking a cigar, too."

Main Street, Greenwater (Photograph by Larson, Nevada Historical Society)

The tough and legendary Charley Brown, sheriff of Greenwater,
later Inyo County Supervisor and California State Senator.
(Death Valley National Park Museum)

The lady was none other than the well-known Diamond Lil, pro-
prietor of a house of sinful pleasure in Rhyolite, who was on her
way to do a different kind of prospecting. Evidently, she liked the
view at Greenwater, for Lil soon had a place alongside the Murphy
Brothers store, the post office, the unique *Death Valley Chuck-Walla*
office, and several drink emporiums.

Diamond Lil was a larger than average woman, with a wasp-
sized waist encased in the tightly-laced corset of the day. She had
a leopard skin coat and a penchant for wearing it a bit late in the
spring or early in the fall. She ever flashed a toothy smile in greet-
ing customers as "dearie." The reason for the smile was Lil's proud-
est adornment, a table-cut diamond set in an upper incisor, which
gave her the Diamond Lil trademark. In early Greenwater days, she
was called "Diamond Tooth Lil" or just "Diamond Tooth" but later,
at both Silver Lake and Crackerjack, where she and her girls held
court, it was just Diamond Lil.

Arthur Kunzie and Frank McAllister filed Greenwater's first copper claims in 1905, but it was not until late that year that ore samples displayed in Barstow brought Joe Harvey, a mining engineer, to the scene. He took more samples and started for Daggett only to be caught in a cloudburst near Cave Springs, in which he lost his outfit and ore samples. What he had seen, however, caused him to backtrack after a second Daggett visit for supplies. The second time, he took a span of mules he had freshly shod at Seymour Alf's blacksmith shop. Harvey's second bunch of samples were so good he forwarded them to the mining magnate Patsy Clark. Clark authorized Harvey to buy the claims of Fred Birney and Phil Creaser. Tasker L. Oddie, later U. S. Senator, F. M. "Borax" Smith, and Patsy's brother, Senator W.A. Clark came and bought. A big bunch of claims were combined and sold for over $4 million. The Greenwater boom was born with scores of newcomers arriving daily from all points of the compass.

Bonanza finder Frank Shorty Harris appears elsewhere in this book. He had staked out a bunch of Greenwater claims and had given them to Judge Decker at Rhyolite. The judge left for Independence but his cruise ship got stuck on a bar in Rhyolite, and the claims were never recorded.

How long Greenwater could have remained a siren for stock sale money is a guess. When the bottom dropped out from mining stocks Greenwater became deserted, by all but two. Fairbanks stayed on, moving buildings to the new town of Shoshone that he was building at an old Indian campsite along the Tonopah & Tidewater Railroad. Charley Brown, the husky young constable stayed too, as Fairbanks' helper. He became a partner of Fairbanks, married his daughter Stella, and almost singlehandedly reared a modern community astride a state highway he promoted. Today, it is hard to find even the site of Greenwater, but Shoshone is the metropolis of eastern Inyo County.

What happened to Diamond Lil? Glasscock, who was a partner in both the *Greenwater Times* and the *Chucka-Walla* related Lil's departure. It seems that when the newspaper partners had urgent

Advertising in a 1907 issue of *The Death Valley Chuck-Walla*
extols the benefits of investing in Greenwater mines.
(Collection of Andy Zdon)

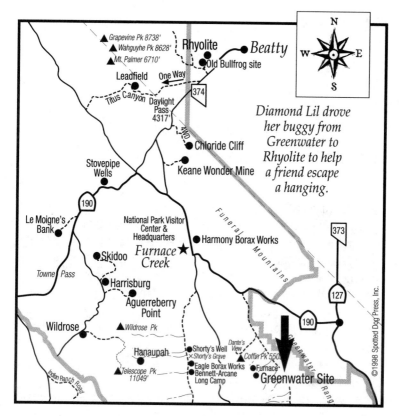

▲ Grapevine Pk 8738'
▲ Wahguyhe Pk 8628'
▲ Mt. Palmer 6710'

Rhyolite
● Beatty
● Old Bullfrog site

Leadfield
One Way

Titus Canyon
Daylight Pass 4317'

374

4WD

● Chloride Cliff

Stovepipe Wells

● Keane Wonder Mine

190

Le Moigne's Bank
●

National Park Visitor Center & Headquarters

● Harmony Borax Works

Funeral Mountains

373

Furnace Creek ★

● Skiddoo

Towne Pass

● Harrisburg

Aguerreberry Point

127

190

Wildrose
●

▲ Wildrose Pk

Hanaupah

● Shorty's Well
✕ Shorty's Grave

Dante's View

▲ Coffin Pk 5500'

Greenwater Range

▲ Telescope Pk 11049'

● Eagle Borax Works
● Bennett-Arcane Long Camp

● Furnace
● Greenwater Site

Indian Ranch Road

N
W   E
S

Diamond Lil drove
her buggy from
Greenwater to
Rhyolite to help
a friend escape
a hanging.

©1998 Spotted Dog Press, Inc.

business in Rhyolite one week, they left one Billy Robinson to put out the paper. Billy undoubtedly thought it funny when he swiped a high society ball item from a New York paper and made it a local item by substituting names of the more proper Greenwater matrons. The wives saw no humor in being libeled thusly and depicted in opera gowns. Their husbands took up the cause. Billy was tried and actually sentenced to hanging. He escaped, and hid in Lil's house. Lil knew full well that the matrons and social arbiters had no use for her either. She hitched up, put Billy on the buggy seat beside her and headed back for Rhyolite.

BULLFROG
SHORTY LIKED TO TALK

✦ — ✦

ED L. CROSS and Frank "Shorty" Harris had their bedrolls spread at the Keane Wonder Mine, south of Daylight Pass in the summer of 1904. Both were out prospecting. According to the expression that still persisted after nearly 40 years, they were "brey-fogling." Despite the season, neither thought of going "outside" to a cooler spot, though Ed had a home over in Lone Pine. Harris had been prospecting around southern Nevada and the Death Valley region for over a decade. He had reached both Tonopah and Goldfield just a bit too late to get in on the good claims. Shorty also had missed the better stuff that was found around the Keane Wonder Mine.

It is difficult to picture two more different men than these two who teamed up to discover the Bullfrog Mine in Rhyolite Hills. Shorty Harris was aptly named for his under-length legs, ever talkative ways and animated jumping about, while Cross was tall, spare, and soft-spoken. It was this writer's great privilege to have interviewed each of the co-discoverers.

The Bullfrog claim sold at a good, figure. It should have been, for it touched off a rush equal or superior to that at Goldfield. Shorty took most of his pay in whiskey. Ed pocketed his and bought a ranch down in Hemet Valley where he lived until the late 1950's.

Cross and Harris moved out from the Keane Wonder on the morning of August 9, 1904 headed for a blowout in the hills to the north that Harris had seen on an earlier trip. Out in the flat, about where the Death Valley-Beatty road is located, Harris picked up a piece of greenish float. It was flecked with gold. He called Cross and they found other gold-bearing pieces of quartz. Harris turned his rock over and over. From every angle he could see gold flecks. He exclaimed, "Ed, that rock just lays in my hand and squints at me like a green bullfrog." The prospectors peered about — doing some squinting of their own, then decided to look toward the hills for the lode.

Late that afternoon they found the mother vein, and decided to set up camp. The next day, they made out location notices. Ed hurried away to file them. Not too certain of county lines, he filed in 14th, Esmeralda and Nye counties. Shorty moved about — doing what he could do best — publicizing the strike as the "biggest thing yet." Soon the stampede was on from the Nevada camps. Bob Montgomery staked out the Montgomery-Shoshone some three or four miles away. His first ore ran $500 a ton. He turned down a cool $1 million for it. The Bursch brothers came and laid out the townsite of Rhyolite near the Montgomery Mine. Walter Beatty, his Indian wife and family lived at nearby Beatty Springs. Beatty sold the spring water for more money than he believed existed, resulting in it being piped to Rhyolite. Beatty started a town on his homestead, south of the springs. A rag town at first, it grew into a commercial center. Beatty was named the first postmaster, a job he was forced to relinquish when a nosy government man came along and found that Beatty could not read nor write. His successor was a young storekeeper, R. A. Gibson, who had set up business with a load of lumber, hay, and other provisions he had trucked up from far off Ivanpah by Rose & Palmer.

Tasker L. Oddie, Tonopah's fearless sheriff, arrived and organized the Bullfrog Mining Company. One of the directors was Key Pittman, who years later was Oddie's colleague in the Senate.

Bullfrog, the discovery town, continued to grow — while Rhyolite did so in a more spectacular way. It boasted a Jay Cook Bank housed in a three-story concrete and steel building, the one whose ruined facade delights so many present day photographers. Rhyolite had a whole street of stone and concrete structures. Bullfrog had one of the finest and strongest jails in the whole state. It is still there.

Colorful clientele of the Northern Saloon in Beatty, just east of the Bullfrog. (Death Valley National Park Museum)

In the big names of mining, Charles M. Schwab, Senator W. A. Clark, and Malcolm Macdonald came and invested. Rhyolite boasted not only piped water — it had an ice plant and a brewery, in addition to its numerous mercantile houses, brothels, and saloons.

Senator Clark and F. N. "Borax" Smith were rivals in bringing railroads to Death Valley and the west. They started as partners with Smith starting rails from Clark's San Pedro, Los Angeles & Salt Lake at the Nevada siding named Las Vegas. Then, while Clark was vacationing in Europe, he read more and more about the Bullfrog boom. He decided to make the feeder line a Clark one. Of course, that didn't suit Smith, the borax king — who thought he had a firm commitment to build from Las Vegas to his big borax mine, the "Lila C," near the present Death Valley Junction. When Clark returned from Europe, Smith's crews were already 22 miles on their way from Las Vegas toward the Lila C. A Clark attorney came out and in effect read Clarence Rasor and John Ryan, Smith's surveyor and superintendent, the riot act. They were ordered to cease and desist, and very plainly told they could not connect with the Clark railroad at Las Vegas or any other point. The Clark and Smith agreement had been a verbal one — reached over dinner at San Francisco's *Palace Hotel.*

The infuriated Smith announced he would never ship a pound of borax over Clark's railroad. He even went further — he moved his construction crews to Ludlow, 55 miles east of Barstow — on the Santa Fe. Even before the survey could be completed, they were laying ties and rails toward the north, over Broadwell Playa and on toward Soda Lake. Smith announced that his railroad, the Tonopah and Tidewater would, as its name implied, give a tidewater outlet to Nevada's mines. In practice, however, he was happy over the Santa Fe junction at Ludlow for his southern terminal. Smith's T&T was held up by heavy construction in Amargosa Canyon, the canyon of hanging rocks, and reached the Bullfrog area after Clark's Las Vegas & Tonopah — which had both a shorter and an easier route. Then, the LV & T erected a magnificent station at Rhyolite, one that has been preserved long after the tracks were gone. A third railroad also

The Tonapah & Tidewater — one of the great desert locomotives of a vanished era.
(Death Valley National Park Museum)

entered the picture, the Bullfrog & Goldfield, a little line which was to all purposes, save ownership, a southern extension of the existing Tonopah & Goldfield. LV&T extended its tracks north to Goldfield, but the T&T was content with a B&G junction. Now, all three lines are but memories. T&T, the last to go, was torn up in 1942 to furnish iron for the War effort — which action, incidentally had been opposed by its owners — Pacific Coast Borax. During the boom years, the mining railroads had been big money earners. The first months after the T&T was completed, solid pullman trains ran from Tonopah to Los Angeles and back each weekend.

While the railroads were coming, the southern Nevada towns were on the downgrade. After the B&G and LV&T dropped out, the T&T picked up the big Rhyolite depot which served as an admirable terminal for the trains hauling the suckers to C. C. Julian's gyp excursions to his highly touted Leadfield in 1926.

There was rivalry between Beatty and Rhyolite. Beatty sought to corral travelers by building the Montgomery Hotel. The Montgomery was not at all modest in advertising that it had the only bath in Nevada south of Goldfield. It was absolutely true. What passed for a hotel in Las Vegas was just a big tent fronting the tracks. But Rhyolite raised the ante when it advertised that its new Southern Hotel had TWO baths. They were really catering to the carriage trade.

At the end of 1906, Rhyolite had 10,000 people, if the "residents-for-a-day" were counted. Not even a reservation would assure one a bed unless the hotel clerk was given his tip. The profits to merchants were almost as big as those going to the mine promoters. The Porter Brothers of Randsburg took 18 wagonloads of their stock, moved it across Death Valley — selling half the supplies by the time their long caravan was unloaded. A poor lunch counter had a line so long it took an hour to get served. It was no town for a prohibitionist. Even the coffee smelled and tasted of liquor. The beaneries kept their water in whiskey barrels.

The *Rhyolite Herald* appeared in 1905. It had competition in the *Bullfrog Miner* and the *Rhyolite Bulletin* along with the *Death Valley Magazine*, which was a monthly. There is a copy of the latter down in the Death Valley Museum now. Its inside cover is devoted to a preview of the next issue and announcing the feature article would be by Colonel John B. Colton who was to tell of his crossing Death Valley in 1849 with the Jayhawkers. Despite the fact that references to the Colton article have appeared in many of the bibliographies, don't take the trouble to look for it. It never existed. When the next month rolled around the *Death Valley Magazine* had a sign on its front door: "Gone to Rawhide."

Over to the west of the business district of Rhyolite, there is the shell of a large concrete building. It was the schoolhouse built with a $20,000 bond issue in the fall of 1907. Rhyolite had 270 school-age kids the previous June; by the time the new building was ready there were only enough left for classes in a single room.

Today Rhyolite and Bullfrog are ghost towns — easy to reach for winter tourists. Rhyolite's ruins were still impressive in the mid

One of the fanciest buildings in town.
(Nevada Historical Society)

1980's before being completely dwarfed by the massive pile of mine tailings from Barrick Gold's recent operations at the Bullfrog Mine, just up the highway on the way to Beatty. There is still a museum or two at Rhyolite, and the famous L. J. Murphy bottle house. Two or three houses are occupied and the old-timers who like to show visitors where millionaires of the day lived. The Montgomery-Shoshone Mine is certain to be high on the list and the visitor will likely be told that it was discovered by an old Indian named Johnnie who gave it to E. A. "Bob" Montgomery in trade for a pair of overalls. It is a good yarn, but it isn't so. Montgomery found his own mine. Those who prefer truth to fiction owe a debt of gratitude to Harold Weight of Twentynine Palms who published a book entitled, "Rhyolite, Death Valley's City of Golden Dreams." Weight dug up an early copy of the *Inyo Register*, old Bill Chalfant's paper over in Bishop. It gives a true story of the Montgomery-Shoshone discovery as printed before the Indian and overalls yarn was invented.

In the fall of 1957 the writer called on Ed Cross at his daughter's, home in Hemet, and with the retired mine owner checked over salient facts in the story of Bullfrog and Rhyolite. In parting, the aged man was asked, "Mr. Cross, how is it that so much has been written about Shorty Harris at Bullfrog, and so little about you?"

Cross laughed and said, "Shorty liked to talk."

Luckless fellow found by a search party just two weeks after he and his friend tried to walk from Rhyolite to Skidoo. His friend met the same demise.
(Death Valley National Park Museum)

SKIDOO
HE WAS HANGED TWICE
— ❧✟❧ —

SKIDOO, a mining camp perched high on the northern brow of the Panamints where it overlooks the famous Stovepipe Wells sand dunes, has been known far and wide as "the town that had the hanging." Perhaps this is none too fair a distinction. In 1966, Skidoo was a small collection of buildings — one of which housed the bank and general store; one housed the mill — while others served as miner's cabins. Back then, one or two old-timers could be found occupying one of the remaining cabins and picking over the veins for high-grade. Today, all of the buildings have collapsed and only the wooden skeletons of a few large mills are all that remain of the boomtown once known as Skidoo.

Nearly a hundred years ago, things were different in Skidoo. The camp boasted a post office, a bank, a phone line that stretched all the way across Death Valley to Rhyolite, a weekly newspaper known as the *Skidoo News*, general store, lumber yard, blacksmith shop, several saloons, and running water piped all the way from Telescope Peak — 23 miles distant. It was the 23-mile water line which gave Skidoo its name for the slang expression of the day was "Twenty-three Skidoo." Skidoo meant scram — vamoose.

Skidoo's most famous incident, the lynching of a drunken saloon keeper, Joe "Hooch" Simpson, on a night in April 1908 made Skidoo the most advertised mining camp in the West. Perhaps it was not just the lynching itself, but the congeniality of the Skidoo-ites that brought the wave of publicity, for 24 hours after Simpson had been interred on boot hill, a Los Angeles Herald reporter arrived. He had come all the way from Lone Pine in a livery rig to get the story about the hanging. Skidoo folk were right proud of such notice and promptly set out to show their appreciation. They disinterred Simpson's corpse and hanged it a second time just so the reporter could take a picture.

The editor of the *Skidoo News* chronicled his big scoop in the issue of April 5, a copy of which has, fortunately, been preserved in the Inyo County Library at Independence. The headlines read:

"MURDER IN CAMP. Murderer lynched with general approval. Joe Simpson shoots Jim Arnold dead and is hanged by citizens."

Fifty-two years after the lynching, visitors to the annual Death Valley '49ers Encampment were given eye witness accounts of "Hooch" Simpson's lynching by two of the few onlookers still living. They were George Cook of Lone Pine and Bill Keys of Joshua Tree who spoke at a campfire among the sand dunes. This writer interviewed the pair whose answers to questions were carried by loudspeakers to the hundreds of campfire visitors. The following is a composite of the two stories. Simpson and a partner ran a tent saloon near the big store and bank. One morning business may have been a bit dull so Simpson took to drinking his wares. It was not uncommon, one surmises, for he was universally known as "Hooch." It was Sunday morning and Joe was not only drunk — he was drunk and armed. Jim Arnold was the town banker, at what was named the Southern California Bank. Simpson weaved into the bank, pointed his gun and demanded $20. Bystanders overpowered him and took his gun. Joe became abusive and Arnold threw him out.

Three hours later Joe recovered his gun from the stove where his partner had hidden it and went back to the bank. Confronting Arnold again he asked:

"Have you got anything against me, Jim?"

Arnold answered, "No, Joe. I have nothing against you."

"Yes you have," Joe retorted, "prepare to die."

With that he shot Arnold near the heart. Then he turned his gun on Joe MacDonald, also of the bank, and would have shot him had not his attention been diverted by a reeling drunk — Gordon McBain

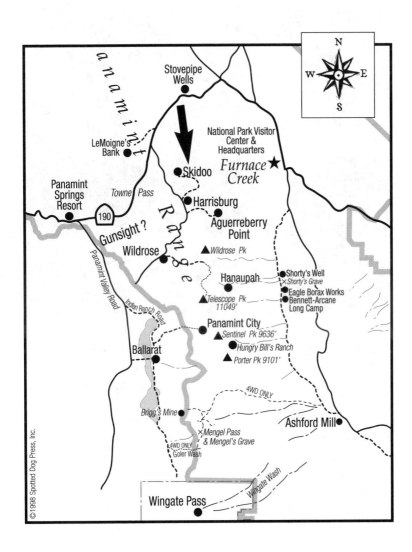

Stovepipe Wells

National Park Visitor Center & Headquarters

LeMoigne's Bank

Panamint Springs Resort

Towne Pass

190

Gunsight?

Wildrose

Skidoo

Furnace Creek

Harrisburg

Aguerreberry Point

▲ *Wildrose Pk*

Hanaupah

Shorty's Well
✕ *Shorty's Grave*
Eagle Borax Works
Bennett-Arcane
Long Camp

▲ *Telescope Pk 11049'*

Panamint City

▲ *Sentinel Pk 9636'*

● *Hungry Bill's Ranch*

▲ *Porter Pk 9101'*

Ballarat

Panamint Valley Road

Indian Ranch Road

4WD ONLY

Brigg's Mine

Ashford Mill

✕ *Mengel Pass & Mengel's Grave*

4WD ONLY
Goler Wash

Wingate Wash

Wingate Pass

Workings at Skidoo. (L. Burr Belden).

who, though unarmed, attempted to arrest Simpson. McBain, incidentally, got between Joe and a rifle-aiming physician only 100 feet distant. Bystanders soon disarmed and handcuffed Simpson. Arnold died that evening.

Simpson showed no remorse. In fact, he became boastful over his marksmanship. The poker parlor, Club Skidoo, was converted into a temporary guardhouse.

The sheriff was not expected until Thursday. The miners determined that Simpson should pay with his life then and there.

On Wednesday night the guard watching Simpson was overpowered by Skidoo vigilantes. The prisoner was taken outside and hanged to a telephone pole. The next day, Thursday, Judge Thisse conducted an inquest.

The *Skidoo News* remarked on how quietly the lynching had been conducted. A joker had told the drunken McBain that he was to be a second victim. McBain promptly left camp.

The *Skidoo News* editor remarked that McBain's running from imaginary pursuers made more noise than the hanging.

On Friday, the Los Angeles reporter arrived. The second hanging was decorously staged with a tent frame — a far less public spot than the telephone pole. The *Skidoo News* editor closed his full-page coverage with a bit of moralizing about the stoutness of the town's telephone poles — which he opined should stand as a warning to evil-doers.

Oh, yes. The coroner's inquest found Simpson had died of strangulation at the hands of persons unknown.

In April 1908, Keys was mining in Skidoo. Cook was hauling supplies back and forth to Rhyolite. At the Death Valley campfire on November 10, 1960, Cook and Keys met each other for the first time in nearly 50 years. Around the fire, Cook admitted he was one of the two men who went inside the guardhouse and hauled Simpson outside — turning him over to the vigilantes. Keys recalled that there was a crowd of 60 men surrounding the tent of Constable Sellers when Simpson had been moved.

The once wild and exciting town of Skidoo is quiet now. The famous water line was hauled away during World War I. There is plenty of ore left, but it is no longer lying loose on the ground. Legend has it, that one foggy night back in 1906, Harry Ramsey and "One Eye" Thompson became lost on a trip from Furnace Creek to Harrisburg. Having lost the trail, they prudently halted and bedded down. Morning revealed promising ore-bearing rocks within arm's reach of their blankets. When they left Skidoo, all of the ore lying on the ground was gone.

ASHFORD MILL
THE FORT
—✴— ✴—

NEARLY 45 miles south of Furnace Creek, there is a major Death Valley road intersection where the east and west high-ways join. Another road heads east via Jubilee and Salsberry passes to Shoshone, while a fourth route goes south to join State Highway 127 at Salt Spring. A bit west of the present junction is a sizable rectangle of massive concrete walls — the abandoned Ashford Mill. Ever since Death Valley National Monument was created in 1933, countless thousands of tourists have asked park rangers:

"Who built that fort down south of Badwater, and why?"

Death Valley specializes in the unusual — and the story of Ashford Mill certainly stands near the top of this category. It happened this way, according to the late Senator Charles A. Brown, who was managing the Fairbanks and Brown establishment at Shoshone when the mill was erected. The Ashford brothers lived in "Dublin City," in the summer months when it was a bit too warm for Death Valley prospecting. This namesake for Erin's capitol consisted of nothing more than caves dug into a cutbank and fitted with doors and windows — a favorite summer camp of the old-timers.

The Ashfords developed a prospect in the Black Mountains, some three miles up the canyon to the northwest of today's road junction. In addition to some spectacular high grade there were broad veins of milling-quality gold. A mill on the spot was the preferred way to mine the ore at a profit. An engineer was consulted, and he proposed a crusher and stamp operation. A test of gravel in nearby Rhodes Wash showed it suitable for the making of concrete. A carload of cement was ordered from Crestmore, 250 miles away

Ashford Mill ruins. (L. Burr Belden)

by rail. When the cement reached the Shoshone siding of the
Tonopah & Tidewater Railroad, the Ashfords were surprised to find
they had two carloads instead of the one they had ordered.

A telegram was sent to the Riverside Cement Company advis-
ing them of the mistake, and asking for instructions. The cement
company figured the freight cost back over the T&T and Santa Fe,
and decided it was more than the product was worth to its makers.
"Keep it with our compliments," was the answer to the Ashfords.

Alex McLaren was boss of the mill erection. He used a rich four-
to-one mix, then used his extra concrete in thickening the walls. It
is a safe wager that Ashford Mill will continue to be a Death Valley
landmark for a long time. It was built in 1915. Machinery was
hauled off during World War II when no piece of metal was safe
anywhere in the desert.

The three Ashford brothers were Harry, Henry, and Rudolph.
They had located their mine in 1907 and were hauling away picture
rock in 1914 when one B. M. McClausland came along. He liked the
prospects so well he agreed to pay $100,000 for the mine and the
then projected mill. The Ashfords copied what they thought was a
printed sales contract they saw in a book. They had no lawyer and
in copying the printed form, it seems they left out some important
words. When it came time to pay, McClausland refused. The
Ashfords sued. After a year, the suit was decided against the
Ashfords. The mill cost was now on their backs and their debts
were so heavy they couldn't operate the big mill. It was closed. For
a time the brothers took ore out by wagon, past their idle mill, to
have it processed elsewhere. Then the operation ground to a halt.

Bill Keys, whose Desert Hound Mine was in the next canyon
over, claims there is still plenty of untouched ore in the Ashford.

After being forced to the wall by the McClausland suit the
Ashfords negotiated a partnership — headed by a Magyar nobleman, Count V. A. Baranoff, and William Cody, nephew and namesake of "Buffalo Bill." Count Baranoff was minus a leg which he
said he had lost in a duel. He rather startled desert folk when he
appeared at Silver Lake wearing Hapsburg court decorations as an

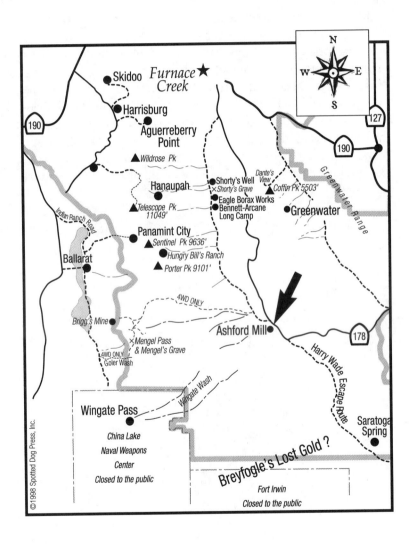

N
W   E
S

Skidoo
Furnace ★
Creek
Harrisburg
190
Aguerreberry
Point
▲*Wildrose Pk*
Hanaupah
●Shorty's Well   *Dante's*
✕*Shorty's Grave*   *View*
▲*Coffin Pk 5503'*
●Eagle Borax Works
▲*Telescope Pk*   ●Bennett-Arcane
11049'   Long Camp   ●Greenwater
Panamint City
▲*Sentinel Pk 9636'*
Indian Ranch Road
●*Hungry Bill's Ranch*
Ballarat
▲ *Porter Pk 9101'*
Greenwater Range
127
190
4WD ONLY
Brigg's Mine ●
Ashford Mill ●
✕*Mengel Pass*
& Mengel's Grave   *Harry Wade Escape Route*   178
4WD ONLY
Goler Wash
Wingate Wash
Wingate Pass
●
Saratoga
Spring ●
China Lake
Naval Weapons
Center   *Breyfogle's Lost Gold ?*
Closed to the public
Fort Irwin
Closed to the public

© 1998 Spotted Dog Press, Inc.

added touch to his prospector's garb.

In mid-summer the count decided he wanted to see "his mine." A rig was outfitted at Silver Lake. Four days later when the party was unreported, W. H. Brown, the T&T agent set out on a rescue mission. He found the Baranoff party hopelessly mired. He bundled the occupants into his rig and hurried back to Silver Lake. The nobleman, badly dehydrated, and craving water, sought to supplement his carefully doled-out water with ice he secretly swiped from the bag on his head. He died and was buried at Silver Lake. Later, his family had the body removed. Since the Baranoff-Cody episode, the Ashford mine has been quiet. After all, most mines are quiet these days.

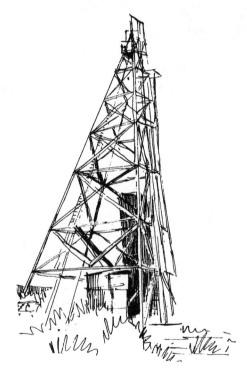

JEAN LE MOIGNE
AND HIS BANK

JEAN LE MOIGNE, a graduate in engineering and chemistry from a university in France, deserves the title of "dean" among Death Valley's prospectors. He sought and found ore everywhere from Calico to Pioche, but it was in Death Valley proper that his story begins and it was in the same blistered trough that it reached its tragic end.

The titanic borax chapter of the valley and its environs has no place in this book. A mere chronicle of its high spots would require a sizable volume, but it was borax that brought Jean (the Americans soon knew him as John, and later as "Cap"), to Death Valley and dropped him there alone, and jobless, 5,000 miles from home and friends.

Jean was called from Paris by his fellow countryman Isadore Daunet, who headed Death Valley's first borax enterprise, Eagle Borax, in 1882 — a year before William Tell Coleman's larger Harmony Borax started near Furnace Creek. Daunet had trouble refining his cottonball and sent for Jean, the young chemist son of old country friends. Between the time Daunet offered Jean a job, and the time of his arrival, the little Eagle Borax plant went belly-up. A heartbroken Daunet, took his own life.

Eagle was probably the simplest and least efficient borax plant ever devised. It consisted of an open vat which had an Indian-tended fire beneath. Native American workers dumped cottonball borax they had gathered on the valley floor into the vat. After boiling, the solution was drawn off into small tanks where it cooled. The borax crystallized and was harvested. It contained so much foreign material it sold at too low a price to pay expenses.

Very possibly, the young chemist would have devised a more efficient operation, but he arrived too late to save the ill-fated Eagle Borax works.

Death Valley was a far different land than Jean Le Moigne had expected. Yet, despite what must have been an initial forbidding picture, he stayed for 40 years. Along with the news of Daunet's death, Le Moigne learned that Eagle Borax was without funds. His trip to Death Valley from France was made on advanced funds — and, there was no money for a return trip. He instead turned prospector. The change from brilliant university graduate to "desert rat" was so complete that Le Moigne soon came to avoid all of the trappings of civilization, including companionship. He also developed quite a disdain for money. In the 1890's, he was known to have expressed a desire to once again visit France, but a decade later, after he had profitably sold a mine or two, Le Moigne did not want to leave his beloved desert.

Throughout the 1910-20 decade, Le Moigne lived in a rock cabin in the Cottonwood Mountains. The cabin location was in a canyon which now appropriately bears the name "Lemoigne." A quarter mile upstream from the cabin was Jean's silver mine, the one he called his "bank." The mine was a small one, but consisted of a ledge of almost pure silver. He knew the ledge would give out if worked regularly. He did not even sink a shaft — but worked it from a trench, which with depth, he stoped, preferring to handle waste rock twice rather than to install machinery which might,tempt him to "overdraw the bank."

Despite his taciturn disposition, Le Moigne is known to have taken a partner, Bill Stewart. That was in 1916. Bill lived up Emigrant Canyon in a tent while Jean stayed in his rock cabin. The partners were ten miles apart at bedtime.

Earlier, Le Moigne had lived for several years down at Bicycle Lake (now located on the Fort Irwin army base), where he briefly ran a store, and had a house built of lumber hauled from Barstow. When the house burned, Le Moigne went back to his cabin in the canyon — close to his bank.

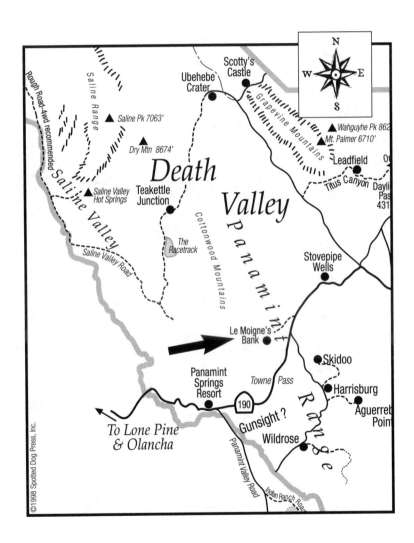

Rough Road-4wd recommended

Saline Range

▲ Saline Pk 7063'

▲ Dry Mtn 8674'

Saline Valley

▲ Saline Valley
Hot Springs

Teakettle
Junction

Saline Valley Road

The
Racetrack

Death

Valley

Cottonwood Mountains

Ubehebe
Crater

Scotty's
Castle

Grapevine Mountains

▲ Wahguyhe Pk 862
▲ Mt. Palmer 6710'

Leadfield

Titus Canyon

Dayli
Pas
431

Panamint

Stovepipe
Wells

Le Moigne's
Bank

● Skidoo

Panamint
Springs
Resort

Towne Pass

190

Gunsight ?

Wildrose

● Harrisburg

Range

Aguerreb
Poin

To Lone Pine
& Olancha

Panamint Valley Road

Indian Ranch Road

N
W   E
S

©1998 Spotted Dog Press, Inc.

As a storekeeper, Le Moigne was quite unique. Since he was out prospecting much of the time, he always left the door to his store unlocked. A plate on the counter served as the cash register. Customers served themselves and left what they considered the right price in the plate. The strange thing is that the system seemed to work. Those were the good old days — during the years when few but the old-timers moved across desert trails.

Le Moigne's return to his Death Valley mine did not last long. He told his partner one day that he was not feeling well. Stewart advised him to go see a doctor. Le Moigne hitched up his burro team and started for Furnace Creek. He never arrived. Later, on the old road between Stovepipe Wells and Salt Creek Le Moigne's body was found curled under a mesquite bush. Evidently, he had taken suddenly ill. He had halted, and set the brake. The burros could not pull away, and died with him.

Today the USGS quadrangle maps carry a notation "Le Moigne Grave." It is on the old trail, now a jeep road. The tales about Le Moigne are numerous. "Cap" is famous, or infamous for hitching himself alongside one of his burros to produce a team, when he lived down by Bicycle Lake. When one of his animals was ill and rather than wait to break in a wild one, Le Moigne just cast himself as a temporary replacement.

Another good Le Moigne yarn was told by Stewart. It seems a fellow learned the "bank" was for sale. He had seen some of that rich ore and offered $10,000 cash. Much to his partner's disgust, Jean turned down the offer, not because the price was not right, but because the money was in the form of a check. Old Cap just didn't trust banks, and anyway the nearest one was way over in Lone Pine. It was much too far to go for $10,000.

Cap was known all over the desert for his coffee. Up in Olancha, around World War I, Jim Nosser of Johannesburg asked for the recipe. "I take a hell of a lot of coffee, damn little water, and let it bile and bile and bile," Le Moigne once said.

HANAUPAH
THE BURRO WORE A BATHROBE
— ❧✦❧ —

PROSPECTORS OF THE OLD SCHOOL knew the meaning of work —
hard backbreaking work. A prime example was Alexander Shorty
Borden, onetime US Cavalryman, who switched from chasing
Pancho Villa down below the Rio Grande to hunting ore in the
Death Valley region.

The No. 1 exhibit to prove the foregoing thesis consists of a road
up the Panamint Range from below sea level to the 8,000 foot contour on Telescope Peak. It was built by Borden, with a crowbar,
pick, and his two burros. Where Shorty's road joins the west side
road, below Furnace Creek, is a hand dug well — Shorty's Well,
also Borden's single handed work.

Borden arrived in Death Valley early in the 1920's and put blankets down in an Emigrant Canyon cave which he enlarged, fitting
the opening with a door and window. It served as a base from
which he made prospecting trips that ranged from north of
Ubehebe Crater south to the Avawatz Mountains. They were slow
painstaking treks lasting for days or weeks, which were devoted
entirely to careful sampling of rock. On one such trip, Borden
became intrigued with some deserted Indian shacks grouped
around a spring in Hanaupah Canyon. He learned that the shacks
had been occupied by Indian draft-dodgers during World War I.
Borden put down his blanket, tethered his burros, and stayed. In a
shelf cave he found a little native shrine with charms such as bird
claws and snake rattles, each carefully protected in a bottle.

More important than the shrine however, were several outcroppings of ore he discovered. One silver prospect that appeared to

Shorty Borden (L. Burr Belden Collection)

carry considerable lead was given prompt attention. All evidence indicated an extensive vein. Borden dug out as much as his burro could pack and headed back for camp, a three-day journey. The assay reports were encouraging. He decided to develop his prospect into a mine. It would not pay, however, unless he had a road. No pack train operation would be profitable.

Others might have quit then and there — but not Shorty. The obstacles only made him more determined. A bulldozed road could have been blasted out up Hanaupah Canyon in a matter of weeks. Shorty, however, had no such equipment, nor money to hire any.

With his crowbar, pick, and two favorite burros Shorty Borden went to work on his road. In summer he packed into the little mountain oasis and worked down toward Death Valley floor. In winter he camped on the valley floor, dug his well, and pecked out the road up the canyon.

Shorty and his burros were great companions. His two favorites were "Hanaupah Jack" and "Tule Hole." They were animals he loved so much he would spend his last dollar to buy them feed, even denying himself sufficient grub. They were the best fed and fattest members of the burro tribe in all the Panamints. Shorty thought Hanaupah Jack suffered from the cold winter nights. On one of his infrequent trips "outside" he bought a flannel bathrobe in Lone Pine which he manipulated into a "burro coat." Hanaupah's fore legs were worked into the sleeves, with the main part of the robe serving as a blanket for the burro's back. The robe was secured in place by a liberal winding of rope and rawhide. To man, Hanaupah was an object of wonder — but to other burros he appeared possessed with evil spirits. The wild herd up on Harrisburg Flats would snort and gallop away in fright whenever Jack trotted up to exchange friendly greetings.

Present day road maps indicate the road from Shorty's well is open for about five miles. A map printed 20 years ago shows it to be nine miles long and terminating at Hanaupah Spring where Shorty had his mine. The United States Geological Survey topographical sheet also shows a road to the spring. To those who may wish to go there — a word of caution: those USGS crews might laugh at having to roll aside a few boulders — but few others would. The route should be a good challenge to the four-wheel drive fraternity.

Borden started on his one-man road project in September 1932. He had it completed before March 1933, after six months of ceaseless labor, labor that meant long days and no weekends off.

Back in his cave dwelling days at Emigrant, Shorty lived on a budget that approximated zero. He had a quantity of oatmeal which he cooked for his meals three times daily except for some welcome additions obtained in an unusual way. The hard breed of traveler who assayed to reach Death Valley on tires was in no hurry. The road didn't permit speeds of more than 10 or 15 miles an hour. In his cave, Shorty could hear autos coming long before they rounded the bend upstream. He had a gold pan salted with pay dirt. Come afternoon he would sit by the cave door. When he heard a vehicle he would step down beside the road and appear to be panning gold. Travelers would invariably stop and inquire as to the prospects. Borden let them see for themselves the telltale streak of gold on the pan bottom. Conversation would follow and the prospector would issue a dinner invitation.

The dining was done in the cave with its ingeniously fitted interior. When the guests found out that the meal was to be oatmeal — just oatmeal — back to the car the visitors would trot to return with an armful of canned goods. Shorty's strategy worked quite well. Fellow prospectors Jack Stewart and Bill Corcoran, in their tent some 200 feet away, would chuckle:

"Shorty has caught another mess of fish," they said.

Shorty's ore samples, which averaged $24 in silver and lead after eliminating the high grade, caught the eye of Miss Katheryn Ronan, manager of the Furnace Creek Inn. Shorty was encouraged by a small grubstake she provided. He sacked and piled up 40 tons of his better ore. He had an informal offer for hauling to the Tonopah & Tidewater at Shoshone. Now with his ore ready he found that even his depression period costs were far higher. It

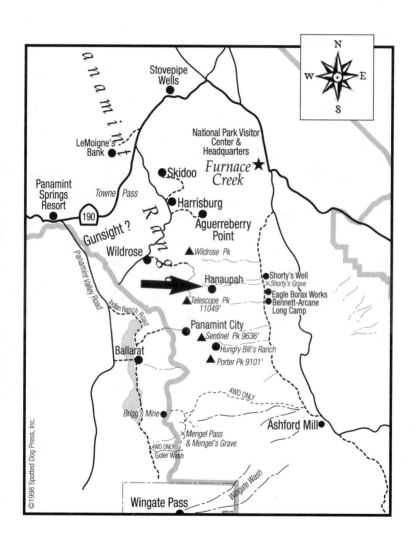

would cost him $20 a ton to get his sacked ore to the railroad. This plus rail fare meant a cost of $26.50 a ton to take $24 ore to the smelter at Salt Lake.

The ore was left neatly sacked opposite the spring. A regretful Shorty took his burros north to try new prospects in the Inyo Range. He never returned to keep up his assessment work.

There isn't any 40 tons of sacked ore up at Hanaupah Spring anymore. The 1940's brought war, soaring lead prices, and a smelter right at Bonnie Claire. One day some trucks drove up Shorty's abandoned road, and the ore was taken to that smelter.

By World War II, Shorty was in his 70's. He gravitated to the Sanitarium in Big Pine, where he was a resident until the mid-1950's. Then he sold a prospect in the Inyos and moved to a rest home in Lone Pine. He suffered a stroke, which affected his speech, but in slowly pronounced syllables he told this writer, in January 1958, about his Hanaupah discovery and his big disappointment over being unable to market his ore profitably. No, he had never been paid by the truckers who took his ore to the smelter. He could still laugh though, over his oatmeal dinners. Shorty was a great little guy.

AGUERREBERRY
AND HARRISBURG
— ❖❖❖❖ —

IN JUNE 1906 two prospectors were camped on the floor of
Death Valley alongside an irrigation ditch. The place, now Furnace
Creek Ranch, was then known as Greenland. One was little Frank
"Shorty" Harris, ever-roaming prospector. The other was a quiet,
soft-spoken Basque, Pete Aguerreberry. Both were taking a breather
after long ore-searching tramps into the rapidly building summer
heat of the area.

Harris, as this writer heard it second hand from one of Shorty's
numerous partners, proposed the two strike out for Ballarat and be
there for the traditional Fourth of July celebration. Aguerreberry
had no immediate plans and was agreeable, so they set out on the
morning of July 1, crossing the spongy sink south of the present
Death Valley Airport over the trail which had been corduroyed in
places to prevent man and burro from sinking deep into the soft
crust. Then they climbed the trail up the steep east slope of the
Panamints, bedding down near the trail.

The next morning the pair descended over a broad upland mesa
now called Harrisburg Flats. At the mesa's north side were intru-
sive black hills. Harris and Aguerreberry took a course diagonally
southwest, a course which in a few more miles would lead them to
Wildrose Spring, Wildrose Canyon and then to the fleshpots of
Ballarat.

At the base of the little hills Aguerreberry picked up a rock that
intrigued him. He showed it to his companion who responded,
"Hell! it's lousy with gold." Pete suggested a halt to stake out
claims. Harris objected saying, "We'll come back and do it. If we
don't get to Ballarat tomorrow night all the likker will be gone."

With that, Shorty started off. Reluctantly Pete followed.

During the evening of July 3, and the following day, Aguerreberry apprehensively heard a loose-tongued Harris boast of another bonanza discovery "right up there in the Panamints."

Dawn Came on July 5th and Pete Aguerreberry headed back up Wildrose and on north to his discovery site. He reached the spot after dusk to find a hillside swarming with fellow prospectors. The next morning revealed that the newcomers had ignored Pete's little markers for they had staked out the land for hundreds of yards around. Pete protested. Shorty Harris came to his rescue, and the original Aguerreberry discovery claim was restored.

The new camp was a producer from the grassroots down, at least for a time. When the population numbered in the hundreds a name was wanted. Harrisberry was proposed and voted for, but when the name reached the papers it had been changed to Harrisburg.

The boom days came and went. For years, Harrisburg and Skidoo, some 12 miles north, were rivals. Both produced gold — lots of it. Harris soon sold his claims, but not Aguerreberry. He tunneled deep into the little hills and built a cabin, black-smith shop and storehouse nearby. For the next 35 years Pete worked his mine, installed air pumps, a baby-gauge railroad and compressed air drills. In marked contrast to the average miner's cabin, Pete Aguerreberry kept an ultra neat house. He even had lace curtains at the front windows.

The Panamint Range topped out in a ridge some five miles east of Aguerreberry's camp. There a flat-topped promontory offered an unsurpassed panoramic view of Death Valley's awesome magnificence thousands of feet below. Pete thought that others would be interested also. He accordingly scraped out a road from his mine to the lookout spot which he called "Fine View" or sometimes "Great View."

About a year or two after Death Valley National Monument was established in 1933, a distinguished visitor stopped at Aguerreberry Camp and asked directions to Fine View. He told Pete there would be road signs put up and that the viewpoint turnoff would be marked.

Blacksmith shop and ore cart at Harrisburg. (L. Burr Belden)

No one could have been more surprised than Pete Aguerreberry when an Automobile Club of Southern California road sign crew came down the Emigrant Canyon road, two or three months later and erected a sign at the Harrisburg turnoff. It carried an arrow pointing east and the name read "Aguerreberry Point." Pete's inquiring visitor of weeks before had been Phil Townsend Hanna, public relations director for the Auto Club. Hanna had learned of Pete's arduous road building just so his fellowman could share with him the magnificent panorama — and Hanna had appropriately felt the modest Basque miner deserved to have his name on the viewpoint. It is there today.

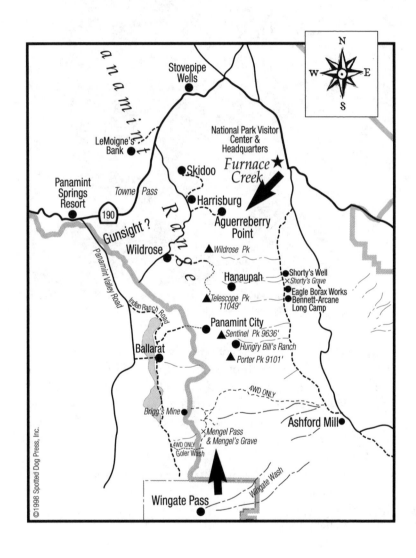

GREATER VIEW
WOODEN LEG MONUMENT
⌒✳⌒

ONE BALMY SPRING EVENING IN 1918, two well-known Death Valley miners were passing time at Wildrose, then an old stage station on the way to Harrisburg and Skidoo. One was the Basque, Pete Aguerreberry who owned and operated the Harrisburg mine. As noted in the preceding chapter, Pete had broken out a rough road from his camp to the 6,650-foot ridge at the head of Trail Canyon, because he wanted others to enjoy the panoramic view of the great valley below. Pete, usually taciturn, surprised his friends that evening by telling of the lookout he termed either "Fine View" or "Great View."

When Pete had finished, another spoke up. From his cabin he had a "greater view" he asserted. This second miner was Carl Mengel, owner of a good gold producer on the west ridge of Butte Valley. Mengel, an ever friendly chap and a native of San Bernardino, was a well-educated mining engineer who had filed claims all the way from Barstow to Belmont, and from Kawich to Saline Valley. Mengel's mother, of German extraction, had taught both English and German in the San Bernardino schools. Carl had gone through public school and the Sturges Academy there, and then had taken engineering in Denver.

The death of an uncle in Tulare County suddenly turned Mengel from a miner to an orange grower. The grove proved profitable, but Mengel contracted tuberculosis. He sold the grove and spent two or three years "chasing health" as he termed it. Buying a buckboard, he drove up and down the Redwood Highway, taking a leisurely pace with 12 hours sleep at night and a nap during

Carl Mengel in Butte Valley. (Death Valley National Park Museum)

the noon hour. Eventually, his team took him to Puget Sound where he found the air invigorating. For two years, Mengel operated as a commercial fisherman, then decided he was strong enough to return to mining once more.

He landed at Silver Peak, Nevada, east of the massive White Mountains and west of Tonopah. He promptly went to work as a miner, only to be promoted when the superintendent overheard him discussing rock structure in geological terms. A tunnel in the mine, one that had been dug along a broad vein, had pinched out. It intrigued Mengel. He decided an earth slippage had moved the vein to one side and he could pick it up. He and a partner were working alone in the abandoned tunnel when, without warning, quantities of overhead rock fell. Both men ran, but one of Mengel's leg was caught by the falling rock and he was pinned down —

while scores of other rocks cascaded down burying him. Miraculously, Mengel's companion received only minor injuries and eventually wormed out of the debris.

For the next 24 hours men worked feverishly in relays to reach the imprisoned man. Doctors, who were waiting at the mine entrance, examined the seriously injured Mengel. They found crushed bones and the beginnings of infection. Few thought Mengel could live — but live he did, for another 39 years. This time the convalescent period was spent on the desert. With summer advancing he moved into the Panamints and, as he felt stronger, began some prospecting. Near the head of Anvil Spring Canyon in Butte Valley, Carl Mengel dug a prospect hole which, after a few months, he decided was really a mine. It was indeed a mine and he worked it until his death in 1944.

Below the mine, around a projecting butte was a spring. Mengel filed for the water and curbed the flow. With open rock flumes he diverted some of the flow to irrigate grape vines, apple and peach trees. Adjacent to this he built his cabin, a tasteful rustic one with a trellis of roses shading the entrance. Running water was a luxury as was a screened summer bedroom.

The view from Mengel's cabin — Greater View — was down Anvil Spring Canyon, across the Death Valley floor, up Jubilee and Salsberry passes, then clear over into Nevada. It is less known than Aguerreberry Point, partly so because it is remote and best reachable by a car with high road clearance.

Mengel kept lifelong friends in San Bernardino. During the 1920's he would come "outside" two or three times a year. He stayed at the Augustine Hotel where he loved to talk with Charley Rouse, the owner.

The 1940's saw Mengel doing less mining due to advancing age. On a visit to San Bernardino in 1944 he died. Friends arranged to have cremation, and after a service at Kremer Mortuary, the little urn of ashes was taken back to Death Valley. Atop Mengel Pass, 50 feet outside the Monument boundary, a round stone cairn was erected in which the urn was placed. Loving friends took Carl's

Carl Mengel's monument at Mengel Pass. (L. Burr Belden)

wooden leg and placed it with the urn. At the monument base, a piece of granite was inscribed:

"Carl Mengel, 1868-1944."

LATER DAYS
TALC, LEAD, AND EPSOM SALTS

PRECEDING chapters have offered selective chronicles of mines and mining camps of the Death Valley area. Undoubtedly there are as many more equally as colorful. For instance, Jack Keane discovered unbelievably rich ore in the Funeral Mountains, near Chloride Cliff, which started a rush that immediately preceded the Bullfrog discovery. The Keane Wonder ore was so good, that the mine sold for $150,000 before any development was started. Some later owners claimed Keane Wonder was the true "Lost Breyfogle." It was not the impressive $150,000 sale, however, but a later day "battle" that gets top billing when old timers talk of Keane Wonder. Around 1912, J. R. Lane, a Calico merchant, bought the mine and decided to haul his ore to the railroad at Rhyolite with a steam tractor. The one that Lane bought was the matriarch, Old Dinah, originally purchased in the 1890's by Pacific Coast Borax and used to haul colemanite from Borate in the Calico Hills to the company's roaster at Marion. Retired when the Daggett & Borate narrow gauge railroad was built, the old veteran was shipped to Ivanpah where it was started north to open a tractor road to the Lila C. On Stateline Pass, Dinah blew a flue and was left to rust.

When the Carbonate Mine was developed down near Confidence Mill, a corduroy road was built across the Amargosa Sink to Rhodes Wash. A new tractor was bought and Old Dinah brought up from her temporary gravesite along Stateline Pass. When Carbonate folded, Lane picked up the tractor, converted her to an oilburner and gave Death Valley its event of the year for 1913, when his crew took the mechanical horse to the Keane Wonder. She made two trips to Rhyolite, again blew a flue and was abandoned alongside Daylight Pass.

Nearly 20 more years elapsed. H. W. "Bob" Eichbaum built his toll road from Darwin over Towne Pass and down to historic Stovepipe Well, where he planned a resort. At the sand dunes Eichbaum's trucks bogged. He unloaded and built his resort which he first called Bungalow City, the present motel at Stove Pipe Wells. He scoured the valley for colorful relics to spice up the somewhat plain exterior of the bungalows. He found the famous lost wagon from up near Mesquite Spring, and then he turned his eye on the old tractor rusting up in Daylight Pass. Before he got it, however, the Borax Company, which was converting its Death Valley holdings into resorts, decided it wanted the tractor, and sent a mule team after it. The borax crew under Harry P. Gower collided quite unexpectedly with Eichbaum. The borax truck and teams were already hooked to the relic, when Eichbaum came driving up the road. He parked his car sideways to block the road and threatened suit. Gower just laughed and reminded Bob that the local justice of peace was also on the borax payroll. The tractor still stands in front of Furnace Creek Ranch.

Carbonate was a camp with advanced ideas, even though it didn't last long. It boasted transplanted palm trees and a swimming pool, one that filled with sand during every windstorm.

Wingate Pass, the scene of the famous Eichbaum-Gower battle, boasts a later chapter when it and Layton Canyon were given over to a monorail built to haul Epsom salts to the Trona Railway from a deposit in the hills south of the top of the pass. The first motor proved to be too weak to haul loaded trailers up the grade. A heavier engine arrived. Its added weight pushed the monorail footings through the Searles Lake crusts which hastily brought an end to the project.

The valley's road north turns up Grapevine Canyon past Scotty's Castle to join US 95 near the former town of Bonnie Claire. Southwest of the castle there is a fork. The west branch goes to Ubehebe Crater and beyond to Racetrack Valley. Today it is a rough

The Keane Wonder Mine in its heyday. (Eastern California Museum Collection)

road best traveled by jeep or pickup, but it taps much historic mining country. Some 15 miles south of Ubehebe is a fork, called
Teakettle Junction. The Racetrack is on the western fork, but on the
way is another side road which heads west to the Ubehebe ghost
town, site of a major lead operation during World War II. On south
side of the Racetrack, perched high on a hill, is the Lippincott lead
mine and from there, a rough jeep trail used to lead down into
Saline Valley.

Back at Teakettle Junction, the east fork heads up Lost Burro
Gap and forks again. The left branch ends at the colorful Burro
Spring. The right one traverses Hidden Valley, location of numer-
ous old mines, a wild burro herd and many joshua trees. The Lost
Burro and the Keeler were principal mines of the area north of
Ulida Flat, followed by Goldbelt Spring, once an active camp. A
graded county road which continues past Hunter Mountain,
Jackass Spring, and Lee Pump eventually reaches State Highway
190 near Darwin Junction.

East of the Furnace Creek resort area is the ghost town of
Schwab where a few cabins of the old cabins remain. Up the old
T&T right of way from Death Valley Junction was a station named
Leeland, and some six miles back in the hills is Lee Camp, a profitable mine sold by members of the well-known Lee family of cat-
tlemen who bore names like Philander, Meander, Salamander and
Cubander. Because of the remoteness, writers of a half-century and
more ago felt they could fictionalize the Lee's with impunity. One
was quoted by a Sacramento paper as finding "Cub" Lee at Furnace
Creek — then called Greenland — with a daughter "Peanuts" and
a son "One Sock." The yarn continued to state that Lee lived there
because he had deserted the Union Army in the Civil War. It was
color — but not truth. Cub Lee was caretaker at Amargosa Borax
Works south of Shoshone, some 80 miles from Greenland. He and
his wife had no children. His elder brother Phil passed away in the
San Bernardino County Hospital. Phil's death record indicates his
younger brother, Cub, was all of 12 or 13 years old when Lee surrendered to Grant at Appomattox.

Along with the World War II boom in lead and the compulsory shut down of gold mining came more expansion in non-metallics. In fact, interest had turned to deposits of abrasives, driller's clay and manganese even before the war. There was a sizable manganese operation at Owl Holes at one time. Another in Wingate Wash has since closed down.

There were two principal fields of talc mining. The largest producer was the Grantham Mine located in Warm Spring Canyon. At its height of operation, it provided jobs for at least twenty-five men.

Tom Kennedy also had a sizable talc operation in the vicinity. Down near Saratoga, the Pfizer Corporation had succeeded with Southern California Minerals. Farther east were Western Talc and Sierra Talc. Up at Sheep Spring in the Avawatz was a lithographic stone quarry whose operation ended with the arrival of offset lithography. It is probable, however, that dollarwise, Death Valley mining will never match the glory of days past when miners and their loyal burros roamed the silver and gold boom camps. Today's operations are far more steady though admittedly, they lack the storybook character that made the Panamint, Bullfrog and Skidoo the legends they are today.

Coso to Yosemite & Beyond

❦ ⚜ ❧

"I crawled about the ground, seizing and examining bits of
stone, blowing dust from them or rubbing them on my
clothes, and peering at them with anxious hope. Presently,
I found a bright fragment and my heart bounded!
I hid behind a boulder and polished it and scrutinized it
with a nervous eagerness and a delight that was more
pronounced than absolute certainty itself could have afforded.
The more I examined the fragment the more I was
convinced that I had found the door to fortune."

Roughing It
Mark Twain

"Callahan was drinking in front of Jack Murray's Saloon

one night and getting tired of Joe Lee's tirade.

Callahan hit Lee square in the face with the

butt end of his gun.

Lee staggered for a minute and, reaching

down for the gun under the bar, he shot Callahan

square in the abdomen, and Callahan dropped to

the floor mortally wounded.

There was a free for all fight with guns popping every place

until some far-sighted miner shot the lights out."

Nightlife in Lundy, eastern Sierra mining town
The Story of Early Mono County
Ella M. Cain

Rare photograph of a woman with men working a rocker in the Sierra.
(Nevada Historical Society)

THE HIGH SIERRA RUSH

Gold madness!

The Eastern Sierra was a harsh land at the time of the '49ers. That great wave of fortune seekers which swept westward over the crest avoided some 200 precipitous miles of this great barrier, as they sought out the most favorable routes.

The brown mountains and bitter valleys paralleling the Sierra Nevada on the east were known to only a few early explorers and trappers. That beauty and wealth might be found on that side was no concern to those first eager Argonauts who rushed to claim their shares of California gold. They just could not afford to hesitate.

Within a decade, the backwash of that wave was to flow over and around the Sierra, as restless men who had missed their pots of gold sought out new bonanzas. Mexicans came too, from the south, still feeling some claim on this land which their country had so recently been forced to cede to the United States. Their own quest for silver in the southwest had dated back to the days of the Spaniards' conquest. Perhaps this background and their under- standing of desert country were factors in Mexicans locating some of the greatest producers in the area.

Gold madness lost little of its intensity as it spread eastward, and silver and other minerals were sought out as wealth producers too. New camps sprung up almost overnight, many existing on lit- tle more than hope, courage and excitement. Rumors were ram- pant. Glorious reports appearing in newspapers of the day predicted a fabulous future for each new strike. The fact that many mines of the eastern Sierra were relatively isolated or inaccessible seemed to lend enchantment. The very momentum of a booming mining camp seemed to overcome any and all obstacles, at least for a time. If the mine did produce, there was the additional challenge of getting ore reduced and bullion transported.

Placer mining was first in popularity in the earliest days. Anybody could afford a gold plan or could rig up a dry washer, and there was little loss if the claim proved barren.

Companies with money to invest could operate on a larger scale using equipment for hydraulic mining. But rich placer areas were limited and, in time, exhausted. The best known mines were lode claims, with their shafts and tunnels and dumps as enduring evidence of their development. The fact that expensive equipment was required for any extensive operation of lode claims led to mining companies and the promoters who created them. Financiers in the east seemed eager to have a part in the frenzied activity out west, often investing astonishing amounts on little more than a promoter's vivid imagination. Prospectors staked out claims with the hope of selling out to some company.

In contrast to the promoters and camp followers who created the frantic rushes to new bonanzas were the quiet mining men who were content to work their claims in a small way on a long range basis. Their mines have not made a splash in history, but they provided independence and a reasonably good living for many an individualist.

When California became a state in 1850, it was hardly prepared to govern its far outposts. Certainly it was not too much concerned with its eastern border beyond the Sierra barrier. Mariposa and Tulare, and later Fresno County stretched over to take in the area covered in this book, but there was no attempt to furnish any civil control. Each mining camp, largely populated by people who were there to escape restrictions, was responsible for its own procedures of law and order. These were as loose and varied as they were colorful.

Mining districts were organized in each new region, the boundaries being established by members of the district. Officers were elected and rules and regulations adopted, including provisions for registering and transferring mining claims. When Congress enacted a general mining law, it was to legalize what was already common practice and to establish some uniformity. A copy of the Act of May 10, 1872 was used as a guide in each district. Local laws still governed, however, when not in conflict with the rather broad provisions of the United States law. To this day there is considerable variance within the state of California. Mineral rights took precedence over any other claim on the land, and provisions were enacted for patenting mining claims, by which procedure the owner gained actual title to the land.

Mono County was established in 1861. The prosperous town of Aurora, its chief reason for existence, was made the county seat. What a cruel blow it was to the county to find, by a later survey of the state line, that its courthouse was three miles over the line on the Nevada side. After two and one-half years of occupancy, during which the citizens of Aurora voted for two sets of county officials, one in each state, Mono County finally yielded to the fickle line. Its recorder and treasurer picked up the county records and funds, leaving the bills, and moved across to Bodie until a special election in the spring of 1864 determined a new county seat. Bridgeport, a little settlement in Big Meadows, where the footbridge crossed the East Walker River, won the honor over the lively mining camp of Monoville down by Mono Lake.

Inyo County did not come into being until 1866, after the creation of Coso County had failed by default. The new town of Independence, and the Kearsarge mining camp west of it were main contenders for the county seat, Independence being selected as the better location. Two important boundary changes were made later. The first, in 1870, changed the northern line of Township 6 south of the Mount Diablo baseline, with the provision that Inyo County was to pay $12,000 to Mono for the land lost to that county.

In 1872 a new southern boundary line was established, which added the southern portion of Panamint Valley and that portion of Death Valley which lies between Stovepipe Wells and the present southern line of Inyo County, as well as the Tecopa-Shoshone region.

The establishment of Mono and Inyo Counties gave eastern California an identity and the right to assert itself in state affairs. Civic pride demanded law and order — communities began to mature — but a mining community is not tamed overnight. After the turn of the century, mining documents were recorded in their respective counties and the districts ceased to exist, except as a means of describing the general location of a given claim. Little change has been made in the mining laws since the movement was legalized in 1872. If the laws are now obsolete as the burro prospector with his pick and shovel, perhaps it is because we are romanticists at heart and reluctant to change this tie with our colorful past.

As the influx of miners created an interest in the country east of the Sierra, the earliest settlers were finding favorable spots for farming and grazing in widely separated locations. Mushrooming mining camps created a ready market for grain, hay and beef. Supplies of any kind commanded inflated prices. Stockmen came, driving their beef cattle from the San Joaquin Valley over Walker Pass to the mining camp at Coso and northward as far as Bodie and Aurora. Many returned to take advantage of the good grazing lands they found in Owens River Valley, and an increasing number of framers were attracted to the new land.

It was inevitable that conflicts should develop between the Native Americans and the newcomers who were taking possession of their lands, just as it was inevitable that the Indians would be subdued in the end by a force greater than their own. The natives, who occupied traditional hunting grounds and had a sparse supply of food at best, naturally were alarmed over the increasing number of settlers. An unusually severe winter in 1861-62 made the situation even more critical. Raids on herds of cattle and subsequent reprisals developed into a bloody war, marked more by shameful incidents than by righteous victories. Remote settlements were vulnerable to attack by desperate natives, and travel was hazardous. Many frightened newcomers left the region and activity slowed to a standstill. It was during this critical period that U.S. soldiers were sent to Owens Valley to protect the new settlers. They founded Camp Independence on Oak Creek on July 4, 1862, at a site that is now a portion of an Indian Reservation. Although the turbulence was to continue for another five years, the presence of the soldiers created some sense of stability in the valley.

Miners, in general, had no quarrel with the Indians, but they, too, were subject to acts of reprisal. Prospecting diminished during that period of conflict, and some mines had to completely cease operations until the Indian raids had subsided, but the mining movement was too great to stop. It had not yet reached its peak. During peaceful interludes, soldiers joined in the prospecting, especially in the Inyo Range east of Camp Independence.

Mining still holds an important place in the economy of the eastern Sierra, although the picture has changed. Now, more emphasis is placed on nonmetallic products, such as talc, dolomite and sulfur, and the salines of desert sinks. Today's prospector dreams of being skyrocketed to fame and fortune on a discovery of "rare-earths" that can be used in the processing of pharmaceuticals or computer chips. During the 1960's, new claims were being filed at a rate of 500 or so each year in Inyo and Mono counties, but have tapered off in recent years due to economic demand and stricter environmental laws, which have made it more difficult for small mining operators to get started. Mining today is big business, a powerful blend of the old and the new. Bulldozers have replaced the pick and shovel for assessment work, and a good road is an essential for any operation — but in many ways the old atmosphere resists the veneer of the times.

Much of the romance of the early mining era is in the eyes of the beholder. The sight of an abandoned mine development creates an intense desire to know all about its moment of glory and what caused it to fail. The chance discovery of a lonely tunnel or an interesting dump immediately sets off speculation as to the kind of a person the miner might have been, his hopes and the degree of his success. One book cannot cover all the mines of the eastern Sierra — there are hundreds — but it is hoped that this book will furnish some background, guide the reader to a few new places, and lead to happy hours of speculation.

It should go without saying that great caution is necessary in exploring old mines. Timbers rot in time, and rocks shift, deep shafts may be entirely uncovered. *Never, under any circumstance,* should anything suspected of being dynamite or blasting caps be disturbed.

Consideration and good manners are just as important, and more vital, in remote locations as in one's own community. Any property on a mining claim belongs to the owner, no matter how weathered or dilapidated it may appear. He may resume operations next week and need everything on the place.

Be careful, be considerate, have fun and leave no trace.

Mary DeDecker

Coso
ANCIENT HOT SPRINGS
—⟫✛⟪—

Coso was an exciting word in the mining world of the early 1860's where it meant a source of untold wealth. Actually, "Coso was a Paiute-Shoshone word which referred to the thermal region nearby. The Paiute-Shoshone used the springs found there for medicinal purposes. Obsidian outcroppings in the area were extremely valuable too, furnishing material for arrow points and spearheads. Numerous petroglyph sites indicate that the Coso area must have been an important place, even in prehistoric times. These pictures and symbols carved in the rock by natives of the past could, no doubt, tell a fabulous tale of their day, if we only knew how to interpret them.

Rich ore ledges were discovered at Coso in March 1860 by Dr. Darwin French and party on their expedition to search for the lost Gunsight mine. With this goal in mind, they were not unduly excited over a lesser find. The "Gunsight" story came from one of the Mississippians of the '49 Death Valley party, who had picked up a piece of silver float so pure that he used it to make a sight for his gun. This was presumed to have occurred in a mountain canyon west of Death Valley. Several well organized parties, such as that of Darwin French, and many a lone prospector, have searched in vain for the source of the silver gunsight. It has not been found to this day.

The party continued its search northward until the decision was made to turn back. In the meantime, they had discovered a rugged canyon containing a fine stream of water which flowed over a

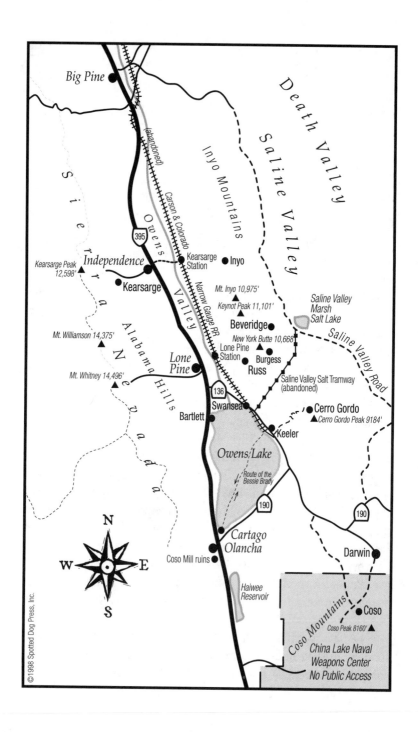

Big Pine

D e a t h V a l l e y

S a l i n e V a l l e y

(abandoned)

I n y o M o u n t a i n s

S i e r r a

O w e n s

395

Carson & Colorado

Independence

Kearsarge Peak
12,598'

Kearsarge
Station

Kearsarge

Inyo

Mt. Inyo 10,975'

V a l l e y

Keynot Peak 11,101'

Narrow Gauge RR

Saline Valley
Marsh
Salt Lake

Beveridge

Mt. Williamson 14,375'

A l a b a m a

New York Butte 10,668'

Lone Pine
Station

Saline Valley Road

Lone
Pine

Burgess

N

Russ

Mt. Whitney 14,496'

Saline Valley Salt Tramway
(abandoned)

136

Swansea

Cerro Gordo

e v a d a

Bartlett

Cerro Gordo Peak 9184'

Keeler

O w e n s L a k e

Route of the
Bessie Brady

N

190

W   E

190

Cartago
Olancha

Darwin

Coso Mill ruins

S

Haiwee
Reservoir

Coso
Mountains

Coso

Coso Peak 8160'

China Lake Naval
Weapons Center
No Public Access

© 1998 Spotted Dog Press, Inc.

series of delightful falls, a pleasant oasis in the desert country. The party named the canyon and falls "Darwin" in honor of their leader.

Returning by way of Coso, the party showed more interest now in the ledges they had passed over. Enthusiasm mounted as they gathered samples to take back to the coast. Assay figures proved to be fabulous, both in gold and silver, as proclaimed in San Francisco's Alta California. The Coso Mining Company and the Coso Gold and Silver Mining Company were formed immediately and the Rough and Ready Mining Company the following year. Each claimed to be backed by an impressive amount of capital.

The Slate Range District, east of Coso, was organized in November 1861. More fabulously rich ledges were reported there and new companies formed to furnish capital to work them. Promoters were exceedingly active. Prosperity fluctuated, affecting both districts alike. When enthusiasm rose, both districts benefited and when it fell, both suffered.

Visalia was the source of supplies for the desert camps. The distance was long, mostly by trail. When Captain George, a local Native American, established an express over the route, making it in four days by horseback, it was hailed as a great improvement. An ambitious plan for a wagon road over the Sierra, to come in between Owens Lake and Little Lake, was submitted to the legislature and chartered in 1862. It was said that there were twenty-eight applicants for the franchise, but nothing came of it. In the meantime, the Tulare supervisors granted authority to build a trans Sierra trail with a thirty-three foot right-of-way, to be completed in two years. A condition calling for completion of a sixteen-foot wagon road in five years was included in the grant. The trail was completed as reported to the supervisors to be completed, "to a point in the Owens River Valley at the foot of the Big Meadows and the Lone Pine Tree," at a cost of $1,000. It became well known as the Hockett Trail.

Operators at the mines did not seem to do as well at producing as the promoters were doing at organizing mining companies. Some ore, however, was being taken from the Josephine Mine and processed in arrastras. A steam mill was making a good recovery on ore from the Winoshilk Mine. But stockholders were far from satisfied and their restlessness eventually led to an investigation. This revealed that inferior equipment had been purchased, including that found at the Josephine Mill. Wood in lieu of iron had been used for many of its parts. Certain procedures of management were questioned — the public had lost confidence in both the Coso and the Slate Range operations. Continued conflict with the local Paiute-Shoshone had added to their problems. Mines had closed completely during periods of extreme danger and the Indians took advantage of such times to destroy or carry off as much as possible. They eventually burned the Searles mill in the Slate Range. The Josephine mill also was burned and its owners made a claim against the government for $250,000, charging that the Indians were responsible. There was doubt that it had been done by Indians and the amount was considered excessive in any case. The owners failed to collect. The Josephine was finally sold at sheriff's sale for $40,667. The great Coso boom had ended.

As Americans moved out, Mexicans came in to work the abandoned mines. On March 23, 1868, when the district was reorganized, the minutes of the meeting were written entirely in Spanish. The place became known as the "Spanish Mines." Since the Mexicans were capable miners, content to operate on a small scale, they worked them profitably for some years.

There was a renewed interest in the mines again in the 1890's when the Josephine was relocated as the San Jose. Pat Reddy, famous as a criminal lawyer and always active in mining affairs, had an interest at Coso for a time. Flurries in more recent years brought other generations of miners to the scene, but none of them operated on a large scale.

In later years, the thermal area became better known than the mines. Health seekers came from far and near for mud baths and hot water therapy. A health resort located at the hot springs and put out ads with claims as extravagant as those of the miners before them. Water from the springs was sold for medicinal use.

An attempt to mine sulfur there during World War I was unsuccessful. Cinnebar deposits discovered in 1929 did prove profitable. Processing was done in a small way until 1938, when a mill capable of handling 25 tons of ore per day was built. The deposit was exhausted the following year after yielding nearly $17,000 worth of mercury.

Both the hot springs and the mines were withdrawn from pubic use in 1945 when the entire area was set aside for the China Lake Naval Weapons Center, a restricted area. The government made property settlements in favor of those who had legitimate claims, but many a miner felt that he had been deprived of a valuable strike. People who had enjoyed the hot springs were shocked at their withdrawal. Paiute-Shoshone elders were stunned to find that they were forbidden to enter the healing place that had eased their people's aching bodies for hundreds of years.

Old Coso, at the time of withdrawal, was a picturesque little mining camp, almost a ghost town then. Some of its better rock cabins were still occupied, but the street was quiet — its boom days long past.

CERRO GORDO
LAWLESS COMSTOCK EAST OF THE SIERRA

Cerro Gordo, the Mexicans' "Fat Hill" was the Comstock of California's eastern Sierra. Its great silver, lead and zinc deposits were found on the west slope of Buena Vista Peak, at the south end of the Inyo Mountains. The story of its productive year, when silver-lead ingots were stacked around camp like cordwood and present day cities were then vying for the lucrative business of supplying the mines on the hill, is a fantastic chapter in mining history.

Pablo Flores is credited with the original discovery in 1865. Mexicans were on the ground floor and had first choice in filing claims. They worked the mines on a small scale for some time without interference from the impatient Americans who failed to realize the store of wealth east of Owen's Big Lake. Most of their ores were smelted in vasos, their own type of crude ovens. But the richness of their find was too good to keep. A Mexican prospector, on a visit to Virginia City, could not contain his excitement and proudly displayed ore samples to support his claims. His specimens were promptly tested and the results convinced even the skeptics that this was a place worth investigating. The word flashed across the state.

Among the Americans who rushed to the scene was Mortimer W. Belshaw of San Francisco, who was to become the mining baron of Cerro Gordo. He looked it over and immediately went to work to acquire claims. Abner B. Elder became his junior partner. Both men had gained valuable experience in working silver ores in the mines of Sinaloa, Mexico, so were well qualified to take on "Fat Hill.'"

Arriving back in San Francisco with a shipment of ore, they had no difficulty in securing financial support. Their new corporation was named the Union Mining Company, for the Union Mine, which they intended to acquire. Belshaw had already obtained a third interest in the mine in exchange for a fifth interest in the smelter he expected to build. His particular interest in the Union was typical of his foresight. It contained the best galena orebody on the hill and he well knew that lead was an essential item for processing the rich silver-quartz ores. With his power of persuasion, he anticipated no problem in acquiring control of that mine.

The Lone Pine Mining District, taking in an entire cross section of the Inyo Range, including Cerro Gordo, was organized April 5, 1866. A thousand locations were filed by 1870. the original claims were long and narrow allowing the miner to follow his ore vein as far as 3,000 feet in some cases. When federal mining laws were established in 1872, the district was reorganized and named Cerro Gordo for its center of activity. Its local laws were altered to conform with the new United States regulations, including maximum dimensions of 600 by 1,500 feet for lode claims.

Back on the scene at Cerro Gordo, Belshaw, now financially secure, proceeded to establish his kingdom on the hill. Three basic needs must be met — a wagon road, a smelter and a water supply. The road came first, a narrow, winding eight-mile ascent, but, nevertheless, a way for four-wheeled vehicles to reach the mines. It was hardly completed when Belshaw and Elder set up their toll station at the narrows. Here was the first example of Belshaw's ruthless business procedures. Other miners who had helped in building the road were given no consideration at the toll gate. In the years to follow, control of the road provided an effective means of penalizing competition which could not be squeezed out.

No time was lost in hauling the heavy machinery for their smelter up the new road. Belshaw's remarkable energy had the furnace in production by the fall of 1868. He was not satisfied with

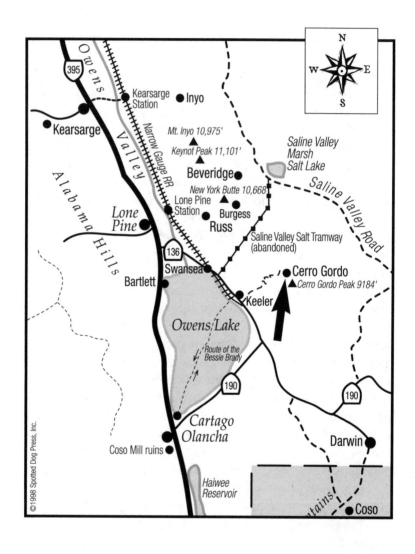

normal production. His plans called for an output of four tons of bullion per day, which would require greater ore loads than that type of furnace could treat. Driven by his own demands, he found it necessary to invent a new appliance to equalize the heat. The Belshaw water jacket so increased the efficiency of his smelter that it yielded five tons per day, an unheard of achievement. The daily monetary yield was approximately $3,500. The shining bars of silver-lead bullion were shipped by way of Los Angeles for further refining at the Selby Smelting Works in San Francisco..

By 1871, Cerro Gordo was well established as a mining town; Buena Vista Peak looked down on a scene of bustling activity. The canyon walls were well scarred with mine diggings. Two blast furnaces and numerous vasos were treating ores as fast as they could be dug from the earth. The town's main street was lined with good frame buildings which housed all the stores and offices essential to a thriving community. More were being built as fast as lumber could be obtained from sawmills in the valley. Simple shelters of all kinds — dugouts, rock and canvas cabins — extended the residential area far beyond the main streets and, of course, there was a Chinatown. Daily stagecoaches carried passengers up and down the winding road. The new two-story American House welcomed visitors who preferred the best. Proper social functions were held here. Most of the important business in town was carried out at the Cosmopolitan, although two other saloons also enjoyed good patronage. Night life centered about Lola Travis and Maggie Moore and their painted girls whose houses were conveniently located at either end of the town. Their centers of dancing and revelry were disturbing elements to some of the town's leading citizens, but they were obviously a minority group. Gunplay was frequent, fatal shootings all too common. Cerro Gordo was considered a lawless place, even in those days of turbulent mining camps. It attracted more than its share of tough characters, in addition to a normal quota of quick-draw local residents.

Victor Beaudry, who built the town's second fine new blast furnace in 1870, came to Cerro Gordo as a merchant in 1866. Being a good businessman, he gradually acquired valuable mining property by attachments on unpaid bills. Among these acquisitions was half interest in the Union Mine, the portion which Belshaw had never obtained. Actually, Beaudry was smelting ore before the Belshaw furnace was completed, but was hardly a competitor until he built the efficient new model. Production of the hill leaped again! This called for a steady flow of freight wagons down the Yellow Grade. Belshaw, in meantime, had bought out the interest of A.B. Elder in their smelter, and also the one-fifth interest of the Mexican who had traded his share in the Union Mine. It seemed wiser then to join forces with Beaudry than to fight him. So it was Belshaw and Beaudry henceforth who ruled the hill and reaped its profits together.

Transportation of bullion was an everlasting problem. The freighting contractors were hardly able to keep up before the new smelter was fired up. After that it was impossible. If they made it down the Yellow Grade without losing control of the heavily loaded wagons, they faced the long haul through sandy wastes and rocky washes to a shipping point. The trip took about three weeks. On their return they were laden with supplies for the booming town, machinery for the mines and hay for the ever essential strings of pack animals. The best they could do was not enough to keep the output moving. Backlogs of ingots collected at the smelters. The situation became desperate. What good was their fantastic rate of production if the bullion was not delivered to the refineries!

The roles played by ambitious young cities in their attempts to furnish adequate transportation, and so capture the Cerro Gordo trade, makes a fascinating story. Visalia and Santa Barbara had already tried to claim the Owens Valley trade, but it was during Cerro Gordo days that an intense competition developed between

Ventura, Bakersfield and Los Angeles. That the latter city was the ultimate winner was a great factor in its early growth and prosperity.

James Brady of the Owens Lake Silver-Lead Company was
responsible for one interesting phase of the transportation story.
His company had established a camp at Swansea, on Owens Lake,
and had built a smelter there. The cost of hauling ore down the
grade from Cerro Gordo had to be met by savings elsewhere, so
Brady conceived the idea of freighting across the lake. This would
save three days of hauling through the sand around the shore. A
little steamer was built on the Owens River, just above the lake and
a wharf was constructed at Swansea, but the great earthquake of
March 26, 1872 delayed both projects. The upheaval caused the
lake to recede in the area of Swansea so the wharf had to be built
150 feet longer than planned. The ship, 85 feet long and 16 feet
wide, was finally launched June 27, 1872. She made her maiden
voyage across to Daneri's Landing, later named Cartago, loaded
with thirty tons of bullion. A week later, as part of the Fourth of
July celebration at Ferguson's Landing, south of Lone Pine, she
was christened the Bessie Brady by Brady's little daughter. The
steamer performed so well that the backlog of ingots was soon
transferred to Cartago, but Belshaw was more desperate than ever.
The bullion still was not reaching the refinery. In January, there
were 18,000 bars awaiting shipment, mostly at Cartago, where
they were being put to use for building temporary huts roofed
with canvas. Thirty thousand of these bars had collected by the
middle of May. They averaged 87 pounds in weight and were each
valued at $335.

At this point, Remi Nadeau, who had previously freighted for
the mines, returned through Owens Valley from a contract in
Nevada. Belshaw and Beaudry intercepted him near Owens Lake
and made a deal then and there. Together they formed the Cerro
Gordo Freighting Company, which set up a chain of stations a day's
haul apart all the way to Los Angeles. They bought out former

Cerro Gordo Townsite — circa 1958. (Mary DeDecker)

freighting contractors and acquired little Bessie Brady, putting every possible effort into a plan for a maximum performance. Once more the bullion was moving! By 1874 the now enlarged smelters were putting out eighteen tons per day and the Cerro Gordo Freighting Company had the situation well in hand.

The time came when the greedy furnaces were running out of fuel. For miles, the Inyo Mountains had been stripped of pinyon and juniper. Even any of the accessible limberpine and bristlecone were sacrificed for fuel or mining timbers. Recognizing the need for a new source of timber, a Colonel Sherman Stevens built a sawmill high in Cottonwood Canyon west of Owens Lake. A flume was constructed down the canyon to deliver logs and lumber to the wagon road. The Stevens Mill went into operation in 1873 and by 1876 it was doing so well that its business was incorporated as the Inyo Lumber and Coal Company, and the flume extended to the lake shore. Besides mine timbers, lumber and wood for fuel, the company sold charcoal, making it in two large kilns beside the lake. Since most of its products were shipped on the Bessie Brady, the company decided to build its own ship. The keel was laid at Cottonwood in the spring of 1877 and this little steamer made her maiden voyage in June. She was named the Mollie Stevens for the daughter of Colonel Stevens. One of its first assignments was to carry 30,000 feet of mining timber ordered by the Union Consolidated Company, probably one of the last orders from that company.

Cerro Gordo had no natural springs, so it was necessary to import all the water used in the smelters as well as for domestic purposes in the town, except where it might be collected from occasional snowfalls in the winter. In 1870 Belshaw ran a pipeline to capture a supply of 1,300 gallons per day, but the system was not protected adequately against freezing weather and was out of order much of the time. The usual supply came in by pack animals and was sold to small consumers at ten cents a gallon, while the wholesale rate was five cents and up. One can well imagine how conservative the townspeople must have been in using the costly item. The normal water bill for the American Hotel was $300 per month. There were times when the furnaces were forced to shut down for lack of water and this was indeed serious. After enduring some years of this unsatisfactory situation, Stephen Boushey, a mine owner, secured financial backing to organize the Cerro Gordo Water and Mining Company. This was based on a bold plan for tapping the bountiful waters of Miller Springs, ten miles north of Cerro Gordo and 1,800 feet down from the Inyo crest toward Saline Valley. This meant pumping up to the crest and then conveying the water to town through ten miles of pipe buried deeply enough to prevent freezing. It took weeks to haul the necessary pipe and equipment up from Los Angeles. Winter weather interrupted the project, but, finally, in May 1874, the town was deluged with 90,000 gallons a day of the precious fluid. There followed such an era of luxurious cleanliness as had never been known on the hill.

Belshaw's aggressive moves had made him and Beaudry the undisputed masters of Cerro Gordo, but by the early 1870's the Owens Lake Silver-Lead Company was becoming a threat to their domain. This was the company that had its smelter at Swansea on the northeast shore of Owens Lake. Their managers were strong, shrewd men who were not inclined to yield to Belshaw's high-handed ways. It was this company which had the vision to build the Bessie Brady and, later, to finance Colonel Stevens in building his sawmill, both of which benefitted Belshaw. But the very existence of its operation was a great irritation to the baron on the hill. When it began acquiring valuable mines at Cerro Gordo, it was not to be tolerated. His toll road was the Swansea company's ore line, so Belshaw deliberately let it deteriorate until the ore wagons were forced down to hauling at only half capacity. John Simpson, who owned an interest in the company's tunnel, forced the issue into court when he refused to pay at the toll gate. A judgment was issued in his favor and the aroused citizens of Owens Valley joined in protest of Belshaw's stranglehold on transportation to Cerro Gordo. Petitions were presented to the County Supervisors, who reduced the toll rates by one-half.

The Owens Lake Silver-Lead Company had won a moral victory, but it never recovered financially. Foreclosure of a $98,000 mortgage caused it to suspend operations in the spring of 1874. That summer a cloudburst swept a layer of debris over the camp and smelter at Swansea, a sad burial for a courageous enterprise.

Belshaw, in the meantime, was occupied with subduing another rival. He had never succeeded in acquiring the San Felipe silver-quartz claim which crossed the side line of the Union mine. When the owners of the San Felipe extended a tunnel, which they had acquired from John Simpson, to meet their silver vein, they came upon galena, the lead ore so important for smelting silver. Noting galena on the San Felipe dump, Belshaw was beside himself. Claiming that they were working his Union lode, he boldly took possession of the disputed portion. Thus began a long, bitter struggle.

A blast furnace at Cerro Gordo. (Mary DeDecker)

When the matter was taken to court, judgment was given in favor of the owners of the San Felipe, in spite of the fact that Belshaw and Beaudry were represented by the wily Pat Reddy. But Reddy proved a master at delaying tactics, which tied up the San Felipe so the owners could not operate. Finally, in May 1875, he obtained a new trial before the State Supreme Court. The suit dragged on for another year. Then the Union Consolidated Company was formed to include representatives of both factions. The costly litigation, in addition to increasing costs of operation, ended the lusty days of Cerro Gordo. The furnaces shut down early in 1878.

When the Carson and Colorado narrow-gauge railroad came to Keeler in the early 1880's, there was a revival in activity on the hill. With cheaper transportation assured, the mines were worked periodically, but without any great success until Louis D. Gordon discovered that the dumps were rich with zinc ores. His perseverance led to a new era, from 1911 to 1915, when Cerro Gordo again took its place at the top of the silver-lead, and now zinc, production in the state.

Mineral surveys of the mines showed a criss-cross pattern concentrated below Buena Vista Peak. Fifty of the claims were patented, including the San Felipe, Santa Maria, San Benito, La Despreciada and Ygnacio, which were among the early Mexican locations.

The next productive period was brought about by a raise in the price of metals in 1915. A picturesque feature of mining days entered the picture then, a Leschen aerial tramway running from Cerro Gordo to Keeler. Its cables spanned the canyons from tower to tower for 29,560 feet, its buckets silhouetted against the sky. The system, powered by electricity, had a capacity of 16 tons per hour. It was used again in the 1920's to transport limestone, mined through the Union tunnel, to Keeler for use in the Natural Soda Products Plant and for the Clark Chemical Company's plant at Bartlett.

Considerable exploration work was done again in the 1940's and some ore shipped. Wally Wilson, who acted as caretaker following that period, eventually sued the company he was serving for back wages and came out as possessor of its mines. Inadvertently, he failed to list the tramway among the assets, so had no hold on it. The company promptly sold the tram system to a Nevada concern which removed it from its lofty towers only to let it rust away, unused, at its new location.

Cerro Gordo is credited with producing $15,000,000 worth of ore. No other group in California has matched its record for silver, lead and zinc.

The site of the old town is dominated by Buena Vista Peak (now known as Cerro Gordo Peak), its white marble face capped with a slanting dark band. The Union Mine dump spills from the mountainside above the town and the canyon slopes are dotted with lesser dumps. One can only guess as to the miles of tunnels and slopes underground. The two-story American Hotel stands on Main Street, a little uphill and across the road from Beaudry's Smelter. Buildings of later years were grouped at the main intersection. A sad little cemetery with a marvelous view is situated on

The Carson & Colorado — first train to cross into California, circa 1883.
(Courtesy, L. Burr Belden via the Hugh C. Tolford Collection)

the slope of the hill north of town. Just over the Inyo crest, by way of a saddle north of Buena Vista Peak, are more mines and the site of Belmont Camp.

The peak may be seen for miles from Highway 395 across the lake. The mines are reached by a dirt road turning east from the highway at Keeler, a distance of eight miles. There are several rather steep grades which discourage making the trip in a conventional passenger car.

It appears that Cerro Gordo has come to life once again. There is a small bread and breakfast establishment at the townsite, and various private owners have acquired mining properties on the hill. Notices of a quiet title action naming familiar Cerro Gordo claims have been published. Heavy earthmoving equipment rolls up the Yellow Grade. Along with private ownership, come the "no trespassing" signs, but not even the interested residents of Keeler, at the foot of the grade have any idea as to the meaning of it all.

RUSS & INYO DISTRICTS
PIONEERING THE OWENS RIVER VALLEY

The Owens River Valley, a narrow 100-mile corridor between two great mountain ranges, was a little known land when it was first used as a thoroughfare north and south. The mighty Sierra Nevada on the west and the Inyo-Whites on the east were effective natural barriers to any cross travel. The valley was named in 1845 by John C. Fremont for his companion, Dick Owen, though neither ever saw the valley. Few actually entered it until the discovery of gold at Monoville attracted miners from all directions. All travel from the south came through this long, narrow valley and soon it was to become the direct route between Aurora and the Coso bonanza.

Those first travelers came for business in the mining centers and took no time for unnecessary stops, though some note must have been taken of the country as they passed through. A "Hill Party" did come into our valley purposely to prospect. From a base camp at the present site of Lone Pine, they prospected on both sides of the valley and located in Mazourka Canyon what were probably the first mining claims in this region. No development work followed these first projects.

Early in 1860, the New World Mining and Exploration Company arrived on the scene under the leadership of H.P. Russ. Financiers, ever alert for new opportunities, had organized the company in San Francisco and sent it over Walker Pass to investigate the potential of Owens Valley. Camping on the river south of Independence, the party surveyed the front of the Inyo Range with field glasses, then went to inspect some prominent outcroppings southeast of their camp. They found a gold bearing ledge that looked so promising that they moved camp to a site nearby. A number of claims were located, including the Union, Ida and Eclipse, which were to become well known producers. The Russ District, taking in a long central section of the east wall of the valley, was organized April 20, 1860. But little development was accomplished until two years later. The district was reorganized at that time and its laws revised.

It was here that the name "Inyo" first became known to white men. A Paiute-Shoshone name for the mountain range in which the mines were located; Chief George explained its meaning as "the dwelling place of a great spirit." The fact Paiute-Shoshone relied on the range for food may have had some bearing on their high regard for it.

The establishment of Mono County in 1861 had its effect on the entire eastern Sierra. Pioneers settling in remote locations felt some security in the existence of a county government on their side of the Sierra Nevada, even though its practical value must have been doubtful. Prospectors scattered throughout the region searching for new strikes. They had a definite foothold in the new land and, hardy souls that they were, were doing well. But fate was cruel in bringing in an unusually difficult winter in 1861-62. Severe winter snows were followed by a flooding rain in late January, resulting in melted snow to add to the disaster. The pioneers were to suffer losses and the plight of the Paiute-Shoshone was to be just as desperate. The critical situation precipitated incidents which were to lead to serious hostilities. It became so dangerous for the settlers to venture out unguarded that even prospecting and mining slowed to a standstill. Many of these pioneers left the country.

The arrival of the Army at Camp Independence in 1862 was followed by a peaceful interval during which activity was resumed. The soldiers stationed at the camp soon became vulnerable to mining fever and it was a prospecting soldier who discovered gold to the east where the Owens River curves against a spur of the Inyo

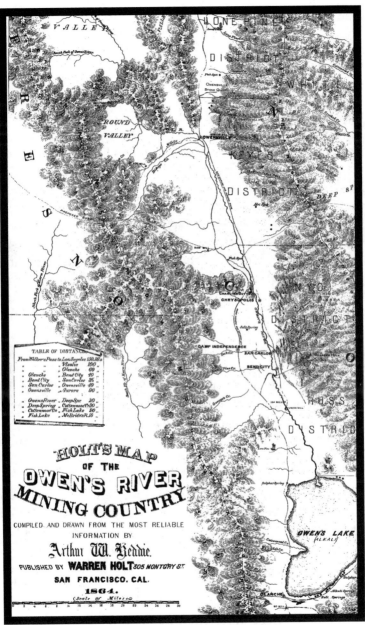

Map of the Owens Valley, circa 1864, during the Civil War.
(Bancroft Library Collection)

Mountains. Samples were sent to San Francisco, with encouraging results. The San Carlos Mining and Exploration Company was organized and a delegation of three men came to investigate the lode. It took them a month to make the trip by way of Mono Pass and Bloody Canyon and the mining camps of Monoville, Aurora, and Hot Springs. No doubt their enthusiasm was fired en route. Upon reaching the lode, they immediately found a vein of galena which increased their excitement. They frankly liked what they saw.

So the stage was set for another mining boom. But Indian trouble intervened and the people of San Carlos were occupied for some months preparing for a possible attack. It was not until the summer of 1863 that the real influx began. San Carlos and Bend City, three miles down the river, grew at a rapid pace. Chrysopolis, up river, was recognized as a promising camp. Claims were filed all along the front of the Inyos and up the gullies and canyons eastward. Mining companies were organized in the coastal cities to reap the profits. Development proceeded at a frenetic pace. The San Carlos Company announced that its ditch, running southward from the curve of the river, was 2,700 feet long, though the purpose of the ditch was not explained. Down river, the twelve-stamp Ida Mill was operating, the Union mine was turning out rich bullion from its eight-stamp mill, and the Eclipse was said to be the richest mine in all of California.

The year 1864 found the adobe villages prospering. Bend City and San Carlos, together, were predicted soon to have a population exceeding that of Visalia. Considerable rivalry was building up between these two towns. Free ferry service was furnished at San Carlos. Bend City was not proud of its own primitive toll ferry, so decided to build a bridge over the river. The question of its location became a lively one. Downtowners carried the vote to locate the bridge at the lower edge of town. Uptowners came up with the money and the imposing structure was built at the upper end. The village boasted sixty to seventy buildings, including two hotels. It appears that saloons did not rate the prominent billing given them in most mining camps. The first Union delegation from Owens Valley sent to the county convention at Visalia was instructed to vote for no man who drank whisky or played cards. Even the mining men took pride in giving names of refinement to their claims, such as Silver Cloud, Olympic, Chrysopolis, Calliope, Romelia, Golden Era and Prosperine. Culture was finding its way to Owens Valley. The first wedding, the marriage of a Mr. Woolsey to a Miss Warner, took place at San Carlos.

The great need of the district was for improved communication. Express routes to Aurora and to Visalia were lifelines to an outside world. A Visalia trip of only two days set a record, to the delight of the people of San Carlos. When San Francisco newspapers only four days old arrived by the same route, it was truly cause for rejoicing. California was coming closer!

The mining communities were well supplied by products of the farms along the river and westward. A sawmill at Big Pine was turning out good lumber, which had been a scarce item in the river towns. The San Carlos Mill, by the river at the corner of Romelia and Silver streets, was ready to go by the fourth of July. Life had not been easy, but comfort and prosperity were within reach at last.

It was during this year that the Inyo District was created from the original Russ District, being that portion lying north of a line running west from Winnedumah. One of the laws of the new district provided that, in case of potential problems with the local Indians, the claims would be honored without assessment work until the danger was over. Provision was made for soldiers to file free of charge or labor until ninety days after terms of duty had ended.

Bend City was named provisional county seat of the new County of Coso, approved by the state legislature. Procedure was set up for electing county officials and a Republican convention at San Carlos came up with a nomination for each office. June 6, 1864 was designate as election day, but the election was never held due to failure to establish legal notice. Coso County failed by default.

Before the year was over, the Owens River settlements were suffering from hard times. Mines had not provided the wealth that had been anticipated. Perhaps the newspaper editor from Visalia correctly analyzed the difficulty after making a trip over. He reported that he saw only one mine operating on correct principles. Periodic skirmishes with the local Native Americans, added to the discouragement. The Union Mill down the river was burned by Indians in June 1865. When the town of Independence was founded across the valley on Little Pine Creek, the dwindling populations of San Carlos and Bend City moved to the new community which was shortly to become the county seat.

W.A. Goodyear, in the "Eighth Annual Report of the State Mineralogist," published in 1888, describes the mining towns as he found them then. By the bridge at Bend City he saw ruins of an attempt at reduction works and a horizontal water wheel. Two large arrastras were noted and parts of reducing equipment. Ruins of 33 houses, mostly adobe, were counted at Bend City and 26 at San Carlos. Both towns were found to be completely deserted. The large stone building housing the quartz mill at San Carlos was falling to ruin. Down river, the Ida and Union mines were both idle. The Union Mill had burned and the Ida Mill, about a mile north, was crumbling. Its owners were preparing to build a mill on the old Union Mill site. Modern machinery being shipped from England for the new plant was expected to crush fifty tons of ore per day.

A later report stated that the ore was transported from the mine to the river by tramway. The company's twenty-stamp mill operated for many years.

The Eclipse mining claim (later the Reward) was patented in time, as was the Brown Monster claim. The Reward Consolidated Mining Company worked them both, along with six unpatented claims, from 1880 until 1914. In 1935 they went into production again for an extensive period. The Eclipse was one early discovery that proved its worth.

The Reward Mine in the Inyo Mountains. (Eastern California Museum Collection)

There is hardly a trace of the old towns left now. Bend City was located on the present road to Mazourka Canyon, where a tower of the transmission line stands near the bend of the old river bed, 4.3 miles from Independence. It was fortunate that the town was abandoned prior to the great earthquake of 1872. Had the adobe buildings been occupied, there would have been many more lives lost, without doubt. Besides, the town would have suffered the indignity of having the river abandon it for a new channel. The present traveler, en route to Bend City, may see convincing evidence of the shifting of the valley floor which took place during that quake. About three miles east of Independence, the road drops down over a 15-foot scarp on an earthquake fault that runs north and south between the present aqueduct and the old river bed.

The site of San Carlos may be reached by taking the first dirt road turning north from the Mazourka Canyon road after crossing the abandoned railroad right-of-way and driving about three miles. The town was just west of the curve of the hill that crowds the road into an old canal bed. The abandoned railroad right-of-way runs close beside the canal at this point. The writer, in the late 1930's, found the building outlines still well defined by melted adobe walls and the mill still recognizable as a stone structure. Since that time, weathering has taken its toll on the adobe and the mill and any other rock foundations have been sadly dug apart. A well worn slate pencil was found inside the largest rectangular outline, which our children had already decided must have been the school. A few coins, dated in the 1850's, were found in the sand toward the mill. The San Carlos ditch, smaller than the canal east of it, is still surprisingly well preserved. The narrow-gauge railroad has come and gone since San Carlos days and the Owens River waters now flow down the Los Angeles aqueduct.

Mazourka Canyon and the area west to the foot of the range have been the scene of mining activities since the Hill party filed the first claims. Both lode and placer claims have been worked intermittently until the present time. Santa Rita Flat was named for an early mine — Bonanza Gulch for its placer deposits. In July 1894, a cloudburst revealed coarse "colors" on a road in the vicinity of the Santa Rita Flat. The gold ranged in size from ten cents to $10 nuggets. Although water is not available for placering, many miners worked the gravel by a dry process during the next twelve years. In 1936, a placer mining company from Los Angeles leased claims on Pop's Gulch between Al Rose road and Santa Rita Flat. It was a big scale operation. Gravel was hauled by truck to a washing plant at Santa Rita Spring where a well furnished a good supply of water. Evidence of placer days, not too long ago, may be seen in diggings along Al Rose road and the passages "gophered" under the gravels of Pop's Gulch. Farther down the canyon, water has been carried over the hill from Barrel Springs to Bonanza Gulch to placer the gravel deposits there. This location is still active.

Tunnels, shafts and diggings may be found throughout the Mazourka Canyon area. Some are dangerously unguarded. Others are still being worked and should not be disturbed. But there are still many interesting places where it is safe to explore. The Whiteside tunnel, near the mouth of Mazourka Canyon, 7.3 miles from Independence on the right side of the road, is so safe and spacious that it has been approved as an emergency shelter. As a mine, it never did produce. Some say it was a promotional scheme — that there was nothing there when they began and nothing when they finished. A trail up the ridge south of the mine goes to Willow Springs, which was a millsite for the Black Eagle Gold Mine after the beginning of this century. The buildings at the springs have been burned — even the old wooden water tank under the red willow tree has been destroyed — but the site is still an interesting place to visit. A wagon road climbed the ridge north of the mine to reach the millsite by a slightly longer route. The grade proved to be too steep for general use. Lengths of cable secured to iron stakes are located above the steepest grades apparently to assist in hauling equipment and building materials up to the mine and mill. Another

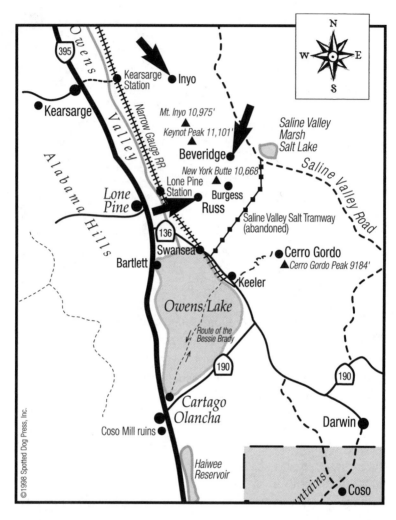

road, a little less precipitous, ran from the mill to the mine high up on the mountainside. It took a cool head and considerable courage to drive a loaded ore wagon down that grade. The company lost one capable driver, a teenage youth, when the young man's father visited this scene. One look at that mountain road convinced him that here was no place for his only son and heir.

BEVERIDGE
HIGH IN THE INYO MOUNTAINS
—❦✳❦—

Beveridge, which was the most important gold producing district in Inyo County, has remained the most inaccessible. Its mines and mills tucked into a maze of canyons on the precipitous east face of the Inyo Mountains were reached only by trails. Although these were well built to carry the traffic of heavily loaded pack trains, many portions of these old trails have since been washed out by cloudbursts. Occasional springs were the only source of water and they were few and far apart. In some instances the flow was enough to create running streams in the canyons before being lost to the thirsty gravel. Such places were blessed with streamside trees — willow, cottonwood or even oak. As a whole, however, wood was extremely scarce, except for a fair amount of pinyon at higher elevations and a fringe of bristlecone and limber pine on the peaks. Most of the important requirements for mine production were scarce or missing, but the gold was there, so hardy miners appeared on the scene and proceeded to overcome the obstacles.

The organization meeting was held December 7, 1877, at Big Horn Spring in Hunter Canyon about midway between the summit of New York Butte and the lake in Saline Valley. This spot was about as remote as could be found, even in those days, but it was typical of the district. The occasion was important and the miner members were present. W.L. Hunter, discoverer of the first claim, was elected chairman of the new district. He proposed that it be called "Beveridge" in honor of John Beveridge, a worthy citizen of the time and one who had been active in discoveries east of Cerro

Gordo. This same Beveridge had been named justice of peace at Bend City by the Tulare County Board of Supervisors in 1865 and had continued in that capacity after moving to Independence. He was elected first district attorney for Inyo County, but failed to qualify. W.L. Hunter served as Inyo County clerk, auditor and recorder in 1885 and 1886.

According to the record of that meeting at Big Horn Spring, boundaries of the Beveridge District were described as:

"Commencing at a point in Saline Valley, at the Northeast corner of Cerro Gordo Mining District, thence North fifteen miles, thence West to the summit of the Inyo Range of mountains, thence Southerly along the summit of said Inyo Range to a point where the Northern boundary line of Cerro Gordo Mining District crosses said summit, thence East along the Northern boundary of Cerro Gordo Mining District to the Northeast corner of the same and place of beginning."

Among the laws adopted to govern the district, No. XV affords an interesting comment on local conditions:

"That in consequence of the scarcity of timber, the miners of this District claim all the timber of Hunter's and Robles' Canyons for mining, building and fuel for the District and any wanton destruction or location of the same for private use will not be tolerated."

The Big Horn Mine, discovered by W.L. Hunter in 1877, became an active group of eight claims and a millsite located between Hunter and Beveridge Canyons. Hunter built three arrastras in the canyon named for him. These he operated until 1893, claiming to have recovered up to $10,000. This property has been worked from time to time until recent years, although transportation of ore has always been an expensive item. Selected ore was transported by pack mules over the Inyo crest to the roadhead in Long John Canyon, then by truck to Owenyo. Here it was transferred to the railroad for shipment to smelters at Salt Lake City. Reports show a total production figure of $40,000.

The Sierra Nevada from the Burgess Mine in the Inyo Mountains.
(Mary DeDecker)

The Keynot group of seven claims on the ridge north of Keynot canyon made the record for the greatest production in the district. It also had the most extensive development, including seven tunnels from 150 to 750 feet long. Its deepest mine went down 1,800 feet. Ore was carried three miles by pack mules to a five-stamp mill in Beveridge Canyon, formerly Hahn's Canyon. This amazing accomplishment of transporting heavy mill machinery so far by trail paid off in savings of costs for carrying ore. Beveridge camp below the junction of Cave and Beveridge Canyons was, and still is, by far the most inaccessible of the mining camps of the Inyos. Hence, it has had few visitors since it was abandoned and shortage of water along the route makes the trail a difficult one. The mine operated continuously from 1878 to 1886, and then intermittently until 1907. The total production figure is $500,000.

The Burgess Mine (Iron Sides), which included nineteen claims, was a later gold producer. It too had impressive development figures, a shaft of 156 feet deep, a tunnel 700 feet long and 2,000 feet of drifts. A gasoline hoist and compressor were used in this operation. Located on the Inyo crest, one and a half miles southerly from the summit of New York Butte, it provides a dramatic view of the snowy High Sierra to the west, as well as a glimpse of the salt flat of Saline Valley down Craig Canyon. Burgess can be reached from the west side by a foot trail from Long John Canyon. There was a time when the jeep trail up from Swansea could be followed, but severe thunderstorms and subsequent washouts over the years have taken their toll on the unmaintained road. The only other possible jeep trail is a hair-raising road that parallels the crest of the range from Cerro Gordo. The walk from Cerro Gordo to Burgess makes a nice overnight, though waterless backpack trip. A cabin and outbuildings provide shelter in case it is needed at this exposed location. From the cabin at Burgess, a pleasant hike of about 1.5 miles north along the crest can be made to the summit of New York Butte with its spectacular view across Saline Valley.

Other mines in the district include the Chilula, Gavilon, Montano and San Antonio mines near the head of Robles Canyon (Robles Canyon, a small canyon not named on modern maps, runs northerly from Hunter's Canyon near the Big Horn Mine), the Laura and McAvoy Mines north of Keynot Peak and the Cinnamon Mine which had its own two-stamp mill near the Big Horn Mine. The Gold Standard (Vega) Mine of a later date was in the vicinity of the Craig and Little Hunter canyons. The camp for the Vega operation is located just south of the mouth of Hunter Canyon, overlooking the salt lake of Saline Valley. A good dirt road branches from the main Saline Valley road and climbs the alluvial fan to the camp, where a caretaker greets visitors and offers a pleasant spot of shade. Springs in the green canyon above furnish a good supply of water which flows through a small pool and is channeled about the place. It is worthwhile to take a short walk into Hunter Canyon. A small stream confined between its rugged rock walls falls into refreshing pools bordered by maidenhair fern and columbine, a surprising oasis in this desert land.

KEARSARGE
NAMED FOR A CIVIL WAR BATTLESHIP

High in the canyon of Little Pine Creek (now Independence Creek), a mile downstream from Onion Valley, one may find stone rubble and remnants of the cabins of Kearsarge, although the site is almost covered by fill for the road. Lower in the canyon overlooking the switchback approaching the "county cabin" is the rock foundation of Kearsarge Mill. At intervals up the slope northward are rockwork footings for the pipeline that carried water to the mill from a spring up in the cliffs. Still lower on the stream, half a mile above Seven Pines, was the five-stamp Rex Montis Mill. Its foundations are plainly visible from the old Onion Valley road.

Kearsarge Peak, the beautifully triangular mountain west of Independence, was the scene of great activity as the Coso mines declined. It was said to have supported 3,000 men, but that, no doubt, was an exaggeration typical of the times.

The original discovery was made in 1864 by woodcutters who were doing a little prospecting on the side. They were camped at Todd's (later Hill's, for one of the woodcutters and now Gray's Meadows) to whipsaw lumber for the nearby settlements. Searching for a worthy name for their mine, they decided to call it Kearsarge in honor of the Union battleship which had so recently sunk the Confederate raider, Alabama. That would show those Confederate sympathizers down in the Lone Pine Hills what was thought of their Alabama mines. Kearsarge Peak was named for this first mining claim.

Prospectors arrived on the scene as if by magic and soon there were claims filed on every likely ledge. The Kearsarge Mining District, taking in an extensive segment of the eastern Sierra, from Big Pine Creek to the Alabama Hills, was organized in September of that year. It was then in the county of Tulare. Rich ore attracted the attention of prominent mining men — the Little Pine silver ledges were said to be the richest ever discovered on the Pacific coast — and so financing was forthcoming. A shipment of ore, to a mill in Nevada, netted $900 a ton. Wealth was here for the taking.

Development of various claims progressed through 1865. Dreams of rich prospects carried enthusiasm through the long months of winter, even though it was necessary to suspend activities on the mountain. The year 1866 was one of achievement. Machinery for the ten-stamp Kearsarge Mill was hauled up the canyon of Little Pine Creek and set up on the Sister Mill site north of the creek. By July, the $40,000 installation was ready to operate. Up canyon, along the stream, the busy mining camp of Kearsarge was flourishing, claiming a population of 1,500 people. In the meantime, the town of Independence had been established down in the valley on the same creek. Kearsarge, being the largest town in the newly created county of Inyo, tried for the county seat, but lost out to Independence which was more centrally located. Nevertheless, the future looked bright. As part of the new county with most of their problems behind them, and the wealth of their mines within their grasp, the people of Kearsarge had every reason to feel secure.

As claims on the mountain were developed, three main groups in widely separated locations became the best producing mines. Their ores were rich in both gold and silver. The Silver Spout was just below the summit of the peak on the south side at an elevation of 11,500 feet. The Rex Montis, highest of all at 12,000 feet, was on the north side of the peak's eastern shoulder. Both were considered high-grade, but there were many difficulties in working mines at such extreme elevations. The Kearsarge, at approximately 9,000 feet on the southeast slope, became the best known mine in the district.

The winter of 1866-67 forced another long delay in production up on the peak. Most of the miners and their families left camp for the winter but some remained in their lofty homes, well stocked with supplies. All went well until the end of February when a deep snow fell on the crusted surface of the already white slopes, a condition which should have been warning enough. On the afternoon of March 1st the gleaming canyon wall yielded its weight of new snow with deadly swiftness. The avalanche thundered down on the lonely settlement and, for all practical purposes, finished the town of Kearsarge. Rescuers from Bend City and Independence, as well as the woodcutters from the hill, rushed to the scene. Mrs. C.W. Mills, wife of the mine foreman was dug out of the snow with no worse than a broken leg. When all were accounted for, the shaken residents of Kearsarge went down the canyon to Hill's with plans to finish the winter elsewhere.

Half a century later, one who escaped the avalanche as a young man returned to the site of the old camp to make a memorial to those who were not so fortunate. Selecting a large granite boulder, he cut a monument about four by six feet, with a depth of a foot, then proceeded to smooth the surface in preparation for inscribing the names of the victims. Then came a summer when he did not come back, so the project was never completed.

Work continued at the mines, under a series of different managements, until the problems of operation proved to be too great to overcome. Repeated attempts have been made through the years to make the old mines pay, but the mountain, serene as it appears, has succeeded thus far in resisting them.

One brief period of later development on the Silver Spout was based at a little flat above the falls of the north fork of Independence Creek. The mine is situated precariously at the head of a steep chute and the falls. Evidence of an attempt to build a tramway down from the mine is seen in a rusting cable curled uselessly on the talus below the chute. A more recent attempt was made to work the mine by using water stored from melting snow, but the water came in the form of a cloudburst, wiping out the whole operation. A cable in use at that time still remains in place on the south side of the mountain. Its lower terminal may be reached by going up a short, steep trail from the upper switchback of the road to Onion Valley. The trail to the mine starts at this point.

The Rex Montis, sometimes called the "Ice Mine," last worked from 1875 to 1883, has been under refrigeration since then. It includes four patented claims, the Rex Montis, Arctic, Boomerang and Mountain View. Other claims in the group, including the Rex Montis mill site, were never patented. Three ore veins were being developed by three tunnels when production ceased. An attempt was made in 1935 to remove the ice which had accumulated in the tunnels. The middle one was cleared for a distance of 260 feet, revealing developments long forgotten, but winter weather ended the project. A new approach for working the mine is now underway, the plan being to tunnel through at a lower elevation to intercept the Rex Montis vein. If this is successful, it would avoid the snow problem and allow a reasonably long period of operation each year. A new road is being built, following somewhat the same route as the old trail to the mine by way of Sardine Canyon on the north. It leaves the Onion Valley road at its most northerly switchback on the east face of the mountain. The mine may also be reached by trails which branch from the Silver Spout trail up the south side. Predictions are that the Rex Montis will yet bring wealth from Kearsarge Peak. Who can say when a mine's day has ended?

The Kearsarge, known as the Cliff Mine, includes the Virginia, Golden State, Sister, West Virginia and Keystone patented claims, and the Sister mill site, also patented. Up the canyonside north of the old mill site, a mine dump reveals the location of the mine. It had advantages over the other groups in that it was several thousand feet lower, resulting in a longer working season, and was situated near a road, as well as having a water supply for its mill site. The original wagon road, little more than ruts through the boulders, may still be traced from the little Jewish cemetery on the highway north of Independence up the alluvial slope toward the north side of the mountain to Tub Springs. Turning southward here, it climbs over the saddle to the canyon of Independence Creek, which it follows upward to the Kearsarge mill. The fine rockwork retaining walls used in the building of that portion of the road between the saddle and the mill have yielded to later road work. The entire canyon is now so cut and scarred by various road construction projects that it seems nothing short of a miracle that any of the old sites have escaped. A fine paved road now runs all the way to Onion Valley.

The Kearsarge Mine operated again in the 1920's. Four houses to accommodate employees were built just upstream from the mill site. Lumber for their construction was transported by George Parker, by way of Parker Ranch and Tub Springs. When operations were suspended, the houses were sold and moved to Independence. The machinery used in both the Kearsarge and the Rex Montis mills was sold for scrap long ago, most of it during World War I. That of the Kearsarge mill was hauled out by way of Tub Springs, for the road up the canyon from Gray's Meadows and Seven Pines had not yet been built. Scrap from the Rex Montis mill was snaked down along the creek to the roadhead at Gray's Meadows. Such was the fate of much of the wonderful machinery of the early mining days.

HOMER DISTRICT
MINING AT 12,000 FEET

Lundy, a little town nestled in a glacial canyon at the head of a sparkling mountain lake, was supply center for both the Homer and the Tioga Mining Districts in the early 1880's. The town and the lake were named for William Otho Lundy, who operated a sawmill in Lundy Canyon around 1878, which supplied lumber to booming town of Bodie. The stream was appropriately called Mill Creek.

Promising gold outcroppings, discovered by prospectors Wasson, Nye and Horner, led to the organization of the Homer Mining District in 1879. Most activity centered in the upper or westerly portion of Mill Canyon (also known as Lundy Canyon), and southward on Mt. Scowdan, overlooking Lake Canyon. The May Lundy, named for Lundy's daughter, high on the eastern face of Mt. Scowdan, became the most famous mine in the district, and was by far the best producer. It is said to have yielded $837,000 of the total bullion output of $1,022,000 of the entire district from the fall of 1880 through 1884. Later production was in somewhat the same ratio. Other mining claims filed included such colorful names as Gorilla, Grand Prize, Wolverine, Gray Eagle, Lucky Mortan, Last Chance, Bay Queen and, of course, Bonanza.

Lake Canyon, a beautiful glacial hanging valley, meets the south side of Mill Canyon almost at right angles, 1,500 feet above and opposite the town of Lundy. Mt. Scowdan forms its towering west wall. Most of the above mentioned mines were on that mountain, well above timberline, and were worked from Lake Canyon. The lowest tunnel of the May Lundy was over 11,000 feet in elevation. The amazing developments on these extremely steep, barren slopes

The mill at the May Lundy Mine, circa 1885, high above Mono Lake. (Nevada Historical Society)

are evidence of the intrepid character of the early mining men. The mines were reached by trails and, in some cases, were used to transport ore. All too often these were swept away by snowslides.

Two of the lakes for which the canyon was named, Crystal and Blue lakes, are but mountain tarns, but Oneida Lake is deep and of fair size. The fourth lake lies in a cirque at the head of the canyon. The little mining camp of Wasson, near Crystal Lake, served the mines during the boom days. It included a boarding house, which kept the boisterous miners out of Lundy most of the week, but when they did go down hill, they more than made up for it. Until recent years, the May Lundy Mill was an imposing structure by the outlet of Oneida Lake, and other buildings and equipment were located at the camp by Crystal Lake. Many of these were of the later developments.

A steep and difficult trail zigzagged up the cirque at the very head of Lake Canyon to Dore Pass, and on to the mining camp of Bennettville, a well-traveled thoroughfare during its short existence. Another, less precipitous trail crossed the divide farther east into the head of Warren Fork Canyon, providing access to the fine stand of timber there. A toll road, three miles long, connected Lake and Mill canyons, an essential link between these two centers of activity.

Although Lundy was never very large, it was a lively town in its day. There was the usual mining camp crowd, a Chinatown, the necessary business houses, and hotels and more than enough saloons. The rival gangs, led by lawless characters, kept the populace uneasy until the leaders were eliminated. The *Homer Mining Index*, a weekly newspaper published by a humor-loving editor known as "Lying Jim" Townsend, was extremely popular reading, both at home and abroad. Jim made the most of his available material, including his own shortcomings, and did not hesitate to manufacture good reading copy. In his words, Lundy became a thriving city, to the delight of far away British investors in the Lundy mines. Railroad time tables, advertisements for two busy banks and large stores, and even elaborate and detailed accounts of the opening nights at the theater were all published as part of the game.

Surrounded by the steep mountains, Lundy was a natural for avalanches and the people were well aware of this threat. The season of 1882 is known as the year of the bad slides. Six feet of snow fell that March, a dangerous load on the smooth crusted surface of the season. Six fearful avalanches, bringing tons of snow and debris down their pathways of destruction, resulted. Worried residents had taken the precaution of housing women and children in a building considered out of the path of slides, which proved to be a wise move. Four men were killed at the May Lundy tramway; others narrowly escaped death. The huge property damages were considered secondary at such a time.

As typical of the time, legal processes were slow to catch up with rapidly changing conditions. A map of Lundy, showing blocks and lots, which was a portion of an ambitious town plan, was filed in 1888, after the town was on the decline. A patent to the land came through late in 1895, and deeds were issued too those persons who had purchased town lots or at least to those who were still around to claim them.

The May Lundy Mine suspended operations in 1884 and, although there were numerous renewals during which additional ore, up to $2,000,000 was taken out, the high cost of operation eventually forced the final shutdown. For a period after the turn of the century, the May Lundy and other mines were operated as the Crystal Lake Mine. The most modern equipment was used, including a 20-stamp mill run by electrical power generated nearby. The final effort was made by R.T. Pierce and Tom Hanna, who purchased the properties of the Crystal Lake Gold Mining Co. for taxes in 1921, but they too were unable to make it pay. Wood and water were plentiful, and electrical power for the later developments, but the season was limited to about eight months at the best. The severe winters were costly and the danger of avalanches was ever

Arrastra (Zdon collection)

a fearful threat to life and property.

Other mines were worked intermittently through the years, mostly in a small way by owners, or under lease agreements. The Parrett Mine, discovered in 1877 about a mile west of Lundy, was worked for thirty years by the owner, apparently yielding enough for a satisfactory living. Eleven patented claims were worked, mainly by surface cuts. Ore was packed by burros to an arrastra in Mill Canyon, driven by an 18-foot overshot water wheel. Two other arrastras, operated by similar water wheels, were used to mill ore in Lake Canyon.

Much evidence of this mining activity still exists and the scenic grandeur is still there. It takes but little imagination to transform the rugged canyons into the busy mining scene of the past. The lofty west wall of Lake Canyon is still marked with mine dumps and timbers; trails spared by avalanches can still be found; the old toll road grade down to Mill Canyon still would be a trial to creaking freight wagons; and the foundations of the town of Lundy are still visible at the west end of the lake. Perhaps remains of the old arrastras may yet be found, and even of the water wheels which drove them.

Lundy today is a quiet little resort on the lake. It is about six miles west of Highway 395, the turn-off being just north of Mill Creek, near the northern shore of Mono Lake.

TIOGA
A SHEPHERD FINDS GOLD

Embracing a choice portion of the very heart of the Sierra, the Tioga District stretches southward from Mt. Conness and the Lundy District. Although the "Great Silver Belt" was first discovered in 1860 and seemed to be well-known, it took a boy sheepherder to do something about it. He collected his first samples while herding a flock in the locality in 1874, but his father was not at all enthusiastic. The youth persisted, however, and in 1878 succeeded in filing the first claims along what he called the "Sheepherder Lode." It was through the efforts of a promoter from Bodie that the mines were finally developed. He aroused the interest of eastern financiers, resulting in the organization of the Great Sierra Consolidated Silver Co., backed by 800,000 shares of ten-dollar stock. Undaunted by the inaccessibility of the site, which was reached by trail up Bloody Canyon and over Mono Pass, the company moved quickly to establish a mine settlement up near Tioga Hill at an elevation of nearly 10,000 feet. It was to be named Bennettville for Thomas Bennett, Jr., president of the company. Existing claims were purchased and new claims located as work began on the Great Sierra and Sheepherder lodes. Six of the claims were soon patented.

That the company meant business was evidenced by two remarkable accomplishments, one necessitated by the other. Plans of operation called for the best in mining equipment, and delivery to the eastern foot of the Sierra was no small order. Then they were faced with the forbidding task of getting those heavy awkward pieces of machinery, 16,000 pounds in all, up the final four-thousand feet of mountain wall. But mining men with capital behind them refuse to recognize the impossible exists. Deciding to make the haul over the snow, the most practical route would be by way of Lundy and Lake Canyon and so on up the cirque to the Tioga Crest. This feat, which took three months, was accomplished in the spring of 1882 by the use of six heavy hardwood sleds. As reported in the Homer Mining Index, it took 4,500 feet of one-inch Manila rope, heavy double-blocks and tackle, and all the available trees along the route to boost the machinery up the mountain. No figures can measure what it took in human endurance and fortitude to exert such effort in snow conditions at elevations up to more than 11,000 feet. It was incredible.

That effort was to be enough to convince the Great Sierra Consolidated Silver Co. that a road to the west down the less precipitous side of the Sierra, was essential, resulting in the accomplishment that made the Tioga District famous. The Great Sierra Wagon Road, fifty-six miles long, was built in 1882-83 by way of the glacial dome-land and Yosemite Creek to Crocker's Station.

In the meantime, a tunnel was being driven into solid rock to intersect the Sheepherder and the Great Sierra lodes. It was to be 1,784 feet long by July 1884, when financial disaster forced suspension of operations. The camp closed abruptly. Reports showed that $300,000 had been expended, $64,000 of it on the wagon road — with no returns!

In January 1888, all property of the Great Sierra Consolidated Silver Co., including the wagon road, was sold at sheriff's sale for $164,000 to a group of former shareholders from New England. Development was resumed. The tunnel, a double adit six-feet wide and seven-feet high, was driven to 2,000 feet, when the whole thing was given up as a non-profitable venture. Tioga Hill has not yet yielded the fortune expected of it.

The Great Sierra Wagon Road deteriorated to little more than a trail, but it was to prove of greater value than the mines. Stephen Mather, who was soon to become Director of the National Park Service, with a few friends, acquired the road in 1915 and presented it as a gift to Yosemite National Park. Some of the charm of the old road was lost in its realignment, but in general, west of Tioga Pass, it still follows the old route.

The area of the Tioga excitement was a little north of the present pass of the same name, on its eastern approach. The site of Bennettville was west of Tioga Lake (then known as Lake Jessie Montrose) near the entrance of the great tunnel. Tioga Hill, rising a thousand feet above it, is a portion of the main crest of the Sierra Nevada. An official map of an early survey of the 1880's shows a "Bennettville and Lundy Telephone Line" running through the camp, and the same map shows the trail to Lundy as "Tioga Road." It is possible that these may have only originated in "Lying Jim" Townsend's publication at Lundy. Two buildings of the mining era still stand, but vandalism has take a sad toll. A brass plate countersunk in a rock at the top of Tioga Hill is the U.S. survey point for early mining maps.

PRESCOTT
ALONG THE MONO TRAIL

Prescott District has joined others in obscurity, still the fact that Mono Pass is located on its westerly boundary gives it historical interest. In the early days, the Mono Trail was a main route across the Sierra, used first by Indians and later by the new pioneers. It was on a trip over this trail, in pursuit of Yosemite Indians, that Lt. Tredwell Moore of the U.S. Army found gold in the Bloody Canyon and Mono Lake areas in 1852.

The following year, Leroy Vining came over the same trail to follow up on the gold prospects. Perhaps he found that a beautiful meadow was a more pleasant place to settle than rugged Bloody Canyon or the barren shores of Mono Lake. At any rate, he stayed to prospect on the meadow floor on the prominent canyon that still bears his name, and which later was to become the route for the spectacular highway to Tioga Pass.

The Mono Trail still exists, a direct route from Mono Basin up Bloody Canyon and over Mono Pass to Dana Meadows and Yosemite National Park, but only hardy hikers attempt it now.

At the very summit of Mono Pass, above the timberline, are situated three mining claims, the Ella Bloss, Ella Bloss No. 2, and the Golden Queen. It is interesting to note that patents for the first two were granted to some of the principal stockholders of the Great Sierra Consolidated Silver Company, including Thomas Bennett, Jr., at about the same time that operations were resumed at the Tioga Mines after the sheriff's sale. The Ella Bloss, with one corner in Tuolumne County and in the Tioga District, is of particular interest

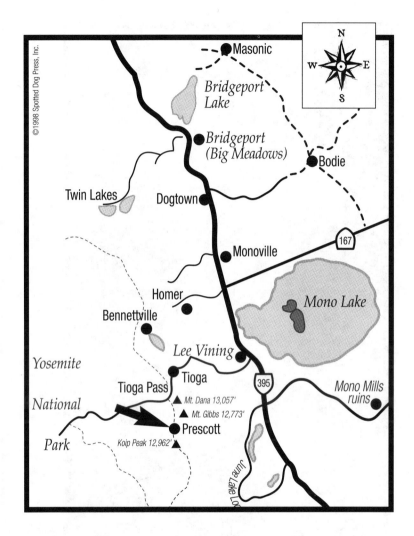

Masonic

Bridgeport Lake

Bridgeport (Big Meadows)

Bodie

N
W   E
S

Twin Lakes

Dogtown

167

Monoville

Mono Lake

Homer

Bennettville

Lee Vining

Yosemite

Tioga Pass

Tioga

395

Mono Mills ruins

National

▲ Mt. Dana 13,057'
▲ Mt. Gibbs 12,773'

Park

Koip Peak 12,962' ▲

Prescott

June Lake Loop

because of the picturesque and well-preserved old log mine buildings located upon it. Down the trail toward Dana Meadows, at the upper edge of the forest, the walls of a primitive log cabin still stand. One wonders if it might have served as the last outpost in the days when the Mono Trail was a well-traveled thoroughfare.

Gold-seeking guests at the Nevada Hotel in Benton. Blind Spring Hill is in the background. (Nevada Historical Society)

BENTON

BLIND SPRING, WHITE PEAK, INDIAN & CLOVER PATCH DISTRICTS

— �֍◉֍ —

Tucked away in its own little basin in the hills between the massive White Mountains on the east, and the Sierra Nevada in the westward distance, Benton Hot Springs today is but a charming ghost of the mining center that it once was. In the beginning, it was a popular gathering place for those Indians who came to make use of the large hot springs located there. Pioneers were quick to appreciate the advantages of the place and began a settlement, then known as Hot Springs, later as Benton, and after Benton Station began operating to the east on the railroad line, the name was changed for a third and final time to Benton Hot Springs. The elevation of 5,600 feet was low in comparison with settlements farther to the north, and the townsite was well-removed from snowy peaks, so the climate was comparatively moderate. The snows that fell did not linger long. The spring, ten feet in diameter, was an outstanding asset as a hot water supply. Its temperature was 135 degrees Fahrenheit and it flowed 400 gallons a minute, enough for the entire town, with a surplus for irrigation. After Bodie and Aurora boomed, Benton became an important waystation on the route from the south.

It is not surprising that this focal point was the scene of a tragic incident during the period of unrest between the settlers and Indians. The well-known partner of William S. Bodey of Bodie fame, E.S. "Black" Taylor, was destined to be the victim. After the loss of his friend in a snowstorm, on the outskirts of Bodie, Taylor restlessly drifted on to other camps. Arriving at Hot Springs, he established himself at a little spring a short distance northeast of the settlement. There he built a stone cabin with a thatched roof, stayed to prospect the area and found it good. Unfortunately, his lonely cabin was in the pathway of an angry band of Paiute-Shoshone heading to the settlement, just at the time when tensions between the settlers and Native Americans had escalated. At Taylor's cabin, they had a chance to vent their feelings. They besieged the place for two days before they finally succeeded in setting fire to the roof. Upon being forced out of his flaming cabin, Taylor was killed. The place is still known as Taylor Springs.

The Cornucopia, Diana, and Comanche veins on Blind Spring Hill east of Benton were discovered in 1862 while the Civil War was in full swing back east. The hill, six miles long and rising 1,200 feet above the town, was soon dotted with claims. As the work progressed, it was found to have a mineral-bearing zone for almost half of its length and about one and one-half miles wide. Enthusiasm soared. Claims were worked in feverish haste with the help of Chinese laborers. The first discoveries continued to maintain their status among the best producers. The Diana was combined with the Karrick, later to become the Wai Wera Mine, and the Eureka and Laurel claims located in 1865 were combined to become the Little Emily Mine. Both mines are well known in the history of Blind Spring Hill.

The White Peak District, seven miles east of Benton in Montgomery Canyon of the White Mountains, was well publicized at the time, but did not prove to be a great producer. Most of the development was on its Phoenix and Mountain Queen (Creekside) claims. The camp of Montgomery never did acquire size or importance and its site is now inaccessible.

Indian District was about eight miles from Benton, westerly. The Tower Mine proved to be the best producer. In the Clover Patch District, some twelve miles southwest of Benton, the Wild Rose and Banner mines did reasonably well, In 1885, the two districts merged to form the Indian District.

Another mining camp named after the high point of the White Mountains, White Mountain City, in Deep Springs Valley across the range to the southeast from White Peak District near Benton. (Nevada Historical Society)

Estimated production from the Benton area from 1862 to 1888 was $4,216,000. This was almost all silver. According to J.F. Millner, Wells Fargo and Company's agent at Benton in the 1880's, estimates by each district for the same period were: Blind Spring, $3,946,000; White Mountain, $60,000; Indian, $150,000; and Clover Patch, $60,000.

Ore reduction went through an interesting cycle. In the beginning ore was shipped to Reno or San Francisco, but the shipping costs consumed much of the profit. There was a cry for local mills. So several small mills were built to serve the area. The Wai Wera Company built a five-stamp mill and processed some ore from other districts as well as the ore from its own mines. It burned in 1888 and was not rebuilt. A different outlook resulted from the appearance on the scene of the Carson and Colorado narrow gauge railroad. It became more profitable to sort the ore rather carefully and send it out by rail, most of it going to the Selby Smelting Works near San Francisco. Although they continued to process some ore locally, mine operators along the route of the railroad became rather

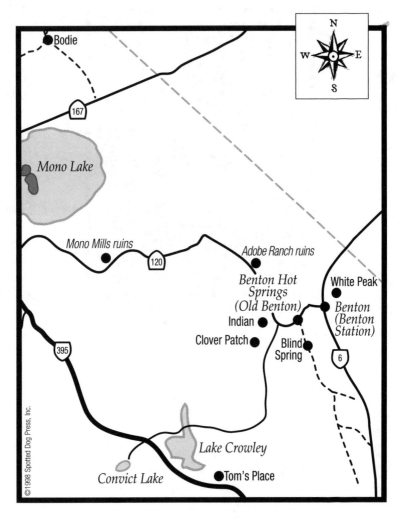

independent. Many of the mills that had been so eagerly sought were now forced to close.

Benton was the logical supply center for all of the nearby mining districts. Never becoming one of the larger boom towns, it endured longer than most of them. It was a busy and exciting place for many years. The mining atmosphere was there, a Chinatown flourished, and travelers stopping over added the cosmopolitan touch. There were lawless incidents, but, as a whole,

Benton's reputation was relatively mild. Communication was surprisingly good for its time. A pony express carried mail between Benton and Aurora twice a weekend, and stages ran on a regular schedule. It was suspected that the Carson and Colorado had a part in discouraging the rival project. The settlement of Partzwick, almost a suburb of Benton on the north, offered some healthy competition to the local businesses and assisted in the social life of the area.

The greatest activity occurred from 1862 to 1889, but the town lived on through lesser periods for many years. The hot springs are an enduring attraction, and the mines renewed operation from time to time, but they have been picked fairly clean in recent times. In later years, Benton Station, over the hill on the railroad became the center of business, such as it was. It also claimed the main highway to Nevada. Old Benton, was left with little more than memories. Several of the early buildings, including the Wells Fargo office, still remain, as well as other buildings of a later period. An old farmhouse called "The Old House" in Benton Hot Springs is a nice place to purchase a cold drink, soak in the famous springs, or spend some time looking at the antiques for sale in the store. Farming equipment and other relics of the early days are displayed throughout town, and the old pioneer cemetery is just above town to the north.

A very scenic and enjoyable loop trip may be made from Bishop by way of Highway 6 north to Benton, then left on Highway 120 (closed in winter) through Benton Hot Springs, westward across vast sage country to Mono Craters, and the south side of Mono Lake to Highway 395, then south on that highway back to Bishop. A short side trip can be made from Highway 120 by turning right on Dobie Meadows Road (approximately 18.4 miles north of Benton) and driving 1.7 miles to the adobe ruins of the Adobe Ranch which still operates today.

LAKE DISTRICT
MAMMOTH LAKES
—❋ ❋ ❋—

Scenic Lake District derived its name from the fifteen mountain lakes lying within a ten-mile radius of Pine City. The name "Mammoth," which could hardly be used to describe any of the lakes, originated with the Mammoth vein on Mineral Hill east of Lake Mary. Soon it was applied to the entire region.

Attention had first been focused on the Pumice Mountain (Mammoth Mountain) area in connection with the Lost Cement Mine. The story has several versions, but all center around samples of red cement-like ore in which grains of gold were set "like raisins in pudding," supposedly picked up in the vicinity of Mammoth in 1857. The account usually heard was that a Dr. Randall of San Francisco came to Monoville in the spring of 1861 with samples of the red cement ore and a crude map showing Pumice Mountain as a landmark. They had been given to him by a grateful patient, a consumptive who was too sick to return to the scene himself. He and his brother had crossed the Sierra with some difficulty, coming over the crest at the head of the San Joaquin River. They found the red cement ledge on a pumice flat east of the crest.

Dr. Randall spent the summer of 1861 in the Mammoth area searching for the treasure. Returning the following year, he hired a crew of men, with Gid Whiteman as foreman, to continue the search. If the Lost Cement Mine was ever found, its location was never revealed. Whiteman devoted his life to the search and hundreds of prospectors tried in vain to find the elusive treasure. There is still speculation as to whether or not it really existed and, if so, what vital clue was the tale missing.

The silver-gold lode that made Mammoth famous was discovered in June 1877 by a group of miners who were searching for the Lost Cement Mine. If it was not the mine they were looking for, it was something just as good. They gave it its impressive name and publicized it as the "largest Bonanza outside of Virginia City." Miners responded, true to form. The rush was on! Comstock investors, eager to profit from the new discovery, secured the Mammoth Mine by option before the summer was over, then waited impatiently to begin development in the spring. Activity had begun and the snows had hardly melted when General Dodge, a well-known mining investor, arrived on the scene. Without bothering to inspect the mine, he bought it for $10,000 cash and $20,000 in company stock and proceeded to organize the Mammoth Mining Company, which incorporated in July 1878. The boom continued with renewed vigor — new claims were located throughout the district and new companies were created to develop them.

Mammoth City sprang up in a gulch below the hill. Pine City was another lively settlement on Lake Mary to the west, 200 feet higher in elevation. Their combined population was said to have been over 1,500 people in 1879. Following the pattern typical of the restless influx to new bonanzas — hopes were high and so were the prices of all it took to supply their needs. Women put lace curtains at the windows of their crude homes to give themselves the courage to share their men's enthusiasm. Families who followed the mining game had long since learned to make the best of their environment.

Mammoth stimulated its share of the roads that were so vital to the development of the eastern Sierra. One was a wagon road from Benton, a well-established mining town situated on the main thoroughfare to Bodie and Aurora. More important, however, was the construction of a toll road over the rugged "Sherwin Grade," creating a more direct route from Bishop Creek to the Lake District. A fifty-four mile toll trail was built by J.S. French over the Sierra crest, from Fresno Flats (now Oakhurst) to Mammoth City, providing a route by which beef cattle were brought in from the San Joaquin

The water wheel at the Mammoth Mine. (Mary DeDecker)

Valley. A railroad route over Mammoth Pass was surveyed in 1881, but by then Mammoth's need for railroads was over.

The company forged ahead, driving tunnels and processing ore. A fine twenty-stamp mill was operating in 1878 and twenty more stamps were added the following year. Each stamp weighed 900 pounds. The mill was driven by a six-foot Knight water wheel. It was a type especially designed for use in the steep watersheds of California's mountainous country, to take advantage of pressure rather than volume of water. A flume brought the necessary water down from Twin Lakes. The mill was also equipped for steam power, which apparently was never applied. Nothing but the finest of equipment was brought in for the mill, regardless of cost. A twenty-foot flywheel was cast in Belgium of high-grade "gray iron"and transported by sea, rail, and Nadeau's freight wagons to its destination on the mountain. The expense of shipping mining machinery was no small item in the cost of setting up a big operation.

By the end of 1879, the Mammoth Mining Company was said to have expended close to $400,000 in extracting bullion valued at $200,000. The unhappy stockholders had differences of opinion — there were implications of mismanagement — and no solution seemed apparent. Operations were suspended and in 1881 the property was sold at sheriff's sale. The towns were quickly abandoned. Severe weather conditions were considered the main factor in forcing the mine to close. Long winters cut down on production time and strong winds were costly. Some experts, however, claimed that it could have been made to pay under proper management; that the mill never should have been shut down.

The Headlight and Monte Cristo companies also suspended operations after driving a joint tunnel 1,500 feet without finding any ore of value. Other mines were developed, the Lisbon, three miles south of Pine City, being the most successful. It began producing in 1881 but its operation was intermittent until 1885 when the Lisbon Company put in a five-stamp mill driven by steam. Continuing in steady production for some years, the yield was reported to average $20 per ton of ore. Several arrastras also were operated in the district.

In the 1890's another effort was made to make the Mammoth mine pay, but it too ended in failure. Only occasional work has been done on various mines in the district since that time.

Little is known of the pathos of mining camps, but a lonely grave below the town remains to tell of the tragic death of a pretty young bride of Pine City. Her husband and his mining partner had decided to stay for the winter, after the rest of the population had gone, hoping to complete a promising lead at their mine. She insisted on staying too. They were very much in love. In March, after the worst of the winter was over, a tragic accident caused her death. The distraught young husband was unable to make a proper burial because the ground was still frozen, so was forced to keep her body covered in the changing snow until the storms were over and the earth thawed. The ordeal was almost more than he could bear. When he and his partner were able to bury her down on the flat, they labored long with their few simple tools to make a picket fence for her grave. She had been an eastern girl and had longed for the day when she might have a lasting home with a picket fence around it. These original pickets have been replaced, but the grave still may be seen on the south side of the road, well below the site of old Mammoth City.

After the mining towns were abandoned, Mammoth was to be enjoyed as a quiet summer retreat for three-quarters of a century. It was a place of tall pines and clear mountain lakes with space for solitude. Now, Mammoth is the scene of a new rush, triggered by a most successful ski development on the slopes of Mammoth Mountain. A combination of natural factors make it one of the most ideal ski areas in the state — the winter snows bring in more gold than the mines ever produced. Year-around resorts cater to skiers in the winter and to other tourists the remainder of the year. Real estate sells for fabulous prices. There was once pressure to build a trans-Sierra highway over the Mammoth Pass where the railroad was surveyed in 1881, but its feasibility was always questioned.

The atmosphere of Mammoth is rapidly changing, but it still carries evidence of its mining days. Highly-colored Mineral Hill, now known as Gold or Red Mountain, east of Lake Mary, was the center of most of the mining activity. Tunnel sites are marked by mine dumps while pieces of mining machinery and timbers are scattered about. Considered a hazard, the Mammoth Mining Company mill was burned in 1929, but remnants of its stone foundation can be seen near the present Mill City campground. Little is left of the great machinery which equipped the mill, except the twenty-foot

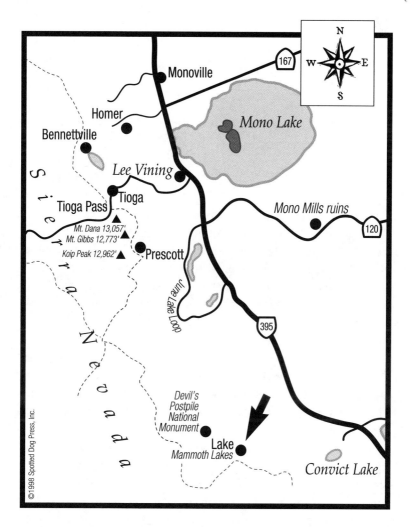

Mono Lake

Monoville

Homer

Bennettville

Lee Vining

Tioga Pass

Tioga

Mt. Dana 13,057'
Mt. Gibbs 12,773'
Koip Peak 12,962'

Prescott

Mono Mills ruins

120

June Lake Loop

395

Devil's
Postpile
National
Monument

Lake
Mammoth Lakes

Convict Lake

167

Sierra Nevada

iron flywheel. Pine City on Lake Mary has been completely obliterated. There are only traces of Mammoth City below, but stone foundations and remains of several log cabins may be found along the old road. A walk through the brush will reveal still more. A road turning left from about a half mile above the Twin Lakes bridge runs down through old Mammoth City.

DOGTOWN & MONOVILLE
LIQUOR STORES OUTNUMBERED HOMES

Dogtown was located just west of present Highway 395, six-tenths of a mile south of the northerly turn-off to Bodie. A California Historical Plaque marks the site. It all began when Cord Norst, a young German, and his Indian wife, Mary, set up housekeeping in a dugout on Dog Creek, where they panned gold for a living. Little could they have guessed the chain of events to follow. The year was 1857, and the location was about halfway between Big Meadows (Bridgeport) and Mono Lake, was far removed from any settlement. It was hardly a place to turn the course of history, but their modest diggings were to lead to the first gold rush east of the Sierra. Mormons in Nevada heard of their activity and moved down to join in this placering. Two years later, Dogtown was a bustling little community.

On July 4, 1859, while festivities honored the date, a Dogtown resident named "Chris" wandered over the hills which form the watershed between the Walker River and Mono Lake Basin. As he stopped to rest, he idly picked up some of the dirt about him and was amazed to find it rich with gold. The news that gold could be picked up right off the ground spread as if by magic. Residents of Dogtown moved quickly to stake out claims ahead of outsiders, who poured in over Sonora and Mono passes, down from Carson Valley, and up through Owens Valley. Soon the ground was claimed for miles; the first gold rush east of the Sierra had occurred. Monoville had come into being. There was a frantic rush to fill all the needs of a booming mining camp. Lumber was whipsawed for use before any of the five sawmills could be brought into production. The first homes were dugouts or log cabins. Of the first thirty-one buildings erected, twenty-two were liquor shops. Important things first! In order to get into big production as rapidly as possible, resources were pooled to build an eleven-mile ditch to bring water from Virginia Creek for hydraulic operations. Enthusiasm waned, however, as winter approached. The placers soon would be frozen out of operation for several months, and the restless miners could find little comfort in the prospect of wasting that time in their crude shelters. The population diminished to a hardy 150 people, who managed to survive that first bitter winter. A welcome spring brought renewed activity and Monoville flourished briefly. It was the report of rich silver lodes in Aurora that finished Monoville as a mining town. Silver had become the magic word — each new find was to be hailed as another Comstock — and lode mining was the new way to wealth. Monoville lost not only its population to Aurora, but its buildings as well, when they were torn down and moved to the new excitement center. Sawed lumber was in demand, too valuable to be left behind.

The fact that Mono placers continued to be worked intermittently was immaterial. They had fulfilled their role in our history by attracting the attention of the mining world and bringing a population over the Sierra. Trails and roads and improved communication with the rest of the state followed.

As for Cord Norst and his wife, they had chosen to remain at Dogtown during the rise and fall of Monoville. This was to be their home for many years, as they homesteaded land nearby and continued to find enough gold on Dog Creek to buy their supplies in the new county seat of Bridgeport.

There is no way of knowing how much was taken from the Dogtown and Mono diggings, but it is estimated to have been in the millions of dollars. Lesser placer deposits extended along the base of the Sierra, at varying elevations, all the way from Bridgeport to

Owens River. For almost half a century, the sluice and rocker were in common use along the entire 80 miles. Hydraulic operations were carried on at the largest deposits, as evidenced by unsightly mounds of gravel. Some work was done in fairly recent years. In the 1880's the Virginia Creek Hydraulic Mining Company operated very profitably on 3,200 acres about the old Mono diggings.

One may still see remains of Dogtown's stone cabins and dugouts along the stream. Monoville was over the ridge southward, east of the present highway, on the north side of Conway Summit. The old water ditches from Virginia Creek may still be traced on the hillside. The "Sinnamon Cut" said to have yielded $80,000 in gold, is a 1,700 by 200 foot scar on the landscape.

Even though gravels of the old Mono diggings have been worked and reworked for over a hundred years, they still may show a flash of color in the pan, which is all that it takes to set your imagination soaring.

DANGERS IN AND AROUND MINES

Travel Safe and Leave No Trace

Various aspects of traveling and hiking in the remote desert and mountain regions of Inyo and Mono counties have certain risks and hazards associated with them. Some of these hazards include, but are not limited to adverse weather conditions, loose rock, exposed rock, rugged terrain, flash floods, potential for insect, snake or animal bites, heat injury, dehydration, or other types of physical injury. Before traveling on any route in Death Valley, or the remote parts of Inyo and Mono counties, be prepared.

Let someone know your travel plans — where you are going, when you plan to return, and have them check on you at your designated time of return. If you will be operating a CB radio, let someone know which channel you will be operating.

Make sure your vehicle is in good running condition — with a tool kit, spare parts, inflated spare tire, and a good jack. Carry plenty of extra water, food, a cell phone (can be used from a highpoint like a hill or mountain top), or a CB radio. If you become stranded, stay with your vehicle and keep your CB tuned to the designated channel as search & rescue personnel may contact you on this channel. Always check ahead with the National Park Service, United States Forest Service, Bureau of Land Management or other managing agencies for pertinent route and weather information. Conditions in Inyo and Mono counties are constantly changing and weather conditions may close roads due to flash flooding and washouts. There is no substitute for knowledge of safety procedures when traveling and exploring the mines and backroads from Death Valley to Dogtown.

Walk safely and Leave Only Footprints

The deserts and mountains of California and the southwest, have been prospected for their minerals since before the Civil War. Shafts, tunnels, rotted timbers and rusted debris are reminders of those early days of mining, and with bits of shiny purple and blue glass catching the sunlight, it is hard to resist exploring the old camps, with their intriguing history. Walk the same footpaths that Death Valley Scotty or Mark Twain may have walked, and take a step back in time to California's frontier past. Take only photographs to remind you of your visit, and leave only footprints.

With the help of the Nevada Division of Minerals, Bureau of Abandoned Mine Lands, we have put together a few pointers that will help you to safely enjoy the many fascinating historic mines found in Eastern California, from Death Valley to Dogtown in Mono County.

Explosives

As mentioned in an earlier chapter on Panamint City, we once camped at Panamint City and explored the ruins of the old mill. One of the guys on our trip found a cache of dynamite left behind during the last prospect of Panamint City when the area was subjected to an intense flash flood. Some blasting caps had been tossed in some old barrels standing outside the man camp. We discovered them when one of our party attempted to burn some camp trash in one of the cans and the caps began to explode like firecrackers.

When we got to a phone, we notified the Inyo County Sheriff. Explosives, become very unstable when left sitting around unattended for years. Only trained explosives experts should handle them. If you find explosives — don't touch them. Leave the area as soon as possible and report your discovery and its location to local law enforcement.

Shafts, Cave-Ins, and Timber

Nature erodes and weakens what is exposed to rain, sun, and wind. Weakened timbers or eroded soils are usually not readily visible. Rain dropped by summer thunderstorms will move down any sloped surface, wearing away its strength. The edge, or collar, of a mine shaft can be extremely unstable, worn away by years of water and wind erosion. These collars have been known to collapse unexpectedly, dragging down anything or anyone who happens to be standing too near. Most shafts are quite deep and a fall is usually lethal. If a person survived such a fall, getting back out would be a challenge. Mine tunnels are also susceptible to cave-ins, which can be caused by minor disturbances such as talking or walking.

The old wood support timbers which were used to stabilize the mine workings a hundred years ago, today are probably rotten, weakened from decay and termites. A well-timbered mine opening may appear solid , but in reality, it may just barely be supporting its own weight. Touching a timber might even cause a tunnel to collapse. Wood ladders and stairways, the flooring, walls and ceilings of old structures are suspect as well. Years of exposure weakens wood and rusts nails.

Water and "Bad Air"

Often times, the floors of tunnels can be obscured by murky pools of water on their surface. Imagine stepping in a pool and falling into a shaft hidden beneath its surface — quite unpleasant. The water in mine shafts and tunnels may also be contaminated with various chemicals and heavy metals.

Remember the old terminology, "canary in a gold mine?" When mining was in its infancy, before technology improved safety below ground, miners used canaries to detect poisonous gases. Canaries were extremely sensitive to "bad air" which could kill a miner with no warning. When the little canary passed out, the miners knew they better hightail it out of the mine. Even today, deadly gases accumulate in low areas or along the floor of abandoned mines and will initially go unnoticed. These gases can be stirred up with even the most seemingly insignificant activity — walking or talking. They can even be disturbed by a slight breeze. The bad air combines with good, and creates a potentially deadly mixture that can cause rapid dizziness, unconsciousness — and even death.

Flash Floods & Wash-Outs

The storms of winter bring snow to the surrounding mountain ranges and high passes of Death Valley. Several times during the winter, Towne Pass can be closed for a few hours due to heavy snowfall. The desert easily absorbs the winter snow which comes to rest upon its bone-dry surface, with plenty of time to melt.

By comparison, summer thunderstorms bring enormous amounts of rain to the desert within just a few hours. The desert terrain with its sun-dried soil, cliffs of limestone and basalt can't absorb the massive amounts of water deposited by these thundershowers. It is these summer storms that have the greatest potential for creating unpredictable, destructive and potentially deadly flash floods. In a matter of hours, they can turn a sudden, dry creek into a torrential river full of desert debris.

Chances are, if you are not inside a car, you will hear a flash flood before seeing it. A thunderstorm has its own sounds— first an oppressive quiet, followed by the sound of rain and thunder — a crack of lightening across the creosote plain. The sound of a flash flood has been compared to that of a jet or plane passing high and fast, but instead of getting fainter, the sound grows louder as the flood approaches.

Move to high ground, above washes and low areas. Flash flood water moves fast and carries with it debris — silt, rocks, trees limbs, uprooted cacti, and whatever else may be in its path As it passes by, you can see the rocks it carries bobbing up and down below the surface of the water and you can listen to them clatter as they strike against each other.

As a result of flash flooding, many of the roads in Death Valley and surrounding areas are prone to wash-outs, which may make them completely impassable to any kind of vehicle, and may require long detours. Usually, road maintenance will sign maintained roads that have been closed due to flooding. This will not be the case on unmaintained roads, so proceed with caution.

Rattlesnakes, Scorpions and Other Creatures

Many venomous creatures live in Death Valley's harsh environment, but despite their frightening appearances, they are only aggressive when disturbed or threatened. A cool mine shaft or the shady ledge of a wood shelf in an abandoned miner's cabin in the heat of Death Valley provides a comfortable escape for desert creatures, most of which are nocturnal — active at night, sleeping during the day. Rarely, are animals, insects and birds seen during the heat of a hot Death Valley day. It makes sense to watch where you put your hands and feet, because you may be disturbing someone's bedtime rest.

Rattlesnakes enjoy coiling up in a cozy place — just under a shaded rocky ledge or beneath the shadow of old mining equipment. With one exception, they all possess one of two types of venom — either a hemotoxin (which acts on the blood) and a neurotoxin (which acts on the nervous system). Only the Mojave rattlesnake has both types of venom. Your chance of being hit by lightening is greater than that of dying from a rattlesnake bite. Rattlesnakes use their venom for two things: to kill their prey and for defense. If you come across a rattlesnake, move away from it as quickly as possible.

Scorpions like the undersides of rocks during the day. They have terrible eyesight despite the fact that they have at least four or five eyes. The sting from a scorpion is usually no more severe than a bee sting and the pain usually goes away within a few hours. There are a few deadly species, which are characterized by a small horn-like growth under their stingers, but they are primarily found in the Sonoran Desert of southern Arizona and northern Mexico.

There are many wild and fascinating creatures in the desert that have carved an existence from the harsh and unforgiving environment. They deserve our respect, not our fear. Observe them and let them go about their business undisturbed.

A Word about Artifacts

All historic and prehistoric sites on federal lands are protected by the Antiquities Act of 1906, and the Archaeological Resources Protection Act of 1979. Defacement, removal, excavation or destruction of such antiquities and sites is prohibited by law.

SUGGESTED READING & REFERENCES
DEATH VALLEY

The books about Death Valley listed below are but a minor fraction of those available about its history and mining booms. The area has served as a strong magnet for both prospectors and writers.

Albright, Horace, *The Story of Death Valley, Its Museum and Visitor Center*, Death Valley '49ers, 1960

Bailey, Paul, *Walkara, Hawk of the Mountains*, Westernlore Press, 1954

Belden, L. Burr, *Death Valley Heroine, Inland Press*, 1954; *Goodbye, Death Valley*, Death Valley '49ers, 1956; *The Wade Story*, Death Valley '49ers, 1957; *Searles Lake Borax*, Death Valley '49ers, (with Ardis M. Walker), 1962 — 1966 reprint
  by American Potash & Chemical and Stauffer Chemical Corps

Brown, Charles A., see *Death Valley Tales*

Carruthers, William, *Loafing Along Death Valley Trails*, Desert Magazine
  Press, 1951

Caughey, John Walton, *Southwest from Salt Lake in 1849*, Pacific Historical Review, 1937, also included in *Far West and the Rockies*, Volume II, issued by
  Arthur H. Clark Co., 1954

Chalfant, W.A., *Outposts of Civilization*, Christopher, 1928; Death Valley, The
  Facts, Stanford, 1930 (seven printings); *The Story of Inyo*, Stanford, 1942 and
Piñon Press, 1965; *Gold, Guns and Ghost Towns*, Stanford, 1947; Tales of
  Pioneers, Stanford, 1942

Clements, Lydia, *Death Valley Indians*, Hollycrafters, 1954 et subs.

Clements, Thomas, *Geological Story of Death Valley*, Death Valley '49ers, 1954

Coolidge, Dana, *Death Valley Prospectors*, Dutton, 1937

Corle, Edwin, *Desert Country*, Duell, Sloan and Pearce, 1941; *Death Valley*,
  Ward Ritchie, 1962.

Death Valley Tales, Death Valley '49ers (revised edition 1965). Chapters on the
  valley's fabulous past by James B. Nosser, John W. Hilton, L. Burr Belden,

Ardis Manly Walker, Harry P. Gower, Phil Townsend Hanna, Carl I. Wheat, Arthur Woodward, R. A. Gibson, and Charles A. Brown

Driskill, Earl C., *Death Valley Scotty Rides Again*, published by the author, numerous printings 1955 to date. (Ranks along with Manly's Death Valley in '49 and Chalfant's Death Valley, the Facts as an all time bestseller

Edwards, E.I., *The Valley Whose Name is Death*, San Pasqual Press, 1940 (contains the best bibliography of any book listed here); Freeman's, A Stage Stop on the Mojave, La Siesta, 1964

Ellenbecker, John G., *The Jayhawkers of Death Valley*, privately printed, 1938

Gibson, R. A., see *Death Valley Tales*

Glasscock, C.B., *Gold in Them Hills*, Bobbs-Merrill, 1934; *Here's Death Valley*, Bobbs-Merrill, 1940

Hafen, Le Roy and Ann, *Far West and the Rockies*, a fifteen volume series by the Arthur H. Clark Co., 1954-61; Vols. II and XV contain diaries of Death Valley travelers of 1849

Hanna, Phil Townsend – see *Death Valley Tales*

Jaeger, Edmund C., *A Naturalist's Death Valley*, Death Valley '49ers, 1957; (also by same author *The California Deserts, Desert Wildflowers*, and *Desert Wildlife*, all published by Stanford Press)

Johnson, Dorothy M., *Some Went West*, University of Nebraska Press, 1997

Johnson, LeRoy and Jean, *Escape from Death Valley*, University of Nevada Press, 1987

Kirk, Ruth, *Exploring Death Valley*, Stanford, 1956

Kockler, Nicolas, *Old Harmony Borax*, Death Valley '49ers, 1962

Lee, Bourke, *Death Valley*, Macmillan, 1930; *Death Valley Men*, Macmillan, 1932

Manly, William Lewis, *Death Valley in '49*, four editions 1894 to 1949, various publishers.

Myrick, David F., *Railroads of Nevada*, 2 volumes, Howell-North Books, 1962-63; covers all of the Death Valley lines

Nosser, James B. — see *Death Valley Tales*

Putnam, George Palmer, *Death Valley and Its Country*, Duell, Sloan and Pearce, 1946; *Death Valley Handbook*, Duell, Sloan and Pearce, 1947

Stephens, Lorenzo Dow, *Life Sketches of a Jayhawker*, Nolta Brothers, 1917

Walker, Ardis Manly, *The Manly Map and the Manly Story*, Death Valley '49ers, 1954; *Freeman Junction, Death Valley '49ers*, 1961; *Searles Lake Borax*, see Belden above; *Death Valley and Manly: Symbols of Destiny*, Death Valley '49ers, 1962

Wheat, Carl I.: At the time of the 1949 Death Valley Centennial this note historian wrote: *Trailing the Forty-Niners Through Death Valley, FortyNiners of Death Valley, a Tentative Census,* and *Pioneer Visitors to Death Valley After, the Forty-Niners,* all of which appeared as separate articles following quarterly publication.
Wheelock, Walt, *Desert Peaks Guide,* Part I, La Siesta Press, 1964
Wilson, Neill C., *Silver Stampede,* Macmillan, 1937
Woodward, Arthur, *Camels and Surveyors in Death Valley,* Death Valley '49ers, 1961; also see *Death Valley Tales*
Zanjani, Sally, *A Mine of Her Own – Women Prospectors in the American West, 1850-1950,* University of Nebraska Press, 1997

HIGH SIERRA – COSO TO YOSEMITE

Austin, Carl T., *Coso Hot Springs,* Maturango Museum Publication No. 1 Maturango Press, 1963.
Cain, Ella M., *The Story of Early Mono County,* Fearon Publishers, 1961.
California, State of, *Annual Reports of the State Mineralogist,* (title varies).
Chalfant, W.A., *The Story of Inyo,* Chalfant Press, 1965.
Doyle, Helen MacKnight, *A Child Went Forth,* Gotham House and The Literary Guild, 1935.
Farquhar, Francis P., *History of the Sierra Nevada,* University of California Press, 1965.
Hobbs, William Herbert, *"The Earthquake of 1872 in the Owens Valley, California,"* (read before the Association of American Geographers at Chicago, December 1907), Wilhelm Engelmann (Leipzig), 1910.
Hubbard, Douglass, *Ghost Mines of Yosemite,* Awani Press, 1958.
Lingenfelter, Richard E., *The Cement Hunters,* Dawson's Book Shop, 1960.
"Desert Steamers" Journal of the West, Vol. 1, No. 2 (1962), Books, 1961-63.
Myrick, David F., *Railroads of Nevada,* 2 volumes. Howell-North Books, 1962-65.
Nadeau, Remi, *City-Makers,* Trans-Anglo Books, 1965.
Schumacher, Genny, *Deepest Valley,* Sierra Club, 1962.
Mammoth Lakes Sierra, Sierra Club, 1962.
Turner, George, *Slim Rails Through the Sand,* Johnston & Howe, 1963.
Twain, Mark, *Roughing It,* The American Publishing Company, 1903
Wheelock, Walt, *Desert Peaks Guide,* Part I, La Siesta Press, 1964.

INDEX

abandoned mines, etc, 179-184
Aguerreberry, Pete, 93-97
Aguerreberry Point, 95
Al Rose Road, 143
Alabama Hills, 150
Alta California, 119
Amargosa Borax Works, 104
Amargosa Desert, 46
Amargosa River, 24
Amargosa Valley, 44
American Hotel, 130, 135
Anvil Spring Canyon, 99
Archaeological Resources
　Protection Act, 40, 184
Argus Range, 30, 36
Arnold, Jim, 74
Ash Meadows, 28, 58
Ashford Mills, 78-82
Augustine Hotel, 99
Aurora, 113, 114, 135, 138, 139,
　165, 171
Austin, 41
Automobile Club of Southern
　California, 95
Avawatz Mtns., 87, 105
Badwater, 78
Baker, 58
Bakersfield, 127
Ballarat, 35, 37, 93-94
Bank of Panamint, 35
Baranoff, Count V.A., 80, 82
Barrel Springs, 143
Barrick Gold, 71
Barstow, 84, 97
Bartlett, 132
Basque, 95
Beatty, 48, 66, 69, 71
Beatty Spring, 65
Beatty, Walter, 65
Beaudry, Victor, 130-132
Beaver Dam Wash, 28
Belmont, 97
Belmont Camp, 133
Belshaw, Mortimer W., 130-132
Belt, Indian Bob, 54
Bend City, 138-140, 142, 145, 151

Bennett-Arcan party, 11, 28
Bennett, Charley, 47
Bennett, Thomas Jr., 159
Bennettville, 156, 159, 161
Benton, 165-169
Benton Station, 169
Bessie Brady, 127, 129, 130
Beveridge, 145-148
Bicycle Lake, 84
Big Dune, 28
Big Horn Spring,145
Big Meadows, 176 – also see
　Bridgeport,
Big Pine, 90, 139
Big Pine Creek, 150
Birney, Fred, 61
Bishop Creek, 171
Bitter Spring, 25
Black Mountains, 78
Black's Ranch, 33
Blind Spring District, 167
Blind Spring Hills, 166, 168
Bloody Canyon, 159, 162
Bodey, William S., 165
Bodie, 113, 114, 154, 159, 171
Bonanza Gulch, 143
Borate, 101
Borax Smith, 6, 67
Borden, Alexander "Shorty," 87-89
　90, 92
Boushey, Stephen, 130
Brady, James, 127
Breyfogle, Charles, 41-46
Bridgeport, 113
Briers, 28, 30
Broadwell Playa, 67
Brown, Charles A., 58, 61, 78
Brown's Toll Road, 33
Buena Vista Peak, 132, 133
Bug-Smashers, 28 – also see
　Georgians
Bullfrog, 44, 57, 64-67, 69, 71,
　105
Bullfrog & Goldfield RR, 68
Bullfrog Miner, 69
Burned Wagons Point, 30

Bursch Borthers, 65
Butte Valley, 99
Cahil, W.W., 26
Calico, 83, 101
Cajon Pass, 22, 33, 35
Camp Independence, 136
Candalaria, 19
Carbonate, 101, 102
Carleton, Major, James H., 25
Carson & Colorado R. R., 132, 167
Carson Valley, 176
Cartago, 127
Cashman, Nellie, 19
Cave Canyon, 147
Cave Springs, 61
Cerro Gordo Water & Mining
　Company 130
Cerro Grodo Freighting Co., 127,
　129
Chalfant, W.A., 33, 71
Chicago Canyon, 44
Chief George, 136
China Lake Naval Weapons
　Center, 48, 121
Chloride Cliff, 46-50, 58, 101
Chris Wicht Camp, 37
Chrysopolis, 138
cinnabar, 121
Clark Chemical Company, 132
Clark, Patsy, 61
Clark, Senator W.A., 61-67
Clover Patch District, 166, 167
Club Skidoo, 76
Cody, William, 80
Cojo District, 27
Coleman, William, 83
Coloma, 16
Colton, John B., 69
Comstock Lode, 31
Confederate Sympathisers, 42
Cook, George, 74, 77
Cooke, Phillip St. George, 22
Confidence Mill, 101
Constable Sellers, 77
Conway Summit, 178
Corcoran, Bill, 90

Coso, 114, 117-121, 135, 149
Coso County, 113, 139, 140
Coso Gold & Silver Mining
 Company, 119
Cottonwood Canyon, 129
Cottonwood Mountains, 84
Coyote Special, 50, 51
Craig Canyon, 148
Creaser, Phil, 61
Crestmore, 78
Crocker's Station, 160
Cross, Ed. L., 64, 71
Crystal, 156
Daggett, 26
Dana Meadows, 164
Daneri's Landing, 127 – also see
 Cartago
Darwin, 36, 119
Darwin, E. French,30
Darwin Junction,104
Daunet, Isadore, 83, 84
Daylight Pass, 46, 101
Death Valley Chuck-Walla, 60,
 62, 63
Death Valley Magazine, 69
Death Valley Scotty, 21, 50-56
Desert Hound Canyon, 54
Devil's Golf Course, 48
Diamond Lil, 60, 61, 63
Dodge, General, 171
Dog Creek, 176
Dogtown, 176-178
Dore Pass, 156
Dublin City, 78
Eagle Borax Works, 47, 83, 84
Earhart-Nusbaumer group, 28
East Walker River, 113
Eichbaum, H.W."Bob," 102
Elder, Abner B., 122, 123
Elliot History, 48
Emigrant Canyon, 84, 87, 90, 95
Enterprise, 27
Esmeralda, 65
Fairbanks, Ralph J. "Dad,"
Fairbanks Ranch, 58, 78
Fat Hill, 112 – also see Cerro Gordo
Father Garcés, 22
Fenner, 44
Ferguson's Landing, 127
Fine View, 94, 95

Fisk, Stella, 44
Fort Irwin, 84
Forty Mile Canyon, 28
FortyNiners ('49ers), 74
Fremont, John C., 135
French, Darwin, 117
Fresno Flats, 171
Furnace Creek, 47, 77, 78, 87, 93,
 104
Furnace Creek Copper Co., 58
Furnace Creek Ranch, 102
Gaylord, Burdon, 50
Genoa, 41, 45
Georgians, 28, 30
Genoa, 41, 45
Gerand, Julian, 52, 54
Gibson, 65
Glasscock, C.B., 50
Gold Center, 58
Goldfield, 41, 44, 57, 69
Goler, John, 30
Goodyear, W.A., 140
Gordon, Louis D., 132
Gower, Harry P., 102
Grand View, 94
Grapevine Canyon, 102
Granite Wells, 33, 48
Gray's Meadow, 149, 153
Great Sierra Wagon Road, 160, 161
Great Smokey Valley, 41
Great View, 94
Greenland, 93, 104
Greenwater, 50, 57-63
Greenwater Times, 63
Hahn's Canyon, 147
Hanaupah Canyon, 87, 89
Hanaupah Jack, 89
Hanaupah Spring, 89, 90
Hanna, Phil Townsend, 95
Hanna, Tom, 157
Harmony Borax Works, 47
Harris, Frank "Shorty," 61, 64,
 93-94
Harrisburg, 77, 93-97
Harrisburg Flats, 89
Harper Lake, 33
Harris, T. S., 36
Harvey, Joe, 61
hazards, mines, etc, 179-184
Hearst, George, 36

Hemet Valley, 64, 77
Hidden Valley, 104
Hill's Meadows, 149, 151
Hockett Trail, 119
Homer Mining District, 154
Homer Mining Index, 156
Horner, 154
Horsebones Camp, 30
Hot Springs, 138, 165
Hungry Bill, 40
Hungry Bill's Ranch, 39
Hunt, Jefferson, 23, 27
Hunter Canyon, 145, 146, 148
Hunter, W.L., 145, 146
Independence, 74, 113, 135, 140,
 142, 143
Independence Creek, 140, 151, 153
Indian District, 167
Indian Ranch Road, 37
Inyo County, 145
Inyo County Library, 74
Inyo District, 139
Inyo Mountains, 92, 115, 122,
 123, 129, 135, 145-147
Ivanpah, 44
Jacobs, R.C., 33
Jayhawkers, 28, 30, 69
Johannesburg, 86
Johnson, Albert M., 54
Johnson Canyon, 39
Johnson, William, 40
Jones, John P., 33
Jubilee Pass, 99
Judge Decker, 61
Julian, C.C., 68
Keane, Jack, 101
Keane Wonder Miine Road, 48
Kearsarge Mill, 152, 153
Kearsarge Mining District, 150
Kearsarge Peak, 149, 152
Keeler, 132-134
Kelso, 26
Kennedy, Tom, 105
Kennedy, W. L., 33
Keynot Canyon, 147
Keynot Peak, 148
Keys, Bill, 21, 52, 74, 77, 80
Kremer Mortuary, 99
Knickerbocker Trust Co., 52, 56
Kunzie, Arthur, 61

Lake Canyon, 154, 156, 160
Lake Mining District, 170-175
Lake Mary, 170, 171
Lane, J.R., 101
Las Vegas, 41, 67, 69
Las Vegas & Tonopah RR, 67
Leadfield, 68
Lee family, 104
Leeland, 44
Le Moigne, Jean, 83-86
Lida, 44, 57
Little Hunter Canyon, 148
Little Lake, 119
Little Pine, 140 – also see
 Independence
Little Pine Creek, 149, 150 – also see
 Independence Creek
Los Angeles, 22, 24, 30, 35, 50,
 56, 127, 140
Los Angeles Aqueduct, 142
Los Angeles & Independence RR, 35
Lone Pine, 64, 73, 89, 90, 135, 149
Long John Canyon, 146, 148
Lookout, 36
Lost Burro Gap, 104
Lundy, 154, 158, 161
Lundy Canyon, 154
Lundy Mining District, 154-159
Lundy, "Otho" William, 154
MacDonald, Joe, 74
Macdonald, Malcolm, 67
Mammoth, 170-175
Mammoth City, 171, 174
Mammoth Mining Company, 171,
 173, 175
Mammoth Pass, 173
Manly, William, 11
Manse Ranch, 44
Mariposa County, 112
Marl Spring, 26
Marshall, John, 16
Massey, Orville, 26
Mather, Stephen, 161
Mazouka Canyon, 135, 142, 143
McAllister, Frank, 61
McBain, Gordon, 74, 76, 77
NcClausland, B.M., 80
McLaren, Alex, 80
McNabb, S.W., 56
Mengel, Carl, 97-100

Mengel Pass, 99, 100
Mesquite Spring, 102
Metallic City, 19
Mexican War, 27
Mill Canyon, 154, 156, 158
Mill Creek, 154, 158
Miller Spring, 130
Millner, J.F., 166
Mineral Hill, 170, 175

MINES
Alabama, 149
Ashford Mill, 54, 57
Arctic, 152
Banner, 166
Bay Queen, 154
Big Horn, 146, 148
Black Eagle, 143, 144
Boomerang, 152
Bonanza, 154
Bonnie Claire, 44
Breyfogle, 46
Brown Monster, 140
Bullfrog, 44, 57, 64-67, 69, 71
Burgess, 147, 148
Calliope, 139
Carbonate, 101
Cerro Gordo, 122-129, 130-133,
 145, 146, 148
Chilula, 148
Chrysopolis, 139
Cinnamon, 148
Cliff, 152
Comanche, 166
Cornucopia, 166
Crackerjack, 61
Creekside, 166
Crystal Lake, 157
Desert Hound, 80
Diana, 166
Eclipse, 136, 138, 140
Ella Bloss, 162
Eureka, 166
Gavilon, 148
Gold Standard, 148
Golden Era, 139
Golden Queen, 162
Golden State, 152
Gorilla, 154
Grand Prize, 154
Grantham, 105

Gray Eagle, 154
Great Sierra, 159, 160
Gunsight, 27-30, 41, 117
Headlight, 173
Ice Mine, 152
Ida, 136, 138, 140
Iron Sides – also see Burgess
Johnnie, 45
Josephine, 120
Karrick, 166
Keane Wonder, 44, 64, 101-103
Kearsarge, 113, 149-153
Keynot, 147
Keystone, 152
La Despreciada 132,
Last Chance, 154
Laura, 148
Laurel, 166
Lila C, 67
Lisbon, 173
Little Emily, 166
Lost Breyfogle, 101
Lost Cement, 170
Lost Gunsight, 41-45
Lost Spring, 24
Lucky Mortan, 154
McAvoy, 148
Mammoth, 171
May Lundy, 154, 155, 157
Montgomery-Shoshone, 65, 71
Montano, 148
Monte Christo, 173
Mormon Diggings, 24
Mountain Queen, 166
Mountain View, 152
Noonday, 26
Olympic, 139
Parrett, 158
Phoenix, 166
Prosperine, 139
Reward, 140, 141
Rex Montis, 149, 150, 153
Romelia, 139
San Antonio, 148
San Benito, 132
San Felipe, 131, 132
San Jose, 120
Santa Maria, 132
Sheepherder, 159, 160
Sierra Talc, 105

Silver Cloud, 139
Silver Lake, 61, 80, 82
Sliver Spout, 150, 151
Sinnamon Cut, 178
Sister, 150, 152
Surprise Valley, 32
Tower, 166
Union (Cerro Gordo) 131-133
Union (Russ District) 136, 138, 140
Vega – see Gold Standard
Virginia, 152
Wai Wera, 166, 167
Western Talc, 105
West Virginia, 152
Whiteside, 143
Wild Rose, 166
Winoshilk, 120
Wolverine, 154
Ygnacio, 132

Mills, Mrs. C.W., 151
Mississippians, 28, 30, 117
Modoc, 36
Mojave Desert, 27
Mojave River, 24
Mono County, 113, 114, 136
Mono Craters, 169
Mono Lake, 155, 158, 162, 169
Mono Pass, 138, 159, 162, 176
Mono Trail, 162, 164
Monoville, 135, 138, 170, 176, 177
Montgomery, Bob, 65, 71
Montgomery Canyon, 166
Montgomery Hotel, 69
Moore, F.T., 22
Moore, Maggie, 125
Moore. Lt. Tredwell, 162
Mormons, 22
Mt. Conness, 159
Mt. Scowdan, 154
Murphy Brothers, 60
Murphy, L.J., 71
Myerstein, Caesar,
Nadeau, Remi, 127, 173
Nevada Hotel, 168
Natural Soda Products, 132
New York Butte, 145, 148
New World Mining & Exploration
  Company, 135

Norst, Cord, 176, 177
Northern Saloon, 66
Nosser, Jim, 86
Nye, 154
Oddie, Tasker L., 61, 65
Olancha, 86
Old Dinah, 101
Old Government Road, 25
Old Spanish Trail, 22, 23, 28 – also
  see Salt Lake Trail
Oneida Lake, 156
Onion Valley, 149, 152, 153
Oregon Battalion, 24
Osborn, J.B., 26
Owen, Dick 135
Owens Lake, 119, 130
Owens Lake Silver-Lead Company,
  127, 131
Owens River, 136, 142, 178
Owens Valley, 114, 115, 119, 131,
  135, 139, 176
Owenyo, 146
Owl Holes, 105
Pacific Coast Borax Corp., 68, 101
Paiute Indians, 25, 26, 136
Paiute-Shoshone Indians, 45, 46,
  117, 166
Pahrump Road, 44
Pahrump Valley, 44, 46
Panamint Annie, 19-21
Panamint City, 31-40, 46, 105
Panamint Range, 21, 31, 37, 77,
  89, 94
Panamint Valley, 30, 33, 35
Parker, George, 153
Parker Ranch, 153
Partzwick, 167
Perry, J.W.S., 47
Pfizer Corporation, 105
Pine City, 170-174
Pioche, 19, 83
Pittman, Key, 65
Pop's Gulch, 143
Porter Brothers, 69
Postoffice Spring, 35
Prescott District, 162-164
Pumice Mountain, 170 – also see
  Mammoth Mountain
Racetrack, 104
Ralphs, John C. 51, 56,

Ramsey, Harry, 77
Randall, Dr., 170
Randsburg, 69
Rasor, Clarence, 67
Reddy, Pat, 120
Reese River, 44
Reno, 167
Resting Spring, 23-25, 27
Reward Consoildated Mining
  Company, 140
Rhodes Wash, 78
Rhyolite,37, 60, 63, 65, 67-71, 77
Rhyolite Bulletin, 69
Rhyolite Herald, 69
Rhyolite Undertaking Parlors, 70
Robinson, Billy, 63
Robles Canyon, 146, 148
Ronan, Katheryn, 90
Rouse, Charley, 99
Russ District, 137-137, 139
Russ, H.P., 135
Ryan, John, 67
safety, around mines, 179-184
Saline Valley, 97, 104, 130, 145,
  146, 148
Salsberry Pass, 99
Salt Lake City, 23, 33, 92, 146
Salt Lake Trail, 23, 26, 42
Salt Spring, 22-26, 44, 78
San Bernadino, 33, 35, 99
San Carlos, 138-140, 142
San Carlos Mill, 139
San Carlos Mining and Exploration
  Company, 138
San Joaquin River, 170
San Joaquin Valley, 171
Sand Walking Company, 23, 27
Sandy, 44
Santa Barbara, 126
Santa Fe, 22
Santa Fe RR, 35
San Francisco, 122, 123, 125, 167
Santa Rita Flat, 143
Santa Rita Spring, 143
Saratoga, 44
Sardine Canyon, 152
Sarras, Ferminia, 19
Scott, Walter – see Death Valley
  Scotty
Scott, Warner, 52

Scotty's Castle, 102
Scwab, Charles, M., 57, 67
Schwab Lake, 102
Searles Mill, 120
Selby Smelting Works, 125, 167
Sentinel Peak, 37
Seven Pines, 149, 153
Seymour Alf's, 61
Sheep Spring, 105
Sheepherder Lode, 159
Sherwin Grade, 171
Shorty's Well, 87
Shoshone, 58, 78, 80, 90, 104
Silver Peak, 98
Simpson, Joe, 73, 74, 76
Skidoo, 9, 72-77, 94, 105
Skidoo News, 73, 76, 77
Slate Range, 119, 120
Smith, F.M. – see Borax Smith
Smith, Joseph, 22
Smith, O.K., 27, 28
Soda Lake, 67
Sonora Pass, 176
Southern California Bank, 74
Southern Hotel, 69
Southern Pacific RR, 35
Spanish Mines, 120
Stateline Pass, 101
Stewart, Jack, 90
Stewart, William, 31, 33, 35, 84
Stevens Mill, 129
Stevens, Mollie, 129
Stevens, Sherman, 129
Stovepipe Wells, 86, 116
Stump Spring, 44
Sublette, Andrew, 24
Surprise Canyon, 31, 32, 35, 37
Swansea, 130, 131, 140
Taylor, E.S. "Black," 165, 166
Taylor Springs, 166
Teakettle Junction, 104
Tecopa, 21
Tecopa RR, 26
Tejon, Fort, Ranch, 30, 47
Telescope Peak, 37, 87
Thompson, "One-eye," 77
Timbisha Shoshone, 40
Tioga Hill, 159, 161
Tioga Lake, 161
Tioga Mining District, 154, 159-162

Tioga Pass, 161
Todd's Meadow, 149
Tonopah, 42, 57
Tonopah & Goldfield RR, 68
Tonopah & Tidewater RR, 26, 58,
   61, 68, 80, 82, 90, 104
Townsend, "Lying Jim," 156, 161
Travis, Lola, 125
Trona Railway, 102
Trona-Wildrose Road, 37
Tub Springs, 153
Tucki Mtn, 28
Tulare County, 27, 97, 150
Tule Hole, 89
Tule Spring, 28
Tuolumne County, 162
Turner Brothers, 30
Twenty-Mule Teams, 47
Twentynine Palms, 71
Twin Lakes, 173, 175
Ubehebe Crater, 87, 103
Union Consolidated Company, 132
Union Mining Company, 123
Vasquez, Tiburcio, 48
Virginia City, 31, 50, 122, 171
Virginia Creek, 177, 178
Virginia Creek Hydraulic Mining
   Company, 178
Visalia, 126, 138-140
Wade, Harry, 28
Walkara,22, 27
Walker Pass, 114, 135
Walker River, 176
Warm Spring Canyon, 105
Warren Fork Canyon, 156
Wasson, 154, 156
Weight, Harold, 71
Wells Fargo, 18, 19, 31, 33
Wells Fargo Company, 167, 169
White, Mary, 21
White, Mrs.Harsha, 44
White Mountains, 98, 165
White Peak District, 166, 167
Whiteman, Gid, 170
Wildrose Canyon, 30, 33, 93, 94
Wildrose Spring, 93
Williams, Colonel Isaac, 22, 24
Willow Springs, 143
Wilson, Wally, 132 22, 24
Wilson Benjamin D., 24

Wingate Pass, 47, 51-56, 102
Wingate Road, 37
Wingate Wash, 48, 51
Winnedumah, 139
Woolsey, Mr., 139
Yellow Grade, 126
Yosemite National Park, 161
Young, Bringham, 22
Yount family, 44-46

THE BIOGRAPHY

LEONARDO
DiCAPRIO

DOUGLAS WIGHT

For Lorna

THE BIOGRAPHY

LEONARDO DiCAPRIO

DOUGLAS WIGHT

JB

JOHN BLAKE

Published by John Blake Publishing Ltd,
3 Bramber Court, 2 Bramber Road,
London W14 9PB, England

www.johnblakepublishing.co.uk

www.facebook.com/Johnblakepub

twitter.com/johnblakepub

First published in hardback in 2012

ISBN: 978-1-85782-672-2

British Library Cataloguing-in-Publication Data:

A catalogue record for this book is available from the British Library.

Design by www.envydesign.co.uk

Printed and bound by CPI Group (UK) Ltd, Croydon, CR0 4YY

1 3 5 7 9 10 8 6 4 2

Papers used by John Blake Publishing are natural, recyclable products made
from wood grown in sustainable forests. The manufacturing processes conform
to the environmental regulations of the country of origin.

Every attempt has been made to contact the relevant copyright-holders,
but some were unobtainable. We would be grateful if the appropriate
people could contact us.

CONTENTS

Prologue   VII

Chapter 1: Scumsville   I

Chapter 2: Introducing Lenny Williams   11

Chapter 3: Early Rejections   22

Chapter 4: Catching the Eye   31

Chapter 5: Making a Killing   39

Chapter 6: Following the River   48

Chapter 7: A Double Tragedy   58

Chapter 8: A Modern Day Romeo   68

Chapter 9: Leo Rising... and Falling   78

Chapter 10: Creating a Monster   85

Chapter 11: The Launch of 'Leo-Mania'   101

Chapter 12: Losing It   118

Chapter 13: Trouble in Paradise   129

Chapter 14: The Leo Tamer   140

Chapter 15: Owning December   151

Chapter 16: Becoming The Aviator   162

Chapter 17: The Parted   174

Chapter 18: Best Bar None   185

Chapter 19: Going Green   193

Chapter 20: Under Fire   205

Chapter 21: Barometer of Truth   213

Chapter 22: Are They, Aren't They?   222

Chapter 23: Dream Man   233

Chapter 24: Looking Lively   244

Chapter 25: The Most Powerful Man in America   249

Chapter 26: The Modeliser   260

Epilogue   266

Filmography   270

PROLOGUE

Leonardo DiCaprio remembers the exact moment when *Titanic* transformed his life.

It came at Charles de Gaulle airport in Paris. James Cameron's disaster epic was on its way to becoming the biggest movie in history and DiCaprio, then 23, had a young girl stuck to his leg. The delusional fan, overcome with emotion at finally being able to clap not just eyes on the heartthrob she had only dreamt about, rugby-tackled the actor and clung on for dear life.

Amid the chaos and the throng, Leonardo had a moment of clarity and the absurdity of the situation struck home.

'I looked her in the eye,' he would later recall, 'and said, "Whatever illusions of grandeur you have about me, they're not true. I will sit here and I will talk to you. You don't need to cling; you don't need to dig your nails into my leg. It doesn't need to be *this*!"'

But the girl, who was no more than 14, had other ideas. It was as if she believed that by hanging on there, he somehow wouldn't notice – and she wasn't about to give up such an opportunity without a fight.

DiCaprio said: 'She just pressed her head against my leg. I said,

"What are you doing, sweetheart?" And she kept clutching. There was just a sort of obsessed look in her eye. She wasn't looking at me, though, just my leg. I looked at her and I sort of grabbed her face and said, "Hi, it's OK, no, you can… you can get off my leg. It's fine." She kept saying, "No, no, no, no!" and I had to gently pry her hands off.'

If Leonardo had been in any doubt up until that point that 'Leo-Mania' had gripped the world – the most hysterical fan reaction since the Beatles – it was truly confirmed at that moment. Until *Titanic* became the highest-grossing film in Hollywood history, he was pretty much able to live in blissful obscurity. Quietly, he'd acquired a reputation for risky, challenging roles and already had an Oscar nomination under his belt for his performance in *What's Eating Gilbert Grape*, but neither of these factors had sent the girls screaming to his feet. Yet within months of the movie hitting the big screen his life was changed forever.

He topped a list of the 50 Most Beautiful People in the World – an accolade that made him groan: 'You want to be remembered for your work rather than being hunk of the month.'

Soon it became clear there was nowhere in the world he could go without someone knowing his name. On an environmental pilgrimage in December 2003 to the deepest Amazonian rainforest to meet the Alto Xingu Indians of Brazil, with his then-girlfriend, the supermodel Gisele Bündchen, he was astounded when a tribesman instantly recognised him and began chattering excitedly about the 'man from *Titanic*'.

'It certainly follows me,' he admitted after that encounter. 'I'm not exaggerating. I've been to the Amazon, and people with no clothes on know about that film.' Indeed, a few years later he was spotted in a dusty provincial village in Mozambique while filming *Blood Diamond*.

Leonardo has been a tabloid editor's dream celebrity. After *Titanic* it was widely accepted he had gone off the rails somewhat, and in June 1998, *New York* magazine ran a highly damaging expose on Leo's partying, which didn't put him in a good light. For the first time he started attracting attention for womanising and drinking. He made odd movie choices, industry experts insisted, when he might have been making millions, filling multiplexes as the romantic lead. Instead films like *The Man In The Iron Mask* and *The Beach* only made just over $150 million each – respectable hits by any other actor's standards but flops when judged next to the $1.8 billion raked in by James Cameron's epic.

At the same time as his fee per movie jumped from $2 million to $20 million, he was scorned for dating some of the world's most glamorous women. Even the ones he wasn't romantically involved with made for explosive headlines. Over the years he's been linked to some of Hollywood's hottest leading ladies: Demi Moore, Alicia Silverstone, Claire Danes, Liv Tyler, Sara Gilbert, Natasha Henstridge and Juliette Lewis, not to mention models like Bridget Hall, Kristen Zang, Bijou Phillips, Naomi Campbell, Amber Valletta, Helena Christensen, Kate Moss and Eva Herzigova.

Yes, after the success of *Titanic* life was tough for Leonardo DiCaprio! His exploits prompt a comparison with the English football legend George Best and the famous story of the hotel bellboy who, on entering the notorious womaniser's room and finding him sprawled on the bed, with his winnings from the casino and the current Miss World laid out next to him, was moved to remark: 'George, where did it all go wrong?'

Yet, joking aside, the attention heaped on Leonardo after 1997 often made him wonder if perhaps he'd made the right move in turning down the lead role in *Boogie Nights* – a part that eventually went to Mark Wahlberg – in favour of *Titanic*. Bathing in his post-*Titanic* success, DiCaprio soon became a night-life junkie.

'Everything happened so quickly, I began to feel engulfed by it,' he explained, and indeed, it took him practically a decade to recover and find himself again. As Leonardo himself remarked: 'I was 22 or 23 years old, and it was completely surreal. It was insane. Nobody could have predicted it, or the effect it would have in so many countries. I shudder when I hear myself complain about it and so many people have so many more real and monumental problems but it was a bizarre, bizarre scenario.

'After *Titanic* I was focusing on things that had nothing to do with the art. All the business with agents and publicists and managers, that can be extremely frustrating and ultimately a waste of time. There's no real control over how the media or the public perceives you – I know who I am, my friends know who I am. And, hey, I'm not complaining about my life: I'm doing something that I love and that's a precious gift.'

After encounters like the one in Paris with the young fan, Leonardo has grown to accept the level of superstardom that one movie has bestowed him but it wasn't always that way. Initially he'd turned down the role that would make him a star and was apprehensive about the marketing machine behind such mammoth productions. He even shunned the Oscar ceremony where director Cameron and crew cleaned up. Since then, he's grown to love it, however.

'I have always been nervous of big-budget studio films,' said Leo. 'The hype and the marketing frighten me. Overall, though, I was glad to be part of *Titanic*. As an actor I look at movies as a relevant art form, like a painting or sculpture. A hundred years from now, people will still be watching that movie.'

It's just as well his attitude changed. In 2012, the movie was revamped for the digital age and released in a stunning new 3D format – just in time for the centenary of the ship's disaster. Once more, Leo's fresh-faced Jack Dawson will light up the world's cinema screens, sparking a new wave of 'Leo-Mania' and potentially introducing the heartthrob to thousands of new fans.

Leonardo DiCaprio might be the most powerful movie star in Hollywood right now, but it could have been so different. In fact, if it hadn't been for the stubbornness of a German mother nearly 70 years ago, there might not have been a Leonardo DiCaprio at all…

CHAPTER I

SCUMSVILLE

Life for Leo really began not on the mean streets of Los Angeles where, famously, he was raised, but back in semi-rural Germany during the Second World War. For an episode then was to have a massive bearing on whether the world would ever be blessed with his talents at all.

Helene Indenbirken was a young mother whose daughter Irmelin was just two when she suffered a broken leg and had to be admitted to hospital. The local infirmary near their home in Oer-Erkenschwick, in North Rhine-Westphalia, Germany, was under-staffed and over-stretched. As little Irmelin lay in bed supposedly recuperating, as the nurses believed, no one took the time to notice that she was actually, silently, wasting away.

As the wards became flooded with more refugees and war-wounded, the nurses on duty had less time to deal with the apparently non-life-threatening cases. Only Helene, who'd arrived in Germany as a Russian immigrant called Yelena Smirnova, recognised something was gravely wrong with her infant child. Seeing that resources were stretched to breaking point and realising if something wasn't done quickly then her daughter could die,

Helene took it upon herself to diagnose and administer the care Irmelin so desperately needed.

What should have been a routine recuperation turned into an agonising ordeal for Helene as Irmelin developed infection after infection and spent a staggering two-and-a-half years in hospital, fighting for her life. Emaciated and malnourished, her stomach became distended and at times, Helene feared she would not make it. But, thanks to her dedication and determination, the youngster gradually recovered and eventually was strong enough to leave hospital while the war raged on.

When Helene's sole concern was her daughter's life she could never have believed that the outcome of those crucial first few months in hospital would have had such a bearing on the family's fortunes but it is something Leonardo has never failed to appreciate.

Speaking of his mother's battle for life, he said: 'She ended up contracting five or six major illnesses and stayed for two-and-a-half, three years [in hospital]. My grandmother basically came every day and nursed her back to health because the nurses didn't have time; they basically left her for dead. When you see a picture of my mother, it's heartbreaking. It brings tears to my eyes, knowing what she's been through in her life. I have a picture of her – her first photograph, with this tiny little skirt – and she's emaciated, with a belly like this,' he adds, gesturing to indicate the size of a beach ball. 'She had a belly full of worms.'

Incredibly, given her tender years, that episode wasn't the first brush with death Irmelin had experienced. Born in an air-raid shelter, she might not have survived beyond her first few breaths had the aim of Allied fighter pilots been off. That innate sense of survival may have fostered in Irmelin a desire to make the most of the chance her mother had given her. When she was 11, her family left Oer-Erkenschwick and moved to the United States to start a new life in New York. She enrolled at City College and in 1963 it was there that she met and fell in love with an enigmatic young beatnik called George DiCaprio. Born in 1943, George was an American hippie whose ancestors hailed from Naples, in Italy, and Bavaria in southern Germany. He had long, straggly hair and a bohemian air about him.

George's grandfather had made the perilous journey from Italy to America in a wooden boat and the young DiCaprio was to inherit much of that pioneering free spirit. George was emerging as a leading light in the alternative literature scene and would go on to count Beat poet Allen Ginsberg and novelist William S. Burroughs as friends, as well as fellow cartoonist Robert Crumb and the writer Hubert Selby Jr. He was rooming with Sterling Morrison, the guitarist from The Velvet Underground and had already published a comic of his own – *Baloney Moccasins* – with Laurie Anderson, a former girlfriend of his who was also a performance artist.

Despite their initial differences in personality – George was gregarious and outgoing, while Irmelin was more reserved, yet strong-willed – the pair hit it off immediately and discovered a shared a sense of adventure along with a desire to see the world. Two years later they were married and spent the remainder of the sixties immersing themselves in the underground counter-culture. It appeared to be the natural progression of things when Irmelin fell pregnant in early 1974, but cracks were already beginning to show in their relationship. Believing West was best for a young family, they moved to Los Angeles 'in hopes of the great western ideals of a better life', as Leo told *Vanity Fair* in 2004. Landing in Hollywood, they scraped by with enough to pay the bills but their choices were limited and so they ended up in one of Hollywood's poorest districts. The couple had chosen Hollywood thinking it was the exciting centre of Los Angeles. Instead, their son recalled in an LA Times interview, 'they wound up by Le Sex Shoppe and the Waterbed Hotel'. George earned what little cash they had by installing asbestos – still a popular component in heat insulation, fireproof roofing and flooring in the sixties and seventies. In his spare time he distributed comics and beatnik books to local bookstores and arranged public readings for the likes of Burroughs and Ginsberg. Meanwhile, Irmelin found work as a legal secretary.

As if to perhaps convince themselves that their wandering spirit could not be curtailed by diapers and feeding schedules George and Irmelin travelled to Italy on what has been described as a second honeymoon. Visiting Florence, they stopped by the Uffizi Gallery, where they took the opportunity to appreciate the Renaissance art. As Irmelin paused to admire a painting by Leonardo da Vinci she felt a strong kick inside her. Was her baby expressing its first opinion of the arts? Irmelin certainly thought so. She decided there and then that if the child were a boy she'd name him after the Italian genius. George was delighted – his father's middle name was Leon and he loved the artistic element of the moniker.

Sadly, however, the holiday ultimately failed to save the marriage and by the time Irmelin gave birth to baby Leonardo, she and George were drifting apart. It has been well reported that Leo's parents separated before he was one, but the reality seems to be that they were apart before then, certainly on an emotional level at least.

Leonardo himself said: 'My parents were divorced before I was even born, but that's never bothered me. As far as my family is concerned, my parents were the rebellious ones – they're people who have done everything and have nothing to prove.'

Little Leo was born on 11 November 1974 and was 'the cutest kid,' according to doting grandmother Helene, who at that point remained in New York (in a quarter popular with German immigrants). Three weeks after he was born she flew to California to see the new arrival for herself. She recalled: 'Irmelin brought him to the airport in her arms. He had the roundest little face.'

Leonardo's parents might still have been living as man and wife at this stage but it was not to last. George felt stifled by domesticity and before his son's first birthday, had made plans to leave. As his parents did their best to work out how to manage things for

Leonardo's sake and moved into separate households, the youngster was packed off to Russia on a cruise ship with Irmelin's parents.

By the time he was returned to his parents, George had already moved out but the solution was as unconventional as their lifestyle had been up until that point. So that they could raise their son together, George and Irmelin each moved into twin craftsman's cottages with a shared garden in the downbeat LA suburb of Echo Park. Before too long, George had met and moved in a new girlfriend called Peggy Farrar and her son Adam, who was three years older than Leo.

Peggy had recently divorced from her husband – and Adam's father – Michael Farrar, who'd managed a dairy farm in northern California. She'd met George in San Francisco, where he'd been on a business trip and she was performing with a theatre company. While Peggy was arguably saddled with the same commitments as Irmelin (though six years younger), George nevertheless must have felt his options were better with this new woman. However, so as not to deprive Leonardo of a constant father figure in his life, the compromise was to continue living next-door. Somehow, the two families managed to co-exist in relative harmony.

The only early disagreement they had to overcome was settling on a sum of maintenance for George to pay towards the upkeep of his son. Both George and Irmelin were struggling to make ends meet and she felt strongly that her estranged husband should face up to his responsibilities. When his initial offer was deemed unacceptable, Irmelin had to take her husband to court to force him to pay just $20 a week for little Leo's upkeep – all George could afford.

Life was tough for a struggling single mother. Even things that most moms would today take for granted – such as finding a suitable day care nursery, while Irmelin juggled her legal job – turned out to be a trial, particularly when her young son proved to be a handful. The infant Leo wasn't shy about making himself heard and therefore his mother found it difficult to find a nursery that would take him. On one occasion she drove to an outer district of Los Angeles to visit his new pre-school.

Leonardo remembers starting to cry, wailing, 'Am I going to stay all the way out here all day? I wanna stay home!' In the end Irmelin had little option but to solve the problem by becoming a childminder herself, taking in local kids from the neighbourhood.

Getting his own way was something Leonardo was quickly getting used to and an early episode gave him a flavour of what it could be like to be an entertainer. He recalls: 'I was taken to a performance festival when I was two. I had my red jumpsuit on and my tackiest shirt. My father suggested, "Hey, go up on stage."

'I remember looking out at a sea of expectant faces. After a moment or two, I began to dance – tappity, tappity, tappity... the crowd loved it. And I thought, "That's me getting that attention, *me*!" There was no stopping me and my dad had to pull me off the stage.'

He was to have less success with his television debut, which came two years later on the educational favourite *Romper Room*. The show, effectively a televised nursery session, saw several sugared-up kids bounce around with a mumsy presenter and a guy dressed as a bumblebee. It seemed an impossible gig to mess up but Leonardo's dream debut was cut short when he became too boisterous.

'It was my favourite show at the time,' he later admitted. 'I used to sing the songs at home. So I went on *Romper Room* and I got completely excited. They had a little circle and they were all singing and dancing, and stuff like that. I was too excited to be on camera. I was running up and slapping the cameras, trying to pull my mom onstage. So they kicked me off.'

Such an experience might have crushed a less-confident toddler but Leonardo said: 'I got to see myself on television. I went completely neurotic, it was beautiful.'

Although George remained close by, it fell to Irmelin to effectively raise the boy on her own. But the area they lived in –

Hollywood Boulevard – was not dubbed 'Syringe Alley' for nothing. The earliest memories for most children revolve around playgrounds and parks, but for the young Leonardo those images are forever slightly tarnished.

He recalled: 'We were in the poorhouse. I would walk to the playground and see a guy open up his trench coat with a thousand syringes. It was a bit of a shock. I lived in the ghettos of Hollywood, right near the old Hollywood billiards. It was the most disgusting place to be.

'My mom, who thought Hollywood was the place where all the great stuff was going on, took great care of me but I was able to see all sorts of stuff at an early age. It was pretty terrifying – I saw people have sex in the alleys.'

With prostitutes and junkies as neighbours, it was impossible for Irmelin to shield her son from the raw life that raged around them. When he was just five, he witnessed two men having sex outside a friend's balcony. This was an image that would have a profound effect on him, especially when it came to tackling homosexual roles later in life.

While his mother was doing her best to limit Leonardo's exposure to more adult experiences, George was doing exactly the opposite. He continued to hang out with the likes of Charles Bukowski, Robert Crumb and The Velvet Underground. He also made an acquaintance of drugs guru Timothy Leary, then only recently released from prison on drug charges. Leary had been an early advocate of LSD and at one stage was labelled 'the most dangerous man in America' by then President Richard Nixon and facing 95 years in jail for a series of drug convictions. Despite his notoriety, he was feted by hippies and the art community, inspiring John Lennon to write 'Come Together', so it was perhaps unsurprising that George would soon be taking little Leo to meet him. Years later, in 1994, it was said Leary even officiated at a marriage ceremony for George and Peggy, but given the suggestion that Leo's parents never legally divorced, this may have only been a spiritual blessing.

Unwilling to modify his hippy tendencies, George would take Leo to new-age parades, the two of them dressed in their underwear, covered in mud and carrying sticks.

Although Leonardo was used to the alternative lifestyle from an early age, one experience when he was six was something he felt was a step too far.

'We were sitting in a car,' he recalled. 'Dad suddenly announced, "The first time I had sex, I was your age. You should try it." But I wasn't interested. I told Dad, "Shut up, Dad, I don't want to try it. I'm gonna do all my homework instead."'

George later explained himself by saying: 'Leonardo was never excluded from conversations about sex or drugs. He's still on a quest to find out how many things he can do in life and not do them straight.'

It might seem the unlikely ingredients for a successful life but Leo's parents found an educational blend from the anti-establishment scene and the mainstream. By this time, young Leo was attending Corinne A. Seeds Elementary School, an innovative teaching establishment at UCLA, but Irmelin was committed to getting her son the best education and two years later she enrolled the budding star into the specialised magnet school called the Center for Enriched Studies.

The school attracted kids from all over Los Angeles and boasted one of the top performance records in California.

'She drove 45 minutes there every day and back,' Leo recalled. 'So she spent every day, every weekday of her life, three hours a day, to make sure that I didn't go to just any normal school.'

Cocksure and confident the youngster may have been, but those attributes often made things worse in the rough neighbourhood he grew up in. He might have been attending one of the area's top schools but he was still the victim of beatings by thugs on the estate.

'I was small, and I was a smart-ass – that's a deadly combination,' said Leonardo, who by this time was developing his own style, which in the mid-1980s was a punky haircut teamed with leather gloves and silver trousers. He was developing into quite the cute little boy.

His stepbrother Adam shared Leo's contempt for the neighbourhood and its inhabitants. 'East Hollywood was the most disgusting place to live in,' he said. 'We called it Scumsville.'

Adam and Leonardo got into several scrapes together. And DiCaprio needed his older stepbrother to come to his aid during one particularly gruesome episode that would live with him for many years to come.

He explains: 'I remember vividly – for some reason this has been in my thoughts – killing a pigeon. The pigeon was limping and my friend had a gun, so we decided to shoot it and put it out of its misery. And it wouldn't die, so we had to shoot it at least ten or fifteen more times, and it was this gruelling torture of the goddamned pigeon. And I was sitting there, and I was crying, looking at this pigeon who just kept getting shot in the head and the back, and who just kept wobbling. And finally my stepbrother just took a board and went "crkkkk!" and killed it.'

Living in such straightened times meant that Leonardo grew to love any opportunity to get out of Los Angeles and he spent all his holidays with his mother's parents in Germany: Grandpa Wilhelm – Leo's middle name – and his wife Helene, or 'Oma' as he affectionately called her. They had moved back to Germany in the early 1980s after growing weary of the American way of life.

Back in Germany, his grandfather's strong work ethic – contrasting somewhat with the hippy ways of his father – ensured at least that Leonardo could enjoy the sort of holidays that the economic reality of his parents' economic situation would otherwise have denied him. Helene remembers her grandson's visits to Dusseldorf as happy times. 'From the age of about eight,

Leonardo spent all his vacations with us here in Germany,' she said. 'He even got his first taste for the sea when his grandfather and I took him on a cruise. We went all over – to the Bahamas and Canada. We also took him skiing in Austria. He was a very happy child, always ready for fun – and food.

'He loved German dishes. A favourite was pig's trotters with sauerkraut. But his real loves are homemade potato pancakes and German cold cuts and rolls.'

Despite his many visits, Leonardo never really got to grips with the German language. 'The best he could manage was a few sentences,' Helene adds.

Then, from out of the blue, something happened that would change young Leonardo's life forever.

His brother Adam had been sent to audition for a cornflakes advert (his parents hoped it might earn a little spending money). That one advert led to a series – 20 in all – and Adam soon found himself at 12-years-old with a cheque for $50,000.

Leo was amazed. How could so much money be earned from doing what looked like so little?

From that moment on, his mind was made up – he was going to escape his dirt-poor background and become an actor, just like his big brother.

CHAPTER 2

INTRODUCING LENNY WILLIAMS

L eonardo's first foray into showbiz had ended in disaster when
he was kicked off *Romper Room* but for a while it looked as if
that early experience might be a high-water mark in the television
career of the young wannabe. After his bold pronouncement that he
wanted to be an actor, 11-year-old Leo set about finding the right
agent but this proved more difficult than he imagined.

His description of that first meeting with an agent is particularly
painful: 'I remember them lining us up like cattle. There were eight
boys. A woman comes up and says, "OK, no, no, yes, yes, no, no, no,
yes. Thank you."'

The young Leonardo was a 'no' and the ordeal left him distraught
– 'I thought that that was my one chance into the business and that
the community was now against me.'

For the next three years he tried again to find adequate
representation – with the same level of success. Leonardo couldn't
understand it. By that age he'd earned himself a reputation among
his school friends for being a bit of a performer. His impression of
serial killer Charles Manson was a particular hit, although he ended
up in a heap of trouble after he painted a swastika onto his forehead

for one such pastiche of the crazed hippie, whose insane gang butchered actress Sharon Tate and other innocents in a mock protest.

In elementary school, he earned respect from classmates with a killer Michael Jackson impression. 'The next thing I was like the most popular kid in school,' he recalls. 'The coolest kid there walked up and gave me a Street Beats tape and goes, "Hey, this is for you."'

It was only a temporary reprieve, however. By the end of term, after an argument over the most beautiful girl in school, the cool kids threw Leo in a garbage can. In a bid to act tough, he began stealing gum from his local convenience store but stopped because he 'believed in karma.'

One of the few teachers who spotted his talent for performing was Helen Stringos-Arias, who was so impressed by the precocious 13-year-old that she put him forward for a state drama scholarship.

'Leo always wanted to be an actor,' she said. 'On school trips, he would get up at the front of the bus and entertain us with impersonations of his classmates and teachers. But I never saw him growing up into a sex symbol – he would come to school with his hair unbrushed, in jeans and a sweatshirt.'

During this time he also came close to winning a break-dancing competition in Germany but dancing was never going to take precedence over his dream. His body popping did earn him his nickname 'The Noodle', however, thanks to the moves he pulled and that has stuck to this day.

It's hard to imagine now but when Leo was 14, he was short and scrawny. And, although he acted tough, he was prone to being picked on by bigger kids. His most humiliating moment of school life, he revealed, was when he got badly roughed up for refusing to return a thug kid's basketball. 'I woke up about ten minutes later,' he recalled. 'I had about 30 kids all around me, throwing spitballs and kicking me. I tried to run away but they'd tied my shoelaces together, so I took one step and fell flat on my face. I had to hop away while they were still kicking me.'

INTRODUCING LENNY WILLIAMS

During this time, the young Leo didn't have much luck with girls either. His first crush was in the eighth grade on a girl called Cecilia Garcia, or 'Cessi', as Leo remembers her. He recounts a poignant tale of unrequited love.

'I went out with this girl named Cessi, this beautiful little Spanish girl. We had this beautiful relationship over the phone all summer – she was away. We were so close, so bonded, we'd tell each other everything. Then she came home, and we went out to the movies for the first time, and – oh, God! – I wanted it to be so perfect. So I put on my light blue turtleneck, which I thought was cool at the time (it was a turtleneck I bought from Kmart or something).

'When I saw Cessi I was petrified and I couldn't even look her in the eye or speak to her. We saw *When Harry Met Sally...* and I couldn't move, I couldn't look at her or anything. But the movie took me away. For two hours I was at peace because she was watching the movie and I didn't have this responsibility on me to be Superboy. And then afterward, I remember eating French dip sandwiches. She was really shy. Finally she said, "Do you have a problem with me eating this sandwich?" I said, "No, no, not at all." But I was really acting weird. And that was our last date. I was in love with her for a year after that, but I couldn't go near her because I was so mortified.'

When he eventually got round to experiencing his first kiss with a girl, it was an equally excruciating moment. Describing it as the 'the most disgusting thing in my life', he said: 'The girl injected about a pound of saliva into my mouth – I had to walk off and spit it out.'

Leo's yearbook shows why the girls might have rejected him. Long before the dazzling blue eyes and angelic blond hair captivated females the world over, he was an awkward-looking, young-for-his-age teenager. Fittingly, perhaps, his fellow classmates voted him 'most bizarre male freshman'.

One classmate recalled: 'He wasn't the type to sweep anyone off their feet. He was a skinny kid and quite wild and funny. Cecilia was very mature for her age – while Leo was playing basketball and joking around, she was interested in politics. No one could have known that Leonardo was going to become one of the most lusted-after men in the world.'

However, Leo certainly lived up to his jokey image in his second year in high school. Then 15, he is pictured in his yearbook wearing a wig with the caption: 'Elvis Does Live!'

His luck with the opposite sex continued when he reportedly fell for a neighbour's dark-haired daughter called Heidi. She grew up to be the notorious Hollywood madam Heidi Fleiss, jailed for fixing vice girls for the stars.

Former friend Mark la Femina told the *News of the World*: 'Leo used to see her in the street when they were kids. She was at least five years older than him but he couldn't get her out of his mind.'

Whenever Leo was asked in school what he wanted to be, he felt foolish mentioning an acting career that hadn't quite taken off.

'At school, when they asked what I wanted as a career I tried to choose between a travel agent and a biologist,' he says. 'I knew I didn't want to be one of the set things they said I should be at school – doctor, lawyer, blah blah blah…'

And he was convinced he was a better prospect than many of the other kids who cluttered up his television screen – including big brother Adam.

'I was always play-acting at home and in school. I used to watch TV commercials all the time and honestly believed that I was better than any of those kids, including my brother.'

Eventually it was Adam who offered to help put him in touch with an agent. Initially, the move looked promising. Leo landed a role in a Matchbox advert and further parts in a breakfast cereal campaign and one for bubblegum, which was ironic given his previous 'life of crime'.

The role might not have won him any awards but on a local level, he attained a level of fame from it. 'When I started getting into commercials everyone started saying, "Hey, you're the 'keeps it poppin' kid!" People recognise you from stuff like that. That's probably my most famous commercial.'

However, the commercials were a false dawn. After this meagre success it was back to the customary rejections, some for spurious reasons. One producer refused him because he had the 'wrong haircut'. His agent had a brainwave. What was hindering Leo's shot at stardom was his name – he felt it was too ethnic. Instead he should try using the more universal 'Lenny Williams'.

Leonardo was horrified. Aside from the usual teasing he received in school, he loved and was proud of his name. Years later, he recalled: 'They thought my name was a little too ethnic. They dissected it and said, "Leonardo – Lenny". Wilhelm, they changed to Williams. I didn't want to act under that.'

In fact, the only name he changed was his agent's – he sacked him and began the search for someone more on his wavelength. However, that depressing episode plus the mounting rejections were beginning to take their toll on the impressionable young teenager.

'I hadn't gotten a job in a year and a half,' he explained. 'That's like over a hundred auditions. You get pretty disillusioned. One day I just decided I hated everyone. I hated all these casting directors, I hated them all – I was ready to quit.'

He recalls returning home dejected after yet another knockback and complaining to his father: 'Dad, I really want to become an actor but if this is what it's all about, I don't want to do it.'

George replied: 'Someday, Leonardo, it will happen for you. Remember these words – just relax.'

Simple words of wisdom they might have been, but they had the desired effect: Leonardo duly calmed down, refocused and carried on with renewed impetus. In addition, if he ever needed a reminder of why he was striving to make a better life for himself and his mother, it was there on a daily basis.

'Money was always on my mind,' he admits. 'If I am honest, it was what inspired me most to come into acting. I was aware that a lot of people in Los Angeles were earning great money. I was always wondering from where, and how we were going to afford this and that – acting seemed to be a shortcut to getting out of the mess.'

Adam gave his take on early life with Leo and their unconventional family set-up: 'We grew up together as brothers in the same homes, we were a very close-knit family. All the parents lived close to each other and were friendly. We've known each other since I was four and Leo was one: we are as close as two brothers could be.

'Leo wanted to get into showbiz after he saw me in a TV ad and found out what I got paid for it. He decided that was what he wanted to do.'

Then came the little breaks. A friend of Irmelin's knew a talent agent and offered to put in a good word. Within weeks, Leonardo was signed up. In the following months he landed parts in about 20 commercials. Those small roles led to work starring in information films. One, for the Disney-produced *Mickey's Safety Club*, was on road safety. Another, on the dangers of drugs, entitled 'How to Deal With A Parent Who Takes Drugs', saw the 15-year-old Leonardo pose with a crack vial that transformed into a shotgun. This was also somewhat ironic given the substances that had been passed around in George's circle of friends since Leonardo was a youngster. After all, this was the kid who once told friends smoking cannabis looked 'as normal as drinking beer.' Leo was quoted in *The Times* in 1998 saying 'With parents like mine, I didn't need to rebel against anything', and his mother Irmelin backed this up in comments in the *Mail on Sunday*, saying: 'We already did the craziness for him.'

Suddenly, Leonardo's attitude to acting changed. Rather than being disillusioned by the profession, he was remarking: 'I'm getting paid for something I enjoy doing, and I get to miss two days of school.'

Gradually, in small baby steps, he was beginning to get noticed. The information films were one thing, but what Leonardo craved was something tangible. And he got it in the shape of Lassie. Luckily for Leo, the exploits of the clever canine were being revived for a 1980s audience. *The New Lassie* started filming in 1989 and it was just the vehicle to get him on television. He appeared infrequently but crucially more than once, as a pal of the dog's owner, Will Estes. His introduction to the series was a two-parter. 'Lassie was having puppies before the big BMX bike race and I was the sort of cocky kid who just wanted to win,' he recalls.

While the experience was a positive one, it opened the eyes of the impressionable young idealist to the fakeries of TV. As he told David Letterman, years later after hitting the big time: 'Lassie was supposed to be a female dog but they had five different guys who were supposed to do all the tricks – maybe male dogs are smarter or something like that. They had this big pregnancy scene and I first realised how fake this business is because they had to tape over Lassie's bits with special fur. I was little shocked and I was a little disappointed – I thought they'd use the real thing.'

At the same time he auditioned for a part in *The Outsiders*, a television version of the seminal 1983 movie of the same name which had been directed by Francis Ford Coppola and made stars of Rob Lowe, Emilio Estevez, Matt Dillon, Tom Cruise, Patrick Swayze, Ralph Macchio and C. Thomas Howell. Following the success of the movie, which launched the notion of the new 'Brat Pack', a series was devised with Coppola installed as executive producer. However, it was short-lived and Leonardo's role even shorter (he appeared fleetingly as 'Young Boy' in one episode) but it marked a continual development.

That progression furthered with a meatier role on daytime soap opera *Santa Barbara*, where he had the more challenging role of playing a teenage alcoholic called Mason Capwell in five episodes. The journey from the odd bit part to the well-oiled production line of a successful soap proved a wake-up call for the young actor. As Leonardo was still only 15, he was permitted on set for half days at a time but these appearances were demanding and he was required to learn the entire script for his episodes. By this time his soon-to-be-trademark blond quiff was evident and he could throw a look suggesting there was more to come from this confident young actor. Of all his early appearances, this was the one that proved most beneficial. His part was emotionally challenging and demanding for an actor who had never once had a drama class in his life. Leonardo came through with flying colours, though and looked to the next opportunity with relish.

He didn't have long to wait. A one-off appearance on top-rated sitcom *Roseanne* was merely a stopgap until he was cast in another TV spin-off from a hit movie, *Parenthood*. Ron Howard's 1989 film, starring Steve Martin and Dianne Wiest, had been an unexpected hit and NBC hoped to replicate that success with a TV series based on the same characters. This time Ed Begley Jr. took on the lead role of Gil Buckman but the ensemble cast deserved more than the reception they received. Leonardo appeared in all 12 one-hour episodes as Garry Buckman – again, essentially a troubled teenager (and a part played by Joaquin Phoenix in the original movie). It was said he had analysed Phoenix's performance as if studying Olivier to play *Richard III*, but the dedication paid off and he landed the part. However, by December 1990, the series was off the air. Just as he had been settling into some full-time work, Leonardo was once more looking for a regular gig.

He wasn't out of work for long, however, and his next significant break came in the shape of another TV series. *Growing Pains* was a homely sitcom that had been running since 1985 about an affluent family in Long Island, New York. One of the stars of the show had been Kirk Cameron, who played the family's troublemaking teenage son, Mike Seaver. Come 1992, the producers felt Kirk was getting on a bit to still be pulling in the younger female viewers and so the search was launched to find a new heartthrob.

The character of Mike became a teacher in a health centre and befriended a teenage homeless boy, who would eventually move in with the family. The producers hoped the storyline would highlight the plight of America's homeless, while at the same time re-energising a dying product.

'That was when I was sent on, to rekindle the girls' lust for a young man,' Leonardo said.

His character Luke Brower first appeared as a guest addition and then became a regular member of the Seaver family throughout the show's seventh series.

Sam Anderson, who played Principal Willis Dewitt, said of Leo's arrival: 'What a cute kid and what a heart-tugger! He was a real interesting addition to that group because he was different to what we were used to.'

Leonardo's appearance failed to re-ignite the interest in the show that the producers were craving but interestingly, it did serve to get him noticed with young fans. For the first time he began receiving attention from teenage girls, who instantly recognised him from the series.

'I get teenyboppers following me around, like, "Hi, hi, hi, what's your name? You're from *Growing Pains*, aren't you?" I like that, you know. It's pretty fun to have people recognise you,' he said.

Irmelin, who was by now handling her son's publicity, recognised a phenomenon that could be exploited and she set about arranging interviews for Leo with some of the most popular teen girl magazines. The upshot was while the show foundered, Leo's stock was rising.

When the series was eventually canned, Leonardo spoke out with an honesty not often found in young actors still finding their feet. 'The new writing was awful,' he remarked candidly. 'Either that, or I'm not sexy at all. Either one – you tell me.'

He went on: 'I had these lame lines – I couldn't bear it, actually. Everyone was bright and chipper.'

Leo might have been frustrated by the lack of genuine opportunities to test himself and feared being pigeon-holed as a bit-part player in tired TV series but he was at least beginning to forge a reputation as a teenager adept at grittier characters. *Parenthood* and *Growing Pains* might not have been cutting-edge drama but within these saccharine settings he emerged as a credible addition to the casts.

By then, though he had definitely caught the acting bug: 'I was lucky enough to get some auditions and commercials when I was 14 and 15, and then a part in a television show at 16, which turned me on to the whole process. I was hooked – not on the prospect of money anymore, though that was great, but on the simple process of acting itself. Something happened. I found I could think myself into the parts and it gave me the biggest thrill.'

By this time his stepbrother Adam had enjoyed limited success and followed up his success in TV ads with a couple of films – *Looker* and *The Incredible Shrinking Woman* with Lily Tomlin. However, unlike Leonardo and despite the ready cash provided, Adam found he could take or leave the acting game.

He says: 'I had a deal with my mum that at anytime I wanted to, I could stop. In the end I decided I just wanted to be a kid and play with my friends, and my mum was cool about it. She never pushed me into anything and I just wanted to be a normal kid.'

Being a 'normal kid' was the last thing that Leo wanted, though. He wanted to play, too, but his game was movies. And at the same time as he secured the slot on *Growing Pains*, he also landed what was to be his movie debut. However, his dreams of a big screen break would have to be put on hold because *Critters 3*, the flick that would provide him with his first full-length feature, bypassed the cinemas and went straight to video.

The reaction of most people on learning Leonardo DiCaprio's first-ever movie was *Critters 3* is astonishment that there was even a *Critters 2*. The original was a shameless attempt to cash in on the success of the far superior *Gremlins* (1984) and even a sequel felt like a film too many. By the time the third instalment came along, the plot had changed dramatically from a small town attempting to repel the alien invaders to a large city battling with the same problems. Leonardo fans might also have been surprised to learn their favourite actor was in it because he, rather understandably, prefers to leave it off his resume.

The no-budget science-fiction movie was made in a warehouse and Leo played the stepson of an evil landlord, a role he describes as 'your average, no-depth, standard kid with blond hair.' That was him being kind. When pushed, he was equally glowing about the experience as he was about *Growing Pains*: 'It was possibly one of the worst films of all time. I guess it was a good example to look back on and make sure it doesn't happen again.'

He might be harsh but it is interesting to note that the part of Josh, so expertly nailed by Leonardo, was initially turned down by British actor Cary Elwes, who rejected it, evidently, for a bit part in *Hot Shots!* Elwes had starred in *The Princess Bride* and *Robin Hood: Men in Tights* but further leading roles would elude him. That's not to say but for *Critters*, Elwes might have enjoyed the same stellar success as DiCaprio but the difference in their attitudes meant that Leonardo wasn't willing to let any opportunities pass him by at this time.

It was with this same philosophy in mind that he secured his next movie role. He made a fleeting appearance in the thriller *Poison Ivy* (1992), the vehicle that it was hoped would signal *ET* star Drew Barrymore's teenage comeback and arrival as a serious actress. Leo only pops up in the opening sequence as Barrymore's eponymous wild child character ruthlessly dispenses with an injured dog.

These experiences gave Leonardo a taste for moviemaking that he would never shake off. And although he was amused by the reputation he was cultivating as a heartthrob, this wasn't something he was planning to rely on in the long-term.

'Even early on, around the time I left *Growing Pains*, I said to myself I was going to do my own thing and not be hunk of the month,' he said. And as he looked towards his next project, he hoped this would be the break into serious acting he so desperately craved.

CHAPTER 3

EARLY REJECTIONS

As Leonardo and his dad sat in the cinema about to be entertained by a knockabout crime thriller, George turned to his son when the leading man appeared on screen and whispered: 'See this guy? Now, this guy is *cool*! His name is Robert De Niro, OK? You remember that name. He's cool.'

The film was *Midnight Run* – De Niro's surprising hit comedy, where his bounty hunter character Jack Walsh tries to bring in fugitive criminal Charles Grodin. It was 1988, but little did young Leonardo know that just three years on from that night, he would be standing in front of the very same Bobby De Niro trying to impress the pants off him.

Leonardo was auditioning for the role of a kid who has been abused by his mum's volatile boyfriend. *This Boy's Life* was based on the memoirs of author Tobias Wolff and he was aiming to land the role of the young Toby. Scots-born director Michael Caton-Jones, whose stock was still rising after the success of his debut movie *Scandal* (about the Profumo Affair) and modest triumphs with *Memphis Belle* and *Doc Hollywood*, was at the helm. But the man Leonardo had to impress was De Niro. Before it was his turn to read, he could tell just how nervous the other wannabes were. Among them was a then-unknown Tobey Maguire. As the tension mounted, DiCaprio knew he must pull something special out of the bag.

'I just got up and screamed, "Nooooo!" I was right in front of his face and, like, veins pumping,' he recalled. For a moment De Niro paused and in that brief moment, Leonardo felt his life hang in the balance.

He continues: 'I'll never forget his face – he burst into hysterical laughter.'

Of course this wasn't the reaction he was expecting or hoping for – 'I thought I had bombed that ship.' But De Niro, who until that moment had been inclined to go with another boy, was swayed by the newcomer's courage and passion.

Leonardo passed the first test and what followed was a further round of gruelling interviews and auditions because Caton-Jones wanted to be sure his search for the perfect candidate was as thorough as possible. In the end, DiCaprio beat 400 other hopefuls to the part and was ecstatic on learning he'd been successful: Leo was heading for the big-time.

'It was simple,' explains Caton-Jones. 'I knew he was it, but when someone reads for you that early, you don't believe it. So we tried loads of young actors, but we came right back to Leonardo.'

Alongside De Niro (who was cast as Dwight Hansen, Tobias Wolff's brutal stepfather) was smoldering siren Ellen Barkin, playing Leonardo's mum Caroline, but Caton-Jones was left in no doubt upon whose shoulders the fate of the movie would rest.

'I have three excellent actors in this film, but Leonardo is the rock that this movie is built on. If people can't relate to the character of Toby, the story becomes voyeuristic, but Leonardo makes this kid's struggle something you can connect with immediately.'

With the weight of expectation upon him, Leonardo might have been forgiven for retreating into his shell to summon up the intensity needed to pull off such a demanding part. Yet such was his innate confidence, he took it all in his stride and thrived on the pressure.

At the same time, he was adjusting to life in a new school. He'd only recently moved to a more affluent area of Los Angeles – the money generated from his commercials and television roles meant that he'd earned enough to take his mum out of Echo Park and their $30,000 two-bed shack. In one respect he had achieved his goal – to earn enough to get his mum out of 'Scumsville', but poverty was not quite a thing of the past, although he was earning enough to be able to tell his dad that he no longer needed to pay the $20 child maintenance. Leo and Irmelin settled in the hilly neighbourhood of Los Feliz, north of East Hollywood. Although they were away from the slums, they were still in one of the poorest areas of the neighbourhood and the mansions on the hills around them were a constant reminder of how far they needed to climb to be truly affluent.

At 17, Leonardo enrolled at John Marshall High, appropriately a school that had featured in as many films as its new pupil, having provided the set for *Grease* and *A Nightmare on Elm Street*. There he fell prey to Hispanic gangs, who picked on him as one of the minority of white students (when first introduced to his new school mates, he was quickly dubbed 'Leonardo Retardo'). But although he was teased and picked on, it seems his treatment was no worse than normal.

John Marshall High had aspirations beyond simply being a backdrop for teen dramas, however. It held well-run drama classes and naturally, Leonardo signed up. Instantly popular, he was cast as the male lead in the school play. At the same time he was holding down TV show roles.

'Leo had that star quality you only see once in a lifetime,' recalls Gerald Winesburg, his school drama teacher, who was certainly impressed.

Leonardo had not long joined the school when he landed the part in *This Boy's Life* but by then he had already made an impression on his new classmates.

'Leo was the virtually the only white guy in the class,' says pal Pot Ontoun. 'With his shock of blond hair, he stood out like a sore thumb. We used to call him "Shorty" – he was so scrawny.

'Once, the teacher asked Leo to read out a romantic speech from *Romeo and Juliet*. Everyone stopped and listened. By the end, all the girls were staring at him, doe-eyed – while the guys were annoyed that he was attracting so much attention.'

Soon, however, his auditions and TV work were taking so much of his time that Mr Winesburg had to bar Leo for missing rehearsals: 'Next morning, his mother turned up to talk it through with me. She was clearly a powerhouse, who was determined her only son would succeed.

'Leo loved the adulation, but he was obnoxious about it. He never got into trouble, though. He had such an enchanting smile and endearing manner, he could charm any teacher.'

Winesburg remembers: 'Each day, the school newsletter would say: "See our very own Leo DiCaprio in so-and-so!" I knew he was putting those adverts in himself.' But more than that, the teacher adds, Leo was determined to get himself and his mother out of the ghetto – 'He had that drive to succeed and I admired him.'

A struggling young actor he might have been, fighting to escape a poverty-stricken childhood, but Leonardo quickly identified the girl he wanted to be his leading lady: high school Homecoming Queen, Jennifer Faus.

Leo pulled out all the stops to charm Jennifer but, incredible as it seems now, given what we know about the actor's prowess with the opposite sex, she blew his attempts to romance her out of the water.

The teenage Leo thought he'd won her over and ended his run of bad luck with girls when Jennifer let him kiss her – only to be left heartbroken when she turned him down for a date because he was 'too bigheaded'.

'Leo and I had the biggest crush on each other,' recalls Jennifer, who is now happily married and working in a Los Angeles store.

'People say I was so lucky to kiss the world's most beautiful man – and I could kick myself now for not saying "yes" to a date with him.'

She met Leonardo when he started at the high school. 'He was adorable,' she says. 'You just wanted to hug him because he was so little. He was so skinny and scrawny that I used to tease him – and hold his hands behind his back.

'He used to drive this big old Mustang – he was so short that all you could see was his little hands on the steering-wheel.'

Little Leonardo looked to have no chance of winning the prettiest girl in school. But then he suddenly experienced a growth spurt – not to mention a role alongside Robert De Niro – and Jennifer soon began to sit up and take notice.

'Once we left high school, I started to see how cute he was,' she explained. 'At first, we hid our feelings with play-fights – I was always boxing with him. I guess it was just an excuse to touch each other. We would hang out and talk a lot, but there was a sexual tension. I could tell Leo was hiding his real feelings.

'One of my best friends had dated him, so I asked her if she would mind if anything happened between us. When she said it was fine, I was thrilled.'

When the two had to walk back from a friend's house in Hollywood, Leonardo made his move.

'He used to joke about how I should go out with him because one day he would be a celebrity,' Jennifer says. 'He was so talented I knew it was true, but I usually just laughed. That night, we both went silent. He turned round, looked at me – and kissed me. I have to say he was a very good kisser, even though he had dated only one other girl.'

But, to Leo's dismay, Jennifer had second thoughts.

'He had just landed a part opposite Robert De Niro in his first movie role,' she continues. 'Leo had always been a cocky kid and his big-headedness finally put me off. He offered to drive me home and asked me for a date. I was worried he was getting a bit too Hollywood, so I told him, "I think we ought to wait a while."

'You could tell from his expression that he expected me to say yes. Then he kind of gave me this look, as if to say, "Hey, I'm going to be famous. Do you know what you're missing?" But now, Leo has so many girls wanting to date him, I think it's good for him to have experienced a little rejection!'

To other pupils, Leo was 'a whirlwind'. School pal Sky Bushy told the *Daily Mirror*: 'He was always moving and talking and messing around. He had a real big crush on Jennifer.'

When it came for filming on *This Boy's Life* to start, Leonardo put any unrequited teenage crushes to one side and set about producing a performance he would be proud of. As he was to find out, though, the experience of making a film with a screen legend was a real baptism of fire – and unlike anything he'd experienced in acting up until that point. 'This role was different from any other I had played,' he says. 'This was something that was true, that actually happened to this guy. When you are in the moment of a powerful story like that, you just can't but feel emotionally disrupted.'

And he recalls: 'When De Niro showed up on the set, it was like the Pope showed up. Everything is on lockdown. "Shh, shh, quiet!"'

As if the hushed reverence wasn't daunting enough, when it was time for the two to do scenes together, Leonardo found himself totally perplexed when his older co-star and famous improviser strayed from the script. 'I don't know what the hell is going on,' he said, remembering his mind-set back then. 'If he says something that's not on the page, do I say, "OK, that was wrong"? "Oh, Bob, you said the wrong line"? See, no, I was supposed to come back and say something – I had no idea how it worked.'

Despite the steep learning curve he was on, Leonardo was able to be himself and enjoyed playing the joker on set and with the rest of the crew. In short, he was a wiseass but rather than antagonise his more illustrious co-stars, this brought them closer together.

'It was good for the part,' recalled De Niro, who looked on with amusement, but he did have call to reprimand the young upstart on one occasion, which left Leonardo wondering whether or not the Academy Award winner was joking.

'I was filming a scene with him where he was trying to impress my mom, played by Ellen Barkin, with a Zippo lighter. Ellen found this so hilarious; the whole set was in hysterics. Towards the twenty-fifth take I was getting a little agitated because I was usually the one getting the laughs. So I stand up and goes, "C'mon guys, can we be a little more professional here? You're laughing all the time, I have things to do!" I was a bit of a smartass. Bob takes me aside and goes, "You know, there's a line with jokes and you shouldn't cross that line because sometimes you can't get back."'

But there was no real danger of Leonardo crossing that line. From the moment he saw the legendary Robert De Niro on set, he was bowled over by his professionalism and experience.

'Earlier, at 14,' Leo recalls, 'I was already wanting to be recognised as an adult; when I was doing *This Boy's Life*, I wanted to be as old as Robert De Niro and as experienced as him and have the same respect as he did in that movie. I'm just starting to scratch the surface of what really makes me happy.'

During filming – on location in Vancouver, Moab and Salt Lake City in Utah, but mostly in Concrete, Washington (the small Cascade Mountain town, where Wolff grew up, which was transformed to its 1950s appearance) – there was really nothing in Leonardo's rather meagre body of work to suggest he could pull off a part as demanding as this one. It was the first time he'd tackled a real character and the complexity of Toby Wolff's relationship with De Niro's character was nothing he'd ever explored before in any of his lesser roles.

Yet, somehow, with Caton-Jones' careful direction and De Niro's stewardship, Leo was able to produce a performance that showed real potential. Indeed, De Niro was suitably impressed to let director Martin Scorsese know that this was a kid to look out for. Leo, meanwhile, credited Caton-Jones for guiding him through every step and paving the way for him to have 'the ultimate trust in directors, because that's how I was brought into this movie world, by Michael Caton-Jones literally taking me under his wing.'

He added: 'Michael Caton-Jones was very much like a father figure to me when I made *This Boy's Life*. I didn't know how to conduct myself on a movie set, I didn't know what the rules were, I didn't know what kind of investment you make in a movie.'

The film had a limited release when it reached cinema screens in April 1993 but still managed to go top ten, grossing $5 million at the box office. Although financially a modest success, critically it was much better received, with many reviewers raving about the performance of the previously unknown teenage star.

Bob Strauss, film critic of the *LA Daily News*, declared it was 'the profound honesty with which Robert De Niro and young Leonardo DiCaprio inhabit their roles that sells the whole, sadly stirring thing.' Of newcomer Leo, he added: 'DiCaprio exhibits an impressive range and an even more impressive sense of proportion. Called upon to be sensitive, smart-mouthed, naive, hurt, angry, cocky and more, he does them all without ever overwhelming the character's fundamental intelligence. It's as full and convincing a portrait of rebellious adolescence as the movies have given us.'

After the film was completed, Leo reflected on what he'd achieved with the role. He said: 'Everything I've done before *This Boy's Life* is just, I don't want to say below, but doing *This Boy's Life* was such a step up in my career; it was such a difference. It was real acting as opposed to just being cute or whatever.'

His step up was confirmed with his first gong – the New Generation Award from the Los Angeles Film Critics Association.

He celebrated his arrival, after 18 years in Hollywood, by buying himself a $35,000 Jeep Cherokee – 'It's kind of rugged and strong and fierce' – and while he lamented the fact that being a movie star still wasn't a guarantee he could land himself a girlfriend, he was wary of girls only attracted to him now because of his status.

'That's something I have to watch out for,' he admitted, maybe cynically. 'Girls who won't look at me for my personality, but for my pocketbook.'

And, as left school for the last time and perhaps reflecting on his poor run of luck with homecoming queen Jennifer, he said of his time there: 'I wasn't exactly the stud. I tried to make girls laugh. They thought I was cute, but nothing serious like Biff, who was wearing the leather jacket.'

One of the key scenes adding to the buzz around DiCaprio on the release of *This Boy's Life* was a sensitively handled gay kiss between Toby and his sexually-repressed friend Arthur, played by Jonah Blechman. Caton-Jones praised Leonardo's courage in handling this potentially tricky scene but its inclusion – and the lack of female interest from the young heartthrob – prompted speculation about his private life that would ultimately plague him for years.

Leonardo would occasionally hit out at the unfounded speculation, saying: 'I don't see why I can't have friends of both sexes without wild rumours being circulated. It's crazy! If I want to go to a party with a few male friends, it doesn't mean I'm gay.'

On other occasions he'd dismiss such rumours with the contempt they deserved. When asked what were the worst things he'd heard about himself, he replied: 'That I'm gay. I heard that I was going out with Ellen Barkin [nearly 20 years his senior]; that I'm an alien. Nothing that odd, I guess.'

Still, at that age, the worst thing that can happen to an up-and-coming actor is *not* to be talked about and Leo certainly set tongues wagging with his assured 'debut' performance. There were whispers about an Oscar nomination but 1993 was blessed with a number of stellar performances from teenage actors, with Anna Paquin's breathtaking turn in *The Piano*, while Christina Ricci sparkled in *The Addams Family*.

He was in exalted company, but Leonardo DiCaprio hadn't yet finished creating a buzz in that year.

CHAPTER 4

CATCHING
THE EYE

After Leonardo had finished filming *This Boy's Life* but before any buzz about his performance started to circulate, he found himself auditioning for another potentially challenging role.

Like the Caton-Jones project he'd just completed, *What's Eating Gilbert Grape* already had a star name on board. Johnny Depp had been signed up to play the lead character before a screenplay was even written. Depp, who had recently made Hollywood sit up and take notice of his acting talents with a haunting turn as Edward Scissorhands, was taken by the idea that Peter Hedges' 1991 novel was like a modern-day *Catcher in the Rye*.

As with *This Boy's Life*, Leonardo faced stiff competition and a real test of his acting skills as he read for the part of Gilbert Grape's mentally retarded brother Arnie. Initially, Swedish director Lasse Hallström wanted an actor 'who wasn't good-looking' for the part but after seeing Leonardo's impressive audition, he was willing to change his mind.

Still, a large group of hopefuls remained in the running and Hallström tried to whittle them down by setting a challenge. Each actor was given the same tape of a retarded boy and asked to mimic his movements.

'I watched the kid move his eyes and body, and just tried to get into his mind,' Leonardo recalls. 'It was interesting because he was completely unpredictable, so I could improvise pretty much whenever I felt it was right during the scene. I took a lot of his mannerisms and made them more like my own.'

His interpretation did the trick. Hallström was impressed by what he saw. 'Of all the actors who auditioned for the role of Arnie,' he said, 'Leonardo was the most observant.'

As Hedges put the finishing touches to his screenplay, Leonardo was installed as Arnie and the rest of the impressive cast assembled. Juliette Lewis, who'd burst onto the scene opposite Robert De Niro in the remake of the thriller *Cape Fear* and who that year had replaced British star Emily Lloyd in Woody Allen's *Husbands and Wives* (1992), was to play Gilbert's love interest, Becky, while Mary Steenburgen appeared as a housewife who lusted after Gilbert. But the most surprising addition to the cast was unknown Darlene Cates, who was to play the boys' mother.

Gilbert Grape author and screenwriter Hedges saw Cates on US chat show *The Sally Jessy Raphael Show* discussing how she became housebound when her weight ballooned to over 550lb. He spoke to Cates and offered her the part, feeling that someone who lived that life for real was more convincing than an actress told to fatten up for the part. It was a brave move and one that added to the independent feel of the picture. Her performance was key to the story, a subtle, moving drama about a family burdened by her immobilised frame.

To prepare for the part of Arnie, Leonardo conducted further research and gave an early indication of the seriousness with which he would approach his roles: he went into homes, studied similarly impaired children and tried to get inside their minds. He was fascinated to discover that, far from being crazy, these kids were spontaneous and unpredictable.

'I had to really research and get into the mind of somebody with a disability like that,' he says. 'So I spent a few days at a home for mentally retarded teens. We just talked and I watched their mannerisms. People have these expectations that mentally retarded children are really crazy, but it's not so. It's refreshing to see them because everything's so new to them.'

The more Leonardo found out for himself about the role he was about to play, the greater freedom he was afforded by Hallström and he was left pretty much to his own devices. He compiled a list of 'a couple of hundred little attributes' but when he approached the director to go through the ones he wanted to try, the Swede essentially waved him off.

'Lasse didn't really tell me anything about actually what he thought I should do,' explains Leo. 'He just said, "Do what you think." It was the most freedom I had ever had with anything I'd ever done.'

Where Leo was concerned, director Hallström believed it was all in his eyes. 'His two eyes are different,' explains Hallström. 'The left eye is very soft and empathetic; the right eye is more analysing. One eye oozes warmth, while the other is more penetrating. One eye is psyche, the other is intellect.'

Commenting on the character of Arnie, Leonardo said: 'He's a person who does specifically whatever he feels at a singular moment. He'll go off and climb the water tower, or scream or burp, or whatever. He's a real instinctual character. I had a great time playing him for that reason, because I was free to pretty much do whatever I wanted with him. It was really a lot of fun. I've never played a character in my life that had that much freedom.'

And he added: 'Johnny and Juliette were really cool for letting me go off and do my thing with that. They were calming me down because I was very hyper.'

Indeed, the freedom afforded to all of the leading actors helped create a relaxed atmosphere on set and Johnny and Leonardo developed a big brother-little brother relationship. Depp playfully teased his young co-star by getting him to sniff smelly food such as pickled eggs so that he could laugh at Leo's reaction. Eventually the demands to see Leo's facial expressions grew so ridiculous, the teenager began charging Depp $500 a pop for the pleasure. In return, Leonardo used his more experienced buddy to supply him with cigarettes.

Johnny was impressed by DiCaprio's assured performance and recognised a rising star in the making. 'Good fun,' he remarked, when asked what it was like working with the teenage Leo. 'He was really a kid, you know, so he was like a pain in the ass. He was always, "Johnny, give me a cigarette. My mom's not looking, give me a cigarette!" But he was a good kid.'

Both actors were unfaltering in their praise for Cates, who revelled in her role.

Leonardo said: 'To come into a movie for the first time and do the job that she's done and to feel so loving and so comfortable towards everybody on set, including me and Johnny [is something]. To me, playing Arnie, I went in and I was able to be this character, and at the end of the three months, I was done with. She has to live that life – she did a terrific job.'

Depp added: 'Darlene is for me the shock of the film. She is one of the most incredible people I have ever known. To be so brave as to allow herself to unravel emotionally, she's incredible – she should be applauded.'

When the movie was released in December 1993, it took over $2 million on the opening weekend and went on to make a respectable $10 million. What was undeniable, however, was the universal praise for Leo's performance. The *New York Times* film critic Janet Maslin gushed, 'the film's real show-stopping turn comes from Mr. DiCaprio, who makes Arnie's many tics so startling and vivid that at first he is difficult to watch. The performance has a sharp, desperate intensity from beginning to end,' while *Film Review* praised 'a performance of astonishing innocence and spontaneity', bringing 'a touching credibility to a very difficult part.'

On viewing the movie, many industry giants, including Martin Scorsese, found it hard to believe that Leo wasn't really mentally challenged but his performance was far more than a really good imitation of a retarded boy. Any moviegoers witnessing Arnie's heartbreaking realisation that his mother was not about to wake up from her nap would realise that here was an actor with extraordinary range and vulnerability – and a face every bit as handsome as Depp's.

And his performance also amazed one of Leo's kinder critics. His grandmother Helene was overjoyed to see him pull off such a difficult role with style. 'He was so convincing,' she said, proudly. 'Many people who saw it thought he was really handicapped because he acted so well. I'm astounded what he manages to do without any acting lessons, he really has talent.'

As the praise snowballed, the award nominations began to come Leonardo's way. He won the National Board of Review Award and the New Generation Award again. Then the whispers started about an Oscar nomination. A Golden Globe nod for Best Supporting Actor was considered a pointer for a similar nomination in the Oscars. Leonardo tried to put the buzz to the back of his mind but when the nomination was eventually confirmed, he was delighted. Publicly, he played it cool by claiming he went back to sleep after his agent called him.

For a 19-year-old, attending his first Academy Award ceremony as a nominee was an incredible achievement in itself. On the night he was accompanied by Irmelin, George and Peggy. It was a nerve-shredding experience. He was up against some tough competition: Tommy Lee Jones for his scene-stealing stint in *The Fugitive*, John Malkovich as Clint Eastwood's nemesis (*In the Line of Fire*), Pete

Postlethwaite for his gripping portrayal of Guiseppe Conlon (*In the Name of the Father*) and Ralph Fiennes' psychotic Nazi (*Schindler's List*).

Leonardo said of the night: 'I was dreading winning. I didn't even plan a speech – I was worried that I would slip up or do something terrible. I was shaking in my seat, putting on a posed smile. Inside, I was petrified.'

In the end, the speech wouldn't have been needed anyway. The Oscar went to Tommy Lee Jones, who added it to the Golden Globe he'd picked up a month earlier.

Leonardo might have missed out on Academy Award glory but in the media that made no difference. Magazines started putting him on their covers. Suddenly, he was being dubbed the next Brando and DiCaprio started to believe it, too.

'As soon as enough people give you enough compliments, and you're wielding more power than you've ever had in your life, it's not that you become an arrogant little prick, or become rude to people but you get a false sense of your own importance and what you've accomplished,' he said. 'You actually think you've altered the course of history.'

And if he'd been surprised at the impact his films were having on female fans after *This Boy's Life*, this was nothing compared to the reaction to *Gilbert Grape*.

'After I did *Gilbert Grape*, teenage girls became hysterical. What they do is shocking, climbing over walls and stuff. Mind you, I've had more fun being famous than I would have done otherwise.'

Another big difference was that, rather than having to attend endless auditions, he was now a sought-after commodity. The temptation would have been to leap into a big blockbuster – something to put backsides on seats and confirm his reputation as a bankable star. Indeed he was offered many high-profile roles, including Robin to Val Kilmer's superhero in *Batman Forever*.

'I just don't want to be big box-office yet,' he said at the time, showing a maturity beyond his years. 'The more you stay low-key at a young age, the more you have room for that stuff in the future, and as long as I can maintain doing films that I want to do, then I'd rather not blow my load on the work. It seems to me that a lot of people who try to do that just disappear.

'Before I started, I had this view that I was only going to do one film a year and that it was only going to be a really fantastic film,' he continued. 'I still think that I want to limit myself to not working all the time, 'cause that's not good for me and not good for my career, but mainly I'm just trying to be selective and to cut through the bullshit hype about scripts, and what everyone else is telling me to do. It's a really hard thing to learn, and I haven't mastered it yet, but I just want to keep on doing stuff that hasn't been done before.'

Rather than jump into something he would later regret – as Chris O'Donnell discovered to his cost when he took on the role of Robin in two Batman films – Leonardo waited nearly a year before agreeing to a movie after *What's Eating Gilbert Grape*. Of course this was a risk that might have backfired but so confident was he in his own ability – and of the moviemakers not to find a new kid on the block – that he felt able to take his time.

And there might have been another telling reason why Leonardo felt it important to slow things down. In October 1993, five months before the excitement of the Oscars ceremony, DiCaprio had been at a party when he bumped into another actor who once had the world at his feet.

He explained: 'I was at a Halloween party two years ago at the house of these twin actors and I remember it was really dark and everyone was drunk, and I was passing through these crowds of people so thick it was almost two lanes of traffic, when I glanced at a guy in a mask and suddenly knew it was River Phoenix.

'I wanted to reach out and say hello because he was this great mystery and we'd never met, and I thought he probably wouldn't blow me off because I'd done stuff by then that was maybe worth watching. But then I got caught in a lane of traffic and slid right past him. The next thing I knew, River had died, that same night.'

Tragically, Phoenix collapsed from drug-induced heart failure and died on the pavement outside the West Hollywood nightclub, The Viper Room – owned, coincidentally, by Johnny Depp. The young actor's death on 31 October 1993 stunned Hollywood and brought home the pressures on the industry's fledgling stars to live fast.

Leonardo DiCaprio was entering the most crucial phase of his short career and how he handled his next move would have a bearing on whether it would prove to be a lengthy one.

CHAPTER 5

MAKING A KILLING

It's not every 19-year-old boy who has Sharon Stone as his No. 1 cheerleader. And that's *the* Sharon Stone, who just two years earlier had caused moviegoers' jaws to drop in theatres across the globe with her now infamous leg-crossing scene in *Basic Instinct* (1992). And she was not just cheering from the sidelines, she offered to pay half his salary, even to carry him on her back to the set just to work with him!

Yet that was the crazy situation Leonardo found himself in when Stone started to court him to play alongside her in an unlikely-sounding Western called *The Quick and the Dead*. Leo's first, second and third reaction was to reject the offer – 'I thought it was just going to be a commercial film, Sharon Stone and everything.' And he added: 'Commercial films tend to play it safe and are familiar.'

However, as time went on, his refusal to jump into anything suspect, combined with a little misfortune in other roles, meant he was approaching the stage of being out of work for a year since filming wrapped on *Gilbert Grape*. By then he'd completed high school and was considering his next option. 'I'm not ready to go to college yet,' he explained. 'But if I do anything, it might be taking an acting class. I mean – I've never taken an acting class in my life and there are things that might help me with my performances.'

He also reiterated his desire to concentrate solely on worthwhile parts. 'Anybody can be a star with a little make-up and a music video,' he continued. 'I want to do good work in interesting films, with good people. If I set high standards for myself, people will remain interested in my work.'

And he remained confident that he wouldn't have to chase after adult roles – he wanted to explore more challenging teenage parts: 'I'm young, young-looking and young at heart – it's best for me to capitalise on that.'

With this philosophy in mind, his only work during that time was *The Foot Shooting Party* (1994), an obscure short, where Leo played a rock singer conscripted to fight in the Vietnam War. In the French comedy, DiCaprio's singer attempts to dodge the draft but when his bandmates gather to shoot him in the foot, they find pulling the trigger is much harder than any of them expected.

For a while it seemed Leonardo's selection policy might also be: shoot *himself* in the foot. He turned down a role in *Hocus Pocus*, the Bette Midler movie, but lost out to Christian Slater when he attempted to fill River Phoenix's shoes in *Interview with the Vampire*. And it wouldn't be the last time his fate was linked to that of the tragic actor.

Eventually, with one day to go before making a decision, he went against his better judgement and signed up with Sharon Stone. Set in the early 20th century, *The Quick and the Dead* was a tale of revenge centred on a gun-fighting contest in the remote and lawless town of Redemption. DiCaprio was to play 'The Kid' – 'a really insecure kid who puts up this show of bravado to convince people that he isn't insecure.'

He admits that he finally agreed to it because 'I hadn't worked for a year' and his role 'is not Billy the Kid, but a really different character. I'm fast and I'm cool – I'm just into my guns.'

Stone was starring as Ellen, a woman who rides into Redemption to settle an old score. An expert shot, she soon finds herself pulled into the high-stakes shooting tournament staged by the town's kingpin, Herod (Hackman), in which gunslingers put their lives on the line for money and fame.

It was a measure of Sharon Stone's pulling power at the time that TriStar, who had installed her as co-producer on the project, allowed Stone to call the shots on the film's director and co-stars.

'They sent me an approved director list,' Stone recalls. 'I sent them back my list. It had one name – Sam Raimi – who at the time was still probably best known for *The Evil Dead*.'

Raimi was shocked when he got a message that Stone had called. 'I couldn't believe it,' he says. 'I didn't believe it. I wanted to call her back and ask if she was sure she got the right guy. But I didn't – I played along as if she *did* get the right guy.'

When he was 'summoned' to meet Stone at a hotel in Vancouver, British Columbia, Raimi was terrified at the prospect of meeting the sex siren. 'I felt like Dorothy going to meet the Wizard,' he reveals. 'I wasn't sure what to dress like or whether to put on cologne, I just knew I wanted to act real smart.'

Stone was charmed, however. 'He walked in with that Beatles' suit and it was like he was 14 years old,' she recalls. 'But his immaturity is his gift – he makes everybody around him act like they're 14.'

Describing the manic competitiveness dominating the film, Stone added: 'It's a comedy, it's an action-thriller, it's a cult movie. I call it *Twilight Zone: The Western*.'

Also joining the cast was an unknown Kiwi actor called Russell Crowe, who originally auditioned for a different role before Stone asked him to try for the lead male. 'When I saw *Romper Stomper* [a low-budget Australian film], I thought Russell was not only charismatic, attractive and talented but also fearless,' she said. 'And I find fearlessness very attractive – I was convinced I wouldn't scare him.'

Raimi also found Crowe to be 'bold and challenging. He reminds me of what we imagine the American cowboy to have been like.' For his part, Crowe remarked that Raimi was 'sort of like the fourth Stooge.'

Regarding Leonardo, Crowe remained largely silent until years later, when he had the opportunity to appear once again alongside the actor in *Body of Lies* (2008). Recalling his previous work with the teenage Leo, Crowe – who by then had cemented his reputation as one of Hollywood's bad boys – quipped: 'The last time I worked with him was in a Western called *The Quick and the Dead*. I tell people he was 12, but actually, I think he was 18. Miss Sharon Stone was the big star, so people kept asking who we were.'

Back in 1994, Stone was indeed the star and her imprint was certainly all over this movie. Describing her work in packaging the film, she painted herself as a fast-draw producer: 'Normally, I'm patient, but sometimes when time's running short I get aggressive,' she admitted. 'I was aggressive in making sure we did our best to get Gene Hackman. They had me and they had to pay me, and they weren't keen on paying anyone else.'

This was also true when it came to securing Leonardo's services. Stone was adamant she wanted Hollywood's hottest young talent but movie bosses were reluctant to fund her choice. Out of desperation she offered to pay half his salary from her own pocket.

'I wanted him bad and we'd topped out financially,' she explained before adding, 'He's so good, I would have carried the boy on my back to the set if that was necessary! He will be one of the finest actors we have seen in decades. His talent, his gift, is so extraordinary.'

Despite his playing-hard-to-get act, Leo was also apparently nervous about coming face-to-face with his blonde bombshell co-producer. He joined up with the cast and crew in Mescal, Arizona, where shooting was already taking place in the Western set built for Lee Marvin's 1970 flick, *Monte Walsh* (and subsequently used in over 50 other films).

Pals of Leo's reveal the flustered teenager fumbled his lines time and again when Stone first came on set. One said: 'Leo admitted to me he'd been heavily attracted to her. He reckoned she played along with it by flirting with him whenever they were in a scene together.'

The star told his friend: 'I couldn't stop thinking about her. It was really weird because she was nearly old enough to be my mum. I think she's really cool. She let me think we could be real good friends. She was brilliant.'

Publicly, though, he told a different story. 'I expected her to be this big sex vixen, seducing everyone,' he said. 'But she was sweet.'

Kissing his co-star, however, was another matter. He revealed: 'To tell you the truth, it wasn't that great. She grabbed me by the back of my hair and pushed her lips on mine and then threw my head away. It didn't feel like a real kiss.'

Indeed he was more enamoured with the guns that he got to use during filming for the producers provided him with antique Colt pistols. 'It's very bad,' he noted, 'very bad, if I drop one of them.'

Not all the cast were equipped with the original guns, though. Thell Reed was the man hired as gun coach and weapons master to the stars and worked with the cast through three months of training. He also had to age Crowe's Colt 1851 Navy Revolver and the other guns used to make them look authentic and employed a rather basic trick. 'I took them out by my swimming pool and dipped them in chlorine water to let them rust,' he explained. 'They looked rusty and old, but were brand new guns.' Such detail, including the nickel plating and ivory handles on Ellen's Colt Peacemakers, was accurate to the time period.

When Stone finally got to see the young Leonardo up close she was suitably impressed, describing him as 'the most gifted young actor I have ever seen – richly, deeply, profoundly eloquent in his emotional accessibility and delivery.'

Sam Raimi was also quick to lavish praise on Leo's shoulders. 'He is the finest actor of his generation,' he gushed.

One scene that did stretch Leonardo's talents was his first death scene. The poignant moment came when he died at the hands of Hackman's Herod – the one man whose approval he would do anything to win. Dying on screen was a new concept for DiCaprio but it was to become something for which he'd grow rather famous.

As filming went on, Stone had her more than enough troubles to deal with. Several times the production had to be halted because of bad weather. Then, from the very first showing of dailies – the raw, unedited footage – some TriStar executives expressed displeasure at seeing Stone in a man's role. Instead they preferred her to dress in a traditional style, more befitting women of the age.

'Some people who shall remain nameless wanted me to wear a dress to ride into town,' Stone recalled. 'I thought, "Oh yeah, the gunslinger's gonna ride into town sidesaddle!"' Though she might have joked later on, the suggestion made her 'just so darn mad!' And she added: 'There were some people who shall also remain nameless, who were concerned that there really weren't a lot of places for me to be naked in this movie. But there are a lot of ways to be sexy other than flouncing around in your birthday suit. This character's not trying to run around in the nude so she can get control over somebody.'

As if that wasn't bad enough, when filming finally wrapped she was hit with the news that TriStar had decided to delay its release from summer or autumn 1994 until the following year. The studio had concerns over the over-saturation of Westerns, as well as the overexposure of Stone and co-star Hackman. Certainly, there had been a glut of Westerns in the preceding years, including *Tombstone*, *Bad Girls*, *Maverick* and *Wyatt Earp*.

TriStar President Marc Platt said that a late September or early October release had only been tentatively planned at the beginning of the year, while his preference was to release it in the March. 'It was the filmmakers who really wanted the film out in the summer,' he explained.

The filmmakers, however, had no choice other than to bow to the studio's will. 'I've had pictures come out in the wrong time slot before, so I know the price,' said Raimi's producing partner, Rob Tapert. 'I'm sure TriStar knows best.'

Tombstone, Kevin Costner's epic on the gunfight at the OK Corral, particularly concerned the studio, who feared the three-hour length feature would cause box-office takings to drop and sour moviegoers on Westerns for some time to come. This aside, there was also the issue that Gene Hackman featured in too many of the genre. Indeed, the *French Connection* star played Wyatt Earp's father in the Costner movie and also starred in the studio's *Unforgiven.*

Meanwhile, Stone herself was suffering something of a credibility crisis around the time the movie had originally been slated for release. One source on the project said: 'Her last two movies [*Sliver* and *Intersection*] haven't performed well. The word is TriStar wanted to wait and see how *The Specialist* [an action film pairing Stone with Sylvester Stallone] will do. If it does well, TriStar is hoping the success will bleed over for Sharon into this picture.'

Even before the movie was released, Stone was still not happy. She demanded a love scene be cut before distribution because she felt it wasn't in keeping with the rest of the tone. A second smooch with Leo was also left on the cuttings floor.

Eventually the film hit cinema screens in February 1995 and although it took over $6.5 million on the opening weekend and over $18 million overall – considerably more than any of Leonardo's previous movies – it was branded a flop. Raimi blamed himself for the poor showing, saying: 'I was very confused after I made that movie. For a number of years I thought, "I'm like a dinosaur. I couldn't change with the material."'

Reviews on the whole were mixed but some did not hold back in their criticism. Associated Press described *The Quick and the Dead* as 'an amazingly bad movie – so bad that not even the extremely talented Gene Hackman can save it.' Of Leonardo, it said: 'DiCaprio, a talented newcomer with much promise, seems lost in the role of the Kid and plays it like he's seen too many *Bonanza* reruns.'

Jay Boyar, film critic on the *Orlando Sentinel*, also savaged the movie, saying it was 'the first jaw-droppingly-awful movie of 1995.' Sparing none of the actors, he added: 'No one in *Q&D* gets very much acting done. Attempting to ape Eastwood, Stone turns into the Woman With No Personality. Hackman resurrects his little Lex Luthor laugh, a sign that he may consider the entire project beneath contempt.'

He did, however, reserve some sympathy for Leo: 'I think I felt sorriest for Leonardo DiCaprio, who follows up his brilliant work in *What's Eating Gilbert Grape* with the role of the Kid in this godawful mess.'

Among those with kinder words was the *Boston Globe*, who described describing the film as 'a sly, savvy Hollywood send-up of Sergio Leone Westerns [Spaghetti Westerns].'

And the pitfalls of doing a more commercial film – despite its relatively poor box-office showing – became increasingly apparent when Leonardo felt even more of his private life being eroded in the wake of the publicity surrounding him. Already he was lamenting the limitations that his sudden fame put on his life. Journalists began quizzing not only the actor himself, but his family and friends, old school pals and neighbours, in trying to track down his former loves and scandals. As would soon become customary with his leading ladies, he was linked to Sharon Stone.

There seemed little truth in the rumours, but more substance appeared to exist in reports that he was interested in a hot young model called Bridget Hall. The 5ft 10.5in Texan was the most in-demand cover girl during New York Fashion Week in April 1995 and had clearly caught Leo's eye.

'We're just hanging out,' she muttered coyly of their relationship, although she blushed as she said it. Despite her picture being on the front of all of the leading glossy magazines, she revealed Leo didn't even recognise her when they first met because 'I don't look like my Guess pictures.'

That the press were interested in who Leo was dating was an indication of how his star was on the ascent. Reports also suggested that he had a soft spot for Alicia Silverstone, at the time the most talked-about young actress in Hollywood, with some even claiming they were engaged. Two years younger, Alicia had burst onto the scene with a stunningly knowing performance in *Clueless* (1995). Unlike Leo, however, she had accepted a part in a superhero franchise – appearing as Batgirl in *Batman & Robin*. The link and friendship were genuine, the romance it appears not.

'Alicia and I did our first movies at about the same time,' Leo explained. 'We've known each other for years. I'm sure she was asked this question [about them being engaged] and she thought it ridiculous.'

In addition to the speculation about his love life, fans routinely pestered him and while he never publicly objected to the attention, the constant interest was clearly getting to him.

He said: 'I want to be a jerk like the rest of my friends, and have fun and not care about the consequences, but I can't now.'

Leonardo, it seemed, was right in his early suspicions that this latest work might not be best for his career development. Whereas he had been lavish in praise of his most recent films, he was quick to distance himself from this turkey. 'It's not my favourite film in the world,' he admitted. 'I guess it was not that good. It was alright, you know. I had a good time doing the character.'

Luckily for Leo, he had another project released hot on the heels of *The Quick and the Dead*, one that would restore any lasting damage to his reputation as a serious actor.

CHAPTER 6

FOLLOWING
THE RIVER

When MTV asked River Phoenix what he wanted to do after being nominated for an Oscar for *Running on Empty* (1988), he pulled out a battered paperback edition of *The Basketball Diaries* from his pocket and said: 'I want to play Jim Carroll.'

He wasn't the only one. In the 15 years that followed the controversial memoir's publication of 1978, several big names had coveted that role. Matt Dillon, *Weird Science* star Anthony Michael Hall, Eric Stoltz, Ethan Hawke and Stephen Dorff all joined Phoenix in believing they could be the one to bring Carroll's story to the big screen. It was the perfect role for any ambitious, talented young star able to play conflicted, charming yet ultimately doomed characters.

Carroll was a New York teenage basketball prodigy and heroin addict. Since publication, the book was optioned many times but either the project or timing was wrong or it didn't fit with the political climate (in the early- to mid-nineties, heroin was seen as being cool). Suddenly Leonardo found himself in the right place at the right time.

It was director Scott Kalvert who finally got the project off the ground. He toyed with the idea of setting the film in the period of Carroll's trials but it would cost too much to put everyone in costume and so he decided to make it in the present day. Plus, he figured, Carroll's descent into drugs was a universal story that transcended the generations.

Despite the title, *The Basketball Diaries* is only fleetingly about basketball. It covers three years – 13 to 16 – in the life of Carroll, an athlete who at 6ft 1in tall could score 40 points in a game. What set him apart from most other athletes of the day was that he was doing this while hooked on almost every drug known to man. Yet, as the diary progresses, the focus switches from the hoops to the hooked. By the end of the book, all that Carroll has left is an ability to eloquently document his own decline.

Carroll's tortured yet poetic memoir began life in the sixties when extracts started to appear in *The Paris Review* and downtown New York literary magazines when he was still a teenager. When he wasn't doing drugs or playing ball, he was hanging out around Greenwich Village and the St. Mark's Place poetry scene. He made himself known to Allen Ginsberg and Gregory Corso, but preferred Randall Jarrell to the Beats. In 1980, he branched out into rock, recording *Catholic Boy* – an album of spare rock'n'roll and streetwise lyrics that included 'People Who Died'. Carroll was more of a punk than a hippie, however, and for a while, he was the punk movement's Lou Reed. For all these reasons, his work has always had a cult following.

Kalvert described the book as a *Catcher in the Rye* but it's the famous JD Salinger novel laced with William S. Burroughs. However described, this was an ambitious project for Kalvert's first feature. Until that point he'd made a name for himself directing music videos for Will Smith, Cyndi Lauper and Marky Mark and the Funky Bunch. It was also the first screenplay to be optioned for the writer Bryan Goluboff. But that's not the only thing that Kalvert and Goluboff had in common: both were self-confessed Carroll groupies.

'I used to follow Jim around in the Village when I was 14 years old,' recalled Goluboff, while Kalvert read the book at 18 and then 'lent it to everyone I knew.' Though Kalvert did not share Carroll's love or talent for basketball, he confesses to dabbling in drugs, which may well have given him an insight into the writer's psyche. Once he secured the backing for the $4 million project, his next task was to find the right actor to play Carroll.

Leonardo DiCaprio might have been just an average basketball player with only a passing resemblance to Carroll, but in many ways he was ideal for the part. By the time the funding was in place, he was the right age to play the junkie and had already built up a body of work to suggest he could perfectly capture this tortured soul.

Leo had always steered clear of drugs and hated the very idea of narcotics but when the role was put to him, it was the idea of Carroll that appealed. 'The book was so hardcore,' he explained, 'and I loved the detail, how this guy made up his own world. That's the kind of stuff I've been doing a lot. I like young guys who've really been in history, who've done really different stuff. Just to try to deal with this fellow who lived everything at once, you know, was so cool.' Regarding any experimentation on his part, Leo, in an interview with freelance writer Rick Martin during the filming of Basketball Diaries, said: 'Compared to this guy [Carroll], I'm so clean, man, it's ridiculous. I swear I don't do any of those drugs. It's just acting for me. People said, "Why don't you try it for the movie?" and that's just so lame, you know? You do drugs like that and it gives you an excuse to do them again.'

When DiCaprio was confirmed in the leading role, Carroll was bemused. He said: 'When they first told me it was gonna be Leo, I didn't know who he was. If they'd said the kid from Growing Pains, I would have known because when I first saw that kid, I said, "This kid has a lot of presence." I said, "That kid is very pretty, he's gonna do well."' Aside from the shock that someone like Carroll was a regular watcher of Growing Pains, he put aside early doubts and warmed to Leo's casting, counselling DiCaprio on how best to portray himself on film.

Carroll, who has been clean since 1975, told Leo about how he and his junkie friends used to use eyedroppers instead of syringes to take the heroin, how he never got nauseous but would sometimes sneeze for nine hours straight and even how when he was straight, he used to 'trance out' so much that they called him 'Dazey'.

Remarkably, the drug addiction was not the most shocking aspect of Carroll's diaries. Eventually he prostituted himself to feed his habit and a perverted coach preyed on the team, trying to molest them.

Playing the twisted coach (whose name was changed in the film to avoid a lawsuit) was veteran Bruno Kirby of *This is Spinal Tap* and *City Slickers* fame. Freelance writer Rick Marin caught up with Kirby when he was permitted access to the shoot in New York for *The Los Angeles Times*.

Asked how he felt about playing a paedophile, Kirby said: 'I don't really play villains, I play people with problems.' It might of course be argued that 'Swifty' – the character's name in the film – certainly has a serious problem.

Interviewing Leonardo about the pressures of playing Carroll, Marin asked if he had any qualms about portraying a heroin addict.

'I'm just gonna do the films that I'm gonna do,' Leonardo responded. 'You can't always think of public perception because if you get caught up in, "Oh, he's a depressing actor, he just does dark films," you get locked into one thing. You should just do everything, all types of different things.'

Asked if his research of the Jim Carroll experience has extended to his own experimentation with drugs (a persistent rumour before filming began), Leonardo said 'no', his voice rising in astonishment at the question.

Of course the inference surrounding Leonardo was that he'd indulged his curiosity to make his performance more real. And the accusation was poignant: it was a charge levelled at River Phoenix when researching his role in *My Own Private Idaho* (1991). Like *The Basketball Diaries*, *Private Idaho* was a low-budget biopic in which Phoenix played a teen hustler/heroin user. According to legend, this was his introduction to hard drugs.

Leonardo was sensitive to the constant comparisons with Phoenix. Indeed, the similarities were not hard to find. Both men had been raised by unconventional parents who'd taken full advantage of the liberated sixties, both caught the eye with their early roles, both took risks in the parts they took, and both had the boyish good looks to attract a much bigger fan-base than some of their movies might have merited. Additionally, the spectre of the tragic Phoenix loomed large over any young, sensitive actor in Hollywood.

Leonardo said: 'People keep bringing up River with me. It's really ridiculous to experiment with drugs for a movie. For a couple of months of work, you're going to experiment with heroin and get hooked for life? With River, it's sad, but I don't know if it was the effects of the business or his life.'

Recalling the moment when he heard of Phoenix's death, he said: 'I was in bed when I heard. It didn't seem real at first. I didn't really know him, but I wanted to cry – and I still do. There are scripts that come to me, and they say, "two young guys". In my mind, I see River and me.'

Predictably, the prostitution element of the film caused controversy. Sex and drugs permeate Carroll's book and Scott Kalvert was keen to portray this aspect as accurately as possible. So much so that Karen Akers, a New York cabaret singer, turned down a cameo when she was told that her scene entailed whips, razor blades and cruelty to cats.

Mindful of censors, Kalvert insisted the worst had been toned down – the last thing anyone wanted in a film starring teen idols was a strong rating. Instead he insisted that, while moviegoers wouldn't actually see Leonardo stick the needle in his vein, they would be left in no doubt as to its evil effects.

'Toward the end of the movie, when you see some of the stuff that goes down – the prostitution, stealing from his mother – it's not pretty. People aren't gonna say, "Wow, I want to do drugs!" It's sickening.'

As well as Carroll's on-hand knowledge, the producers hired a former addict as a 'drug consultant' in preparation to further authenticity. In *What's Eating Gilbert Grape*, Leonardo had already proved he was a genius at mimicry but with the consultant's assistance, was able to slip effortlessly into junkie mode.

He explained: 'The voice – you go down an octave; even when you raise your voice, it's like you got this frog in your throat. It's not necessarily being tired and it's not necessarily like being drunk, it's sort of like your body becomes jelly and all your bones and everything become completely relaxed. You just feel at peace. Supposedly. I don't know, I've never done it. Right?'

Playing Carroll's friend Mickey was rapper Mark Wahlberg. If Carroll took a while to warm to DiCaprio in the lead role, he needed an age to get used to the idea of the singer known as Marky Mark now being an actor. Indeed he was said to have shuddered when told he was even reading for a part.

On set, however, Wahlberg wasn't afraid to send up the naysayers about his presence in the movie. Impersonating Carroll perfectly, he quipped to Rick Marin: 'The interesting thing with Mawky is he's got such a name and I figure, wow, I can't have him in this movie! But gettin' back to the first time I smoked a bag, wow, I muthta been 13 years old. Leo's great, Leo's fabulous – he just plays bathketball a little differently.'

Wahlberg, who appeared earlier that year in Penny Marshall's *Renaissance Man* (1994), had to read six times for the part of Jim's toughest buddy in *The Basketball Diaries*.

'I felt the character in a lot of ways,' he explained. 'I wasn't strung out on heroin, but I was doing what I had to do – you know what I'm saying? It was more about money for us than getting high.'

On set, the difference between Wahlberg and DiCaprio was clear to onlookers. While Wahlberg, then 24, had the self-awareness of someone who had already experienced the highs and lows of stardom in his career, Leonardo (five years his junior) still carried the air of someone who felt he was invincible.

Marin offered a fascinating insight into Leo's behaviour on set. He may not have had any concerns about the impact playing a heroin addict would have on his career, but he did fret about it getting out that he liked to smoke cigarettes.

'Can I have a cigarette?' DiCaprio asked Wahlberg, before he spotted the reporter was still watching. 'Oh yeah,' he then said. 'I don't smoke.'

If Leo was worried about projecting the wrong image on set, he seemed less concerned away from filming. During down time on the shoot, he earned himself a reputation as a party boy, burning the midnight oil with late nights at some of New York's most exclusive celebrity hangouts. Talk of his fling with model Bridget Hall might have cooled, but he was now being linked to Sara Gilbert, his old co-star on *Roseanne*, and also Juliette Lewis, with whom he had starred with on *Gilbert Grape*.

Jim Carroll remembers DiCaprio's discovery of the nightlife. 'It was Mark Wahlberg who turned him on to the club scene,' Carroll revealed to the *Guardian*. 'The women who had come to *The Basketball Diaries* set – models, all these girls. He ploughed right through 'em, man.'

Although the movie's early drug scenes did not apparently faze Leo, a later scene – where he had to deliver a long monologue to an audience – did.

'I can't focus on doing really long speeches,' Leo explained. 'Looking out to an audience and trying to act at the same time, I sort of got dyslexic. And Lorraine Bracco [who played his mother in the film] was like, "It's all right, calm down. It's not that big a deal – do it tomorrow if you can't do it today." And it's a tough thing –

you get in a situation where you feel that you have to be perfect all the time and it sucks, it really does. Sometimes you just sit there and go, "Jesus Christ, I don't know what to do!"'

On release, *The Basketball Diaries* earned a respectable $2.5 million at the box office. While reviews were generally favourable, some suggested the poetry and heart and soul of the book had become lost in translation. However, Janet Maslin of *The New York Times*, wrote: 'What saves the film from self-destructing entirely is Mr. DiCaprio's terrifying performance during some of these latter episodes. One staggering, isolated scene shows a drugged-out Jim paying a desperate visit to his mother, played by Bracco, whose weepiness here isn't one bit over the top. The wolf is, quite literally, at her door. Mr. DiCaprio's demonic Jim pleads, wheedles, screams and tries to force the lock, begging his mother for money as he breaks her heart. That confrontation is worth the whole film.'

And Jim Carroll had nothing but praise for Leo's performance. 'I saw the movie for the first time with Lou Reed,' he said, 'and he asked me if Leo had lived with me for two years, because he acted so much like me. Lou liked the movie – and he hates everything.'

Carroll had even come round to the idea that Wahlberg was a useful addition after all, remarking that he had done a 'good job' in his portrayal of Mickey.

By now there was a real buzz around Leo and he began to be linked to any major role, both fictionalised and those based on real people. Clamour grew that his next project might see him take on James Dean in a biopic of the doomed actor's life.

'You can see the comparison,' says David Loehr, an archivist who ran the James Dean Gallery in the late actor's hometown of Fairmount, Ind. 'They're both powerful young actors who made a big impact early and they both polished their craft for years before they became widely known.'

But he added: 'I have a whole file filled with people who were "the next James Dean". None of them were. The ones who were successful were the ones who took some inspiration from Dean and added their own style, whether it was Maxwell Caulfield or Bob Dylan. I think DiCaprio is doing that.'

Michael Ochs, an archivist and writer on popular culture, believed the *Rebel Without a Cause* star was 'the logical reference point' for Leonardo because of his looks. He said: 'So far he hasn't done anything that, to me, has anywhere near the intensity of Dean's work. But he's got the talent and by choosing roles that aren't directly reminiscent of Dean, he avoids the comparison trap.'

'It would be a huge challenge for anyone to play James Dean,' says Loehr, who sent DiCaprio a Dean biography when he read about the movie discussion and received a note of thanks in return. 'It might be impossible. That's why I almost think it would be better to get an unknown to play him. But DiCaprio could be very good if he's still interested, which at this point he may not be.'

Despite the speculation, which reached fever pitch around the time *The Basketball Diaries* was released, Leo himself was having none of it.

'I don't believe any of it,' he insisted. 'I think about acting and the business all the time, that's the truth – about roles, about whatever people are doing, what to do next. But as far as what people are saying about me, once in a blue moon I really think about it, you know; I really sit down and say, "Hey, is that true?" But it just doesn't register because I read the stuff about me and it's not who I am. It's a cliché, but it's like they're writing about this guy that I've been made to be.'

He might not have been ready to take on James Dean at that moment in his career but he was to find himself indelibly linked to that other tragic actor, River Phoenix. For his next role, Leonardo would replace Phoenix in what would be one of his most controversial roles yet.

Incidentally, there is an interesting footnote to DiCaprio's experience with *The Basketball Diaries*. The film was blamed in a lawsuit for inspiring the 1997 Heath High School shooting, when three students were killed after 14-year-old Michael Carneal opened fire on a group while they were praying. Disbarred lawyer Jack Thompson included the movie in a $33 million action two years after the shootings, claiming the plot, along with two Internet pornography sites, several computer game companies, and the makers and distributors of the 1994 film *Natural Born Killers*, had caused Carneal to open fire. The case was dismissed in 2001.

But the same year the film became embroiled in more moral panic, this time the resulting furore after the Columbine High School massacre. On that occasion two students, Eric Harris and Dylan Klebold dressed in black trench coats and went on the rampage, killing 12 pupils and a teacher before killing themselves. Comparisons were made to a fantasy sequence in *The Basketball Diaries* depicting Leonardo's character, wearing a black trench coat, shooting six classmates in his classroom. The movie was specifically named in lawsuits brought about by the relatives of murder victims – they were all, ultimately, unsuccessful.

CHAPTER 7

A DOUBLE TRAGEDY

Playing a gay, 19th-century French poet might not have been high on the list of priorities for many 20-year-old American actors but the decision to take on the role of Arthur Rimbaud demonstrated just how different was Leonardo's persona from many of his contemporaries.

It was a part that River Phoenix had signed up for and after his death there were not many similarly courageous young actors willing to risk the likelihood of derailing a budding career for the sake of broadening their range. As it was, Leo was candid enough to admit that, had it been left to him, he wouldn't have had a clue as to Rimbaud's identity. It was his dad George (by then looking over all the scripts sent his son's way) who first drew the role to his attention.

'I give a lot of credit to my father for steering me towards material or directors or subject matters that at a young age I wouldn't necessarily have had any exposure to,' Leonardo explained. 'Arthur Rimbaud in *Total Eclipse*, for example – I wouldn't have known anything about that guy, he's someone whose opinion I've always respected more than anyone's as far as not necessarily as far as career choices, but on interesting or fascinating subject matters, or meaningful art. And I've always continued to speak to him before any decisions are made.'

George had said, 'Let me explain to you who this guy was. He was a rebel of his time – he was the James Dean of the poet world. He was a radical artist, and you need to pay attention to this.' Leo was indeed sold by the anti-bourgeoisie pitch – 'It's like, who wouldn't want to play Louis Armstrong? Someone who came in when most music in America was step dancing and fox-trot and "Grab your partner".'

Leo believes his father has been an important influence: 'He gave me an alternative look on life, which has been reflected in the roles I've been choosing. He really taught me that the normal way of being isn't always the best way of being and you've gotta constantly search for something different, and that's what I've been trying to do in my career.'

And he admits: 'I don't know how to pick films that people necessarily want to see. I have a lot to learn in that respect but I have a lot to learn as an actor as well.'

DiCaprio was offered the script at the same time as the producers of *James Dean* were making one of their attempts to interest him. As well as listening to his father's advice, he also asked Jim Carroll which role to accept.

'Jim said, "Are you crazy? This is Rimbaud, man – you're nuts if you don't play him!" Jim told me Rimbaud was an absolutely cool person, a revolutionary for the art of poetry in his time. Then I read the script and found an outrageous character that I wanted to do.'

Rimbaud was a young genius who unwittingly changed the language of modern poetry and is still held in high regard by modern-day poets, even rock singers through the 20th century. Jim Morrison of The Doors believed he was the reincarnation of the French poet, whose work included the book *A Season in Hell* and influenced the likes of Bob Dylan and Jack Kerouac. Van Morrison wrote 'Tore Down' à la Rimbaud, Patti Smith sang 'Rimbaud Dead', while Tom Verlaine, guitarist for Television, adopted the name of Rimbaud's lover and fellow poet, Paul Verlaine.

It seems incredible that a symbolist poet like Rimbaud, an almost exact contemporary of van Gogh, could be held in such wide regard. A recent Pocket Penguin edition of the poet's last poem sold 60,000 copies. Manchester United's enigmatic French footballer Eric Cantona is a fan and little did the British Press realise that when he was giving his strange critique of its obsession with him, referring to 'seagulls' and 'trawlers' before serving a lengthy ban, he was in fact parodying Rimbaudian imagery.

Rimbaud published one book – *A Season in Hell* – in his lifetime and it sold six copies. Much later, the rest of the edition was found in a warehouse in Amsterdam. The only person who kept the flame alive was Verlaine.

The reason Rimbaud and Verlaine were fêted so much was because nearly a century before the 1960s changed society, the pair were shocking the French bourgeoisie with their outrageous behaviour. Screenwriter Christopher Hampton – who had adapted his own play *Dangerous Liaisons* for the big screen – had developed an obsession with Rimbaud since university.

Hampton wanted to write about the two poets when he was 16, but he thought the project too brash as a first attempt. Aged 20, he wrote about them for his second play for England's Royal Court theatre while an undergraduate at Oxford. Stage censorship was still in force in 1968 and homosexual love was a taboo topic; Hampton thought the theme had been treated 'hysterically' in the theatre and literature. In fact, the police turned out for the opening night of *Total Eclipse* and Hampton received his most vitriolic reviews ever.

'Partly it had to do with the second-play syndrome – critics kind of jump on you the second time around. It was beyond the call of ferocity and the play ran for only three weeks. It was an ignominious failure but over the next 10 years it acquired an underground reputation.'

Hampton had hoped a retelling of Rimbaud and Verlaine's tumultuous affair would similarly shock modern cinema audiences. And with scenes showing full-on gay sex and a pregnant woman being kicked in the stomach, there was a good chance of that. He had been trying to achieve a film version for about 20 years before the script passed before Leo. In fact, it took the centenary of the poet's death (1991) to provide the necessary hook. Prominent Polish director Agnieszka Holland took it on and with an $8 million budget set about making it happen. Initially John Malkovich was to play Verlaine, opposite Phoenix's Rimbaud.

When Holland saw DiCaprio in *This Boy's Life* and *What's Eating Gilbert Grape*, she thought he had 'the beauty, power, charisma and acting technique rare in someone so young. He also looked very much like Rimbaud. It's very difficult to find a young man with this power. If he had refused the part, I would not have done the movie.'

Once Leonardo was on board as River's replacement, however, Malkovich backed out, as he couldn't see himself playing that role opposite anyone but River Phoenix. Holland turned to acclaimed British actor David Thewlis to fill the vacancy. DiCaprio was delighted; he'd been a big fan of the actor since the Mike Leigh drama *Naked* (1993) and relished the chance to work with such an esteemed performer.

One thing he wasn't looking forward to was the sex scenes: 'Yes, there is some homosexual stuff,' he said, 'but if you know anything about Rimbaud, he tried to explore everything and homosexuality was something that came about – not saying that Rimbaud and Verlaine weren't in love for a while, because they were.'

Filming was to be on location in Paris, Antwerp and Blankenberge in Belgium. Leonardo was by then an experienced traveller owing to his regular holidays in Germany. But when he arrived in France, it seemed he'd already had his fill of the locals.

'You know it's such a cliché about the French,' he said, 'but it's the most true thing I've ever experienced in my life, how rude these people are. Terrible! As soon as I got on the plane for Air France, I bring up a big carry-on bag and the guy goes, "What in ze hell are you doing? Have you never been in a plane before, you stupeet leettle boy?" I said, "Look, I've paid money to be on this flight, you can't talk to me like that." The more you stand up to them, the nicer they'll be to you.'

And, once he'd got settled into the film, the prospect of smooching Thewlis was still a concern. He said: 'Kissing a man on screen is not a fun thing to do, but as an actor, you have to overcome things like that.'

Thewlis, on the other hand, was slightly bemused by Leo's reaction – after all, it wasn't the first time he'd done such a thing, after a male kiss in *This Boy's Life* and male prostitution in *The Basketball Diaries*. He even questioned DiCaprio's sexuality in remarking: 'Certainly if anyone was worried about doing it, then that would call their sexuality into question more than if they did it. It's, like, what are you scared of? That you might like it? So what if you do?'

When it came down to it, Leo went to extraordinary lengths to prepare. 'I was sure our lips were clean and everything,' he told *People* magazine. 'I made sure I got a little disinfectant, and we both did that. It wasn't fun, though.'

It's hard to imagine him making the same fuss when Sharon Stone was puckering up, although similarly he didn't enjoy that experience much either. Later he explained himself to *Premiere*: 'I did clean off his lips, 'cause we were like eating food, but it didn't quite happen that way. Actually I got very nauseous, as it was my first time kissing a guy. It was like slow motion, you know what I mean? I saw his lips coming towards mine, and I was like, Oh Jesus, is this really going to happen? Like, enough talking about it: my lips are going to touch yours. It was weird, too because I guess men have more body heat or something, but girls' lips are cooler. His were like hot. Nasty. My stomach really was turning after that.'

The two actors then filmed what looked like a touchingly romantic scene but Leonardo reveals he was actually whispering obscenities in Thewlis' ear.

'He's twirling me round in his arms and I'm going, "This sucks, this is sick, I want to throw up all over you". I think he was fine with it. He kept on saying that if you're scared of it, you're homophobic. Well, I'm sorry. Call me homophobic if you like, but I'm just grossed out by it.'

Then, during a wrestling scene, Leo got some measure of revenge. 'We had like, six takes and I think every time I hit him in the balls with my knee. I didn't mean to, but poor guy, he was really in pain.'

Some comfort came for Leonardo in the shape of his mother, Irmelin. Since hitting the big time, she had taken over responsibility for his finances and publicity and she accompanied him to France for the shoot. *Total Eclipse* would also be the start of a tradition Leo would continue whenever he could on future films – giving his mum a starring role as an extra. This time, she played a nurse who watched as Rimbaud had his leg amputated after developing a tumour on his knee.

Poignantly, art echoed real life as Irmelin had been nursing her sick father, who, by strange coincidence, was due to have his leg removed after blood clots were found on his feet. As it turned out, the operation was postponed due to complications with his health. Curiously, Leo complained of a tingling in his own foot while filming at the same time as his grandfather was undergoing surgery.

Leonardo had been aware of how seriously the illness was affecting Wilhelm, his namesake. Before the release of *The Basketball Diaries* he'd flown to Germany on a visit, realising the grandfather with whom he'd spent so many joyous summers was dying.

'It's really sad to experience something like that,' he said, 'especially for my Grandma 'cause she's been with him for so long.'

And of his mother's scenes in the film, he said: 'All of this stuff has been going on in my mind. My mother's playing a nurse and that's what she's been to my grandfather in the past couple of weeks. My grandfather's always been this really hard man; a German man, a hard worker. And now he's telling everyone that he has a soft heart. And he's saying this on his deathbed. I love my grandpa but that's not what I want to do: I don't want to wait until my last days to tell the truth.'

Sadly, Wilhelm did not recover and died in April 1995, starting what should have been a remarkable year for Leonardo on a mournful note. To add to his sorrow, around the same time his faithful dog Rocky (a Rottweiler) also died.

Previously, Leo had spoken of his pet's travails with health problems but the demise was no less of a shock. 'My dog Rocky is probably one of the most unfortunate hounds in the world,' he had said. 'He's a Rottweiler. He was the runt of the litter. He's got stolen and almost sold to the black market when he was two. He has epilepsy. And he has constant seizures and he's on medication, so he's tired. He's overweight because of the medication and now we've just found that he has cancer. My mom treats him like a newborn child.'

When *Total Eclipse* was ready to be shown to audiences it quickly became apparent that screenwriter Hampton's desire to shock had been achieved. When the movie premiered at the Telluride Film Festival, Colorado, a communal gasp was audible at the scene in which Verlaine kicks his wife in the stomach. Some queasy viewers even left the cinema. Although the scene was based on an actual event, the distributers were so alarmed by the reaction they asked Holland to cut it. Reluctantly she agreed. 'You have to make some compromises,' she explained. 'You don't want your distributors against you, especially with such a difficult movie.'

After the initial reaction, the director feared she might encounter a mixed response. 'I know these guys are very controversial and they wanted to be controversial, especially Rimbaud,' she said. 'He did everything to provoke the bourgeoisie and to fight them. He did it because he believed he could find some kind of truth by going over the border of the normal and traditional. He did it with Verlaine, hoping that Verlaine would be as strong as he was, but Verlaine wasn't.'

When the movie eventually hit cinema screens across the US, however, *Total Eclipse* performed poorly. It made just $350,000 at the box office and was, by a long shot, Leonardo's first commercial flop. Once the negative reviews began to appear, scriptwriter Hampton described it as a case of déjà vu after the reaction his play received.

'It could have been out of the London papers in '68,' he sighed. 'People were scandalised by the play and they seem about to be scandalised by the film.'

The reviews were particularly savage. *Screen International* magazine raged: 'As portrayed by Leonardo DiCaprio, in a potentially career-damaging performance, Rimbaud is a feral savant, suicidally uninhibited, endlessly annoying.'

After years of glowing reviews, this criticism particularly stung DiCaprio. He responded: 'I can't listen to that kind of shit. I really don't think it's gonna be career-damaging and, if it is, then fuck everybody! I'm proud of my work in all the movies I've done. In a few years' time no one will remember the bad reviews; those films will be seen as part of the body of my work.'

Holland blamed the adverse response on the conservative atmosphere of the nineties. She said: 'The media want safe, nice, successful values. I'm not interested in something peaceful, quiet and cute, I'm interested in the search for truth even though it goes through a very dramatic struggle.'

Before he left France, Leonardo took time out to appear in another bizarre project. *Les Cent et Une Nuits de Simon Cinéma* (1995) was a quirky movie about a 100-year-old man who, on realising his memory is fading, asks a young girl to tell him about the last century of film. DiCaprio's cameo was initially uncredited but he appeared alongside such names as Martin Sheen, Daryl Hannah, Emily Lloyd, Harrison Ford and Stephen Dorff.

And, while in Europe – attending a fashion show in Milan as the guest of Giorgio Armani – there was still time for him to have to strenuously deny being the same guest in the exclusive Hotel Principe who'd shocked fellow residents by roller-skating, naked, along the corridors. It was a friend, Leo assured interviewers, and he'd had his underwear on. Interestingly, not that much later, his grandma Helene happened to reveal her grandson's passion for inline skates. Surely this was coincidental, though.

When he returned home to Los Angeles, the exertions of the previous few months began to take their toll. His grandfather's death had hit him harder than he realised. When he met up with his old buddies again, they were shocked at how serious he'd become – they didn't recognise him from the happy-go-lucky Leo who'd left their shores only months before.

In an interview with *USA Today* shortly after he returned home from Europe, he alluded to the misery he felt: 'To tell you the truth, it's such a sad time that, in terms of my personal life, fame seems so miniscule. It's hard to think about when you've got personal problems going on.'

Friend and fellow film-worker Mark La Femina revealed to the *News of the World* that Leo was so heartbroken by the deaths of his grandfather and Rocky, his dog, that he considered, briefly, giving up acting. It appeared the negative reviews for *Total Eclipse* had caused him to contemplate whether his profession was really worth all the hassle. Sure, the money was vital and the opportunities more than he'd ever dreamed of – but at what cost? Already he'd seen how the fame game curbed the freedom his pals took for granted. In a bid to reconnect with what he felt he was losing, Leo suggested to a group of friends that they take off to the desert for a break. But La Femina revealed that when they got there, Leonardo was so upset that his friends were worried he might have summoned them there for a more sinister reason.

La Femina said: 'Leo was in despair and we were worried he might do something stupid. He told friends he'd suffered enough and no longer wanted to work in Hollywood.'

While in the desert, Leo managed to 'get his head together' and was persuaded to change his mind. Although he'd experienced a tough upbringing, the events of 1995 were the first real setback he had experienced in his teenage to adult life. How he coped with the slings and arrows of outrageous fortune at this crucial stage in his development could determine how his future career panned out.

CHAPTER 8

A MODERN DAY ROMEO

After the emotionally demanding roles of Jim Carroll and Arthur Rimbaud, Leonardo seemed to feel it was important to return to what he knew. And fortune continued to smile on him. He was offered the chance to work with Robert De Niro again on a film version of *Marvin's Room*, an off-Broadway play that explored the theme of a dysfunctional family coming together after serious illness threatens the life of the father and a daughter.

Screen giants Meryl Streep and Diane Keaton were to play the central characters in the story – two sisters who no longer spoke. Leonardo was deemed perfect for the role of Hank, Streep's son, who has been committed to a mental asylum after burning the house down. It was familiar territory for Leo and an opportunity to work with some of the finest in the business.

DiCaprio had been aware of the script for a while after De Niro told him playwright Scott McPherson was adapting his play of the same name that had opened in Chicago (1990) to widespread acclaim, scooping several awards following its run in New York. '"Whenever you get it assembled, let me know," I told him,' said Leonardo of De Niro's approach.

When he finally read the script, he was bowled over – 'I couldn't believe the way the dialogue occurred. It was unlike anything I'd ever read. The jokes played as natural as possible, completely in conversation.'

Sadly, McPherson never lived to see his film being made. He died in 1992, aged 33, from AIDS. The play was based on his own experience of AIDS in his family; his lover, Daniel Sotomayor, also died from HIV-AIDS. At the helm of the movie was stage director Jerry Zak in his first big-screen production.

Incredibly, Miramax chief Harvey Weinstein initially refused to consider Diane Keaton for the movie. It was only when Meryl Streep, who'd already been cast, flexed her considerable muscle, refusing to play if Keaton wasn't cast, that she was hired.

'There was no one else,' Streep said. 'If there's anything good about being old, it's that you get a say about who gets to be in the film with you.'

Keaton was delighted her fellow actress had stuck her neck out for her. 'I can't believe she did that. Isn't it incredible? But I don't know why. I mean, why? I'm thrilled to hear it; it's such a great thing to say. I mean, God. From Meryl Streep!'

The film was, surprisingly, the first time the two had acted together. Both had appeared in Woody Allen's *Manhattan* (1979), though not in the same scene. Between them, plus De Niro and DiCaprio, they had 19 Academy Award nominations and five Oscars. Here, Streep played the bad sister, Lee – a tough single mother with one 'nice' son and DiCaprio's delinquent teen. Of Hank's spell in the asylum, Streep said: 'We call it the loony bin, or the nut house, to show we've got a sense of humour about it.' Keaton played the 'nice' sister, Bessie, who stays in Florida to care for their bedridden father Marvin and his doddery sister, Ruth. Her performance was to earn her another Academy Award nomination.

De Niro's involvement was a small part as Bessie's distracted doctor. But linking up with the master method actor helped

Leonardo learn more about his own performances: witnessing the great De Niro up close again confirmed to him that he would never put as much of himself into a role. 'If I had to go through a movie for three months and be that character both on and off set, I'd have a nervous breakdown,' he said.

'I know what I'm doing but when they say "Cut!", I'm fine. I can joke around. I don't go hide in the corner and yell at anyone who tries to speak to me.'

Not long before filming started, Leonardo agreed to help out a friend with a short film he was making. R.D Robb was a struggling director and Leo, together with his actor friends Tobey Maguire and Kevin Connolly, joined Amber Benson, Scott Bloom and Jenny Lewis in the arty black-and-white production called *Don's Plum*. Leo, who donated his time free of charge, played a women-hating drug addict, who rants about life in a Los Angeles coffee shop. 'Girls make me sick!' was among the more choice phrases his loathsome character emitted. The shoot took six days in total and he left thinking no more of it than he'd helped some friends out.

In August 1995, filming on *Marvin's Room* began in New York and on location in Florida, which included a trip to Walt Disney World – the first time any of the theme parks had been used as a backdrop to a movie.

Completely unfazed by the stellar cast around him, Leonardo turned in another compelling performance. Although Hank was essentially another mentally challenged teen, the character called for more reserve and discipline than Arnie in *What's Eating Gilbert Grape*.

Meryl Streep was suitably impressed: 'Leo is possessed of the wild gene – unpredictability – which makes his career seem to defy categorisation, his life careen along the cliff edge, and his work vivid and bright and exciting.'

And Keaton was even more smitten. 'I was in love with him,' she gushed. 'He's great, he's beautiful: that guy has really got it. So talented, so gifted and funny – everything you want in a person.

He's like a light. He walks in and it's like magic. Meryl Streep and I would sit there and go: "God, this kid is so beautiful!"'

While Leonardo was no doubt equally taken with his female co-stars, he reserved special mention for Streep, then a two-time Oscar winner and with eight other nominations.

'Meryl Streep does things I would never have thought possible. She says her lines with such intensity on the set and it comes out so naturally that the result is simply incredible on the big screen. Her presence on screen is outstanding. She was more than impressing to my eyes. In addition, she's an adorable woman.'

Before filming had begun on *Marvin's Room*, Leo had signed up to play the lead in a new version of *Romeo + Juliet* (1996). It would be a game changer in the career of the 22-year-old heartthrob. Suddenly he'd combined credibility with popularity and Hollywood had itself a new superstar in the making. But it nearly didn't happen. Leonardo was at first reluctant to tread the well-worn path of another *Romeo and Juliet* adaptation: 'I wasn't sure at first – I didn't want to run around in tights, swinging a sword. I was given a script and at the time I didn't really want to do a traditional version of *Romeo and Juliet*. I wouldn't have done it, if it had been a period piece.'

He felt little could be improved on Franco Zeffirelli's 1968 treatment with Leonard Whiting and Olivia Hussey excelling in the title roles. 'It has been done so many times and so many people loved the Zeffirelli film,' he said.

But then his father George – who else? – persuaded Leo to have a closer look at what the director Baz Luhrmann was proposing. Australian director Luhrmann had caught the eye with his debut movie *Strictly Ballroom*, which in 1992 transformed the public's perception of ballroom dancing. George appreciated the modern slant Luhrmann was giving to the age-old tragic love story and he helped the director persuade Leo to join him in Australia to hear exactly how the movie would take shape. He stayed for two weeks work-shopping ideas with the visionary moviemaker.

'Then I realised how magical, energetic and electric he wanted his adaptation to be,' said Leonardo. 'What was crucial to me was that this was going to be a genuine *Romeo and Juliet*, the real thing – not another *West Side Story*. Instead of swords and a lot of elaborate costumes, he wanted to bring to the movie a lot of religious themes, the cars, the guns.'

He added: 'What Baz had done was reinvent it and, in the process, he discovered new ways of treating the play and the characters.'

As for Luhrmann, he had been trying to get the project off the ground for years but kept getting knocked back by a reluctant studio. He first spotted Leo around the time of his Oscar nomination and instantly knew he had his Romeo.

'I saw a picture of Leonardo and thought, "This guy looks like Romeo." Then I heard he was up for the Academy Award and thought, "This guy must be able to act, too."'

Luhrmann believed strongly that every generation needed its own version of the Shakespearean classic and he believed Leonardo DiCaprio symbolised the vibrancy of the younger generation.

With Leo on board, a second workshop was arranged so Baz could test out actresses for the role of Juliet. Initially, Natalie Portman was considered ideal. Just 14, she had won plaudits for her debut in the classy thriller *Leon* (1994), but when it came to filming scenes with DiCaprio – seven years her senior – 20th Century Fox felt it didn't look right.

Natalie summed up the studio's reaction. 'Fox said it looked like Leonardo DiCaprio was molesting me when we kissed,' she said.

Another actress eager for the part was a certain Kate Winslet. She longed to play Juliet – 'but I knew I was too old,' she said. As DiCaprio's leading lady her time would come, though.

'I saw many young actresses from around the world,' Luhrmann says. 'I had to have someone who looked 15, but was in control of her craft like a 30-year-old.' Jodie Foster recommended a girl who had dazzled in *Home for the Holidays*, a movie she'd directed. New

Yorker Claire Danes, a graduate of the prestigious Lee Strasberg Theatre & Film Institute, was only 14 when she won the role of Angela in *My So-Called Life* (1994–95). Critics and a loyal core of viewers adored it, but the show lasted only one season. Small-but-sweet roles in *Little Women* and *Home for the Holidays* followed, gaining Danes a reputation as a major talent with maturity beyond her years.

Liv Tyler and Leo's old friend Alicia Silverstone were considered, but when Luhrmann consulted DiCaprio, he was adamant it had to be Danes, then 16.

'I knew she'd be the one,' he said. 'I saw her television show, *My So-Called Life*, and I knew from that point on that she was an extremely intense, emotional girl and possessed a lot of the stuff that we wanted Juliet to be.

'I told the director about her. Other actresses came in with a flowery version of Juliet. We didn't want a flowery, over-dramatic version of Juliet, but somebody that was really forceful, because she actually laid down the law to Romeo.'

In the adaptation of the original play, some alterations were necessary. In the play, the feuding families fought with swords and knives. In the film, the weapons were updated to guns but in order for the script to remain unchanged, the names of blades, like 'Rapier', 'Dagger' and even simply 'Sword', were displayed on the firearms. Some of the characters' names were tweaked from the original text. The heads of the feuding Montague and Capulet families were given first names. Friar Lawrence was renamed Father Lawrence and Captain Prince was a modern interpretation of Prince Escalus. One thing Luhrmann did not want to compromise on, though, was the language. He preferred his actors to stick to the bard's original words.

This was something Leonardo took a while to get used to. 'At first I thought I would have to put on an English accent and try a sort of affected Shakespeare thing,' he recalls, 'but Baz explained he wanted to make it understandable, very clear, and after working with him a while, I began to feel more comfortable.'

He added: 'I'd never done much Shakespeare in school and it was kinda frightening to read through. Then I saw Keanu Reeves in *Much Ado About Nothing* and I knew if he can do it, I can do it, too.'

Similarly, it was Claire Danes' first effort at Shakespeare – both as an actress and a student. 'I studied the text of the play with my tutor and wrote three five-page essays on it. I really embraced the idea of "tragedy,"' she said. 'Doing Shakespeare is easier than acting a bad script – it's so well written. After this, everything seems like crap.'

For Danes though, the idea of playing a tragic love-torn teenager was a little too close to home. 'When I started *Romeo + Juliet*, I was just starting to break up with my boyfriend and I would cry periodically during rehearsals,' she revealed (referring to the musician Andrew Dorff, brother of actor Stephen Dorff). 'It's just so hard to be talking about love when you're supposed to be falling out of it.'

And the thought of doing the role justice kept her awake at night. 'I had such a panic attack when I was about to play Juliet,' she continued. 'I'd just seen the Olivia Hussey version and she was gorgeous. So I had a little breakdown at 3 o'clock in the morning.'

Whereas the original play was set in Verona, Italy, Luhrmann set his version in the fictionalised community of Verona Beach, Florida. To capture the feeling of stifling heat, filming was done in Miami, but mostly in and around Mexico City and Veracruz. The Capulet mansion was filmed at Chapultepec Castle, while the ballroom was built on Stage One of Churubusco Studios; the church is Immaculate Heart of Mary in the Del Valle neighbourhood.

'It was so surreal, the whole experience,' recalled Danes. 'For four months, we were in Mexico City, which is really kind of a magical place, very passionate and vibrant. There are so many colours surrounding you when you're there.'

It took a while for Leo and his co-star to really click – Luhrmann described their early interaction as argumentative, like two kids on holiday – but they eventually grew into the roles together.

'It was a moment-by-moment collaboration,' Luhrmann recalls. 'Those moments of rehearsals were very sweet moments; we had fun trying to understand the text. One of the things we set out to do was to get them to claim the language for themselves, to make the words their own.'

Speaking of her relationship with DiCaprio, Danes said: 'I think we understand each other. I mean, we're two different chemicals and when you put us together in the same container, things start happening. Good and bad things.'

As was customary for most DiCaprio movies, rumours grew that their on-screen romance had spilled into real life. Both parties denied this, but did Danes have Leo in mind when she swooned that 'God did good when he created boys'?

When it came to filming the immortal balcony scene, Danes found herself petrified: 'That was so intimidating to do that scene! I mean, it was ridiculous. I had to go on and say those famous lines that have been made fun of over the years. I had to throw all these other performances and interpretations behind me and start from scratch.'

Luhrmann recalled: 'That scene knocked me dead because I was wondering how we were going to have a young girl talking to herself on the balcony. She went beyond my expectations in that scene – she made it believable.'

For all its triumphs, the Mexico shoot was plagued with difficulties. At one point, Danes' mother was hospitalised with pneumonia (although she later made a full recovery) and a Mexico City crewmember was hospitalised after a taxi he had hailed was hijacked by three men, who apparently slammed his head against the pavement and threatened to kill him if he didn't produce $400. There were attacks by killer bees, multiple broken legs and an outbreak of food poisoning meant production shut down for four days. Leonardo spent much of his time there vomiting from dysentery and whenever he could, he drove back to Los Angeles rather than stay in Mexico City.

'The truth was it got a lot more extreme than anyone really bargained for,' Luhrmann says. 'But part of the reason I chose Claire and Leo was because I knew they could sustain the work and its intensity.'

One of the issues the production crew thought they might have to handle was the young stars going out on the rampage, perhaps led by DiCaprio who, after the gossip column treatment he received in New York filming *The Basketball Diaries*, had developed a bit of a reputation as a party animal. Co-producer Martin Brown admits this had him a little worried before shooting began in Mexico City.

'We thought we'd better have some bail money set aside – but it went much better than we expected,' said Brown.

The film's iconic love scenes, played in front of a fish tank and in a swimming pool, came about as a result of the director's research in Miami Beach. 'I was trying to work out how Romeo is going to see Juliet, and I went into a Miami nightclub that had a fish tank in the toilet,' he explained. 'I thought it could be a great flirtatious device.

'Shakespeare was using an 18-year-old boy to play Juliet, so he kept the lovers apart. But I wanted them to have sex and the water environment fit into that. Throughout the movie I use water purposely – the lovers kissing underwater is the last image.'

The cast were happy to take Luhrmann's lead and he carried an impressive presence on set. 'Baz is so elegant,' gushed Danes. 'Most directors wear T-shirts. Not him. He came to the set looking elegant and graceful every day. The movie's all contemporary dress, set in the present, with guns and cars. I think Baz wanted it to be manic, operatic, heightened, like *Strictly Ballroom*, but he wanted young people to be able to relate to its violent world.'

As for DiCaprio, Danes found him nothing short of 'brilliant'. 'I know that word's overused,' she said, 'but he's smarter and more perceptive than anybody I've met. He's also wild and out of control, which I love about him.'

Yet, although they developed a closeness on set, at the end of the four-month shoot, Danes still had a feeling she had only scratched the surface when it came to her co-star. 'I spent four months with him and I couldn't figure him out,' she admitted. 'I still can't figure out whether he's really transparent or incredibly complex. I think he's the latter, but I don't know.'

Other actors weren't so ambiguous. John Leguizamo (who played Tybalt Capulet), said: 'I just hated him because [acting] came so easy to that little blond, happy, golden-boy. He'd smoke a cigarette, do some laps, [imitate] Michael Jackson, go on the set and there it was.'

When the time came to talk the film up ahead of its release, Leo made it sound slightly incongruous. 'It's like nothing that I can describe,' he said. 'It's just us driving around in cars actually, with guns instead of swords. We've got all this slick gear on, like tight pants and Hawaiian shirts and we're, like, speaking the Bard. My dad dug it, really dug it – he suggested letting me borrow one of his shirts.'

Danes, however, felt the studio's publicity machine shouldn't mention the fact that the actors stick to the traditional dialogue, lest it put young cinema-goers off. But she needn't have worried: the pre-release buzz about how Shakespeare had been given the MTV treatment sparked huge interest. Publicity shots showing Leo looking dashing as a nineties Romeo were designed to set teenage hearts racing. Fox executives believed they had an unexpected smash on their hands. The only thing that could ruin their perfect promotion was if anything should happen to their precious leading man – or if there was any suggestion that Leo wasn't readily available to marry any of his impressionable young fans.

Given the wise head on young shoulders and his failure up until that point to hold down a regular girlfriend, there was little danger of those things happening though, was there?

CHAPTER 9

LEO RISING… AND FALLING

'OK, Leo. Jump!'

The rush of air hit the young actor full in the face as he plunged earthwards. What better way to get his juices flowing again than by taking a sky-dive?

For a brief moment it was everything he hoped it would be – exhilarating and terrifying at the same time, the chance to view the world from 12,000ft. He was one of ten friends who, in early summer 1996, thought it would be a great way to spend the day. Each of them was doing a tandem dive, with a qualified instructor attached so nothing could go wrong. All Leo had to do was pull the chord at 5,000ft. He did so, expecting to float gently to the ground.

Except, instead of the 'chute billowing out above them, Leo's flapped angrily, then twisted and refused to open. Instinctively, his dive buddy cut the chord.

'We started plummeting to earth. I had one of those, you know, flashes – photo – you know, eight-by-10 glossies of my life in front of my eyes, you know, two years old, eight years old, you know, ten. I pulled the second chute; that was clumped up as well. So then I said, "Oh, wow, now I'm really going to die!"

'You have those moments,' he said. 'It's going, "Oh, God, you know, why do I have to die today? Why did this have to happen, you know? This sucks." You know, I'm 21 and I didn't want to die – that's what it's like.'

Luckily, his instructor managed to inflate the second chute and potential disaster was averted although the near-death experience shook Leo to the core.

As he told talk show host Oprah Winfrey years later: 'There's just something fundamentally wrong about looking out of a plane and being thousands of feet in the air and saying, "OK, I'm going to hurl myself out and fall and plummet to the earth."'

It's not known if Fox or director Baz Luhrmann knew how close they came to losing their rising star but back on solid ground, Leo set about promoting *Romeo + Juliet*, as it was now called, to appeal to a younger, hipper audience. Had they got wind of the drama, just weeks before the movie opened, they would be praying nothing else happened to harm the pre-release hype – like their leading man stepping out in public with a stunning model.

But that's just what Leonardo did at the film's premiere at the Mann Chinese Theatre in Los Angeles on 24 October 1996, when he appeared in public for the first time with the ravishingly beautiful Kristen Zang on his arm.

'This is Kristen,' the normally reserved Leo gushed to the assembled media. 'Isn't she gorgeous? We're very serious about each other.'

The couple had met at a showbiz party when Leo was still a virtual unknown. Although by that time he'd earned a reputation as someone who liked to hang around supermodels and enjoyed partying with his attractive co-stars, he had largely been able to float under the radar where love interests were concerned. There had been reports of a romance with model Bijou Phillips, stepsister of the actress/singer Chynna Phillips, after he'd watched her sashaying down a catwalk in New York the year before, but it was a bit of a surprise when leggy model Kristen accompanied him to the premiere.

Zang, on the other hand, was used to dating superstars. At 24, she was three years older than DiCaprio and, although still a relative newcomer to the showbiz scene, gave the impression of being more worldly-wise than her younger beau. Before she was snapped arm-in-arm with Leo, she had already admitted publicly how she'd been left at 'rock bottom' after a three-year romance with movie-star hell-raiser Nicolas Cage ended in heartache not long after they'd become engaged; she had also dated INXS frontman Michael Hutchence.

Strange as it might have seemed for the teenage girls who were suddenly waking up to Leonardo's boyish good looks, Kristen was decidedly underwhelmed when first introduced to him.

'I thought Leonardo was too young for me,' she confided in a friend. 'But then we started talking and the chemistry was there. By the end of the night, I was smitten.'

The couple had hit it off spectacularly quickly. Within weeks of their meeting, Leo had introduced her to Irmelin – a sure sign of intent by any young man – and his mother had been equally taken by the 5ft10in blonde from Battle Creek, Michigan. She had stayed over at their house and was behind his thinking when, after 21 years of living under the same roof as his mum, he made plans to move out from their shared house and into a place of his own. When he was in Mexico filming *Romeo + Juliet*, Zang had flown down to join him on set and comfort him when the demands of the intense shoot became too much.

The sight of DiCaprio seemingly in a stable relationship right at the moment when he could conceivably cash in on a newfound fame with young fans might have been deemed heartthrob career suicide. But Leonardo's new manager, Rick Yorn, could tell the sight of a beautiful woman on his arm would not quell the interest in his young acquisition. Yorn was an experienced agent, manager and producer who had Martin Scorsese, Cameron Diaz and Benicio Del Toro, as well as his own brother, the musician Pete Yorn, on his books. Rick had overseen Leonardo's recent roles and was providing a much-needed calming influence on him now public attention was soaring. Leo's dad, George, was happy that his son was receiving proper representation now that he'd hit the big time, and he remained an advisor when it came to scripts. At the *Romeo + Juliet* premiere, Rick saw for himself the seeds of what he would later recognise as 'Leo-Mania'.

'Leo and I were walking in and there were all these young girls, kids, behind a barricade and they broke through,' recalls Yorn. 'He was like a Beatle. They're screaming and it was like, "Whoa!" That hadn't happened before. I had seen that happen with other people, but not at that level. I called and talked to some people, and I was like, "God, this is going to be just a taste."'

Despite early indications that the movie might confound the studio's initial pessimism and be a success, reviews were on the whole mixed. Many critics believed it was sacrilege to turn a Shakespearean classic into a shoot-'em-up blood-fest, while others found watching the young stars trying to wrap their tongues around Elizabethan language painful.

Jay Carr of the *Boston Globe* led the attacks, saying DiCaprio's 'deliveries are flat, lacking the ardour one might reasonably expect from even a theatrically unschooled Romeo.'

He added: 'Skulking around like a third-rate James Dean impersonator, all listlessness and sullenness trying to pass itself off as soul, he's a recessive presence. In various ways, all the acting is terrible, with the shining exception of Claire Danes. Eyes alive with sentience and spirit, she alone brings Luhrmann's effortful misconception to life, swimming upstream in a torrent of clueless shouting – swimming, in fact, during much of the balcony scene, which Luhrmann transfers to a swimming pool.'

The *San Francisco Chronicle* claimed, 'Leonardo DiCaprio and Claire Danes, who play the leads, aren't up to the challenge. They can neither say the lines nor convey the feelings underneath them. They sound uncomfortable and constrained, and look like people embarrassed to be talking funny.'

Janet Maslin, critic at *The New York Times*, was kinder to the lead stars, saying: 'Fortunately, this film's young lovers, played radiantly by Claire Danes and Leonardo DiCaprio, have the requisite magic and speak their lines with passionate conviction. They remain rapt and earnest even when some of the film's frantic minor players might as well be speaking in tongues.'

In any event, it seemed that the MTV generation didn't look to newspaper film critics to decide their movie choices. *Romeo + Juliet* exploded into theatres on its release in November 1996 and shot straight to No. 1 on its opening weekend, raking in $11.6 million. The movie was credited for its ability to attract swarms of teenagers to the theatres – clearly the antiquated dialogue did not put off the youngsters. Indeed such was the interest that some newspapers sent reporters to investigate the sudden fascination with Shakespeare – and found that it might have had more to do with the leading man than the bard.

Sarah Etherden, 16, of Hamilton, Ontario, admitted she'd had to drag her boyfriend of a year-and-a-half, Ron Johnson (18) to see *Romeo + Juliet*. 'It was better than I thought it was going to be,' said Ron. 'But Sarah cried the whole time.'

Sarah said: 'I think I cried because it was so emotional. I read it in English class, but you don't realise [Romeo and Juliet's] true feelings until you see them. He was just so sensitive – you can't help but fall in love with that.'

Amy Paulse, executive editor of *Teen People*, said the reason why the film was a hit with teenage girls was all down to Leo. 'Aside from the fact he's drop-dead gorgeous, it has to do with the pining factor,' she said. 'Girls feel they could save him. They feel they could've taken the poison away from Romeo. They fantasize and pine away for this unattainable heroic figure and he supplies it.'

Leonardo now became pestered with questions about his own love life and whether Kristen was the Juliet for him. He replied rather diplomatically: 'I believe in love at first sight but it hasn't happened to me yet. I don't know if I'm going to get married and I probably won't unless I live with somebody for 10 or 20 years. I played Romeo, but I don't have the balls he did.'

And, as the hysteria mounted, he was at pains to show that his feet remained firmly on the ground. 'The main thing for me is just to maintain my life with my family and my friends,' he said. 'They treat me like Leo, not like Leonardo, master thespian. That's all I need to maintain my sanity.'

The movie didn't just go down well with teenage girls. After the initial scorn from film critics, it began to build some momentum and featured prominently in the annual award ceremonies. *Romeo + Juliet* was also celebrated at the Berlin Film Festival, where it was recognised with the prized Gold Bear for direction and Silver Bear for DiCaprio's performance. Luhrmann also produced the successful soundtrack albums for the film that collectively went on to sell more than 8 million copies worldwide. DiCaprio also collected the Blockbuster home-video award for Favorite Romance Actor.

A worldwide smash, the movie went on to gross $147.5 million, a decent return on its $14.5 million budget. Now it was confirmed. Leonardo DiCaprio was an A-lister, able to confidently carry a film as the male lead. Yet, although he was trying his best to take things in his stride and enjoy the new levels of attention, he was vulnerable to people trying to take advantage of his newfound popularity.

Not long after *Romeo + Juliet* was released, he told an alarming story about the lengths some so-called fans would go to for a piece of Leo memorabilia. He had been playing basketball with his friend Vincent in a schoolyard near his home in Hollywood.

'So this girl came up and said, "I'm your biggest fan. Give me your T-shirt,"' he said. 'I told her, "I'm not giving you this T-shirt off my back, I'm playing basketball. I'll give you an autograph or something but that's about it." Ten minutes later, she gets her mother to come and tell me she has a daughter dying of cancer in hospital and that I should sign my T-shirt to her. So, trying to be a nice guy, I did.'

He took off his T-shirt and gave it away before remembering that the cancer had started the conversation as a car crash. When Vincent heard this, he chased the woman down and found her laughing with her daughter about Leonardo DiCaprio being a sucker. Thoroughly riled, he said they had a 'damn nerve' and tore the T-shirt into pieces in front of them.

'It really bummed me out,' explained Leo in a 1997 *Times* interview. 'How could this happen? Like I'm not even there, like I'm just some mechanical thing walking around that isn't really human. I took it personally.'

But if he thought that behaviour was off the wall, he would have to get used to it fast. Interest in all things DiCaprio was about to go off the scale.

CHAPTER 10

CREATING A MONSTER

With no guarantee that *Romeo + Juliet* would be the hit it was at the time they signed up for it, Leonardo's manager, Rick Yorn, was keen for his client to secure a major hit. Up until that point the actor had earned a reputation for taking on challenging roles, but widespread exposure had so far eluded him. So, when a script for a movie based on the sinking of the world's biggest liner – *RMS Titanic* – landed on his desk, Yorn gave it some consideration. In fact, it had taken an age for the script to get that far.

Behind the ambitious project was *The Terminator* director James Cameron, whose desire to retell the story of the majestic vessel's ill-fated maiden voyage had become something of an obsession. The disaster of 1912, when the ship sank after striking an iceberg 400 miles en-route to New York, had captivated writers and movie-makers ever since, spawning some 16 films, 18 documentaries and over 130 books.

Cameron's interest first peaked nearly a decade before the idea of the movie took shape. After seeing Robert D. Ballard's 1987 *National Geographic* documentary, *Titanic Revealed*, about the discovery of the wreck, Cameron jotted down these ideas: 'Do story with bookends of present-day scene... intercut with memory of a survivor… needs a mystery or driving plot element'. Although he was to spend the next 10 years producing films such as *The Abyss*, *Terminator 2: Judgment Day* and *True Lies*, he continued to think about *Titanic* – the 'Mount Everest of shipwrecks' – and in 1995, approached 20th Century Fox about funding a similar expedition for himself. 'My real goal was to actually go dive the shipwreck,' he said. 'Making the movie was kind of secondary.'

He had begun to think about a possible storyline, however, and pitched a 'Romeo and Juliet on the *Titanic*' idea to the studio. Against the backdrop of the human tragedy of the ship's sinking, when over 1,500 people died, Cameron wanted to place an unlikely-sounding love story between Jack Dawson, a free-spirited young artist, and Rose DeWitt Bukater, an upper-class teenage girl engaged to someone else.

Cameron recalled: 'They were like, "Oooooohkaaaaaay – a three-hour romantic epic? Sure, that's just what we want. Is there a little bit of *Terminator* in that? Any Harrier jets, shoot-outs, or car chases?" I said, "No, no, no. It's not like that."' After telling Fox that he believed he could make the movie for less than $100 million, he asked for a 'couple of million' upfront to pay for a dive so that he could get footage of the wreck to use in the finished movie. Fox chairman Peter Chernin expressed an interest but wanted to know more before committing.

In September 1995, one of two Russian submersible Mir 1 crafts began its decent in the North Atlantic about 700 miles east of Halifax, Nova Scotia. After a two-hour fall, Cameron arrived at the wreckage of the *Titanic*, two-and-a-half miles below the surface. During 12 dives over the next 28 days, they found the *Titanic*'s 400-foot bow remarkably well preserved. Specially designed cameras filmed surprisingly intact staterooms with ornate woodwork, pristine chandeliers, cabin doors still on their hinges and piles of furniture that looked to have been swept into a corner by a flood of water. It was footage unlike any other before.

Top: A baby-faced teenage DiCaprio before his star exploded.

Bottom left: Playing mentally challenged Arnie Grape in 1993's *What's Eating Gilbert Grape?* for which he was critically acclaimed and which earned him a 'Best Actor in a Supporting Role' Academy Award nomination.

Bottom right: At the premiere of *Romeo + Juliet*, in which he played the male lead, ensuring he became the Romeo of teenage girls around the world.

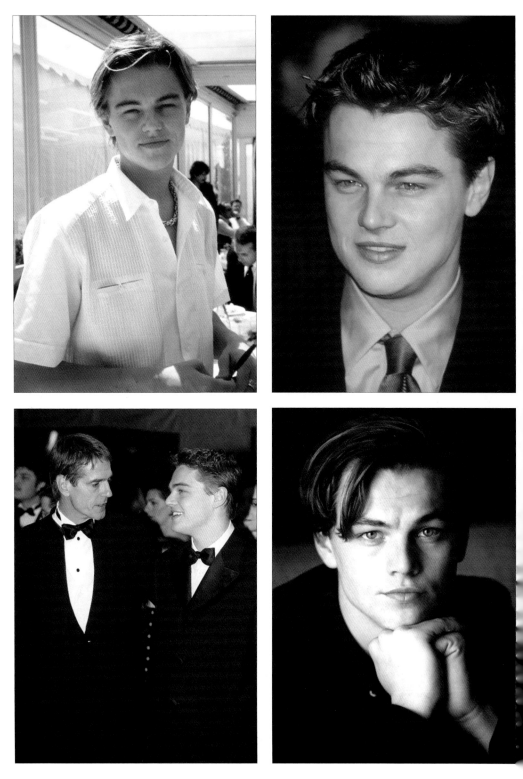

The many faces of a teen heartthrob: Throughout the late 1990s DiCaprio's face adorned many a magazine cover and bedroom wall as he stared in a string of hits, including *The Basketball Diaries*, *Romeo + Juliet*, *Titanic*, *The Man in the Iron Mask* and *The Beach*.

DiCaprio and Kate Winslet at the 1998 Golden Globes, at which *Titanic* was nominated for 8 awards, including 'Best Performance by an Actor in a Motion Picture – Drama'. DiCaprio and Winslet's Jack and Rose captured the hearts of millions and the actors have remained close friends.

Top: The cast of *The Beach* with director Danny Boyle at the film's premiere party in London, February 2000.

Bottom: Proud parents – DiCaprio's parents arriving at the premiere of *The Beach*, Leicester Square, London, February 2000.

Top left: Playing infamous con artist Frank Abagnale Jr. in 2002 on the set of *Catch Me If You Can*, with director Steven Spielberg.

Top right: DiCaprio with his 'Actor of the Year' award at the Hollywood Film Festival Awards in 2004.

Bottom: This is your captain speaking…at the Berlin premiere of *Catch Me If You Can*, 2003.

Top left: A thorn among the roses? DiCaprio with Princesses Eugenie and Beatrice at *The Aviator* premiere in London, December 2004.

Top right: With *Aviator* co-star Cate Blanchett at the film's Italian premiere.

Bottom left: At the Golden Globe Awards, after winning 'Best Performance by an Actor in a Motion Picture – Drama' for *The Aviator*, with actress Hilary Swank, 16 January 2005.

Bottom right: Every bit the modest winner, DiCaprio with his Golden Globe.

Top: At the Rome Film Festival premiere of *The Departed* with director Martin Scorsese and co-star Vera Farmiga.

Bottom: DiCaprio and Scorsese at the Academy Awards Governors Ball, Scorsese winning 'Best Achievement in Directing' for *The Departed*, 25 February 2007.

Top: The London premiere of *Blood Diamond*, a confronting film set in the midst of the Sierra Leone Civil War, January 2007.

Bottom left: DiCaprio with acting legend Morgan Freeman at the LA premiere of *Blood Diamond*.

Bottom right: Seemingly startled by attention from beautiful women, DiCaprio at the Academy Awards Vanity Fair Party with Naomi Campbell, February 2007.

Energised by the adventure, Cameron set about convincing Fox to fund the film and costed a huge replica *Titanic*, speculating the movie would require $75 million. Even at that price, Fox felt a partner was needed and Paramount came on board to share the cost on the proviso that it could distribute in North America. Cameron's last film, True Lies (1994) had cost a whopping $100 million and, although it had made three times that much at the box office, studio executives were skeptical that a movie about a sunken ship would replicate that success. Paramount's investment was capped at $65 million, meaning any additional cost along the way would have to be footed by Fox.

Cameron eventually persuaded the studios that a 770ft model, nearly 90 per cent of the actual size, would save on special effects. To facilitate this, the largest water tank ever constructed would need to be built, capable of holding some 17 million gallons. Increasingly concerned about their potentially spiralling investment, Fox wanted bankable stars to guarantee a return, but as the central characters were just 17 and 21, Cameron's options were limited.

For Rose (who Cameron described as 'an Audrey Hepburn type'), he considered Gwyneth Paltrow, Claire Danes and *Scent of a Woman* star Gabrielle Anwar. Chris O'Donnell and Matthew McConaughey were considered for the role of Jack (envisioned as a young Jimmy Stewart crossed with the Bohemian author Jack London), but Cameron decided both were too old. Tom Cruise expressed an interest, but was almost instantly dismissed because of his wage demands. Casting director Mali Finn then suggested Leonardo DiCaprio and Kate Winslet for the lead.

At 20, Winslet was nearing the limit of an actress required to play a 17-year-old girl but her eye-catching performance in *Heavenly Creatures* (1994) had put her on the radar of the major American studios and her fuller figure made her more suited to the body shape of women in 1912, as opposed to the willowy actresses who were dominating Hollywood. There was also a buzz about her in Ang Lee's soon-to-be-released version of *Sense and Sensibility* – a role that would later earn her an Academy Award nomination.

It was at this point that Rick Yorn was consulted on Leo's interest in playing Jack. Yorn had a feeling that the big-budget epic could be the breakthrough to box-office success he desperately wanted for his client. Leonardo, however, would take some convincing.

'He laughed at me and it's like, "No chance,"' Yorn recalled of DiCaprio's reaction to the script. For Leo there was nothing to recommend the part – no heroin, no angry poetry writing, no mental illness, nothing. What did intrigue him, though, was that Kate Winslet was in the running for the part of Rose. Winslet's involvement, however, was by no means assured.

She recalled: 'I met Jim before I read the treatment and thought to myself, "This is great." He'd been thinking about this film for a year-and-a-half when I met him and that was December 1995. Then I read the treatment and thought, "Wow!", floods of tears. Gotta do this film. I took the bull by the horns and phoned him and said, "I have to do this. Give us a chance, mate!" To me it's a love story – it was never about a sinking ship, it was never about another *Titanic* movie. It happened to be the place where this story was set. That's what it was for me – always, always, always.'

Winslet flew to LA for a screen test but, although she impressed, Cameron still held out. In desperation, she sent him a single rose with a card signed 'From Your Rose' and pestered him by phone. 'You don't *understand!*' she pleaded one day when she reached him by mobile phone in his Humvee. 'I *am* Rose! I don't know why you're even seeing anyone else!'

As soon as she heard Leonardo DiCaprio was being considered for the part of Jack, she was a big fan. 'My God, did I want Leo to play that part,' she said, even counselling Cameron that if he didn't choose her, then he should still do all he could to hire Leo.

What DiCaprio was taking for granted, however, was that

Cameron had set his sights on the young star in the first place. The truth was the Canadian director hadn't yet convinced himself that Leonardo was right for the part.

'He didn't strike me as necessarily having the qualities I wanted for my Jack,' Cameron explained. Like two nervous teenagers on a bind date, eager not to give the impression they like each other, Leonardo and Cameron embarked on a strange sort of courtship to sound each other out. Eventually Leo consented sufficiently to read for the part. Yet so disinterested did he appear that he almost blew his chances.

Recalling the reading, Cameron explained: 'He did something that really rubbed me [up] the wrong way. He sat there smoking a cigarette, slouching as if the whole thing was too much trouble – I didn't even think he was paying attention.'

Indeed the director almost thought about stopping the whole process so as not to waste any more time.

'Then he got up and read the scene, and it was like "boom!"' Cameron continues. 'I saw it and knew – he was the guy.'

DiCaprio still had doubts and asked Cameron if Jack should have something else to make him more endearing, like his characters in *What's Eating Gilbert Grape* and *This Boy's Life*.

'Look,' Cameron told him, 'I'm not going to make this guy brooding and neurotic – I'm not going to give him a tic and a limp, and all the things you want. It's harder to play Jimmy Stewart.'

Meanwhile, Winslet was hired for a fee of just under $1 million. For Leo, that swung it and after holding out for so long, he finally jumped in for the considerably larger fee of $2.5 million, his first million-plus paycheck.

'I was resisting it for a long, long, long time,' DiCaprio revealed of the process. 'I was prejudiced against it at first because I am not enthusiastic about doing large-scale films. It was only after meeting the director James Cameron and Kate Winslet – who was cast before me – that I said yes.'

Now on board, Leonardo was very much on message. 'What I loved about the character of Jack was his artistic side,' he said. 'He was a real Bohemian figure. Another great thing about the film is that, being both the writer and director, James cared so much about the story between Jack and Rose. He knew that, with all the special effects in the world, unless the audience connected with those two people it would just be a visual feast.'

What also might have smoothed the deal was Cameron reportedly agreeing to let Leo have it written into his contract that he could take six of his friends along to the set so they could 'horse around'. But any thoughts he might have harboured that this would be like any other movie were quickly dispelled once he got to work.

Renowned as a virtuoso filmmaker, James Cameron also had a reputation for being a control freak who gets involved in every aspect of his movie, from writing, editing and producing to occasionally operating a camera, testing a stunt or using a paintbrush on the film set.

Eager not to make the same mistakes encountered on Kevin Costner's epic disaster *Waterworld* (1995), the most expensive movie ever made, where an artificial set had been constructed in Hawaii, Cameron decided a fully controllable set on a land-based operation was needed. A new studio complex costing $57 million was constructed in Santa Rosarito, Mexico, about 20 miles south of San Diego. While the massive set and water tank were being constructed, filming began on the modern-day scenes, in which veteran actress Gloria Stuart played an elderly Rose, reminiscing about her dramatic experiences on the ship.

The location was the Halifax area on the *Akademik Mstislav Keldysh* research vessel that Cameron used to film the underwater sequences, a year earlier. Fifty crewmembers made the trip to Novia Scotia for what was supposed to be a pit stop to the main event. However, on 9 August 1996, three weeks into filming, all hell broke loose when several people fell violently ill after a dinner break.

Actor Lewis Abernathy, who played a cynical sidekick to Bill Paxton's relic hunter, recalled: 'There were people just rolling around, completely out of it. Some of them said they were seeing streaks and psychedelics.'

'I thought it was food poisoning,' he continued (luckily he had eaten in his hotel that night). 'Really bad seafood can make you hallucinate and this caterer was big on clams. Jim was being loaded into the back of this van – I was just shocked at the way he looked. One eye was completely red, like the *Terminator* eye – a pupil, no iris, beet red. The other eye looked like he'd been sniffing glue since he was four.'

Later, a lab report confirmed that the director and his crew had been poisoned by lobster chowder laced with PCP, a hallucinogenic drug also known as "angel dust". Although dozens of crew were taken to hospital, many were back on set after 24 hours. The speculation was that Cameron was such a tyrannical director that a disgruntled crewmember had sought revenge. The culprit was never found, though, and the real reason behind the attack was never established. However, the incident was a taste of things to come for a shoot that would be beset by problems.

At the outset, though, cast and crew arriving at the huge coastal facility in Mexico could not fail to be impressed by the sight that greeted them. The huge replica *Titanic* was visible for miles, resting on a steel frame and manipulated by massive hydraulics. It sat in the 600 x 600ft basin, which lay empty for the early part of the shoot and was only filled up when the lifeboat scenes were shot. Cameron had spent six months researching artefacts, drawings and plans to make the replica as detailed as possible.

He chose to build his *Titanic* on the starboard side after studying weather reports to determine which direction the funnel smoke blew but this posed problems for shooting the ship's departure from Southampton, as it was docked on its port side. Of course any writing on props and costumes had to be reversed and if someone walked to their right in the script, they had to walk left during shooting. In post-production, the film was flipped to the correct direction.

For Leo and Kate, who had lessons on etiquette from a full-time coach hired to instruct the cast on the manners of the upper-class gentility in 1912, their first scene together would be the most poignant – a nude scene, in which artist Jack sketches Rose wearing nothing but a stunning 'Heart of the Ocean' necklace. Both the jewel and the drawing – which was sketched by Cameron himself – become centrepieces to the plot. The interaction between Rose and Jack, however, would be crucial if audiences were to buy into their love story.

It was a tough first day on set for Winslet – to be naked in front of the entire crew – but Cameron had little choice because the set wasn't ready for many other scenes. The actress approached this sensitive moment with a remarkably business-like attitude. She arrived on set wearing nothing but a wrap-around gown and gave her startled co-star a sneak preview before disrobing in front of the rest of the crew. Yet, despite her bravado, she was nervous and Cameron felt he'd struck lucky that the scheduling meant they could capture the reality of the couple's vulnerability together.

'It wasn't by any kind of design, although I couldn't have designed it better,' he recalled. 'There's a nervousness and an energy and a hesitance in them. They had rehearsed together, but they hadn't shot anything together. If I'd had a choice, I probably would have preferred to put it deeper into the body of the shoot.' He added that because the set was still being prepared, 'we were scrambling around trying to fill in anything we could get to shoot.'

As the director tried to make best use of the shooting schedule, the set designers prepared one of the most elaborate ever sets used for a movie. The interior rooms, in particular, were breathtaking in their attention to detail. Using photographs and plans from the *Titanic*'s builders, the sets were reproduced exactly as originally built. The liner's first-class staircase, a key location in the script, was made of real wood and ultimately destroyed during the sinking scenes. Also, the *Titanic*'s original suppliers wove the first-class dining room carpet, using the original design and colours. Individual pieces of furniture, decorations, chairs, wall panelling, cutlery and crockery were meticulously reproduced, complete with the "White Star Line" crest on each piece. Even the ceilings – usually left incomplete on sets – were recreated.

For authenticity, Cameron relied on the expertise of *Titanic* historians Don Lynch (considered by many to be the most knowledgeable in the business) and Ken Marschall, an artist specialising in in the reproduction of authentic paintings of the iconic vessel. Many of the special effects shots were exact reproductions of Marschall's paintings, while Lynch was amazed when he finally got to walk around the ship, among the cast in their period costumes.

The initial amazement at the set and the delight in the two leads' ability to accurately convey their vulnerability were short-lived, however. By late autumn of 1996, reports started coming from the set that Cameron's notorious control freakery had hit new heights amid allegations that he wasn't paying due care and attention to crew safety.

As fears grew within the studios that costs were escalating, Cameron was under pressure. Early on in the shoot, he attempted to film one of the trickiest and most crucial scenes: the dramatic moment when the *Titanic* – the ship they said would be unsinkable – is finally submerged in water. Cameron was extremely definite about the circumstances of the vessel's final moments and distrusted earlier Hollywood versions that showed the liner gracefully sink into the water. Instead he wanted to record it, 'as the terrifyingly chaotic event that it really was.'

As the site of the wreckage confirms, the boat split in two before submerging and to recreate this, a section of the replica would be have to be lifted and upended. In order to portray the terrifying effect such an event would have had on the passengers, Cameron needed over 100 stunt people effectively tumbling from the upended hull. One stuntman broke an ankle, another cracked a rib and another cracked a cheekbone during 10 days of chaos as Cameron tossed both ship and crew about in trying to capture the vital shots.

'Luckily, nobody was hurt badly,' says stunt coordinator Simon Crane. 'We padded the set as much as we could so people could hit stuff and bounce.'

The incidents caused such concern within the Screen Actors Guild, however, that it sent a representative along to monitor the shoot, although ultimately found no evidence of negligence. To allay fears and cut costs, Cameron eventually replaced stuntmen with computer-generated versions of them.

Amid all this upheaval, Bill Mechanic, chairman and CEO of Fox Filmed Entertainment, arrived in Mexico for urgent discussions on the budget. He politely handed the director a two-page typed list of scenes that the studio wished to cut from the script in order to save money. According to witnesses, Cameron glanced at the memo and said bluntly: 'If you want to cut my film, you'll have to fire me. And to fire me, you'll have to kill me.'

Mechanic left fearing the worst but within weeks, when Cameron had cooled down, he agreed to certain money-saving changes, many involving computer-generated imagery instead of real action footage. Yet, although Cameron had managed to fend off the studio executives and concerned union officials, he still had to deal with grumbles about working conditions on set. Reports continued to leak about the dangerous working conditions, 90-hour working weeks, endless night shoots and the director's angry outbursts.

Kate Winslet would confirm later: 'If anything was the slightest bit wrong, he would lose it.' She did stress, however, that the director would never scream at the cast, adding: 'I think Jim knew he couldn't shout at us the way he did to his crew because our performances would be no good.' When her comments – made to the *Times*, just after she finished filming – went around, Kate feared she'd been misconstrued and sent a letter to the *Los Angeles Times*, saying: 'At the time of the interview I had just returned to London after months of a long, physically and emotionally demanding shoot, and I must admit I was "blowing off steam".'

Nevertheless, the making of *Titanic* confirmed Cameron's reputation as 'the scariest man in Hollywood'. Cast and crew on the film followed on from their counterparts on *The Abyss* (1989) in nicknaming the taskmaster a modern-day 'Captain Bligh' for his uncompromising stance and dictatorial style of working. According to *The Times*, he became known as a '300-decibel screamer with a megaphone and walkie-talkie, swooping down into people's faces on a 162ft crane.

'"God damn it!" he would yell at some poor crew member. "That's exactly what I didn't want!"'

The trouble wasn't that Cameron wasn't prepared to lead from the front – many times he got into the water himself to search for the perfect shot – but that he expected others to share his own attitude. Responding to a charge from one former crewmember – 'Cameron loves pain' – he replied: 'I don't love pain. I love results, and sometimes results require pain.'

His leading actors would certainly testify to that. Winslet chipped a bone in her elbow and routinely feared she would drown in the huge tank, while DiCaprio was nearly crushed by a horse during one sequence. Then, while shooting a storm scene (which involved them being lashed to the railings), both were left stranded for over an hour when a real storm blew up and the rest of the crew abandoned the set. Indeed Winslet was so upset after that ordeal, filming was reportedly halted for the rest of the day.

'He's so impassioned about what he's doing,' explained Danny Nucci (who played Jack's free-spirited Italian buddy, Fabrizio). 'And because he has the power and the money at this point in his career, he'll redo the shot, change it around, rehearse it, or shoot it again and again if that's what it takes. Yeah, he'd yell and scream, but he was just yelling because he was frustrated. After three months, I got used to it.'

During this time it was almost impossible to find a kind word written about *Titanic*. Persistent reports appeared in the press about the changing release date, abusive working conditions endured by the cast and crew, as well as the fact that the film was wildly over budget. Cameron developed a siege mentality but considered himself unfairly maligned. When a construction worker was seriously injured after falling from a scaffold and had to undergo an emergency splenectomy (surgery to remove a damaged spleen), it was a film company doctor rather than a construction firm medic who got him to hospital. What might have been a tale about how the safety provision on set saved a man's life was spun as further evidence of a director being out of control.

Come December, everyone needed a well-earned break and Cameron granted both cast and crew a three-week sojourn. Meanwhile, the director faced another stand off with Fox executive Bill Mechanic as costs continued to rise.

'Bill was freaking out because they ran the numbers and figured out we couldn't make any money off this film, even if it was a hit,' recalled Cameron. 'So I said, "OK, we're fucked. It's my responsibility, take my salary!"' In waiving his fee and share of the profits, Cameron was potentially giving up millions of dollars, although he did get to keep his sizeable screenwriting fee.

'Nobody was ready for a movie this big,' Mechanic explained. 'It was on a massive scale. No one had ever tried anything like it.'

As the weeks rolled into months – seven in all to complete all the filming – tensions grew increasingly strained on set.

Kate and Leo were required to sit in cool water in wringing wet clothes for an hour a day as they acted out their lead roles in a movie where the budget slowly rose towards the $180 million mark. As the crew worked in wet suits, the 'talent' had to make do with a hot tub to plunge into once the scene was over, lest they recreate the effects of the icy water on the victims for real.

'This experience was new to me because I had never done a film of this size before. A normal action film would be entirely different – this was well beyond that. Some of the things we did were unbelievable,' Leonardo recalls.

He went on to describe some of the situations he was put through: 'There were times when I was sitting up on the back of a hydraulic poop deck, strapped on with Kate – with 20 cranes around me, lights everywhere, Jim Cameron swooping on a crane and a camera directed straight at my face – and I thought, "Where am I?"

'There were people on bungee cords flying below us as the thing was rocking back and forth; stunt guys were tumbling over each other. Then we had to do our lines and scream and everything. It was crazy – I was in genuine terror half the time.'

That he got through it all was thanks in no small measure to the relationship he had built up with his co-star, Kate Winslet. Their closeness did not spill over to an off-screen romance but it's clear they formed a friendship for life. 'I think the movie would have been twice as hard if it hadn't been for Kate and the fact that we got on so well,' he revealed. 'It was important to keep the on-screen chemistry going – we both truly like each other.'

But the stresses and strains on the *Titanic* movie set took their toll on Leonardo, too. He recalls: 'There were many times when I was in tears. It was the toughest shoot, lasting for six or seven months, and Kate Winslet and I were both driven very hard in a lot of difficult water scenes. There was no point in complaining – we were filming in a giant tank in Mexico and the film was costing a fortune.

'So, all the complaining in the world was done in privacy, with just the two of us. We did not have to vent it on anyone else. Sometimes Kate was in tears, other times I was, and occasionally we both were; it was that kind of a job. But Kate is awesome. She is beautiful, tremendously talented, has a great sense of humour and is really down to earth – I don't think England realises yet what a treasure she is.'

And he later confided to talk show host Oprah Winfrey: 'If it wasn't for her [Winslet], making that film we would have been shrapnel. It was the toughest film we ever had to make. We were partners together – we held each other's hand and supported each other.'

After filming wrapped, Kate revealed she'd initially feared she and Leo would have the right chemistry and she even worried his boyish good looks would be a distraction, but her concerns proved unfounded.

'We hit it off straightaway,' she said. 'It really wasn't a problem. I'd thought that possibly it would be a problem. He might have had an incorrect assumption of what I might be like, being English. I was as relaxed as I possibly could be with Leo when I first met him. I did think to myself beforehand, "It's going to be hard because what if I really fancy him?" – I so thought I was going to because he is absolutely gorgeous, there's no two ways about it. The closeness that we have is something a lot of my female friends envy like hell but, to me, he is just silly old Leo.'

There were persistent rumours that Leonardo and Cameron came close to blows at one stage but, publicly at least, DiCaprio paid tribute to the director's expertise at the helm: 'He spent a surprising amount of effort and detail on that. He is extremely passionate about what he does and lets you know right away if you are not giving your best. He demands that everyone is extremely focused.'

And he added: 'It takes somebody with a general-like attitude to storm the beaches of Normandy, to start an epic battle, which is what this film was to me.'

Although the shoot was plagued by negative reports, Winslet

revealed she did her best to ignore them. 'I shut out all those kind of politics and never really knew anything about the budget,' she observed. 'I think it's really sad that when we did finish shooting, eventually – and, yes, we did run over, and it was seven months and all of that stuff – that people hone in on that side of things. It's easy to be negative about something like that. But, no, that money was spent for a reason and it's up there on the screen.'

On 21 and 22 March 1997 came the final two days of shooting – and they were among the most dangerous. The underwater implosion of the *Titanic*'s bridge meant thousands of gallons of water were sent crashing through tempered glass. To make sure the shot went smoothly, Cameron slipped into a wetsuit and manned the camera himself.

When filming was at last completed, there was a huge party to celebrate. The satisfaction of a job well done, combined with a collective feeling of relief, led to a raucous night of revelry. And it was no surprise when party boy Leonardo danced raunchily on the tables.

For the cast, their ordeal was finally over. Yet for Cameron, his battle was in many ways just beginning. He came away from the shoot with about 12 days of footage – three times the length of the original voyage. By then the relationship between Fox and Paramount looked set to split like the hull of the liner. When more editors were needed to sift through the vast volumes of footage, both companies argued as to who should foot the bill.

Money wasn't the only problem, however. A huge row was erupting over *Titanic*'s release date, originally set for 2 July (Independence Day weekend in the States). When it became clear that there was no way Cameron would have the film finished in time, Fox pushed for a postponement to August (Paramount's thinking was that this was too late to cash in on the crucial summer blockbuster market and they believed it would be better to hold off until the November). For Fox, this posed a problem. Already it had two big movies – *Alien Resurrection* and *Anastasia* – coming out for the Thanksgiving weekend.

With the studios at loggerheads, Cameron felt under siege by the constant speculation in the press. Out of desperation, he fought back against his critics, writing to *The Los Angeles Times* on 5 May to call for a sense of perspective. Denying the reports and defending his methods, he ranted: 'Am I driven? Yes. Absolutely. Out of control? Never. Unsafe? Not on my watch.'

Eventually a compromise was reached on the release date, with the studios agreeing to a 19 December launch. The film would hit cinemas in time to be considered for the Oscars, but Fox and Paramount were still squabbling about territories. As Paramount prepared to throw its weight behind the North American release, Fox nipped in and scheduled an overseas launch at the Tokyo Film Festival on 1 November.

After moments when it seemed the movie would never be made, a sense of anticipation greeted the initial screenings. At a final cost of over $200 million, the weight of expectation hung heavily around Cameron's neck. The press, which had gleefully dived in when reports of unrest filtered from the set, now lined up to pen '*Titanic* sunk' reviews in which they condemned the over-bloated waste of money.

Everyone connected with the film took a deep breath; Leonardo was no exception. Breaking with his own tradition, he took the precaution of twice attending screenings ahead of the premiere, 'just to get used to it.' And he was amazed by what he saw. 'For the first, I was watching my own performance,' he recalled. 'On the second, I was just swept away by the brilliant job that everyone has done. For once, this is more than a film – it is an immense experience.'

Leonardo DiCaprio was impressed. It was now a matter of time to see if cinema audiences would feel the same way.

CHAPTER 11

THE LAUNCH OF 'LEO-MANIA'

Standing side by side in front of the ladies' mirror, best friends Ashley and Katie checked their hairdos one last time before emerging. They could have been any two friends about to embark on a date – except they were only 12, they were at the cinema and both only had eyes for the same man.

'Leo is soooooo cute!' swooned Ashley, who was in a hurry to get a good seat for the 4.15pm showing of *Titanic* at the Garden Grove's Four Star Cinema, in Orange County, Los Angeles.

'Yeah,' confirmed Katie. 'They had only front row last time we saw it – but who cares? He's soooo worth it!'

It was February 1998 and *The Los Angeles Times* was conducting an investigation into what was making *Titanic* so popular at the box office, such was its phenomenal performance eight weeks after premiering.

Fellow fan Alex O'Gorman had seen the movie five times by then and she admitted to the paper that she still screamed whenever DiCaprio arrived on the big screen. 'The last time I saw it, the part when he comes in his tuxedo – my friend and I screamed,' she says.

By early 1998, any thoughts that *Titanic* had been a costly risk – and even the $200 million price tag – had been swept away. A shrewd investment was how Fox and Paramount's involvement was now being viewed. At three hours, 14 minutes long, the movie was already being described as a modern-day *Gone with the Wind*. Some analysts were claiming the ship itself – aided by director Cameron's amazing special effects – was the real star but teenage cinema-goers begged to differ.

'Face it, the parts without Leo are boring,' one 13-year-old girl (who'd seen the movie several times) insisted, before adding: 'To be honest, I don't think any of my friends care about watching the *Titanic* sink again – it's Leo we want to see.'

'He's hot!' said Nicole, 14, who went to see the film five times with friends Christina, 15, and Samantha, 15, and was gutted to learn the next two showings were completely sold out.

In the early days of the movie's release few could have predicted it would go on to provide such a strong showing. Renowned film critic David Thomson of the *Guardian* recalled: 'When this film was shown to the press in the autumn of 1997, it was with massive foreboding. The people in charge of the screenings believed they were on the verge of losing their jobs because of this great albatross of a picture on which, finally, two studios had had to combine to share the great load of its making.'

For *The Los Angeles Times*, film critic Kenneth Turan was particularly scathing, claiming the movie bombed, not because of the impressive climatic sinking scenes but because of the lame love story at its heart. 'What audiences end up with, word-wise, is a hackneyed, completely derivative copy of old Hollywood romances,' he wrote, 'a movie that reeks of phoniness and lacks even minimal originality.'

Awarding *Titanic* just one star out of four, the *San Francisco Examiner*'s Barbara Shulgasser ranted: 'The number of times in this unbelievably badly-written script that the two lead characters refer to each other by name was an indication of just how dramatically the script lacked anything more interesting for the actors to say.'

Some reviewers were kinder to the two lead stars. American online critic James Berardinelli praised Cameron for choosing 'two of today's finest young actors' and went on to say that Leonardo, who had 'rarely done better work, has shed his cocky image. Instead, he's likable and energetic in this part – two characteristics vital to establishing Jack as a hero.' And Gene Siskel, one half of the legendary Siskel & Ebert At the Movies TV film critic duo, called Leo's performance 'captivating.'

Yet such was the vitriol aimed in Cameron's direction that the *Guardian*'s David Thomson felt some reviewers just wanted to be kind out of sympathy. He said: 'Some of us came out of the advance screenings and in a simple effort to spread a little comfort, we said things like "Well, really, it's not too bad. I think some people may like it."'

Yet despite the pessimism from the press, some audiences certainly did like it. Opening weekend takings were fairly strong for a film of that magnitude but not overwhelming. *Titanic* topped the US film charts with $28.6 million, fending off a challenge from the latest James Bond release, *Tomorrow Never Dies*. It failed to surpass the figures set by the previous chart-topper, *Scream 2*, which had made $33 million on its opening weekend, though.

But then instead of falling off as most new movies do, takings actually increased the following weekend – up to $35.4 million – as word spread about the spectacle on offer. On week three, it took $33.3 million, while a month after release it was taking an extremely healthy $29.2 million. The film's biggest single day was on Valentine's Day, 14 February, when it raked in $13 million, more than six weeks later. It stayed at No. 1 for 15 weeks – a record for any film – and by March 1998 had become the first movie to earn more than a billion worldwide. Internationally, it would be just as successful ($1.2 billion overseas), helping *Titanic* earn a whopping total of $1.8 billion, a record it would hold for 12 years until Cameron's next epic, *Avatar*.

Although few so-called experts were quick to spot the 'Leo-effect' in the film's success, his publicists were in no doubt as to what the movie was doing for his popularity. 'We get an enormous bag of mail a day from all over the world,' his publicist Cindy Guagenti revealed. 'We are besieged.'

And his stunning popularity came as no surprise to Cathee Sandstrom, editor of *BB* and *BOP*, top US teen fan magazines. 'Leo's the biggest draw as far as actors go right now,' she said. 'We got a huge response to him after *Romeo + Juliet* and now with *Titanic*, they can't get enough of him.'

Sandstrom said she'd heard of some girls going to see the film 17 times, with some writing in that they would 'do just about anything' for the chance to meet their hero. As she explained, fans would 'get pretty creative' to achieve their dream of meeting him. 'One girl even sent us a letter saying her friend would kill herself if she couldn't meet him,' she said, before adding: 'They have a lot of disposable income and they do see movies again and again.'

The 4 Star Cinema in Garden Grove, Orange County was typical of what was happening at multiplexes around the US. Manager Yaron Israel told *The Los Angeles Times*: 'We see the same faces every week, especially the little girls. They have their napkins, they're crying all the time. I don't know where they get the money, but they do. They love Leonardo DiCaprio.'

Fans of the film were also buying the soundtrack in massive numbers, making it No. 1 for three weeks. The main title song, 'My Heart Will Go On' performed by Celine Dion, was a worldwide smash, selling more than two million copies. On radio stations throughout America, however, the most requested version was the one that included clips of dialogue from the movie.

The key sound bite hitting a chord with listeners was the moment when Jack declares his undying love for Rose while freezing to death in the water: 'Promise me that you'll never give up,' DiCaprio utters with his last breath. 'Promise me now, Rose.'

Even Leo's reported first love, Jennifer Faus, admitted to longings for her childhood sweetheart after being taken to see *Titanic* by her husband, Sergio.

'Seeing Leonardo kiss Kate Winslet did bring back a few memories for me,' she said. 'I wish I had appreciated our kissing a bit more at the time, but it was nice to think he had some practice with me. Until I saw that movie, I couldn't understand why so many girls were in love with him. To me, he was just little Leo from high school.'

And the longer the run continued, the more times audiences returned to see it. Some girls claimed they'd seen the movie as many as 40 times. One Leonardo biographer, Douglas Thompson, said of the repeat viewers: 'They go back time and time again just to see the first half of the film, before the ship hits the iceberg. For the real fans, there's not enough of Leo in the second half.'

The growth of 'Leo-Mania' – the phenomenon that did so well for *Romeo + Juliet* – was gold dust for the studio bosses. But quickly had a profoundly negative effect on Leo's life.

It's understood that as the clamour around her long-time boyfriend grew, Kristen Zang began to feel the heat. The couple had been dating since the end of 1995 and they were said to be planning to buy a house together on Malibu Beach before filming on *Titanic* began. Friends revealed that during that arduous process, the model started to realise that she would soon have to share Leonardo with the rest of the world. Showing maturity beyond her years, she foresaw a future where he would have to demonstrate the willpower of a saint not to succumb to temptation as girls threw themselves at him. As the media interest intensified, her feelings cooled and much as it pained her to say it, she had to bring matters to a head.

Kristen, it was reported, took Leonardo out for a meal and told him: 'You're about to become the biggest actor in the world with women throwing themselves at you. It's going to be impossible for you to stay committed to me. To save ourselves grief and heartbreak, it's best we just stay friends.'

Leo, in turn, was devastated. Until that moment he hadn't considered the attention would have a knock-on effect when it came to his personal life. He was swiftly seeing the downside of worldwide fame. Not for the first time he questioned whether this was what he'd gone into acting for.

And so it was that at the London premiere of *Titanic* on 18 November 1997, it was mum Irmelin and not Kristen who accompanied him. Missing from the London event was Kate Winslet, who was in hospital after being struck down by a stomach bug returning from filming her latest movie Hideous Kinky in Morocco. Leo took time out from his busy promotional schedule to visit the actress in hospital in west London, but although she was released two days later it was the beginning of a difficult few weeks for Kate. She would also miss the Los Angeles premiere on 14 December because she was in London attending the funeral of her former boyfriend, the actor Stephen Tredre, who'd died of bone cancer aged 34.

Although the crowds came out in force for Leo in his home city, it was nothing like the reception he'd received in Tokyo on 1 November for the world premiere, where 3,000 fans, screaming 'Romeo, Romeo', had charged the theatre. As 250 police with riot gear tried to control the throng and Leo was smuggled in through a back door. A stunned James Cameron remarked that it was 'the most unbelievable scene I have ever been party to'.

Leo's relationship with Kristen Zang may have ended, but he'd still followed through on plans to move out of the house he shared with his mother. Some reports claimed his new house was a modest place, certainly by Hollywood standards, not far from hers, but the *Sun* described it as a 'fabulous $2 million mansion, with six bathrooms, three bedrooms and a master suite, which boasts polished wooden floors, 18ft ceilings, glittering chandeliers, five fireplaces, a marble Jacuzzi, plus a steam shower, sauna and gym.' There was also a 'media room', complete with 8ft TV and cinema screens, and separate servants' quarters. The landscaped gardens, with a view to the Pacific Ocean, included a koi carp pond and a grotto. Among Leo's new neighbours was the legendary Elizabeth Taylor.

Despite the interest in him, publicly Leo was at pains to stress how desperate he was to remain grounded: 'The main thing for me is just to maintain my life with my family and my friends. They treat me like Leo, not like Leonardo, master thespian. That's all I need to maintain my sanity.'

Also joining him in London was his 'Oma' Helene as he tried to quell suggestions that he would party the night away in England by claiming instead that all he was interested in seeing was some museums. His grandmother, meanwhile, lapped up the high life, telling reporters: 'I sat just behind Prince Charles and then Leonardo and I had dinner afterwards. It was thrilling. But I know all this fame won't go to his head. And he knows he will always be my grandson and I'll be his Oma.'

In January 1998, the movie had turned its success at the cinemas into gongs, picking up the first of an impressive haul of awards at the Golden Globes, traditionally an early indicator of Oscar success. There it scooped four for Best Motion Picture (Drama), Best Director, Best Original Score and Best Song. Although Leo was nominated, as were Kate Winslet and Gloria Stuart, he lost out to Peter Fonda for *Ulee's Gold*. He did, however, pick up the Blockbuster Entertainment Award for Favorite Actor, the MTV Movie Award for Best Performance and further MTV awards with Kate Winslet for Best On-Screen Duo and Best Kiss, but it remained to be seen if his performance would merit a nod from the Academy.

The international success prompted some to adjust their opinions. In the UK, the popular *Empire* magazine tied itself in knots over what stance to take. Initially giving the movie five stars, it then downgraded it to two after a public backlash began against its success, before reinstating the original mark.

Filmmaker Robert Altman was not so forgiving, however, declaring: '*Titanic*, I thought, was the most dreadful piece of work I've ever seen in my entire life.'

As James Cameron allowed himself to hope that he might follow up his Golden Globe success at the Oscars, the director found time to hit back at the critics who had initially panned the scale of the movie. He was particularly scathing towards *LA Times* critic Turan, saying: 'Simmering in his own bile, year after year, he has become further and further removed from the simple joyful experience of movie-watching, which, ironically, probably attracted him to the job in the first place.'

Cameron also attempted to put a finger on the movie's phenomenal success. '*Titanic*' is not a film that is sucking people in with flashy hype and spitting them out onto the street, feeling let down and ripped off,' he said. 'They are returning again and again to repeat an experience that is taking a 3-hour and 14-minute chunk out of their lives, and dragging others with them so they can share the emotion. Parents are taking their kids, adults are taking their parents. People from 8 to 80 (literally) are connecting with this film. Audiences around the world are celebrating their own essential humanity by going into a dark room and crying together.'

When the Academy Award nominations were announced, *Titanic* dominated the field with 14 – the most since Joseph L. Mankiewicz's *All About Eve* (1950). Although Kate Winslet's performance was acknowledged in the Best Actress category and there was a Best Supporting Actress nomination for Gloria Stuart, there were no awards for Leo. It was a particularly cruel snub by the Academy, who chose to overlook the impact his performance had had on millions of fans. And the news infuriated those fans, prompting several hundred to phone and 200 to email in their protests to Los Angeles once the nominations were announced.

There was simply no precedent to the strength of feeling. Sherry Lansing, head of films at Paramount, tried to find one by comparing the heartthrob's fame to Frank Sinatra in his early days. But she added: 'The frenzy is not just about Leo's looks, but his talent.'

Yet while Leo's popularity was being likened to that once enjoyed by John Wayne, Mel Gibson, Tom Cruise, Clark Gable, James Stewart, Henry Fonda, Cary Grant or Paul Newman, stargazers were quick to point out that, far from being the rugged all-action hero, DiCaprio's image was more that of the sensitive poet-hero, the beautiful waif with heart. His androgynous looks reminded some more of a young David Bowie and the hysteria he induced in 14-year-old girls closer to the music world than cinema.

Critic Owen Gleiberman said that Leo's performance in *Titanic* was 'underrated' because his Jack was 'such a jocular, self-sacrificing romantic sweetheart that everyone assumed DiCaprio was simply a nice-kid actor playing himself.' And Lindsay Doran, president of United Artists, said that for those looking for a precedent to Leo-mania, a more apt precedent is the Beatles.

'People are confusing his looks with his talent,' he told *The New York Times*. 'Look at the Beatles. It was the power of the music that created the emotion that got all mixed up with how adorable those guys were. Nothing will change that.'

Certainly, ahead of the Oscars, the fact that Leonardo had managed to carve out a career that so far avoided the clichéd testosterone-heavy action films such as *Top Gun* and *Lethal Weapon* was an achievement in itself.

But although *Titanic* was in the running for so many awards, DiCaprio didn't bother to make an appearance. James Cameron revealed the actor left a message for him the day before breaking the news, saying, 'It just ain't me, bro.' Cameron duly dubbed him 'a spoiled punk' for what he deemed to be his pompous attitude.

Defending himself later, Leonardo explained: 'It wasn't a pompous attitude. My reasoning was that I didn't really understand the reason to go up the red carpet to the Academy Awards if you weren't personally nominated – it's kind of that simple. But to go through that whole ritual is kind of showing up at an awards ceremony just for the sake of showing up – you know, it's just not me.'

With magazine cover stories appearing with titles such as 'WAS LEO ROBBED?', the actor chose to spend Oscars night dining in a sushi bar in New York's Greenwich Village. What he missed was *Titanic* sweeping the board with 11 Oscars, including the coveted gongs for Best Picture and Best Director. The film equalled the success of *Ben-Hur* (1959) and would be matched by *The Lord of the Rings: The Return of the King* at the 2004 Oscars.

Collecting his award for Best Director, James Cameron thanked his 'killer cast', giving special mention to Kate Winslet and Gloria Stuart – two of only three nominees who failed to win an Oscar – but when he came to Leo, he threw his hands up in the air as if to say, 'wherever he may be'. Listing these two women and the other key cast members, he said: 'You guys gave me pure gold every day and I share this gold with you.'

Going on to thank his parents, who were in the audience to witness his finest hour as a director, Cameron closed his speech with a somewhat cringe-worthy declaration that he was 'King of the World' in homage to Leonardo's iconic exclamation on the bow of the ship.

Although Oscar glory continued to elude Leonardo, he could console himself with the knowledge that he and Kate Winslet were considered the Most Romantic Couple in Movie History, according to a poll of US cinema-goers. And his scene where Jack grabs Rose by the waist and takes her flying through the air with the movie's haunting soundtrack in the background was voted One of the Most Romantic Scenes in Cinema History, up there with Clark Gable telling Vivien Leigh he doesn't give a damn in *Gone with the Wind*, Meg Ryan and Tom Hanks finally meeting on the Empire State

Building in *Sleepless in Seattle*, Humphrey Bogart saying goodbye to Ingrid Bergman in *Casablanca* and Patrick Swayze running his hands along Demi Moore's arms as she works pottery in *Ghost*.

Leo may perhaps have turned his nose up at these accolades but one thing he couldn't deny was that he was now ingrained in the nation's consciousness and part of one of the most iconic movies in history. And, at 23, he was also far and away the hottest heartthrob in Hollywood. Named one of *People* magazine's 25 Most Intriguing People, his face was now appearing on the covers of glossy magazines because it guaranteed extra sales.

As the film's takings bypassed *Star Wars* and *Jurassic Park* to become the biggest movie ever, interest in Leonardo DiCaprio showed no signs of fading.

'Aside from the fact he's drop-dead gorgeous, it has to do with the pining factor,' explained Amy Paulse, executive editor of *Teen People*. 'Girls feel they could save him. They feel they could've taken the poison away from Romeo. They fantasize and pine away for this unattainable heroic figure and he supplies it.'

Many critics were now acknowledging DiCaprio's role in *Titanic*'s staggering success. John Burman, the *Hollywood Reporter*'s international news director, said: 'DiCaprio is poised to enter the upper echelon of Hollywood power. He will be able to get a film made based on his name alone.'

However, the next test of Leo's popularity would come all too quickly. The release of *The Man in the Iron Mask* (1998), a movie he had signed up to while still in the throws of his *Titanic* experience, had been delayed because of the overruns of the Cameron juggernaut. It was more the type of film he would have made, had his career not been recently interrupted a major blockbuster. Written, produced and directed by Randall Wallace, the screenwriter behind Mel Gibson's Oscar-winning Scottish epic *Braveheart* (1995), *The Man in the Iron Mask* was by no means low budget. Costing $30 million, it teamed up DiCaprio with a meaty cast of veterans: John Malkovich, Gabriel Byrne, Jeremy Irons and Gérard Depardieu.

Leonardo took on the dual role of the cruel French King Louis XIV and his twin brother, Philippe. Loosely based on Alexandre Dumas' *D'Artagnan Romances*, the story centres on the aging Musketeers Athos, Porthos, Aramis and D'Artagnan and carries many similarities to the 1939 film version. To master the part, Leo had to accurately portray the spoilt and promiscuous King Louis and his brother Philippe, who is imprisoned in an iron mask to disguise his true identity. When the musketeers (who, as disaffected royalists have hatched a plan to replace Louis with Philippe) rescue Philippe, he must try to convince everyone he is king. However, despite the horrendous ordeal of being imprisoned by his own brother, he cannot adopt his sinister ways and is therefore discovered by D'Artagnan, the one musketeer not to go through with the plot.

For Leo, the challenging nature of the two roles and the release of the movie couldn't have come at a better time. Instead of playing the romantic lead in a movie that had audiences of both sexes reaching for their hankies, here he was both villain and hero. Indeed it was a quick opportunity to remind cinema-goers that he was a serious actor: 'For me it was an awesome experience acting with those guys and also playing a dual role.'

Although filming was set in Paris, he found there was no escape from 'Leo-Mania'. Some of his closest friends – Tobey Maguire, Jonah Johnson and Ethan Suplee – joined him in France, but when they tried to take in Leonardo da Vinci's *Mona Lisa* during a trip to the Louvre on a day off from filming, they were chased by a gang of screaming fans. Hordes of teenage girls also discovered their apartment nearby on the Champs Elysées and staked it out.

Attention from adoring fans aside, Leonardo more than equipped himself on set alongside his seasoned co-stars. Randall Wallace recalled: 'From the first day of filming, there was never any question Leo was in their league. He was a peer, absolutely.'

DiCaprio's presence in the historical drama gave an added spice to the film's opening in March 1998. Following his contribution, it was considered the first real challenger to *Titanic*'s dominance, which had comfortably remained in top spot since the December. In movie terms it was being heralded as the iceberg that could finally sink the all-conquering movie.

Wallace said: 'I suspect Leo-Mania helps draw people to both movies. And don't forget, when he was making *Titanic* and I was signing him for *Iron Mask*, it was widely expected that *Titanic* would be one of the biggest disasters in Hollywood history.'

As it was, *Iron Mask* came extremely close to knocking *Titanic* off its perch. On its opening weekend, it grossed nearly $17.3 million, just $300,000 short of *Titanic*, but not enough to dislodge it. Still, for DiCaprio, a total of $35 million from two films was further evidence of his burgeoning power at the box office.

Hollywood Reporter's John Burman said that even though *Iron Mask* failed to get to No. 1, this did nothing to halt Leonardo DiCaprio's rising star status. 'The press can't get enough of him,' said Burman, who predicted he could now make triple or quadruple the $2.5 million he made on *Titanic*, such was the demand for his presence.

Hollywood observers speculate whether he is indeed a new Brando or simply the latest flash in the pan. 'I think he's the real deal,' says film historian and writer Stephen Spignesi, who penned a book on all things *Titanic*. 'When I saw *Gilbert Grape*, I was floored. I couldn't believe it was a performance. And in *Titanic*, he's brilliant. Even a couple of questionable moments for his character, he pulls them off.'

'When you saw him in *Gilbert Grape* and *Basketball Diaries*, you knew he was not just a keen observer of life, but he has a real affection for it,' says Randall Wallace. 'He's a tremendously instinctive actor and also an intelligent actor, which is a fantastic combination. And he's also smart enough not to let his intelligence overwhelm his instincts. Whatever he decides to do, I think he will do well.'

'He proved himself a good actor at an early age,' said Amy Paulse of *Teen People*. 'He definitely has staying power.'

It was impossible to believe that only months before some critics were dismissing Leo as being too young to play a poverty-stricken artist who had lived a bohemian life in Paris, sketching prostitutes and wasn't weathered enough to suggest he might have lived rough by his own wits. He wasn't a man, but a boy-child of an actor, said some. Professional critic Camille Paglia even described him as resembling a '13-year-old lesbian.'

As *Titanic* passed the 1 billion mark, some industry analysts declaring as much as half of that figure might have been generated solely by Leo's presence. Before too long, his own publicists began to fear the hysteria was getting out of hand and worried he was becoming over-exposed. As Kerry Parnell, editor of the British magazine *Bliss* (aimed at girls from 12–18) confirmed when he topped the 1998 *Bliss* Boy Poll by an extraordinary margin: 'He got 70 per cent of the vote from 10,000 readers who wrote in, so he completely swept the board. Last year he came No. 28, so it's all happened incredibly fast. We've never had a phenomenon quite like him.'

Whether he liked it or not, it seemed the world was living on Planet Leo. In London, 8,000 fans stormed Leicester Square on 20 March for the British premiere of *The Man in the Iron Mask*. The cast were asked to stand away from the windows because their shadows were causing fans outside to hyperventilate – this was all before Leonardo had even arrived. One brandished a poster bearing the words 'LEO SEX GOD', while during the movie, many even screamed when a mask worn by DiCaprio simply appeared on screen.

In Japan, schoolgirls organised 'Leo cry parties', during which they gazed upon DiCaprio videos and wept. Then, in May, he chose not to attend the Cannes Film Festival for fear of being mobbed. With the hysteria at its height, *Premiere* magazine rated him No. 25 on its Top 100 Hollywood Power List; one place above Jeffrey Katzenberg, who runs the film studio DreamWorks with Steven Spielberg.

Spielberg himself even bemoaned: 'Any father would be proud to take Matt Damon home and introduce him to his favourite daughter. I know I would. Except, of course, *my* daughter, who is very taken with Leonardo DiCaprio.'

For Leonardo himself, 'Leo-Mania' did have its upsides, however. His astonishing popularity now meant spin-off benefits for his older movies. Blockbuster Entertainment reported that the combined rentals of *Marvin's Room*, *The Basketball Diaries* and *Romeo + Juliet* increased by 61 per cent in the three weeks after *Titanic* opened in the UK, while *Total Eclipse*, at one stage his first genuine flop, was now a highly sought-after commodity after because of Leo's full-frontal nude scene.

In May, the *Daily Telegraph* in the UK reported that Rupert Murdoch, whose 20th Century Fox distributed *Titanic* outside the US, was said to have gone out of his way to seek a meeting with DiCaprio. It said: 'It's unprecedented for studio bosses to seek out actors like that, but the rumour mill suggests Murdoch was concerned DiCaprio should not feel "left out" of all the Oscar acclaim showered on *Titanic*. And, of course, Murdoch would have wanted to assure him that Fox will gladly fund whatever his next film turns out to be.'

But the real craziness was still to come. The surreality of the 'Leo-Mania' crystallised one day when he was travelling in Europe and the previously mentioned 14-year-old girl grabbed his leg and held on for dear life. Even reputable magazines lost the plot, with *Time Magazine* running a bizarre article that focused on his shopping habits. 'He prints my grocery list. It's like, "Chuck steak, and deodorant, and broccoli,"' recalled DiCaprio. 'I seemed like the most immature, juvenile punk in all of these articles that were written about me.'

What was getting lost in the coverage was that Leo was still trying to be a grounded individual. In 1998, he and his mother donated $35,000 for a 'Leonardo DiCaprio Computer Center' at the Los Feliz branch of the Los Angeles Public Library, the site of his childhood home, rebuilt after the 1994 Northridge earthquake and opened in early 1999.

He was the hottest talent in town, of that there was no doubt. Manager Rick Yorn boasted that 15 scripts were waiting for Leo, all with offers of at least $15 million, while *Forbes Magazine* placed him at 34 in a list of the country's wealthiest entertainers. But, as the tills kept ringing, the more wearied by talk of the *Titanic* phenomenon, Leonardo himself became. 'I do not take success or failure personally at all,' he revealed. 'I am told it has made the most money in the world but I hate looking at figures and seeing results. How much and how fast? It is boring.

'I have also done a lot of small films of which I'm proud. They might not have been seen by many people but that doesn't make them worth less in my eyes.'

Increasingly he was starting to yearn publicly for some time off, a break from movie making. The last thing any of his fans wanted to hear was that he was giving up films for a year but he claimed to be exhausted after making 11 films in just five years.

Leonardo had gone straight from filming *Titanic* to work on *The Man in the Iron Mask* in France and he revealed these projects had left him 'emotionally drained' – 'I couldn't resist the film, with such a great cast, and I have no regrets but it was an exhausting process.'

He then added: 'I'm taking a year off. I want to slow down, because I have been working so hard. There are so many things that I have not had the chance to do, just because of work.

'Looking at lions, elephants and zebras in the wild is one of them. The strangest thing about Hollywood for me now is seeing the things I had wished and hoped for becoming a reality. It is a bizarre feeling, because even I don't believe it.

'It is the same with all the stories about my alleged sex appeal. I just don't see it. I am living through the experience and only later will I wake up and know what it feels like.'

Lamenting the sacrifices he had made to pursue movie stardom, he said: 'My problem is that I have not had a chance to live life. I started in films at 16 and I have gone from one to another. I have had to put aside all my other interests. I need to put back some energy and thoughts and experiences in my life. There are a lot of great advantages with this job, but some things that are not so good. Anonymity is to be cherished.

'I enjoy going where I'm not recognised. If I have to go to the wilds of Africa to do that, so be it.'

And when he planned to return to films, he was clear about one thing – he didn't want to play another romantic lead: 'I died as Romeo, and as Jack Dawson in *Titanic*. Perhaps they are trying to tell me something. I feel as if I have done those kinds of leads for now. I am not looking to play the super-hero either.

'At this moment, I feel I would sooner see a herd of wildebeest than face another film crew.'

Cameron might have tried to claim the title for himself but by mid-1998, Leonardo DiCaprio was the undoubted King of the World. The question facing him now, though, was how long would it be before that crown slipped?

CHAPTER 12

LOSING IT

Just like *Titanic*, in early 1998 Leonardo's wholesome image seemed unsinkable. To his army of teenage fans, he was the perfect man: ridiculously handsome, but a boy whose first loyalty was to his mum and who made sure his beloved grandma was seated next to royalty at premieres.

But within months of becoming the most sought-after heartthrob on the planet, Leonardo DiCaprio was heading straight for an iceberg. Amid the wild hysteria in the wake of *Titanic*'s sensational success, there had been little to suggest that Leo's public image could be holed below the water line. Sure, he had been linked to every available (or not) supermodel and actress, from Helena Christensen to Liv Tyler. Reports of his wild partying were now commonplace during any movie shoot, while allegations of an extreme bender in Miami Beach to bring in the New Year hadn't even come close to dampening public opinion about the golden boy.

And he'd survived reports following his Oscars' no-show: the reason being he ducked out because he was sporting a black eye after an allegedly bizarre altercation involving *Showgirls* star Elizabeth Berkley and her boyfriend. The story went that Leo –

whose favourite trick in getting a girl's attention was to slip his phone number into her bag – had come a cropper when Berkley's boyfriend Roger Wilson suspected she was flirting with the actor. Wilson had apparently tracked him down to a New York restaurant and got involved in a fistfight with the star's entourage. Leo's publicist insisted his shiner was simply the result of a run-in with a door but did seem to confirm a fight had indeed taken place. Cindy Guagenti said: 'Leo was never involved in the fight. He stayed inside until it was all over.' New York Police investigated the incident but detectives did not take things further with Leonardo.

As quickly as he'd become the world's biggest star so he had also emerged as one of Hollywood's biggest Casanovas. Un-named 'friends' were quoted in newspapers saying that Leo, who in many respects had been a late starter when it came to women, now had a new motto: 'So many girls, so little time.'

An unsubstantiated story started circulating that after seeing a picture of the beautiful model Amber Valletta in a magazine, he asked his people to fix up a date. And sightings of the couple walking the streets of New York suggested he'd got his wish. Pals seemed to be growing concerned for the star: 'He needs to settle down and find out what real love is all about', said one. 'He will go after any good-looking girl, famous or not,' declared another. 'He told one girl they'd join the "Mile High Club" by making love in a plane. He hired an executive jet, served her champagne with fresh strawberries and ice cream, and they made love while looking at the stars.'

Meanwhile, actress Nicole Becher now claimed to be the first girl to kiss Leo when they were teenage classmates. In what would soon become celebrity folklore, she said their noses bumped and they burst into giggles. 'I was the first girl he had kissed and we were both trying too hard.'

At the turn of the year he had been linked to stunning 20-year-old Vanessa Haydon – who was tipped to be the next supermodel –

after they were apparently spotted kissing and cuddling in New York and strolling in Central Park. His management denied a romance but by now it was becoming increasingly difficult to determine what was a genuine love interest or what was a PR stunt launched by ambitious young women who sensed a way of capitalising on Leo's reputation.

At the Paris after-show party of *The Man in the Iron Mask*, Leonardo was said to have been openly flirting with former Wonderbra model Eva Herzigova, despite the fact that she was married. And while he was in Havana and staying in the same hotel as supermodels Naomi Campbell and Kate Moss, his friend Eric Donovan said: 'Leo was really interested in Naomi and said he had to have her.'

Donovan claimed Leo and Naomi ended up in the hot tub together at the end of a party – 'It was hot and heavy between them and Leo wanted her badly but from what I understand she said no to a further relationship.'

Despite this, the world was being told that Naomi reacted angrily when she believed the then full-figured model Sophie Dahl was trying to muscle in on her man at a Paris party. Sophie confided in a friend that she was sitting at a table chatting to Leonardo, when Naomi, four years his senior, suddenly shrieked: 'Stop talking to my boyfriend!'

Outside, Sophie apparently tried to join the couple in their limo but Naomi, never one to knowingly walk away from an argument, was having none of it. She quickly slammed the door and slipped down the lock, leaving a bemused Sophie alone on the pavement.

Perhaps on a mission to wind Campbell up, Leonardo was next reported to be making a beeline for her friend Kate. He met up with Kate in London – at the time he was apparently seducing lap dancer Karen – and there was instant electricity. Whether that developed into anything more is open to question but while publicists might have been privately fretting over where all the constant speculation about Leo's love life was leading, he himself was more blasé. Talking about his romances, he said: 'Well, isn't that exactly what men my age are supposed to do? When you're my age, your hormones are kicking in and there's not much besides sex on your mind. But seriously, I don't want to be thought of as a party animal, the stereotypical young actor – I'm not like that.'

'I had fun,' was all he would concede, pointing out that he couldn't sleep with every woman he wanted, and that actually liking women was important to him, too – 'You always ask yourself, [Could I be in love with this one?] You're always yearning for a partner in life.' He went on: 'I like girls who are intelligent, funny and pretty, with a nice personality. I'd definitely say I am romantic when I'm alone with a girl. I'm doing the baby voices, all that stuff – rubbing noses, the whole thing. I'm getting embarrassed now...'

In an attempt to put across a more wholesome image he began talking about the pet lizard that he claimed he missed more than the company of women when he was away from home.

The bearded dragon, Blizz, accompanied him where possible. 'He's my pet lizard, a bearded dragon lizard,' he explained. 'I had him with me on the set of *Titanic*.'

He was at pains to convince people that he was still the vulnerable adolescent at heart. Although he enjoyed the company of supermodels, he was never happier just hanging out with friends playing ping-pong or on his PlayStation. He still liked to play the role of prankster on set, mimicking his directors and fellow cast members and playing pranks on crewmembers (mostly revolving around breaking wind). And he still missed his mother Irmelin. Even though he'd moved out of their house the previous November, he now admitted: 'You never realise how much you need your mum until the day you leave her.'

Yet, despite his attempts to dispel the myths surrounding his reputation, the claims kept coming. Soon it wasn't just kiss'n'tell girls hoping to make a fast buck who were lining up to discuss Leo's sex life. Ex-girlfriends and former co-stars couldn't help talking about DiCaprio's prowess, or so it seemed.

Kate Winslet, who told how she and Leo took turns to wee underwater while filming their sinking scenes, also revealed they would sneak off during breaks in filming on *Titanic* and snuggle up in DiCaprio's trailer to swap intimate secrets. She said: 'We were comparing notes on some very, very personal things and it got really graphic. He's very good at it and a lot of the sexual tips he gave me have worked!'

Then his former girlfriend Bridget Hall was quoted, albeit through a friend, chastising Leonardo for breaking her heart and being such a flop in bed. 'We had been good friends before we finally slept together,' she reportedly confided in a friend, who helpfully told the *Sun*. 'It was my first time and I wanted it to be so special. Then Leo dumped me and I was devastated.'

According to the paper, after taking the 5ft 11in Ralph Lauren model's virginity, Leonardo callously parted ways with Bridget. The 20-year-old model further confided: 'We had been good friends and we finally slept with each other at New York's Royalton Hotel.'

A source went on: 'After that she did not hear from him for weeks. Then he began calling her from the set of *Titanic* in Mexico, asking her to come down and see him. She went, but it just wasn't the same.'

Close friend George Wayne, a contributing editor for *Vanity Fair* magazine, was then quoted as saying: 'After that very important moment in the girl's life, he dumped her like a hot potato. Leonardo has to be attacked for having the nerve to deflower one of my very dear friends.'

A spokesman for the Arkansas beauty said: 'Bridget had a very short-lived friendship with Leonardo. They are not really friends any more.'

If Leo badly needed some positive PR, it came from an unlikely source. Kristen Zang chose that moment to go public with her feelings on the now much-maligned star. Zang came out to say what a passionate, tender lover he was. She was quoted as saying sex with him was 'the most wonderful experience in the world', adding: 'Being Leo's lover is like living out a glorious fantasy, even better than his millions of female fans have imagined it. I still tremble with excitement when I recall his lean body pressed against mine.'

The swimsuit model's breathless description of their 18-month affair appears in the US magazine *Star*. She says the 23-year-old actor doggedly pursued her 'like Jack did with Rose in *Titanic*', adding: 'He was determined to bed me, but I never wanted him to think I was easy. Leo was my knight in shining armour. He's a tender lover who could make any girl putty in his hands.'

Leonardo's astonishing prowess with women was even rubbing off on his lookalikes. Oliver Martin, an 18-year-old student from Berkshire, England, revealed how his life had been transformed ever since *Titanic* came out simply because he was the spitting image of Leo. He said women liked to call out the name of his famous alter-ego during sex and told how many of his conquests requested he recreate scenes from the world's biggest movie.

Oliver revealed: 'I met this beautiful blonde at a club called Harpers in Guildford. When we left together, she said we couldn't go back to her parents' house so we stripped off in the back of her Fiesta. All the windows got steamed up just like they did in *Titanic*. Only there wasn't quite as much space in the Fiesta as there was in the motor in the film.'

After months of unprecedented interest, DiCaprio was definitely fighting a rearguard action. In March 1998 he took legal action to prevent American magazine *Playgirl* from publishing his nude shot from *Total Eclipse* in their July issue. The magazine's move had already prompted editor-in-chief Ceslie Armstrong to claim she'd quit because of the invasion of the star's privacy. Then *New York Magazine* took a pop at his lifestyle, claiming Leonardo and his showbiz pals were now essentially a marauding gang called the 'Pussy Posse' with DiCaprio as its leader.

The magazine claimed the gang was a regular feature of New York nightlife, prowling clubs looking for action. And it termed the hordes of young girls willing to offer themselves to the gang's every whim 'Leo-Maniacs' – the models, actresses and affluent hangers-on desperate to be associated with them.

'When he goes to a club, people start screaming and jumping over the security guards, and elbowing and pushing to get near him,' *New York Magazine* reported.

The Pussy Posse's core members included long-time pal Tobey Maguire, *Witness* actor Lukas Haas, Harmony Korine, writer of *Kids* and director *of Gummo*, David Blaine, then a budding young street magician. Sara Gilbert, the one-time romantic interest for Leo, was also a long-standing buddy. Scores of other young actors whose names were not yet recognisable had apparently dropped everything to be a part of the gang. 'All they do now is hang out with Leo,' one young actor, who did not wish to be identified, explained.

According to *New York Magazine*, every night was a party and Leo's gang was becoming known as the new Rat Pack. Upstairs at Moomba, downstairs at Veruka, in the special extra VIP room at Life, everyone wanted a part of 'Leo-Mania' and his posse was only too happy to oblige. 'The models are all over him,' Jeffrey Jah, director of Life, said. 'He's got rock stars, Puff Daddy, and Donald Trump going over to his table to sit with him. Leo just comes in to hang out with his friends.'

The unnamed actor continued: 'If Leo wants to go to Paris, it's let's go to Paris. Las Vegas? No problem.' On Oscars night, when the posse was getting into trouble with Elizabeth Berkley's man, he said DiCaprio was shouting: 'Let's rent a plane! I want to go to India!' The same actor added ruefully: 'The people closest to him have Leo-Mania worse than anyone.'

Indeed the scene described above seemed to loosely resemble the plot of *Don's Plum*, the independent film Leo and Tobey Maguire had helped out with a few years previously but now, perhaps unsurprisingly, they were less enthusiastic about a wider airing. In that short film (which would eventually launch, but only outside the US – in Berlin, in 2001), their characters apparently 'sit around, smoke, talk, say "bro" a lot, insult the waitress, try to have sex with girls in the back room and fight', as one person who'd seen it said to *New York Magazine*.

In real life, the posse accompanied Leo to movie sets, with the actor sometimes travelling with over ten people in tow: 'That's not an entourage,' said an observer when his gang recently arrived in Paris. 'It's a delegation.' In *New York Magazine*, it was suggested they acted as unofficial bodyguards and even carried his cash. One dancer, at Ten's strip club, told the magazine: 'He comes in here with all his friends and sits back like the Mac Daddy – he doesn't even tip!'

'They're all about seeing the girls,' quipped a magazine photographer in *New York Magazine*.

During press events, the man who the *Daily Mirror* said was described as a 'little upstart' by Gérard Depardieu, his co-star in *Iron Mask*, invited journalists out on the town, impressing them with his ability to down tequila slammers, vodka, champagne and wine without ending up face down on the carpet; always with his friends in tow, actively encouraging him to take advantage of the limitless free booze on offer.

Leonardo was quick to distance himself from the term 'pussy posse', however, saying: 'I think it's the most degrading thing toward women I've ever heard, and I've never used that term in my entire life.' Yet the allegations continued. He was hanging out with Hugh Hefner at the Playboy mansion and commentators speculated that, while the reports might not be damaging in terms of his position as Hollywood's hottest star, there was a real danger he would fail to mature as an actor and jump straight from being juvenile to boorish.

The backlash was well and truly in full swing and Leonardo's reputation as a bad-boy womaniser now meant he was a target to send up. Although he won an MTV Movie Award, a spoof video showed a crew swaddled in bandages, all claiming the actor had assaulted them. At the Razzies, the annual celebration of all that's bad in movies and an event designed to prick the most pompous of egos, Leo picked up the Golden Raspberry Award for Worst Screen Couple for both his roles in *Iron Mask*.

His partying, of course, was nothing new. The reputation he built during *The Basketball Diaries* in New York continued while filming *Titanic* in Mexico, when he was ejected from a club because of the way he and his friends were cavorting with each other. He was then photographed in another club looking very drunk, cross-eyed, sticking out his tongue and grabbing his crotch.

By the turn of the year, he'd celebrated the success of *Titanic* by living it up in fine style. Renting a private jet, he'd flown a dozen friends from the so-called posse to Miami Beach for an extended New Year's Eve bash and spared no expense, splashing out on lavish dinners complete with Beluga caviar and Bollinger Champagne. While partying in a nightclub he'd jumped on top of a table and grabbed his crotch again in a raunchy gesture.

True, he had been working hard but playing hard was beginning to take its toll and this, combined with the negative attention he was receiving, convinced him that he needed to take some time out.

Cinema-wise, the only other film Leonardo was to feature in that year would be Woody Allen's *Celebrity* (1998), where he had a cameo role – funnily enough, as 'an overbearing, cocky, young Hollywood actor'. At the time of filming he'd been careful to select parts that wouldn't lead to his over-exposure but the nature of this particular role only served to reinforce the public's perception of him. Art was in danger of imitating life but it was an opportunity Leo felt he couldn't turn down.

'I don't want to have my face everywhere. I want to trust my instincts with everything I choose. I want to go with things that have integrity and that I feel I'm doing for me. It was just a cameo part. I play the stereotype of what a young, disgusting actor should be,' he explained.

Perhaps fortunately, the film was neither a critical nor a commercial success, taking just $5 million at the box office and being described as 'flat' by *The New York Times*, while it was described as a 'rehash of mostly stale Allen themes and motifs' by *Variety*.

After the stunning highs of *Romeo + Juliet* and *Titanic*, for the first time in his career Leonardo was experiencing the downside of fame. Overly relying on his instinct, he impulsively rejected parts that another time he might have considered. In particular, the idea of being sucked into another blockbuster repulsed him. He therefore had no hesitation in turning down the role of Anakin Skywalker (Darth Vader) in the latest *Star Wars* series and rejected *Spider-Man* (2002), a part that would work wonders for best pal Tobey Maguire. However, he also let slip by *American Psycho*, a film that had earlier hugely interested him. The character of Patrick Bateman from Brett Easton Ellis's cult novel, would have allowed him to once again explore his darker side as a successful city worker who goes on a killing spree in Manhattan. Instead, the role went to Christian Bale.

'It was never my intention to have my image shown around the world,' Leonardo bemoaned, as news surfaced that barbers in Afghanistan had been arrested by the strict Taliban rulers because they were offering Leonardo DiCaprio-style haircuts labelled 'The *Titanic*'.

Indeed he seemed to be suffering from some kind of 'post-*Titanic* distress syndrome' – the sort of fame where everyone wants to talk to you but nobody wants to listen to what you've got to say. In spite of the supposed great sex with models, the whole chapter seemed to give him a downer. There were many times in that year following the movie's release when he wondered if he'd done the right thing in taking the part. How would his life have been different, had he taken *Boogie Nights* instead as initially planned?

There was talk of DiCaprio taking a sabbatical, perhaps to study more Shakespeare or do something completely different. He desperately needed a break and so he announced: 'I'm taking time off right now – I need it. Hopefully I'll have a year to do the stuff I haven't done since I was 16, like travelling, reading the books I wanna read, taking the exercise classes that I wanna take, meeting the people that I wanna meet.'

And he added: 'I've just got to maintain my passion for what I do. That's the only thing to do as an actor and as an artist in this business. No matter what position you're in with your career, the business is so shifty. You're a hero one minute and then you can be out the door the next, a nobody.

'If you can do what you do best and be happy, you're further along in life than most people.'

What Leo wanted was some peace but would he ever get it?

CHAPTER 13

TROUBLE IN PARADISE

It could have been a scene from one of his movies. The young Leonardo hesitating as a sultry older woman beckons to her sofa. Almost giddy with excitement, he fumbles with her clothing, all the while trying to contain his teenage lust. It would have been a nerve-racking episode in any teenage boy's life but what made it even more so for the young heartthrob was that his giggling friends were peeping in through the bedroom keyhole.

This wasn't a movie, however. It was the graphic detail of how Leonardo DiCaprio lost his virginity and it was splashed all over a newspaper. If he had thought that by stepping back from the public gaze, this would quell interest in his private life then he was to be sorely mistaken. The greater the mysteries surrounding him, the more people wanted to find out what makes him tick.

According to Barbara Jane Rohling, she was 32 when she seduced the 18-year-old Leo after agreeing to attend a party with the actor and his teenage pals.

'Everyone else said they were going to bed or leaving for home,' Barbara told the *News of the World*. 'Suddenly only Leo and I were left. He started stroking my hair and telling me how much he liked me. I fell for him, even though he was such a baby.

'He kissed me and grabbed my breasts in an immature way. He was feeling me to see how far he could go, but in a strange way I found it exciting. He wasn't a great lover because he was so inexperienced, but I still enjoyed it. I remember noticing he didn't really have any muscles. He told me that he'd fooled around with girls, but never gone the whole way. I thought it was strange that he was still a virgin in Hollywood when he was 18.'

Barbara said she didn't realise his friends were watching until the music went quiet and she heard rustling from behind the door. The pair allegedly stopped what they were doing and she tiptoed over and threw the door open to see Leo's pals running all over the house, laughing. Barbara told how Leo had initially cracked up at their infantile behaviour but soon his mind was back on the job to hand.

Once she'd transformed him into a man, she said her toyboy lover couldn't contain himself. From that moment, according to Barbara, Leo turned into such a brazen sex machine that he even persuaded her to romp with him in the stairwell of a crowded Hollywood club, a week later.

'I was at a party at a place called Bar One, a real celebrity hang-out,' Barbara told the newspaper. 'Leo saw me and rushed over. I remember he was wearing a gold lame headband – as he often did – and looked a bit girlie.

'He whispered in my ear: "What are you doing right now?" I thought he was pulling me towards the dance floor but he took me outside by the stairwell and started undoing his trousers. I could see his sexy black Calvin Klein boxers. When he told me what he wanted me to do, I was shocked but I'd had a pink schnapps cocktail and I felt light-headed because I don't normally drink.

'I agreed to do it and it was all over within a minute. I was thinking, "I can't believe I'm doing this to a guy wearing a gold lame headband!" When I finished, he had a big grin on his face and thanked me.'

According to Barbara, Leo's first sex sessions had taken place five years earlier, shortly after he signed up to star in *The Basketball Diaries*. She'd met the teenagers by accident at a club on Sunset Boulevard and agreed to go out with them the following week. Barbara was a regular on the Hollywood scene and had previously dated Julian Lennon. In keeping with the Beatles' theme, Barbara termed the two-day bender that resulted in Leo losing his virginity her 'lost weekend.'

'After we made love we cuddled on the sofa for a while and I asked him to take me home. But he said he'd had too many beers and, anyway, he wanted me to stay the night,' she added.

Possibly ruining many young girls' fantasies about their movie idol, Barbara said after their first sex session, Leo promptly fell asleep. The following night, however, he made up for his initial lethargy by passionately stripping her off for a rematch. After she complimented him on being a fast learner, she says he quipped that she'd taught him well. The following day she cooked them both breakfast before Leo drove her home.

Although they enjoyed the risqué liaison in a public place the following weekend, that was the last she saw of him. 'I see him in clubs and parties a lot and he is always very sweet,' says Barbara.

At the time the revelations hit the newsstands, Leo was in Thailand filming his latest movie *The Beach* (2000) – and possibly grateful that he was on the other side of the world.

The Beach was his first major project and the long-awaited follow up to *Titanic*, which was always going to be a hard act to follow. At the time he spoke of the overwhelming expectations he felt, following on from its success: 'I really wanted to take my time and not rush into anything. The misconception was that I was slacking off, but I needed to find a project that I connected with, that really spoke to me. Not something that somebody else told me was a brilliant story, or was going to be a brilliant movie.'

The film was based on the 1996 novel of the same name by Alex Garland, which had become a seminal read for Western backpackers travelling through the Far East in search of paradise. DiCaprio was paid $20 million to play the lead role of Richard, requiring the character of a British backpacker to be turned into an American. In the original book, Richard travels to Thailand in search of adventure and meets Daffy, a hippie traveller, who tells him about a secret island undiscovered as yet by tourists. Before committing suicide, he leaves him a hand-drawn map. Richard meets a French couple, Étienne and Françoise, and they agree to join him on his quest to find 'the beach'. However, they must risk their lives in order to get there and on the journey, have to pass gun-toting marijuana farmers. Eventually they do reach the paradise beach and discover what seems to be a utopian community living there. Predictably there is soon trouble in paradise and the presence of the newcomers causes tensions to surface. Richard inadvertently invites others to the islands but all hell breaks loose when they are killed by furious dope farmers. He then faces a desperate fight to escape with his life.

A film version of the book was begging to be done. At the helm was directorial golden boy Danny Boyle, who'd worked wonders with small budgets on the gritty Scottish films, *Shallow Grave* (1994) and *Trainspotting* (1996), the brilliant adaptation of Irvine Welsh's underground bestseller about heroin junkies in Edinburgh. Utilising the same screenwriter, John Hodge, and producer Andrew Macdonald, who had so successfully adapted *Trainspotting*, it looked a sure-fire winner, particularly when initially it appeared Boyle would be reunited with Scots talent Ewan McGregor and Robert Carlyle, who'd been instrumental in making the last venture such a success.

Almost immediately there was controversy when McGregor was abruptly dropped. The story circulating at the time was that Boyle had been promised more money from 20th Century Fox if he could get a big Hollywood name on board. But Boyle, who had talked with Leonardo DiCaprio at the Cannes Film Festival about hooking up on the right project, only had one name on his list.

'Yeah, Ewan was upset,' recalled the director, 'but we needed to make the character an American and it just didn't fit Ewan. The guy in the book is just sooo British. He's very passive, and although it's very cinematically written, it's an illusion. Because when you boil the book down to adapt it, there's actually nothing happening.'

McGregor only recently, in an interview with *The Times*, broke his silence about the rift that opened the door for DiCaprio: 'You just don't treat your friends like that. They absolutely made me think that I was playing the character in *The Beach* and we talked about dates and moving dates and so on, and all the while they were keeping me there just in case Leonardo pulled out – which is really nasty. And then afterwards, I just didn't hear from Danny for years.'

He went on: 'When he told me, he was very conflicted and he was very upset, and I spent a lot of time making him feel better and saying, "No, it's all right. I understand." And when I went home, I thought "F***! That doesn't feel very nice." And my wife was furious. So I phoned up the producer, Andrew, who I felt was part of the team. And I said, "Andrew, I've just had lunch with Danny and I don't understand. I didn't think that's really what we were about. I thought we were about something else. I really thought we stood for something." And he went, "Oh come on, it was gonna happen sooner or later." And then I never heard from them for years.'

Already a huge fan of Danny Boyle's work, when the opportunity arose to work together, DiCaprio jumped at the chance. Yet, although Boyle had a track record of delivering successful movies, some still considered it an unusual choice for the actor. Many industry watchers in the US claimed he was taking a huge risk in agreeing to star in a movie that was dark and dangerous and in complete contrast to *Titanic*. However, Leonardo revealed he was drawn to the character of Richard because he believed, 'This was one of the more complex characters that I'd ever read.'

'My character really represents a lot of themes that I think are going on with my generation, of being really, truly desensitised to real emotions and real, tangible experiences because of the media, movies, television and video games. I identified with that,' he said.

Leo's character, Richard, has to adapt quickly to the laws created by the island community and as the story unfolds, these rules lead to death and deception. Yet, despite this, DiCaprio said he felt his character remained sympathetic – 'I think he's a real human being. He's someone who's constantly contradicting himself and constantly looking for the real thing. He's quite selfish in a lot of ways and always thinks the grass is greener on the other side. And once he achieves his goal, he dismisses it and goes on to the next one and thinks there's got to be something better. So, he's neither a hero nor a villain.'

He added: 'The character goes on this journey and ends up finding this Utopia that seems to be cocooned away from the normal laws of society. It seems like the answer to everything he's ever hoped for but, eventually, he realises that paradise in itself is an imaginary concept.'

Although the seemingly ruthless move to bring in Leonardo DiCaprio upset Ewan McGregor and ruined the almost brotherly relationship he had previously shared with Boyle, the cast change was the least of the director's problems in a controversy-strewn production.

From the outset the movie was beset by problems. To capture the idyllic location set in the novel, the production crew settled on Maya Bay on the tropical island of Koh Phi Phi Leh, off the southern coast of Thailand. No sooner had the crew arrived, however, than there was a protest to halt filming. As local authorities started to negotiate with 20th Century Fox, English-language newspaper, *The Nation*, said in an editorial that the film project would violate laws designed to protect the island from certain kinds of activities and developments.

'The island needs quiet preservation and not Hollywood fame and mass-market tourism,' *The Nation* declared.

Environmentalists also protested the fragile eco-system on Maya Beach would ultimately be destroyed by the intended newly planted coconut trees and dune shaping. However, the movie was eventually given the go-ahead, with film bosses promising to repair any environmental damage caused.

In a statement, Leonardo spoke out on the issue: 'Preservation of the environment has always been of utmost concern to me and I would never be part of any project that did anything to harm nature. I have seen extraordinary measures being taken to protect the island and I pledge to remain vigilant and tolerate nothing less than these maximum efforts.' He added that he had been assured the island would be returned to its natural state after shooting.

Later he said: 'When we came in, that island was a wreck. We improved it to pristine condition but it was next to impossible to counteract the charges – it was a lot of political propaganda.'

The four-month shoot in Thailand was constantly disrupted by the crew being stung by jellyfish; also by the stormy weather: when 10-ft waves capsized the boats used for filming, Boyle, DiCaprio and about 15 crewmembers fell into the sea, a few miles off the coast of Koh Phi Phi Leh. 'All the cameras and film and steel boxes were churning around us in the water,' said Boyle afterwards. 'We really thought we were going to die. But Leo is a good swimmer and he calmed the other crewmembers, who were not strong swimmers. Eventually, after about 15 minutes, these boats came out and rescued us but I'll never forget the sight of these huge, macho crew guys – grips, gaffers – uncontrollably sobbing once we finally reached the shore. But Leo was pretty cool through it all.'

When the film was finally released in February 2000 it received a mixed reception. Fans of the book were critical of the decision to change key aspects of the story. For the movie version, Richard embarks on an affair with Françoise (played by French beauty Virginie Ledoyen) even though he has befriended her lover Étienne (Guillaume Canet). Richard is also blackmailed into having sex with Sal, the community leader (played by Tilda Swinton) in order to stay on the island.

Although *Empire* magazine gave the movie four stars out of five and praised it as 'engrossing', largely the film was panned by critics and received lukewarm reviews at best upon release.

'Empty-headed', 'seriously confused' and a 'Benetton take on *Lord of the Flies*,' said the critics. Rupert Mellor, writing in *The Times*, called it a 'washout, a bloated wreck; its hollow layering of hipper-than-thou pop culture references buckled the book's already clunky character arc. Desperately seeking complexity, DiCaprio's descent into lunacy was spectacular in its awfulness – a cameo from a bald-headed Leslie Nielsen as a blundering Colonel Kurtz-a-like would barely have jarred.'

Naturally disappointed, Leonardo said: 'I don't think people really gave it a chance but I totally expected whatever might follow up [*Titanic*] was going to be looked at under a microscope.'

But he put the tepid reviews behind him in the only way he seemed to know how: by becoming embroiled in another 'did he-didn't he?' sex mystery. This time, the actor reportedly spent half an hour locked in his hotel bathroom with All Saints' beauty Nicole Appleton after the pair got chatting at a party for his new film.

What gave the story extra spice was that Nicole's band had hit No. 1 with the theme song from *The Beach*. She'd also had a history of celebrity romances, having once been engaged to Robbie Williams.

The London premiere of the movie, on 11 February 2000, was a big deal in showbiz, with 10,000 screaming fans in Leicester Square all vying for a glimpse of the returning Leo. But, according to the *Sun*, he only had eyes for blonde singer Nicole. Sources claimed the two were 'all over each other' at the party before Leo invited her back to his £1,600 penthouse suite for a private bash. As 40 guests partied into the early hours, Leo and Nicole sat in a corner cuddling, then chatting intently on his king-sized bed. At around 4am, he led her into the bathroom. One guest was quoted, saying: 'When they came out, he had the biggest smile on his face and Nicole looked a bit embarrassed.'

Such was the frenzy surrounding the story that British tabloid reporters followed Leonardo to Germany, where he was appearing at the film's premiere in Berlin. When asked about his dalliance with Nicole, he seemed confused and queried: 'Nicole Appleton?'

When he was gently reminded that she was the girl in the bathroom, he said, rather sheepishly: 'Oh, *her*,' before adding, more diplomatically: 'Nicole, oh yes, she's a very nice girl.'

As the liaison became part of celebrity folklore, it was left to Nicole to pour cold water on the claims a few months later. In an interview with *Esquire* magazine, she refuted the allegations that anything happened between them, but after starting off by paying tribute to Leo in saying what a 'sweet guy' he was, she then launched into a bitter attack on the actor, suggesting that perhaps he had done something to upset her.

'Basically we were all hanging out in this VIP bar at *The Beach* premiere,' she said. 'A friend of mine introduced me to him and he said, "Yeah, I heard your song. It's really good and the video – I saw it twice. Come on, let's have a drink to it." He's a sweet guy. He didn't say anything nasty to me. He was just observing the room and seeing girls, the way they were with him. And that's what really f***s me off because he probably did go off and get someone and sleep with them. And I get the blame for it.'

She added: 'He was already wasted before I met him. And, er, it's not my scene, the whole thing – I can't get into that.'

But she wasn't finished: 'He's quite like a child. Like a big, immature child. And he's surrounded by a bunch of idiots as well.

To be honest with you, he acts like a spoilt brat. A big one though – he's very tall.'

Appleton didn't hold back when it came to voicing her opinion about Leo's usual posse of friends and family, who, as was customary by then, joined him in London.

'They all seem really young,' said Nicole, who at 26 was a year older than DiCaprio and many of his chums. 'One of his friends kept on coming up and pulling my hair. I said "Ohmigod, your friend is a freak!" It was like little schoolboys having fun. It totally changed my impression of Leonardo DiCaprio. My niece doesn't even act like that and she's seven years old.'

Despite the miserable reviews and caustic comments from women he met at parties, Leonardo was still clearly enjoying a high personal approval rating among cinema audiences, who had waited patiently to see him for two years since *Titanic*. The film made $144 million worldwide and earned its money back in the US alone. Sadly, though, the healthy box-office takings failed to mask DiCaprio's lacklustre performance and he was nominated for another Razzie Award (Worst Actor) for his work.

Yet, while the critical acclaim was hard to find, the movie did have a positive but short-lived legacy, though. After the initial protests and concerns, Thai tourism received a welcome boost on the back of it. Sadly, however, four years on the perfect paradise was ended by the massive tsunamis that devastated the region on 26 December 2004. On Koh Phi Phi Leh, 200 bungalows at two resorts were swept out to sea, with many foreign tourists among those missing.

Leonardo was devastated by the news and responded by making an undisclosed donation to UNICEF for tsunami relief efforts in Thailand. At the time he also set up a link on his website so that visitors could make a donation to UNICEF. 'It is a horrific, horrific situation for all involved,' he said before describing Koh Phi Phi Leh as, 'one of the most pristine, beautiful places I have ever been in my life. I had such a wonderful experience there, and the people were wonderful to me.'

The actor could also claim, with some justification, to be the star that helped turn Hollywood green. He returned from Thailand with a strong desire to be more environmentally conscious burning within him and was the first among the showbiz elite to start driving an eco-friendly Toyota Prius hybrid car, sparking a trend that saw George Clooney, Harrison Ford and Cameron Diaz among those to follow suit.

At the same time, he also changed his travelling habits, ditching the private jets for commercial airlines. 'I am an eco-geek and like to endorse new technology,' he explained. 'We have to find an alternative to fuel which is going to run out. It is only a matter of time. Thinking about the future got me started in the first place.'

Leo wasn't always so planet-conscious, though: his first car, bought when he was 16, was a 1969 Ford Mustang. 'It broke down on the freeway three times,' he says. 'I nearly died.' But, as he explained, working on *The Beach* opened his eyes to the environmental problems affecting the planet. 'It occurred to me that we inevitably ruin wherever we go,' he said. 'What starts off as paradise does not seem to last too long. It was an important time for me – I had to face life head-on.'

He most certainly did. As so often happened with Leo, no sooner was he back on the showbiz circuit than there was more trouble in paradise.

CHAPTER 14

THE LEO TAMER

'LEO'S HOTEL SUITE-Y!' was the somewhat ingenious headline that announced DiCaprio's latest girlfriend in March 2000, just a month after *The Beach* had hit cinema screens. Much incredulity greeted the name of his latest flame: Paris Hilton.

Paris was just an 18-year-old debutante on the New York social scene when she appeared on Leonardo's radar. He'd been chilling in a Manhattan club with his usual gang of buddies when the heiress – bubbling with the confidence that only a multi-million dollar inheritance will give you – sashayed over to his table, swished her long, blonde hair at him and boldly asked for a glass of champagne. He was smitten, apparently.

According to press reports, the tabloids had been playing catch-up as Leo's romance with Paris had begun a few months earlier before they were first spotted together. As she was based in LA and a regular on the party scene there, it had been easier for them to conduct any meetings in private.

Yet, as Leo was enjoying with yet another association with an attractive blonde, more pressing issues were closer to home. His stepbrother Adam had been arrested on suspicion of attempted murder following an incident with his girlfriend that also involved 'terrorist threats'.

Adam Farrar had been detained when police swooped on his home in the upmarket area of Marina del Rey following an emergency call from the girl, who claimed she'd been savagely attacked. Amid the frenzy of the arrest, Leonardo was said to be devastated as the family tried to get their heads around the circumstances of the incident and Adam's bail, which was set at $1 million.

Pal Ash Baron-Cohen, who directed Adam in his debut movie *Pups* (1999) with Burt Reynolds, attempted to shed some light on the proceedings by saying: 'She's been making some allegations against him although I'm not sure what she has been accusing him of.' However, Los Angeles County Deputy Sheriff Jim Tatreau was marginally more helpful: 'We don't yet know the details of the attempted murder or the terrorist threats although they usually refer to comments like, "I'm going to kill you". We do not know how the girlfriend is.'

Despite public ambiguity, it was a shocking situation for Leo to deal with. Sadly, by then, his brother was no stranger to run-ins with the police. In 1998, just weeks before *Titanic* was released, he had been clubbing with Leo at Hollywood's trendy Argyle Hotel when police swarmed in to arrest him for allegedly spitting on a photographer. Pictures of him, cuffed and shirtless, appeared splashed all over the press.

A witness said at the time: 'As Leo, his brother and some other guys were leaving the hotel, there was a crush outside and Adam spat on a cameraman. The guy reported it and the police turned up and put Adam in handcuffs.'

However, just when things were looking bleak for Adam with the attempted murder allegations, he was freed unexpectedly after police claimed to have received new information. Under US law, cops only had 48 hours after an arrest to press charges and as they were not at that stage, they had no choice but to set him free. It seemed there was a distinct lack of evidence to back up the allegations, but although the case quietly drifted away, the screaming headlines were damaging to Adam, who had already struggled to emerge from his younger brother's shadow.

He'd all but given up hope of making it as an actor but seeing Leo do so well had rekindled his desire. Despite Leo's success, he'd been determined not to rely on his little brother for assistance, though.

Before the arrest, Adam – speaking about his part in *Pups* – had said: 'I haven't ridden on Leo's coat tails at all – I got this job on my own merit and will get future acting jobs the same way. I don't flaunt the fact that I'm Leo's brother; there's no way I'd boast that I'm Leo's brother. If the name got me the part and then I turned out to be a really bad actor, there's no way I'd get any more roles. I am a good actor, so I'm going to get by on my own merits and my own name.'

And he continued: 'Obviously watching Leo's meteoric rise over the years finally pushed me into thinking I could do that – and he is supporting me the whole way. He wanted to come to the premier of *Pups* at the LA Film Festival, but he was still in Thailand filming his new film, *The Beach*.'

Adam talked about how Leo had invited him to join him on most of his sets and he'd learned a lot from watching him up close. He also spoke of his dream that he and his brother might one day work together – something that seemed increasingly unlikely in the wake of his arrest, even though this had not amounted to any charges.

'Me and Leo have talked about working together in the future, if the right project came along – it would be great to work with him, he's a fantastic actor. But it would have to be a good project that showcased both our talents well.'

If Leo had needed a welcome pick-me-up to take his mind off family troubles, it came in the shape of a woman *Rolling Stone Magazine* would describe as the most beautiful in the world. Brazilian supermodel Gisele Bündchen – at the time the world's

No. 1, commanding $7,000 an hour – at first turned down an approach from Leonardo when he spotted her on a runway and sent her flowers in a bid to impress her. She had been dating male model Scott Barnhill at the time. But as the months progressed, she met the actor properly through a mutual friend. Gradually, as her relationship fizzled out, she began to fall for DiCaprio, who had conveniently, if you believe the gossip columns, made himself available by cooling things with Paris.

Initially it was tough finding opportunities to meet, when she lived in New York and he was based 2,462 miles away in Los Angeles. Early on, Gisele revealed in a rare interview what attracted her to the world's hottest heartthrob and millionaire movie star: 'I met him through a very good friend of mine. I thought Leo was a nice, chilled-out guy. He was smart and didn't have a stupid-type talk. After that, I just became friends with him. We have a lot of friends in common and we all hang out together. He lives in Los Angeles and I live in New York, but we see each other when we are in the same city.'

The supermodel was obviously a woman after his own heart as she revealed the one thing that might come between her and her new man was her pet dog, Vida – 'My only companion at the moment is my doggy Vida. Wherever I go, I take her with me, even when I go on modelling assignments.'

In fact, listening to Gisele talk was not unlike hearing the young DiCaprio when he first established himself as a Hollywood actor. Like Leo, Gisele had an old head on young shoulders and a maturity that belied her years – she was only 19 yet already a millionaire. She descended from German immigrants and, similarly, she'd had to drag herself out from a modest background and had adopted firm principles for the way she wanted to work – not easy in a notoriously ruthless industry like modelling.

Leo was able to counsel Gisele on the pitfalls of the movie business, something she'd been trying to get into at the time they started dating. She'd auditioned for the *Charlie's Angels* movie (2000), filmed the year before, but had missed out to Lucy Liu. 'Acting is beautiful,' she said. 'But I wouldn't feel comfortable doing something unless I was ready for it – and I wasn't. If you go for a movie, you have to do it well and go for it 100 per cent and I don't have that time right now. I prefer not to do it than to do it badly.

'I want to train for a few years as an actress so I can do a good job. For now, I am just working hard with modelling.'

Legend has it that the gorgeous Gisele was discovered in a McDonald's in São Paulo, but as she explained: 'I left the tiny village in southern Brazil where my parents are from and moved to São Paulo, where I went to school and worked at the weekend.

'I was approached to be a model while I was shopping in a fashion mall. I immediately said, "No way, no way." But then I thought it was cool as I could support myself.'

She arrived in London, where the English designer Stella McCartney gave Gisele her first big break and her reputation as a stunning newcomer to be reckoned with was assured when she confidently handled a slippery runway in towering heels for Alexander McQueen's memorable spring 1998 'Rain' show. As McQueen heralded her as 'the body' – a name adopted by Elle Macpherson ever since *Time* magazine coined the phrase for her in 1986 – the bookings soared and within a year she was the world's hottest cover girl, posing for Missoni, Dolce & Gabbana, Valentino, Gianfranco Ferré, Ralph Lauren and Versace campaigns. The sultry 5ft 10in beauty was hailed as the antidote to the 'heroin chic' era of modelling, famously started when British photographer Corinne Day snapped Kate Moss for her first *Vogue* cover in 1993.

By 2000 the plaudits kept coming. The famously difficult-to-impress Anna Wintour, editor-in-chief of *Vogue* magazine declared her 'model of the millennium' and, like something straight out of Ben Stiller's model world spoof *Zoolander*, she was fêted for pioneering the 'horse walk' – a move where she picked her knees up and kicked her feet out in front. By the time she landed a $25 million contract as the face of Victoria's Secret lingerie boutique, her position as the world's most successful model was secured.

Yet, despite her success, she remained a committed Christian, who prayed every day and who famously asked for forgiveness when she broke the heart of former boyfriend, actor Josh Hartnett. Her lofty moral stance extended even to the catwalk, where she refused to sell sex. Although she'd been dubbed the 'Boobs from Brazil' and had been credited with inspiring 36,000 breast enhancement surgeries in her homeland, she steadfastly refused to wear revealing see-through clothes or to bare her breasts, much to the annoyance of photographers covering the Paris fashion shows, who responded by setting up a humorous pressure group called 'Free the Gisele Two'.

And, like Leo, Gisele had already sampled the downside to success when she became the victim of a vicious attack by former boss John Casablancas at Elite, who branded her the 'monster of selfishness' when she jumped ship to join bitter rivals, IMG. Even her new contract was the subject of scrutiny when it was claimed it contained a 'no marriage' clause, prompting Gisele to respond: 'Seriously, like I'm going to give up my life and sign a contract that says I cannot be married and have children? Please. That's the craziest thing I ever heard!'

In those early days, Gisele also revealed she was looking forward to taking Leo on at basketball, as she was having a court built at her home in Woodstock, outside New York. 'I'm fanatical about it. From the age of 10, my dream was to be a professional player,' she said. 'Leonardo likes to play and he will be getting an invite. He will take a real beating on court.'

To the outside world, it certainly seemed Leonardo had finally met his match, someone as successful as he was in their own field and someone who had learned how to do things their way, often at the risk of upsetting other people. Before long they were the hottest couple in showbiz and were even spotted smooching in public at a celebrity-packed Saci Night Club in New York.

Their public show of affection, in front of the likes of Sean 'Puffy' Combs, Carmen Electra, Jayson Williams and Tommy Hilfiger, was also the first time Leonardo had confirmed a falling out with previous posse member: David Blaine. Since the gang had been vilified in the media, Blaine – who by then had moved on from his days as a street magician to performing odd public feats of endurance – had distanced himself from Leonardo and his friends. But, at Saci, with Gisele on his arm, Leo gave Blaine the cold shoulder, his second snub to the trickster in less than a year after he also body-swerved Blaine's birthday bash at Joe's Pub the previous year.

It seemed Leonardo was showing signs of finally settling down, but on the career front, he still had some way to go to convince critics he had survived the post-*Titanic* fallout. The time was right, then, for the entrance into his life of one of Hollywood's most experienced and respected directors: Martin Scorsese. A die-hard fan of the director's, for years DiCaprio had been desperate to work with him but the opportunity had never presented itself.

Now Scorsese wanted him on board as he attempted to put into fruition the plans he'd harboured for 20 years to make a film about New York's Five Points district in the mid-19th century. Scorsese, whose work with Robert De Niro was legendary in movies such as *Mean Streets*, *Raging Bull* and *Goodfellas*, had acquired the rights to Herbert Asbury's historical take on the period – *The Gangs of New York* – in 1979, but for years lacked either the clout or the cash to make it happen. One of the reasons why Leonardo had hired the services of Rick Yorn was to get closer to the director and to the project.

Yet, as it turned out, Scorsese had been quietly staking out DiCaprio, too, ever since Robert De Niro had given him the heads-up to the actor's potential, back in 1993 and *This Boy's Life*. The call finally came while Leo was shooting *The Beach* – 'I remember eating my pad Thai and being overjoyed.'

Indeed the chance to play a poor Irish immigrant in *Gangs of New York* was a dream come true. 'When Marty told me I was cast in the movie, it was one of the greatest moments of my life,' says DiCaprio, a Scorsese fanatic since he first discovered the 1976 masterwork, *Taxi Driver*.

For Scorsese, *Gangs of New York* was a labour of love he'd developed since growing up in the Little Italy district of Manhattan and the realisation that his neighbourhood had been built on settlements from the past. Researching the history, he began to understand that the old districts of the lower island were a battleground for immigrant communities. In 1970, he read Asbury's book (first published in 1928) and nine years later, acquired the rights to it. *The Gangs of New York* was filled with blood-thirsty detail about gangs such as the Bowery Boys, the True Blue Americans, the Plug Uglies, the Short Tails and the Dead Rabbits (so called because they carried a dead rabbit on a pike as their battle standard) and notorious gangsters like Bill 'the Butcher' Poole, Red Rocks Farrell, Slobbery Jim, Eat-'em-Up Jack-McManus and Hell-Cat Maggie, who filed her front teeth to points and wore artificial brass fingernails to tear adversaries apart in street fights.

As Scorsese explained: 'The country was up for grabs, and New York was a powder keg. This was the America not of the West with its wide open spaces, but of claustrophobia, where everyone was crushed together. On one hand, you had the first great wave of immigration – the Irish, who were Catholic, spoke Gaelic and owed allegiance to the Vatican. On the other hand, there were the Nativists, who felt that they were the ones who had fought and bled, and died for the nation. They looked at the Irish coming off the boats and said, "What are you doing here?" It was chaos, tribal chaos. Gradually, there was a street by street, block by block working out of democracy as people learned somehow to live together. If democracy didn't happen in New York, it wasn't going to happen anywhere.'

By that time he had established a reputation as an ambitious director, whose movies *Mean Streets* (1973) and *Taxi Driver* documented the struggles on New York's own streets, the scale of what he wanted to achieve with *Gangs of New York* was beyond his reach then and at any other point over the following two decades. In fact, it was only in 1999 when Scorsese managed to form an alliance with Miramax boss Harvey Weinstein that his dreams became a reality.

Scorsese's vision was breathtaking, certainly by modern filmmaking standards. He wanted to construct a set replicating large sections of mid-nineteenth century New York and so more than a mile's worth of buildings was constructed at the vast Cinecittà Studios in Rome, under the direction of production designer Dante Ferretti, a protégé of Federico Fellini. A five-block area of Lower Manhattan, including the Five Points slum, a section of the East River waterfront including two full-sized sailing ships, a 30-building stretch of lower Broadway, plus a patrician mansion, replicas of Tammany Hall, a church, a saloon, a Chinese theatre and a gambling casino were all built from scratch. 'Nothing is fantasy – everything was built to look precisely as it did at the time,' said Ferretti. 'When I make a movie, my goal is not just to recreate the past, but to imagine it as if I were a person living in that world.'

Further attention was paid to the fashions of the time and the vast array of accents that would have been flying around the Five Points. Many of the characters were based on people from Asbury's book. The key character of Bill 'the Butcher' Cutting was largely based on Nativist gang leader Bill 'the Butcher' Poole. Over six feet tall and weighing more than 200 pounds, Poole was a 'champion brawler and eye-gouger' (Asbury's words) who rented muscle to Nativist candidates in local elections. He led a gang of thugs based around Christopher Street, in the heart of present-day Greenwich

Village. Poole developed an intense rivalry with Irish prizefighter and gambler John Morrissey, who was savagely beaten by him when the Butcher and his henchmen attacked the Nativists' clubhouse, vowing revenge.

The Butcher finally met his end when one of Morrissey's hoodlums (Lew Baker) shot him dead. As he was dying, Poole seized a carving knife and lunged for Baker, yelling that he would 'cut his heart out' before he died. His death was soon depicted on stage and always ended with him draped in the American flag, gasping out the alleged final words: 'Goodbye, boys – I die a true American!'

Scorsese's initial idea was to have Robert De Niro play Bill the Butcher, with Leonardo playing Amsterdam Vallon, son of Priest Vallon, the leader of the Dead Rabbits, who witnesses his father being murdered by the Butcher. Vallon vows revenge and the main storyline centres on Amsterdam's attempt to avenge his father's death as the Draft Riots during the American Civil War threaten to disrupt life in the city as the gangs know it forever. The movie would have been the perfect showcase for the two actors and a chance for them to work together again for the first time since DiCaprio's big screen debut.

Much to Scorsese's dismay, however, problems with the set and the shoot caused the production to dramatically overrun and when De Niro realised he would have to commit to longer than the original six months already agreed to, he was forced to pull out. Veteran actor Willem Dafoe also pulled out. Scorsese then turned to Oscar-winner Daniel Day-Lewis, coaxing him out of a self-imposed exile from movies to take on the role of Bill. That he managed to do so was testimony not only to Scorsese's powers of persuasion but also to the quality of the role – one that Day-Lewis, as was customary, would throw himself into.

Leonardo would be equally well prepared. Yet before filming began he'd already signed up for his next project – playing real-life conman Frank Abagnale in the biopic of his autobiography, *Catch*

Me If You Can (2002). The idea was that he'd spend six months on *Gangs of New York*, then move straight onto his next project (at the time to be directed by Gore Verbinski). Due to lengthy delays on both movies, though, that one would have to wait a while.

DiCaprio's first priority was to prepare for the role of the young apprentice thug, Amsterdam Vallon. To do so, he approached it with the kind of intensity that Robert De Niro brought to playing Jake LaMotta in *Raging Bull*, transforming his physique from the waif-like traveller of *The Beach* into a street fighter. 'I came into that movie looking like a Billy goat,' he recalled. 'I was Johnny Protein Shake.'

He had to bulk up for fight scenes with Day-Lewis. 'We'd want to really get into it, so we'd wrestle for five minutes before. We'd beat the crap out of each other and then really, like, try to make these hits look real. And we'd have tons of leather on, and straps, and make-up. Blood bursting, blood caked on our face and then the dirt getting in the blood, and then our eyes. Doing this all day.'

As the shoot overran and costs soared by 25 per cent to over $100 million, Scorsese felt pressurised by Weinstein to produce a more commercial, streamlined version. According to *The New York Times*, the director initially tried to stand his ground as Saul Zaentz (a producer who battled with Weinstein over money after working with him on the Academy Award-winning *The English Patient*) confirmed: 'Marty is only interested in making the right picture. He will make it no matter what he has to do. And he is strong enough to fight for what he believes in. Harvey's interest, on the other hand, is not the same as Marty's: it is about making money.'

Eventually DiCaprio and Scorsese agreed to pay a combined $7 million to help offset any costs due to the overrunning shoot. Even so, *Gangs of New York* would still become the most expensive movie in Miramax's 22-year history. And when Scorsese presented a three-hour 40-minute version for Miramax executives, Weinstein couldn't take any more. 'It was like watching a miniseries,' said one person, who saw the film then. 'There was so much slosh in between the things driving the story it was impossible to get through.'

Fearing a commercial flop, Weinstein demanded Scorsese slash the movie, which only served to get the director's back up. 'He was very rude with Marty and he did not like that,' a colleague of Scorsese told *The Times*, although publicly the arguments were described as 'healthy, creative discussions'.

DiCaprio had nothing to say about the conflict but said of *Gangs*: 'All I know is that I've never committed so much time, thought and effort, and felt so attached to a movie as this one.'

Filming over, there were other issues to contend with. With the movie originally slated for a December 2001 release, there was concern that scenes depicting corrupt firemen participating in a riot and of a police officer hanging from a lamppost would cause offence so soon after the terrorist attacks of 9/11.

A compromise was reached: Miramax announced that the release date had been moved back from December to July 2002, which bought Scorsese more time to edit it down. Even then it was a mammoth job and the film was further delayed until Christmas 2002, presenting Miramax with the awkward dilemma of putting *Gangs* up against another DiCaprio movie.

In the time it had taken Scorsese to finally complete his historical epic, Steven Spielberg had taken over the reins of *Catch Me If You Can* and his DreamWorks company intended to release it on the same day. Leonardo DiCaprio movies were now like London buses – wait two years for one and then two come along at the same time.

Leonardo himself was torn. Which film did he throw his weight behind when it came to pre-release publicity? It was a dilemma he never thought he'd find himself in, and one he never even considered when he signed up in July 2000.

CHAPTER 15

OWNING DECEMBER

The story of how Frank Abagnale's conman caper made it to the big screen was almost as circuitous as Scorsese's *Gangs of New York*. Abagnale was a confidence trickster who became notorious in the 1960s for passing $2.5 million worth of meticulously forged checks in a crime spree across 26 countries over the course of five years, which began when he was just 16 years old.

The youngest individual ever placed on the FBI's Most Wanted List, he assumed eight different identities but famously posed as an airline pilot, doctor and prosecutor. Leading police and the FBI on a game of cat and mouse for five years, he was actually caught twice but escaped custody on both occasions. When finally caught, he spent less than five years in prison but was so proficient in his criminality that the FBI hired him to work for the government on release.

Abagnale published his autobiography, *Catch me If You Can: The True Story of a Real Fake*, in 1980 and in the same year sold the film rights to producer Michel Shane for Paramount Pictures. Yet the work remained on the shelf until December 1997, when Barry Kemp acquired the rights for DreamWorks, which had just celebrated its first releases. In charge of the script was Jeff Nathanson, who had a somewhat checkered history with credits including the little-seen *For Better or Worse* (1995) with *Seinfeld* star Jason Alexander and the universally panned *Speed 2*. He was keen to follow Abagnale during the years 1964–74, beginning with his youth in New Rochelle, New Jersey before moving on to his time as the nation's most hunted cheque forger and counterfeiter, with the story climaxing when 'the Skywayman', as the media coined him, accepts the FBI's offer after his imprisonment in France.

David Fincher was the first director attached to the project but by early 2000, he had dropped out, instead preferring to make *Panic Room* (2002) starring Jodie Foster and a young Kristen Stewart. It was July 2000 before Leo was sounded out about the lead role, with Gore Verbinski now at the helm. Previously he had directed *Mouse Hunt*, DreamWorks' first family film, and was considered ideal to add the necessary light touch to Abagnale's knockabout story. Watching over him would be Steven Spielberg himself, who signed on as a producer. After a 21-year wait, filming was due to begin in March 2001.

Alongside DiCaprio, Verbinski had cast *Sopranos* star James Gandolfini as Carl Hanratty (the FBI agent who obsessively pursues Abagnale around the world), Ed Harris as Frank Abagnale Sr. and acclaimed actress Chloë Sevigny, still riding high after her Oscar nomination for *Boys Don't Cry* (as Brenda Strong). But, just when the pieces all seemed in place, Leonardo was unable to commit because of the troubled *Gangs of New York* shoot and Verbinski had to drop out because of the delay. In the intervening period, Lasse Hallström, who directed Leo in *Gilbert Grape*, was in negotiations to step into the hot seat in May 2001 but by July of that year, he too had dropped out.

At this stage Harris and Sevigny also left the film owing to other commitments, but Gandolfini was hanging in there. Spielberg offered the job of director to Miloš Forman (best known for *One Flew Over the Cuckoo's Nest*) and also considered hiring *Almost Famous* director

Cameron Crowe, but eventually he decided to take on the project himself. It would mean dropping out of his own projects, *Big Fish* and *Memoirs of a Geisha*, but the two-time Academy Award winner officially committed to directing *Catch Me If You Can* in August 2001. By this time the role of Hanratty, the FBI agent on DiCaprio's tail, went to double Oscar winner Tom Hanks, continuing a prolific run that had seen him star in six hit films in four years since *Saving Private Ryan* in 1998, including *Cast Away* and *Road to Perdition*.

Spielberg admitted he hadn't even heard of the story before DreamWorks acquired it and had no idea of its history up until that point. 'This movie wasn't even on my radar until the product was purchased,' he explained. 'I didn't even know the history of the project, didn't know this incredible journey the project had taken. I didn't realise that Frank had actually bought and sold his book four times. I mean, which is *very* Frank.'

Once he got to know the story, he was amazed at the ingenuity of Abagnale's deception and had no concerns that he might be glamorising criminality. 'I don't think they can get the wrong idea because Frank Abagnale is the only person who ever did it to this extent and that was 37, 38 years ago. He was just this 16-, 17-, 18-year-old kid, so you have to understand these things.

'There were no electronic safeguards that we have today with this kind of thing,' he added. 'It's a lot harder to pass a bad check today than it was eight years ago. Frank was a 21st-century genius working within the innocence of the mid-sixties, when people were more trusting than they are now. So, I don't think this is the kind of movie where somebody could say, "I have a career plan."'

Spielberg tweeked with the story and changed elements of Abagnale's life to fit with a more rounded idea he had of his journey. In particular, the director boosted the role of Abagnale's father, played by veteran virtuoso, Christopher Walken.

'The whole body of all the scams are true, but the poetic license is in the details,' Spielberg explained. 'For instance, keeping his father in the story longer than he actually was in Frank's life. When Frank ran away from home, he never saw his father again. And I wanted to continue to have that connection where Frank kept trying to please his father – by making him proud of him, by seeing him in the uniform, the Pan-American uniform.'

Abagnale endorsed the changes, telling the master storyteller: 'Even though I didn't see my dad again, every night after living a brilliant day and meeting many women, and making much money, I'd come back alone to a hotel room and I would just think of my mom and dad and fantasise about getting them back together again and cry. That's the justification for the fantasy that you put in there.'

But even with Spielberg at the helm there were further delays. The original start date of January 2002 was pushed back to February. When things finally did get underway, the shoot was a little like Abagnale's life: 147 locations in only 52 days. Compared to what he'd recently endured on *Gangs of New York*, this was a totally different experience for Leo – 'Scenes that we thought would take three days took an afternoon.'

Although Frank Abagnale did not act as a consultant on the film, Leonardo got to meet him and he acknowledged that he could never be as cool a customer as the conman. 'The truth of the matter is, I don't have the gusto of Frank Abagnale,' he said. 'I wouldn't be able, for example, to walk into an airport riddled with FBI agents and bring in 10 stewardesses, even though I knew everyone had a picture posted of me and was trying to catch me. But these are the things that he did.'

Spielberg also admitted he did have preconceived ideas about how Leo would be and confessed that he believed the media hype about him being an unruly party boy. But he revealed he was impressed by what a family man he was, as usual inviting his parents and his 'Oma' onto the set.

'Leo is the party boy,' said the director, but he added: 'I got to know Leo really well with this movie; to know his mom and dad and his grandmother. They were on the set almost every day. He's such a family-guy. I realised things about him that I'd never realised before because I did believe the tabloids, I did believe these news stories.'

Indeed the illustrious filmmaker argued that little should be read into claims that Leo had a wild-boy image – 'He's gone to parties. He's a young kid. I went to parties too when I was his age – I just wasn't that good looking and couldn't get all the girls,' he laughed. 'But I went to as many parties as Leo ever went to, but nobody wrote about my involvement at parties in dating.'

He also hoped *Catch Me If You Can* would create a new phase in DiCaprio's career after it had stalled in the wake of *Titanic*. 'I think *Titanic* actually kept Leo from working,' Spielberg mused. 'And I think right now he's reborn. He's gonna start working a lot now. I think *Titanic* created a gap in Leo's filmography because he couldn't go anywhere – he was too much the focus of rumuor, innuendo.'

Describing him as a 'very inventive actor,' Spielberg said he was impressed by how much Leonardo was his own 'best critic'. 'There were times I'd accept a certain take,' he recalls, 'and Leo would say, "No, no, I think there's something I haven't found yet. Let me do it again." And he'd invariably come up with something that was just brilliant.'

And, after admitting he was swayed by the public perception of his leading man, Spielberg said what convinced him Leo was right for the part of Frank was that he shared the same cunning in his eyes as Abagnale.

'I didn't think of Leo being right for the part just because of the party stuff – Leo had such a wily intelligence in his eyes, he had such a great presentational style. Frank got away with everything he got away with based on 80 per cent presentation, only 20 per cent imagination. It's all about presentation.'

Indeed, presentation was something DiCaprio was already working on. Tired of his reputation as a womanising playboy, he hoped his settled relationship with Gisele Bündchen would keep the gossips off his back. But he was wrong: tabloids and magazines pored over every detail of his relationship with the Brazilian, who was now so massive she was being touted as the world's first 'übermodel'.

In November 2000 it was reported Leo had proposed to Gisele in a bid to show his commitment to her. While she was working in Milan, he had apparently sneaked into her hotel room and filled it with flowers. When she returned, he went down on one knee – with a $125,000 diamond ring in one hand and a bottle of bubbly in the other – and proposed.

Although both parties remained coy about the development, only weeks had passed before it was then suggested the engagement was off. According to sources close to the couple, he'd upset Gisele by ruining her plans for a romantic weekend together in Los Angeles by deciding instead to head for Las Vegas with his pals for a World Title boxing bout.

Reports said Gisele threw her ring at him and said: 'It's either partying with your friends or me.' Leo, perhaps unwisely if true, chose the fight – featuring British champ Lennox Lewis – but returned instead to find it was his relationship heading for a knock-out with a note simply telling him: 'It's over'. A friend of Gisele's was quoted as saying: 'She deliberately arranged to do a photo shoot close to where Leo lives so she could spend time with him. When Leo told her he was going to Vegas, she flew into a rage.

'He said he would be straight back in her arms after the fight, but all he found when he got back was the note. There are millions of men who would give their right arm to be able to go out with a girl as beautiful as Gisele.'

Leo made a desperate attempt to patch things up and bombarded her with calls begging for forgiveness. It seemed to do the trick because soon the gossip columns were full of news that the world's hottest celebrity couple was back on.

Even when it seemed they were quietly getting on with life – he in the middle of the demanding shoot for *Gangs of New York*, she strutting the world's runways – speculation was rife that they would soon be tying the knot. As it was, it seemed the relationship ran its course in June 2002, just after Leo had finished filming *Catch Me If You Can*, a role for which he'd slimmed down considerably after piling on the pounds for Scorsese.

This time the reason given was that Leo was simply too dull for his jet-setting young fiancée. It seemed the poor boy couldn't win. She also had a thinly veiled dig at his suitability as a romantic leading man in claiming her ideal Mr Right 'has to be taller than me.' Soon he was once more linked to any actress or model within a three-mile radius. Par for the course, his steamy on-screen clinches with Cameron Diaz had spilled into real life according to newspaper reports, particularly when they were seen cosying up to each other in public.

In October, however, he was at a Halloween party Hugh Hefner threw at the Playboy mansion. Leo left arm in arm with Jennifer Paulsen, a production assistant at the E! Entertainment network.

Publicly, as he prepared for an intensive round of flesh pressing with two major movies opening at the same time, he would only confirm his two-year relationship with Gisele was indeed over but refused to bow to pressure by discussing the nature of the split. All he would say was that, after the failure of his romance with the supermodel, he feared it was impossible to have a relationship with someone in the public eye. 'It is tougher to date another celebrity,' he conceded. 'You have a lower-percentage possibility of having a successful relationship. There are just that many more people chasing after that person. How many Hollywood relationships have been successful? [Spencer] Tracy and [Katharine] Hepburn… I don't know.'

And, as he looked to the future, there seemed to be a longing within him to one day be in an established relationship. 'I want a kid some day,' he revealed. 'I would love to have a wife I feel comfortable with. It just has to be the right person, where you still treat each other as equals, and you're both independent enough to a point where you can go off to Alaska at a moment's notice with your friends and leave for two weeks, and it won't be an issue. And that it won't get monotonous, so you don't feel like you're wasting your life just lying around all afternoon with your wife. You know what I mean?'

Having said that, he wasn't about to put his days as swordsman behind him just yet. 'I'm not going to sit here and say that I wasn't a little bit of a Don Juan in the past but I'm certainly not like that any more. Not that I'm sitting here saying I'm ready to settle down.'

Back in the business of movies and Leo relished the change of pace *Catch Me If You Can* gave him after the intense grind of *Gangs of New York*. '*Catch Me If You Can* felt almost like an indie film,' noted DiCaprio. 'It was more fun to shoot because it was extremely fast-paced. *Gangs* was a three-year effort for me. So, it's truly coincidence that both films are coming out at the same time.'

For him, playing the cat-and-mouse chase with FBI Agent Tom Hanks on his trail was as good as it gets. He said: 'There's only a handful of scenes where we get to interact, and those were some of the most riveting days for me.'

And, although at face value there didn't seem much to connect his two most recent characters – a street-fighting Irish immigrant and a slick conman in the 1960s – Leo said he felt a similarity at their core.

'The more I talk about these movies, the more I realise how similar these two coming-of-age stories are,' he explained. 'They're completely different genres of film, different stories, different characters, different time periods. And yet, at the heart of both films is a character who discovers a surrogate father in the person who's opposing him the most.'

Naturally, the father-son theme struck a deep chord with Leo because of the close relationship he shared with George. 'The more you're out there in the public eye, the harder it is for people to buy you in different roles,' he maintained. 'I don't want to divulge too much about myself. Eventually, if people know every little intricacy of who I am, they'll look at me on screen and say, "He's not believable as a poor Irish immigrant!"'

It's hard to conceive of either film without DiCaprio. Spielberg hails his 'amazing naturalism.' Scorsese raves about his drive: 'I had the luck to team up with De Niro when he was young and now I feel the same way about Leo. Leo has this honest truth as an actor.'

Although *Gangs'* delay made it likely to go head to head with *Catch Me If You Can*, few could have predicted both Miramax and DreamWorks would slate their movies for Christmas Day, 2002. Delicate negotiations took place between Weinstein and DreamWorks' chief executive Jeffrey Katzenberg to take consideration of all parties' concerns, including DiCaprio's. It was Miramax who blinked first. Weinstein accepted that the violent nature of *Gangs* made the film less suitable for Christmas and therefore moved it forward by five days.

For Leo, the compromise was a welcome one. As the *New York Post* put it, he was going to 'own December'.

Own it, he did, despite reviews for *Gangs* being ridiculously mixed – critics failed to agree on even the right length for the movie. DiCaprio's performance divided opinion, with *Variety* hailing a 'dynamic physical and emotional force throughout'. For the magazine, Todd McCarthy wrote that the film 'falls somewhat short of great film status, but is still a richly impressive and densely realised work that bracingly opens the eye and mind to untaught aspects of American history.' In the other corner, the *Boston Globe* sneered that Leonardo was 'outclassed even by the scenery'.

Overall, *The Los Angeles Times* condemned the movie as 'boring and violent,' but the *Chicago Tribune* chimed: 'There's not a boring moment.'

One thing most critics agreed on was that Daniel Day-Lewis's performance was a tour de force. Deservedly, it earned him an Oscar nomination – one of 10 for the film, including Best Picture and Best Director. Day-Lewis also won a Golden Globe.

In spite of some impressive reviews, Day-Lewis lost out to Adrien Brody in *The Pianist*. Scorsese lost out to Roman Polanski for *The Pianist* in the Best Director category.

Commercially, the film was a hit, taking $10 million on its opening weekend and posting healthy box-office receipts of $194 million worldwide, recouping more than double the original cost. But, if that was a modest success, it was merely a warm-up act for *Catch Me If You Can*.

Taking $30 million on its opening weekend, it had the critics in unison – Spielberg had triumphed in directing, unusually for him, with a light touch. But the most praise was reserved for Leonardo. Roger Ebert in the *Chicago Sun-Times* described him as 'breezy and charming here, playing a boy who discovers what he is good at, and does it. There is a kind of genius flowing in the scene where he turns up for classes at a new school, walks into the classroom to discover that a substitute teacher is expected and, without missing a beat, writes his name on the blackboard and tells the students to shut up and sit down and tell him what chapter they're on.'

According to Stephen Hunter in the *Washington Post*: 'the revelation is DiCaprio, who shows the range and ease and cleverness that Martin Scorsese so underutilised in *Gangs of New York*. In the movie, little Leo is a gang of one, and he's a formidable presence in one of the most enjoyable films of the year.'

The movie went on to generate over $350 million worldwide, making it Leo's most successful film since *Titanic*. Indeed his performance was nominated for a Golden Globe and although he was overlooked, Christopher Walken received an award for his turn as Frank's father.

He might have missed out on awards once more but one thing was clear – Leonardo DiCaprio was back. For him, the big test now was: could he sustain it?

CHAPTER 16

BECOMING THE
AVIATOR

'I can't even comprehend it, honestly. Being able to work with Scorsese two movies in a row is pretty incredible for any actor at any age. I never imagined this would happen.'

So said Leonardo DiCaprio as he rolled from the twin triumphs of his latest pictures into his next project – his own idea to do a biopic on the life of enigmatic Hollywood and aviation mogul, Howard Hughes. It was a remarkable result after Leo had spent years trying to get the movie off the ground with little success.

But at the end of 2002 he was in a good place. His second coming had been greeted as such and, in a remarkable turnaround since his last great wave of success when *Titanic* came out, he was now being attached to every big movie in the pipeline – rather than turning his back on them.

He was to star in the Robert De Niro-directed *The Good Shepherd* (2006) about the formation of the CIA and would appear as Alexander the Great in 20th Century Fox's historical epic. Anyone who was anyone wanted to associate themselves with DiCaprio and for the first time in a long while, he seemed relaxed and comfortable in his own skin. He was also far enough removed from the hysteria to assess the last few years with a bit of perspective.

'Post-*Titanic* was a pretty empty experience for me,' he admitted. 'Being in the public eye like that, and having the media define me as a certain thing. I do not want to be categorised as one thing.' Acknowledging it would have been impossible for him to predict the effect that would have on him, he said: 'I hadn't really had any education in Hollywood – I was just a young man trying to figure things out. You know, for most things, when you have a problem, you can go to a book store and read up about it. But there's no book on how to deal with success, with the public's perception, what to do and what not to do.'

He was even confident enough to refute a claim by Steven Spielberg that Leo was a 'young man in a plastic bubble, so wary about appearing in public that he had to do reconnaissance before venturing out' – 'I can go wherever the hell I want. I blend in. I dress like everyone else because I feel like everyone else, not because I'd normally be wearing snakeskin pants but because this is what I want to wear. People may recognise me but when you dress like anyone else, they don't come running.'

One of his tricks to blending in, he revealed, was a tip passed on by Bob De Niro to buy a pair of ordinary glasses. 'Those are key,' he said. 'I remember De Niro saying to me, "Leonardo, get yourself one pair." I said, "What do you mean?" "One pair of glasses. Don't ever switch them, always wear them."'

Leo had been forced to accept the unpleasant truth that some of those he trusted the most might not have his best interests at heart. While the actor was involved with shooting *Gangs of New York*, his financial adviser Dana Giacchetto had been investigated for fraud and eventually admitted stealing $17.2 million from celebrity clients, including DiCaprio. It was a bitter episode for Leo, who had trusted and befriended Giacchetto and allowed him to influence many of his business interests. Other celebrities stung included Cameron Diaz, Matt Damon, Ben Affleck, Courteney Cox and the Smashing Pumpkins. Although Giacchetto issued an apology, in February 2001, the 38-year-old broker-to-the-stars was sentenced to 57 months behind bars and ordered to pay back $9.9 million.

The Giacchetto episode had partly influenced DiCaprio's decision to streamline his posse to a core group of ten male friends and although he still liked to hit the clubs, it was all done closer to home now.

'That's the other side of fame,' he acknowledged, 'questioning people's intentions around you. Questioning how people came into your life. With me, now, most of the time, people are guilty until proven innocent. Before, it was the other way round. I went into it blindly, not knowing I was being used by some people, or who I should get involved with. It was pretty difficult for me, and pretty overwhelming, and I certainly had a lot of people come into my life who were less than favourable.

'I just have a great nucleus, 10 great friends who I love to hang out with,' he continued. 'You know, hang out with my buddies, drive around in my electric golf cart [his hybrid electric car, a Toyota Prius] and scream at people, stuff like that. That's actually what we do; it's hilarious. One of my boys and I made such a joke out of it that we were in the golf cart, and he was shouting at other cars: "You're all a bunch of polluters! You're poisoning the environment!" At the top of his lungs… Hilarious.'

Being a thorn in the side of gas-guzzling Americans was something high on Leo's list of priorities for 2003. As well as teaming up with Scorsese again for the Hughes project, he was making plans to produce and narrate his own environmental documentary: 'Being an actor and being an environmentalist are things that I'm going to do. One of the things coming up is a new documentary on PBS. I'm going to produce it and be the, I don't know, the anchor kind of guy. It's going to be pretty cutthroat about what we're doing to our environment, how the US is terrible in that respect. Because we're the worst, we're the worst of the worst.

'Take frogs,' he added. 'The frog is the barometer for the condition of a certain habitat. They're amphibians, and they're really susceptible to the forces of nature. I remember when I was a kid and I used to go frog hunting in Malibu. They're wiped out now, never to return.'

It was a theme he would return to many times over the next few years and a key issue used to explain his support for Democratic Presidential candidate John Kerry, who was hoping to unseat George W. Bush in the 2004 poll.

But, if saving the environment was a topic Leonardo was passionate about, this was nothing compared to Hughes, a character it was clear he saw something of himself in. Leo had wanted to make a film about the life of the reclusive genius ever since he first read Peter Harry Brown's *Howard Hughes: The Untold Story* biography while making *Titanic*. Rather than focus on a Hughes who was sometimes unkindly described as a racist, germ-obsessed freak who shuffled around in a pair of Kleenex boxes for shoes in darkened Vegas hotel suites, storing his urine in jars, DiCaprio wanted to base his movie on the boy millionaire of the 1930s, with the matinee idol looks, who designed and flew his own experimental planes and broke flight speed records while taking on Hollywood with his own overly-ambitious projects.

Although Leonardo was fast approaching 30, there were striking similarities between his status and that of Hughes at the height of his fame. Just as Scorsese had referred to DiCaprio as 'kid' on the set of *Gangs*, so Hughes tired of being called 'junior' and demanded due respect for his achievements.

For the first time in his career, the role of Hughes was not one offered to Leo, nor one he had to fight to land. Originally, he took the project to Michael Mann, director of *Heat* and *The Insider*, but probably best known for his association with the TV series *Miami*

Vice (1984–90). Mann brought in screenwriter John Logan, who'd achieved phenomenal success on Russell Crowe's *Gladiator* but by the time the project came to fruition, Mann had concerns about doing another biopic so soon after his epic on Muhammad Ali (2001). And so it was that DiCaprio and Mann joined forces as producers to persuade Scorsese to take up the helm.

'When I saw the title, I thought it was about flying,' the director confessed. 'And I hate flying. But the more something scares me, the more I want to explore it.' Having Leonardo on board helped convince him, however – 'He doesn't so much play the roles as he becomes consumed by them. It's fascinating to watch.'

Leonardo could not have been happier: 'When I read the book about Howard Hughes, I knew nothing about him being a pilot, this man flying around in these airplanes – crashed them four times. I knew nothing about him being this rebellious figure in Hollywood, this anti-studio renegade producer who made the most expensive movie of his time, *Hell's Angels* – cost four million bucks, all his own money. Then went and did *Scarface*, the most violent film ever; then *The Outlaw*, the most sexually explicit.'

Scorsese and DiCaprio chose to focus their movie on Hughes' younger years – from the start of filming *Hell's Angels* in 1927 to the confrontational Senate hearings of 1947, when Hughes was accused of war profiteering, and before he surrendered to drug addiction, paranoia, Nixon, the CIA and his obsessive-compulsive disorder.

Leo spent a year preparing for the role and painstakingly researching Hughes' character. Devouring books on his character, he also spent days listening to recordings of Hughes testifying before the Senate in 1947. Hughes, for all the aeronautics in *Aviator*, never actually put an airplane into production; his infamous 'Spruce Goose' – the largest plane of its time, made of wood – flew just once, with Hughes at the controls. His spy plane and fighter never made it into the air during the Second World War.

'The hearings were the most important thing,' said Leo. 'Hearing

Hughes, this voracious bulldog, attack against the Senate. A man who was his own boss, anti-government control, taking on the system, taking on corporate monopoly with Pan Am, fighting tooth and nail; actually turning the tables, saying I'm afforded the same rights. A man gutsy enough, powerful enough, saying I have enough resources on my own, let me cross-examine you.

'There's this thing about Howard Hughes,' he continued. 'As many different conflicting reports as there are. Some people think he's a homosexual; some think he's a megalomaniac. Some think he's this shy, coy billionaire. No one really knows, though some know more than others. But in trying to define the man, one thing is consistent: from all the people I talked to – Jane Russell, his mechanics – they all loved him and thought he was such a kind man.'

One of the aspects that Leo was keen to pay particular attention to was Hughes' chronic obsessive-compulsive disorder: plagued by a need to constantly wash his hands, living in fear of dust and germs and stricken with the constant repetition of phrases. 'That was the most interesting stuff to get into. Howard Hughes didn't know what he had – you couldn't diagnose OCD at that time. There was no medication for it. Even if you could find it, Hughes couldn't, because he didn't like to talk to doctors.'

The OCD was something Leo felt he could identify with, as he told Oprah Winfrey on his first appearance on her show in July 2005 – 'I remember as a kid doing things like that constantly. You know, walking to school and seeing a crack on the street then having to walk back, you know, 80 feet and touch that crack again and go, "Oh God, I can't go to school now."

'And I sort of, for the role, let all that stuff come out so sometimes, you know. It would take me ten minutes to get to set 'cause I'd have to walk to set and say, "There's that damn gum stain," and walk back and touch that and they go – you know, the people in the mike, "Waiting for Leo on set again." They go, "Oh Jesus, OK, here we go again."'

Clearly he not only admired the single-mindedness of Hughes but also perhaps envied his determination to stifle bad news – something the actor himself wished he'd been able to do over the years: 'There is this great story of Howard Hughes, I think *Life Magazine*, maybe not *Life*, but whatever,' he recounted. 'I wish I could do something like that, such an awesome thing to do. They printed a story about him, he didn't like. He said, "Kill the story" and they wouldn't kill the story. So he went and bought every single copy of *Life Magazine* (or whatever it was) and stored it in a warehouse for 10 years.'

While in charge of TWA, Hughes was also romancing some of Hollywood's most glamorous women, including Katharine Hepburn, Ava Gardner and Jean Harlow. Australian actress Cate Blanchett was entrusted with the daunting role of playing Hepburn and she, too, immersed herself in research to prepare.

'It was great fun trawling through her films,' she recalled. 'It's one thing to play on screen someone who people have an image of and regard as an icon but it's another thing to play her in the very medium in which she has become so revered. The truth is that I don't think I would have attempted it for anyone other than Martin Scorsese.'

Leonardo agreed. He said: 'Marty's got such an encyclopaedic knowledge of film, especially old movies. You have to know your character inside out, or he'll let you have it.'

A love of beautiful women, a stubborn approach to filmmaking and a discomfort at what he perceives to be an unhealthy interest in his private life – yes, it was easy to see why Leonardo DiCaprio would empathise with someone like Howard Hughes. He was quick to point out some key differences, though. 'I think Howard thought of women the same way he thought of planes,' he said. 'He wanted the fastest thing, the newest model – that is not how I approach dating.'

And it certainly wasn't. Since Leonardo had split from Gisele he seemed to be doing his best to show her that he was a reformed character. Although she had appeared to put the relationship behind her by hooking up with wealthy businessman Ricardo Mansur, he hadn't ruled out reconciliation. And in May 2003, he got the chance he'd been waiting for when he spied his old flame in a New York nightclub.

According to the *Sun*, the Brazilian beauty had attended celebrity hairdresser Harry Josh's annual party in New York with her fellow top models Eva Herzigova and Heidi Klum. Leonardo just happened to be there with a group of friends. Sources at the party said Gisele was transformed when she realised Leo was there and put on a sexy dance routine to catch his attention. And if he failed to notice her sultry moves, then the fact that she knocked over several cocktails definitely did the trick.

One eyewitness said: 'Gisele was enjoying herself so much on the dance floor, she knocked over several cocktails. Leo was watching open-mouthed from the side of the room and couldn't take his eyes off her. After a few minutes, she moved over to where he was sitting and gave him a much closer view.

'He was left speechless. It obviously did the trick because they spent the rest of the night chatting and drinking together. At around 1am they left together but then got into separate cars, not saying where they were going.'

The next day, the pair were spotted strolling around New York with Gisele's pet dog, Vida. 'He had his arm around her waist and she didn't seem to mind at all,' said an onlooker. 'They looked very much together again.'

For a worldwide media desperate to pair Leonardo DiCaprio off with a gorgeous girl for years, this was a dream come true. Within weeks the couple was said to be planning a wedding in her native Brazil. Her five sisters had been sounded out as bridesmaids.

The wedding invitations might not have been quite on the verge of being sent out yet, but Leo and Gisele were clearly enjoying each other's company again.

Jilted Mansur went public, insinuating that it was tricky to maintain a healthy relationship with a world-famous supermodel amid constant speculation about her superstar ex. 'If a man is to stay with Gisele, he has to be very secure and sure of himself because he will read and hear things which can drive one mad,' he sighed. 'Of course I will miss Gisele. Our relationship was wonderful while it lasted but nobody is irreplaceable. The No. 1 woman in the world will always be the one at my side and who treats me with total respect.'

Enjoying the first flush of a rekindled relationship, Gisele joined Leo on the set of *The Aviator* once filming got underway in Montreal, where they were able to take advantage of some rare privacy. The couple were seen kissing and cuddling during breaks in filming and appeared genuinely loved up. Writer Ian Halperin, who blagged his way onto the set as an extra despite not having any previous experience, told in his book *Hollywood Undercover* how Leo was very down to earth on set, praising the local acting talent and reminiscing about his time working on smaller films before *Titanic*. Halperin wrote: 'He is a surprisingly nice guy. Considering that he may at the time be the number one box office star in the world, he appears completely normal.

'He tells me he actually preferred his life before *Titanic*, when he could go into a grocery store without being accosted.'

Leo and Gisele ended the year by travelling to South America on a vacation that took them to the model's homeland of Brazil, plus Chile and Peru. If they hoped by trekking to the Amazon rainforest or high up to the Incan city of Machu Picchu, they would escape the hordes and the usual press attention stalking their every move in the US, they were woefully mistaken, though.

Leo revealed: 'I tried to go to Brazil to the middle of the rainforest, thousands of miles from any type of city, or anything like that. I went to this Indian village and met this tribe. I met the chief of all chiefs and he didn't speak a word of English. He was naked and he had his face painted.

'I was like, "Wow man, I'm really gonna get to disappear! This is amazing to commune with nature." His son was sitting next to me and we had an interpreter and he was talking to us about his village and everything.

'The son looked at me and went, "Leonardo?" I said, "Yeah." He goes, "DiCaprio?" I go, "Yeah." He goes, "*Titanic*, right?" "Yeah, that's me."

'Pretty much, I started to realise that everyone in the entire village had seen *Titanic*. I looked in the corner of this straw hut and there was a tinny little colour television with a little satellite dish and they had been watching American movies for years, man. I was shocked!'

And at Machu Picchu, the 15th-century Inca site located 2,430 metres above sea level, there was a similar reality check. Initially, the pair had wanted their mothers to join them, but both were struck down with altitude sickness and had to wait for the young lovers in a hotel in Cuzco. Instead, Leo and Gisele were joined by minders and hid under umbrellas, trying to mingle with rain-soaked tourists at the ancient ruins on a Saturday afternoon after Christmas. Sadly, their hopes of a quiet pilgrimage were ruined and they were forced to move on when a teenage film fan spotted Leo, asked for an autograph and then alerted all her friends.

Christmas time also meant the moment of truth for DiCaprio and Scorsese. A lot of care had gone into making the movie feel as authentic as possible. Keen to avoid the mistakes made on *Pearl Harbor* (2001), where dramatic flight scenes were recreated using computer-generated effects, Scorsese had instead used scale models of two of Hughes' most ambitious planes – the Spruce Goose and the XF-11 spy plane.

And, as a homage to the early bipack colour movies and the Multicolor process owned by Hughes, he coloured many early scenes in shades of red and cyan blue to give the effect of a 1930s film, the colour then changing to glorious Technicolor.

With a $100 budget there was possibly even more pressure on Scorsese to deliver a hit for Miramax than with *Gangs of New York*. DiCaprio's decision not to pursue *Alexander the Great* seemed sensible when Oliver Stone's plodding epic bombed at the box office but it meant all eyes were on *The Aviator* to deliver.

After early screenings, industry analysts were calling the film Scorsese's best work since 1990's *Goodfellas* and much was made of the beneficial effect the director and DiCaprio had on each other.

'Marty has helped bring out the man in Leo,' said film critic Emanuel Levy, author of *All About Oscar*. 'No one believed Leo could play Howard Hughes, who has always been seen as a man's man. But that's changed now – Leo is a lock for a Best Actor nomination.'

DiCaprio, in turn, 'seems to have brought out the kid in Scorsese,' he said, before adding that the film was 'more reminiscent of his brilliant early work like *Taxi Driver* and *Raging Bull*, just more commercial and enjoyable.'

Scorsese also paid tribute to the positive influence Leo had on him: 'Directing is a real headache but working with Leo, who forces you to talk and talk and talk about your movies, gets you excited about what you do.'

Before he got down to the business of promoting *The Aviator*, ahead of its release in December 2004, Leo had some more campaigning to do of a different nature, however. In a final push to win votes for Kerry ahead of the presidential vote on 2 November, he spoke at rallies in Oregon and Florida, urging voters not to back President Bush.

'George Bush has made the wrong choices, disastrous choices when it comes to the environment. It's time for a change,' he said in Tampa, Florida. He also starred in a political ad campaign on the internet, rafting in celebrities including Justin Timberlake and Samuel L. Jackson to take part in 'Rock the Vote', MTV's campaign to boost voting among young Americans, where once again he spoke out about the environment.

The film was released on Christmas Day to generally rave reviews. Writing in *Newsweek*, David Ansen summed up the feelings of many critics: 'DiCaprio is astonishing – wily, impulsive, paranoid, lurching from manic highs to crippling lows. I couldn't imagine him in this part but after seeing the movie, I can't imagine anyone else.'

Time Magazine film critic Richard Corliss echoed that sentiment, praising DiCaprio for carrying 'this big picture with grace', while *Empire* magazine gave it four stars, and raved: 'Leonardo DiCaprio shines, dispelling fears that he hasn't the weight to carry such a complex, forceful role. He's mesmerising in the moment when Hughes rears back from the brink of madness to face down a corrupt senator (a superb Alan Alda) over allegations that he cheated the US Air Force.'

Interestingly, *The Aviator* was up against a movie with more modest prospects, but one which was nevertheless a significant one for Leo. Opening a week after the Scorsese epic was *The Assassination of Richard Nixon*, a dramatisation of Samuel Byck's plot to kill the President in 1974. The movie, starring Sean Penn and Naomi Watts, was Leonardo's first as a producer (although he had been credited as an executive producer on *The Aviator*), through his recently set-up Appian Way company. It garnered similarly positive reviews to *The Aviator* but there would be only one winner at the box office.

Indeed DiCaprio's take on Howard Hughes would go on to rake in $213 million worldwide. The plaudits and profits signalled a personal triumph for him after pushing so hard to get the project off the ground but as the annual awards buzz grew, would he crown a remarkable return to form with Oscar glory, or was he purely destined to be overlooked again?

CHAPTER 17

THE PARTED

'Growing up in this business and truly wanting to be a part of the world of film, I'm a truly privileged person standing here today...' It might have been a speech Leonardo DiCaprio had secretly prepared for his Oscar nomination but in January 2005 it was aired as he collected his Best Actor Award at the Golden Globes.

Although it was a proud moment for Leo – his first such award from the Hollywood Foreign Press Association – he made sure that he used it to pay tribute to the man who, arguably, had helped save his career.

'I must say,' he added, 'that the pinnacle of all that has been to be able to work alongside one of the greatest contributors to the world of cinema of our time and that is the great Martin Scorsese.'

DiCaprio's triumph at the Globes intensified speculation that he might repeat the same feat at the forthcoming Oscars but he faced stiff competition, not least from Jamie Foxx, who had turned in an equally mesmerising performance as Ray Charles in the hit biopic *Ray*. Foxx had already picked up the Golden Globe for Best Actor in the Comedy or Musical Category and there was every chance he would get the nod ahead of Leo, come the Academy Awards. There was further triumph as *The Aviator* picked up the Best Picture Award at the Globes, meaning it was definitely in contention for major honours to come.

Although much of the guesswork was being done by other industry insiders, Leonardo acknowledged winning an Oscar would be a dream come true: 'Anyone who tells you that they don't want their work recognised by their peers is lying,' he commented on the chances of Scorsese or himself triumphing for *The Aviator*. 'I'd love this film to be the one, especially for Marty. That he didn't win an Oscar years ago is still a mystery to me.

'But he's the reason you make movies,' he added. 'You learn after you've been in the business for a while that it's not getting your face recognised that's the payoff, it's having your film remembered.'

While being recognised by the Academy would be a career high for DiCaprio, he was already looking ahead to his next movie: another collaboration with Martin Scorsese. *The Departed* was to be a Hollywood remake of the 2002 Hong Kong thriller *Infernal Affairs*, about deception and betrayal in the underworld. Re-setting the drama in Boston, DiCaprio would play a cop who is sent undercover to gather evidence on a mob boss, while Matt Damon was already signed up to play the gangland enforcer who infiltrates the police at the same time.

Leonardo risked upsetting Robert De Niro in accepting the role, because it meant that he had to pull out of appearing in *The Good Shepherd* (2006) – a role that, funnily enough, went to Damon instead.

Also on board for the movie, which was due to start filming the following spring and was co-produced by Brad Pitt and Jennifer Aniston's company, Plan B, were Jack Nicholson, Ray Winstone and his *Basketball Diaries* co-star, Mark Wahlberg.

Scorsese was delighted to be getting back in the saddle so soon after *The Aviator* and to be reunited with Leo, even if at De Niro's expense: 'After I finish a movie, I think, "Wow, that was really hard work! What the hell am I doing this for?" But then you meet an actor like Leo and start talking about movies and storytelling, and suddenly you're interested again. I'm ready to go start another one.'

Come the Academy nominations, both DiCaprio and Scorsese featured in a strong list of contenders that included *Ray*, plus Clint Eastwood's female boxing weepy, *Million Dollar Baby*.

Ahead of the ceremony, as much talk seemed to be devoted to DiCaprio's potential wedding plans as to his Oscar prospects. Even after directly picking up his Golden Globe, he was asked why it was that everyone was so obsessed with whether he would marry Gisele. 'I have no idea,' was the reply.

Publicly, the 24-year-old model seemed to be dropping hints, while at the same time scotching those earlier reports that Leo had already presented her with an engagement ring.

'I want three children,' she said, somewhat presumptively, 'but I want to be in a happy marriage. I've never been proposed to.'

Leonardo seemed to be making the right noises in interviews, saying how he'd now accepted that monogamy was key to a healthy relationship – 'I've been with Gisele for four years now and we're happy together. When I was younger, I had a lot of fun – I've had my fair share of models.'

Yet, at the same time he told *Daily Variety*, 'I have no wedding plans.'

As the Oscars approached, speculation mounted, though not about who would win, but who Leo would choose to accompany him. 'We'll see,' he told broadcast journalist Diane Sawyer. 'My grandmother, who I'm very, very fond of – if she comes out here, I think she's got the ticket. Even though she does not care about that type of thing at all, I just would love to have her be there with me. Because she will be my, you know, my own private critic throughout the entire night, talking about everyone and who deserved what.'

Already Helene had joined Leo and Irmelin at the BAFTAs in London. There, Leonardo lost out to Jamie Foxx, an ominous indicator of how the judging might go at the Oscars. But, although Scorsese also missed out on glory, with the BAFTA for Best Director going to Mike Leigh for *Vera Drake*, both were smiling by the end of the night when *The Aviator* took the coveted Best Picture.

The 2005 Academy Awards was significant, not least because it was the first time in four years that Leonardo attended a public event with Gisele Bündchen. And the model made the most of her prime-time appearance, looking stunning in a large, white, billowing Christian Dior gown, which wasn't to everyone's taste but certainly ensured she was talked about in the fashion round-ups. DiCaprio, who was wearing Prada and a touch of hair gel, also secured tickets for Irmelin and Gisele's mother Vânia.

Sadly, the entourage would not witness Leo being crowned Best Actor. In a repeat of the BAFTAs, he lost out to Jamie Foxx. While clearly disappointed, he was suitably gracious in defeat. 'I wasn't surprised that Jamie got the award,' he said. 'But I knew that cameras would be stuffed up my face so I had my response ready. Anyone who says they don't practise is a liar.'

Although her man had missed out on Oscar glory, Gisele was clearly glowing with pride at finally being seen in public with him. Before the evening there had been renewed rumours that their relationship was on the rocks but the public show of affection quelled any speculation, at least for a week or two.

When asked whether the judges got it right, Gisele was less than diplomatic, though, saying: 'I was really there to support Leo. He's not just my boyfriend but he's an amazing actor. He's really talented and I was so proud of him. I figured I should go and support my man, so I went there just for that reason.

'I don't think he was expecting to win. I think I was more upset because I thought he deserved it more. I was like, "He did a better job than Foxx!"'

The Aviator did, however, pick up five awards from 11 nominations, notably Cate Blanchett for her convincing portrayal of Katharine Hepburn, but Scorsese again missed out, this time to Clint Eastwood for *Million Dollar Baby*.

A month later, both he and DiCaprio were hard at work in Boston for *The Departed*. The shoot was problematic for many reasons, not least because Leonardo was viciously attacked during a brief break in filming; the actor had attended an early summer party when a woman wielding a beer bottle battered him over the head, leaving him with cuts to his head and face that required 12 stitches.

DiCaprio hadn't known the woman, who'd arrived at the party at 4am in a highly agitated state looking for an ex-boyfriend. Hosting the event was Hollywood restaurant-owner Rick Salomon, notorious for the sex video he made with Paris Hilton that became an Internet sensation.

According to witnesses, another guest – Jonah Blechman, who acted alongside DiCaprio in *This Boy's Life* – shouted out: 'My God, she has slashed open his face.'

Leo was left bleeding and in shock; Blechman and another friend had to support him as he was bundled into a car and driven to the nearby Cedars-Sinai hospital for emergency treatment.

It soon emerged that his attacker had been repeatedly asked to leave the party, but refused – then turned violent. There were also suggestions that Leonardo might have somehow unwittingly provoked the woman by saying something she disliked. It was also thought that she may have been high on drugs and alcohol at the time.

DiCaprio's spokesman, Ken Sunshine, confirmed the incident to the media: 'While leaving a small private gathering, Leo was attacked by a woman who was trespassing and had been repeatedly asked to leave the property. The attacker struck him with a glass object before being restrained by witnesses. She was reportedly looking for an ex-boyfriend, who she had apparently physically assaulted on prior occasions.'

After doctors patched Leo up, Blechman then drove him back to his home above Sunset Strip. 'Leo's been attacked. She smashed his face in and we rushed to help,' Blechman told the *News of the World*.

A close friend told the paper: 'He's obviously still very shocked over what happened to him. One minute he was enjoying the party and the next he was hit in the head. We can't believe what's happened. He's recovering but he's still in pain.'

From the description of the injuries sustained, it appeared Leonardo had been lucky to escape serious injury. One doctor, Victor Storey, was quoted as saying that if the bottle had severed a main artery, he could have been 'dead in seconds'. 'It's almost impossible to staunch an injury like that. And just beside it is the jugular vein. If that gets cut, you have to have immediate treatment otherwise you'll just black out and die within minutes from loss of blood,' he explained before adding: 'Twelve stitches could well cover up to two inches of Leonardo's face and shows that he must have been hit with some force.'

As the Los Angeles Police Department investigated the crime, Leo returned to the shoot on time but would grow frustrated by the now-customary overruns and budget issues. Most of the delays, it seems, were down to Scorsese striving for perfection with every scene.

'Scorsese is a perfectionist,' a source revealed to the *Boston Herald*, 'but he's an icon, so the studio can't say too much.'

One scene, where DiCaprio's co-star Vera Farmiga chases him in front of the Edward Brooke Court House (amounting to about 70 seconds on film), took six hours to shoot, with 10–12 rehearsals and over 15 takes. Scorsese's attention to detail was so intense, it was reported he even requested a lamppost in the background of a chase scene be replaced by one that looked a little different.

According to reports, Jack Nicholson also further complicated matters by re-writing each day's shoot, forcing the director to shoot his doctored script before shooting his own version, just to keep Nicholson happy.

'The set is not a happy one,' confirmed the sources, while describing DiCaprio as 'frustrated'. However, bosses at Warner Bros hoped that Nicholson's over-the-top performance, combined with Scorsese's skill at the helm and contributions from Leo and Matt Damon, two leading young actors at the top of their game, would give the director his first big hit since *Goodfellas*, 16 years earlier.

And, certainly, although Nicholson worked on just 25 of the 99 shooting days, his presence made a huge difference. Scorsese himself said, 'With Jack, a little bit goes a long way.' In fact, the veteran's often unpredictable and eccentric antics left his younger co-stars bemused.

'When Jack came on the set, he would do things that were just nuts,' Damon recalled. 'If you look at Leo and I in all our scenes with Jack, we are like deer caught in the headlights.'

Nicholson was playing Frank Costello, a crazed and violent Mob boss who sends a mole to infiltrate the police, not realising that he already has one in his own organisation. 'It's a guessing game,' explained DiCaprio. 'Who is a person with integrity? What's your true identity? How much does that ultimately matter?'

When Warner Bros first sent Scorsese the script he was initially wary about taking on a remake, especially as this was another film about organised crime. 'But maybe that's what I do,' he resolved. 'I've tried different milieus and different types of stories – I even tried a musical, *New York, New York* – but I am more comfortable with stories like this. Maybe it's because I was brought up in a little Sicilian-American village in New York that doesn't exist any more.'

Incredibly, this was the first time Scorsese had worked with Nicholson, despite knowing each other for 30 years. 'I wanted a real presence to carry over the whole picture so that even if he was only in three scenes, you would still feel the presence of this larger-than-life, almost God-like figure,' the director explained. 'Jack and I have known each other for 30 years, but for some reason we had never quite connected on a movie so I thought it would be interesting to see if he had any desire to take on the role of Costello. I wanted something iconic from Nicholson. It may have taken a long time, but it was worth the wait.'

Nicholson relished the challenge and constantly kept Scorsese and screenwriter William Monahan, not to mention the rest of the stellar cast, guessing by continually improvising during the shoot. During one scene with Damon, when they were in a seedy cinema showing porn movies, Nicholson produced a sex toy and waved it menacingly in front of his young mob prodigy, only explaining later: 'I thought the scene would look better with a dildo.'

It was the first opportunity Leo had to see the unique three-time Oscar winner up close. He revealed Nicholson kept him on his toes with a performance that was both inspiring and intimidating.

'He's a force of nature and you have to be prepared to roll with the punches,' he explained. 'There were moments during filming when I didn't know what was going to happen next.'

He went on: 'If you hire Jack Nicholson to play an Irish Mob kingpin in a Martin Scorsese film of this genre he's going to make the role his own and that involves going into the set every day, expecting the unexpected. He is going to throw curveballs at you and you have to be completely prepared for anything. There was tons of improvisation with him – I was never sure which side of Costello he was going to be playing on any particular day. It makes you terrified as an actor and it ups the stakes.'

That was certainly true when it came to filming one of the key scenes in the movie: when Nicholson's mob boss confronts DiCaprio's character, suspecting he could be a mole. After one take, Nicholson said to Scorsese: 'I don't think he's scared enough of me – I have to be scarier.'

Leo takes up the story: 'So, I came in the next day and Jack's hair was all over the place. He was muttering to himself and the prop guy tipped me off that he had a fire extinguisher, a bottle of whisky, some matches and a handgun somewhere. So I sat down at the table not knowing what to expect and he set the table on fire after pouring whisky all over the place and stuck a gun in my face.

'It changed the whole dynamic of the scene and that's what he does – he makes you so much better and he makes you react as an actor, and you take more chances because your character is reacting to this homicidal maniac.'

Indeed, the unpredictability of Nicholson helped draw out one of Leo's most convincing performances to date.

'Leo is remarkable,' raved Scorsese. 'He conveys the conflict of a young man who has got himself into a bad situation and then wonders what the hell he is doing there. You can see it in his face; you can see it in his eyes. He knows how to express emotional impact without saying a word. It's quite extraordinary to watch.'

As if there hadn't been enough going on during the shoot, it didn't take much to remind Leo that the usual circus accompanying his life was never far away. On one occasion they were shooting all night in downtown Boston next to a strip club. No sooner had the cast arrived than 20 scantily clad girls in G-strings descended on the set. As Damon and Wahlberg started to become interested, it was soon clear they were on the lookout for only one man. 'Where's Leo?' they asked as bemused security wondered how best to manhandle them from the shoot.

Filming finally over, it was time for Leonardo to take stock of his life. One of the key dilemmas was whether Gisele would be in it. Although publicly they'd seemed more together than ever, there were signs that perhaps they wanted different things from the relationship – or the same things, but with different people.

In July, Gisele turned 25 and when asked what her dream present would be to mark her quarter life, she returned to a theme of earlier interviews – 'I want a baby. My life dream is to have a baby, but it's not only up to me. It's up to the father, too. I don't know anything, though – I wish I had a crystal ball.'

A crystal ball might have shown her that in just a few months she

op left: Does DiCaprio's future lay behind the camera? Watching takes on the set of *th Hour*, an environmental documentary which he co-wrote and narrated.

op right: With co-star Russell Crowe at the *Body of Lies* premiere in New York, ctober 2008.

ottom: Reuniting with his *Titanic* co-star Winslet, the cast of *Revolutionary Road* at its remiere in LA, late 2008.

A passionate environmentalist,
DiCaprio speaking at the New
Jersey location of the Live Earth
concerts in July, 2007. 150 musical
acts performed at eleven different
locations around the world, with
guest speeches from influential
individuals in a variety of fields, all
to raise environmental awareness.
The event was broadcast to a
global audience.

Top: With Live Earth founder, Al Gore, and rock musician, Jon Bon Jovi, at the Academy Awards Vanity Fair Party in 2007.

Bottom: Continuing his environmental support, DiCaprio at the 20th Anniversary of the Natural Resources Defense Council in April 2009.

Top: DiCaprio with then-girlfriend and now friend, Bar Refaeli, at an LA Lakers NBA basketball game in mid-2010.

Bottom: The cast of *Shutter Island* with director Martin Scorsese at the Berlinale Film Festival in Berlin, February 2010.

Left: At the London premiere of *Inception* – or is it all just a dream? – with co-stars Marion Cotillard and Ellen Page, July 2010.

ight: DiCaprio on the set of *Edgar* with director Clint astwood, February 2011.

Top left: DiCaprio looking sharp at the AFI Festival World Premiere Opening Night Gala for *J. Edgar*, 3 November 2011.

Top right: On the set of the much anticipated new adaptation of F. Scott Fitzgerald's *The Great Gatsby*, in Sydney, Australia, October 2011.

Bottom: Introducing musical legend, and one of his favourite artists, Stevie Wonder, at the Darling Hotel and Star Casino opening party in Sydney, Australia, October 2011.

Charming, serious and just a little bit cheeky, DiCaprio at the *J. Edgar* film photocall in LA, November 2011.

Arriving at the Golden Globe Awards in 15 January 2012, a dapper DiCaprio is now one of Hollywood's most respected actors.

would be single once again. After five years together, the couple called time on their relationship in November and this time the split looked permanent. The suddenness of the development – there was no public announcement – kept the tabloids guessing as to the cause. Some speculated that it was Gisele who made the decisive move and there were claims she'd been unhappy after Leo had been spotted getting close to *Layer Cake* actress Sienna Miller in an LA club.

Quick as a flash she was being linked with US surf champ Kelly Slater, a former squeeze of Pamela Anderson's. Eventually, *Newsweek Magazine* quoted Gisele's manager, confirming: 'Yes, they broke up.' However, she scoffed at the suggestion that her client had jumped into another relationship so soon after splitting from Leo, but friends of DiCaprio were reminded of how quickly she'd hooked up with Rico Mansur after their last break-up.

Leo's split with Gisele caused an unexpected fall-out throughout the entertainment industry. Legendary swordsman Mick Jagger became unwittingly embroiled in it, after he was reported to have offered the heart-broken (and potentially available) supermodel a shoulder to cry on. This, however, was much to the annoyance of his lover L'Wren Scott. The Rolling Stones' frontman was said to have taken Gisele to Manhattan hot-spot The Big Cheese for some 'fatherly advice' but maintained it was 'all innocent'.

The fact that Leo was single once more also meant he was once again ripe for approaches by any up-and-coming young starlet keen to use an association with the playboy to boost her fledgling career. Rising star Mischa Barton, then of *The* OC fame, gave an insight into the attitude of perhaps many managers when she revealed her publicist suggested she sleep with the *Titanic* heartthrob to get noticed. She had spotted the actor during a photo-shoot in Malibu and her PR remarked: 'For the sake of your career, go and sleep with that man.'

But teenager Mischa gave a further insight into how her fellow teenagers in the profession were viewing Leo when she reacted with dismay to the suggestion, claiming he was far too old. 'Isn't Leo like,

30, or something?' she was quoted as saying in society magazine *Harpers & Queen*.

It wasn't long before DiCaprio was back in the dating game, however, with suggestions his friendship with *Spider-Man* actress Kirsten Dunst had moved to a new level. They were seen cosying-up in a Los Angeles nightclub. He was then spotted holding court in Manhattan's über-trendy Bungalow 8 until the early hours with a bevy of beautiful hangers-on 'flirting up a storm with anything with a pulse,' according to the *New York Daily News*. 'He looks like he's on the prowl,' an onlooker told the newspaper. 'He was checking out all the ladies.'

What the press failed to notice, though, was that Leo had made a quick trip to Las Vegas for a party thrown for Irish rockers U2. There, his attention had been drawn to Bar Refaeli, a ravishing blue-eyed blonde Israeli model. Although 11 years his junior, he was captivated by her beauty – and possibly her curvaceous 35C-24-35 figure.

Conveniently forgetting his 'I've had my fair share of models' assertion from the beginning of the year, Leonardo endeavoured to get to know the alluring Bar better. Any romancing had to be put on hold, though, because when he returned to Hollywood, he had to rush to hospital to be at his father's bedside. George had been riding his motorbike in Los Angeles when he was struck by a car and left unconsciousness.

For a horrifying moment, Leo feared the worst and kept a two-day vigil. Mercifully, no lasting damage was done and once he regained consciousness, the 62-year-old was expected to make a full recovery.

'Leo was a bit shaken up,' a friend told reporters. 'But his dad is going to be OK.'

For Leo, it was a timely reminder of the fragility of life. And as he looked to a new chapter, it was with an even greater sense of purpose: he would only get one shot and he was determined not to waste the opportunity he'd been given.

CHAPTER 18

BEST BAR NONE

In many ways it was a familiar sight – DiCaprio hitting the bar again, surrounded by those only interested in getting something from him. But this was Mozambique and, instead of glamorous cover girls for company, he had ruthless African mercenaries.

Leonardo had sought out the soldiers of fortune to prepare for his latest role – that of a diamond smuggler whose activities helped fund the bloody civil war in Sierra Leone. It had been said before, but in many ways *Blood Diamond* would be his most challenging movie yet. Filmed on location in Mozambique, he was playing the bad guy, but in a movie with a social conscience – and one that was to cause ructions back in Hollywood.

Leo had already earned a reputation for caring about global issues but the trade in conflict diamonds was a distinctly unfashionable one when DiCaprio signed up to star in Edward Zwick's gritty thriller. He immersed himself in the role of a tough ex-mercenary who teams up with Djimon Hounsou, cast as a victim of Sierra Leone's civil war. For their own reasons, the two men set out to hunt down a priceless diamond. The action, set in the early 1990s, shows how rebel soldiers (funded by the sale of diamonds) forcibly recruited children and terrorised civilian populations, murdering and amputating arms and legs. Although by no means Leo's first foray into action/adventure, *Blood Diamond* required him to do 'research' of a sort he wasn't entirely unfamiliar with.

'I had never really spent time with any South African mercenaries,' he said, somewhat light-heartedly in explaining his research. 'So, it was a matter of seeking some of these men out, hearing their stories, spending as much time as possible with them and getting them drunk.'

He went on: 'There aren't many metrosexuals out there, you know. They are very alpha-male guys: hardcore, direct and blunt. I was somewhere in the middle – not as extreme as some of those dudes, but not the other thing either. I had to hear their stories, I didn't know the situation – I took a lot of my character from the conversations I had with them.'

Another task was mastering the 'extremely difficult' South African accent. 'I spent weeks and weeks just asking people cuss words, ways to insult one another. How you ask for a drink or a cigarette, about their attitudes towards America and each other. It was a long, long process.'

Mozambique was the perfect place to set the movie, being a southeast African country, with a history almost as troubled as Sierra Leone. Many parts were given over to local actors, painfully aware of the human cost of the trade in conflict stones – diamonds that are smuggled out of countries at war to fund arms.

Working on the movie was to have a profound effect on Leonardo, who witnessed first hand the problems faced in cash-starved African countries. 'There was a particular girl in Mozambique, who was working on the movie,' he recalled. 'And I came to learn that both her parents had passed away from AIDS and she was living in this orphanage. How could you not be drawn to helping out in a situation like that, where children have lost everything?'

So moved was he by her plight that he and the makers of *Blood*

Diamond tried to do their part by raising hundreds of thousands of dollars for amputees, orphans and other victims of war and disease in the country.

'This film has changed me, you know,' he continued. 'It really has. You have to do something, you have to give back.'

But this was not simply some patronising gesture for a bit of positive PR. Leo and his crew were awe-struck by the fortitude of the people they met, who were resolutely determined not to let circumstances ruin their lives.

'What impressed me most was that, amid all the atrocities that have gone on in Africa and the poverty and hardships, there was still such a positive attitude to life,' he acknowledged. 'You could go drive around Mozambique and people would be dancing in the streets, they were just so happy to be alive.'

DiCaprio had come a long way since those confusing months in the aftermath of *Titanic*, but the farther he moved from those days, the more he appreciated the doors opened for him by films. 'It gave me so many more opportunities as an actor, on so many different levels,' he explained. 'It put me in the driver's seat to place myself in movies that are important and get a lot of those movies financed, which is hard to do.'

Blood Diamond was one of those 'important' movies and one he hoped would entertain, as well as deliver a message 'without forcing it down people's throats.'

It was a small British charity's fight to expose how illegal gems fuel war in Africa that inspired director Zwick to make the movie. Global Witness started in a backroom in London nearly 20 years ago when two of its three founders, construction boss Patrick Alley, and Simon Taylor, a biologist, gave up their jobs to campaign against the plunder of natural resources in poor countries. Their partner, PR executive Charmain Gooch, funded the charity from her own salary. Struggling to get by on donations from collections tins, they enlisted the help of The Body Shop founder Anita Roddick, who provided a grant allowing them to open an office in the west of the city. The charity's investigation into *Blood Diamonds* in Angola is dramatised in the movie, with *Beautiful Mind* star Jennifer Connelly taking on the characterisation of Charmain Gooch when she posed as a journalist to collect evidence that diamonds were being used to fund the war.

Oxfam and Amnesty International added their weight and eventually the campaign led to an industry campaign, but as the finishing touches were being put to the movie, scheduled for release in December 2006, Global Witness reported blood diamonds were still coming out of Africa.

Campaigner Alex Yearsley said: 'There is hard evidence that rebels in the north of the Ivory Coast are smuggling diamonds out through Ghana. These stones are reaching world markets and people are buying them.'

The movie appeared to have an instant impact, even before it was released. When news of the film first emerged, the De Beers Group went on the offensive, hired a Hollywood PR agency and joined with the World Diamond Council in a costly damage-limitation campaign. The trade in diamonds is worth £30 billion a year and the industry moved fast to stop diamonds becoming the new fur.

The two organisations claimed that, under the Kimberley Process – the scheme designed to certify the origin of rough diamonds – trade in blood stones had dropped to just 1 per cent. And the Word Diamond Council even tried to persuade Zwick to add a balancing statement to that effect.

DiCaprio argued companies like De Beers were missing the point. 'The movie isn't necessarily saying don't buy diamonds. It's saying that every time you write a cheque for something, you are endorsing the way that company does business. When it comes to diamonds, I for one am going to get proof that it's not a conflict stone. Diamonds funded these warlords in Sierra Leone and 4 million people died. It's the awareness we have to have as consumers. It's been a natural resource that should benefit that country, but instead has caused destruction and the displacement of people.

'To me, it's a movie about corporate responsibility, because who we are and what we do as consumers in more fortunate countries affects people in places like Sierra Leone and other countries halfway across the world. That goes for environmental issues, too. Every time you buy something as a consumer, you're essentially endorsing the way a company does business, and you're essentially advocating their policies.'

Leo says he was moved to take direct action himself because he believes consumers back home were experiencing fatigue when it came to appeals on behalf of African issues: 'There's a detachment we've formed from watching infomercials because there's a certain amount of disconnect. But I got to see places like SOS, where children have lost their parents because of AIDS or poverty, and they're getting a completely new opportunity. It's wonderful to see those contributions turn into something really tangible and it changes how you look at things. It makes you want to come home and not want to hear about anybody's problems, because people there have maintained such a positive attitude about life.'

'The good thing about this movie,' he added, 'is that the gem industry is now saying it will go in and re-examine what's going on in Africa; the film has had a social impact.'

When it did hit the screens, it produced the odd effect of garnering mixed reviews from critics, yet an overwhelming thumbs up from the public.

Leo was praised for his South African Afrikaner accent, a particularly tricky one to get right without sounding Australian, but BBC Radio 5 Live's Mark Kermode summed up the critic's response when he described the movie as 'issue-tainment'. He praised *Blood Diamond* for putting 'the issue of conflict diamonds in the public eye' but added: 'Whether or not that makes it a great drama is a slightly different question.'

Elsewhere, it allowed critics to dust off their jewel-themed puns, prompting lots of references to 'flawed diamonds', suggestions that it 'failed to shine' and the overall effect was 'more Gerald Ratner than Harry Winston'. DiCaprio, though, was generally thought to have 'sparkled'.

Writing in *The Times*, James Christopher said: '*Blood Diamond* is so bleak and depressing you will never look at a gemstone again without idly wondering how many lives it might have cost.' He also praised DiCaprio's gritty performance as the ruthless mercenary, 'even if his heart isn't quite the concrete brick he pretends it is.'

Yet, while the critics were divided, the manufacturers were not hanging around to see if cinema-goers shared their indifference. DiCaprio's presence meant the film was sure to do big business at the box office and already there was talk of an Oscar nomination for Leo – nicely adding to the buzz he'd already generated with *The Departed*, released just three months earlier.

Leonardo's performances in both *The Departed* and *Blood Diamond* were each nominated for a Golden Globe, meaning effectively he was up against himself. Co-star Djimon Hounsou as Solomon Vandy was also a contender for his supporting role.

Ahead of the ceremony, the diamond trade upped the ante, recruiting celebrities including Beyoncé Knowles and Jennifer Lopez to wear dazzling diamonds to the Awards in return for donations of $10,000 to the African charity of the star's choice.

When it came to the small matter of the gongs, Leonardo missed out, his performances perhaps cancelling each other out. In a curious echo of 2005, when his portrayal of Howard Hughes lost out to another take on a real-life personality, so it was that in 2007 he lost out to another African film. Forest Whitaker triumphed for his performance as ruthless dictator Idi Amin in *The Last King of Scotland*.

By the time the London premiere of the film came around, a week after the Globes, Leonardo was celebrating as he was named one of the movie's five Oscar nominations – his turn in *Blood Diamond* being preferred by the Academy over *The Departed*. Huge crowds greeted his arrival showing his star still shone brightly as he grew older. Before the screening, he spent 45 minutes chatting to fans.

He arrived without Bar Refaeli and it wasn't long before the gossip columns were full of reports suggesting the year-long relationship was, like his movie, on the rocks. Amazingly, given the attention Leonardo continued to attract, the couple had been able to keep their affair largely under wraps and refused to speak publicly about each other. Sightings of them in Paris, Prague and New York were the only indications they were still an item. And when the *Daily Mirror* tried to interview Bar shortly before *Blood Diamond* came out, a PR warned: 'No questions about Leo!'

Now it appeared all was not well in camp 'LeoBardo'. A pal of Leo's told the *Mirror*: 'He was really into Bar in the beginning but now he's kinda getting to the end of his tether. He finds her really clingy and being apart because of work causes rows.'

The Academy Awards of 2007 was supposed to be the year that the jewellery would be conflict-free. Leonardo arrived, girlfriend free, but wearing a ruby-red, diamond-free teardrop pin, circulated by Amnesty International and Global Witness to raise awareness. Many other actors also sported the pins. But the diamond companies fought back, with Patricia Arquette and Sarah Jessica Parker among those wearing diamond rings in return for a donation to South African charities. Not everyone read the script, though.

Despite being nominated for five awards, *Blood Diamond* ended up with none. With all the pre-Oscar hype around the diamond issue, it was easy to forget Leo had another reason to celebrate. *The Departed* was the biggest winner of the night, scooping four Oscars, most notably for Best Picture and finally, a Best Director gong for Scorsese, after being five-times nominated. Looking genuinely shocked, he praised the cast, singling out Leo as he said: 'Leo

DiCaprio, six-and-a-half years work we have done together. I hope another 12, another 15.'

The Oscars provided Leonardo with an opportunity to further another cause close to his heart: the environment. He took to the stage with former vice-president Al Gore to announce that, due to the policies adopted by the Academy, 'for the first time in the history of the Oscars, this show has officially gone green!' Quite how this was achieved wasn't mentioned, but the skit allowed Leo the chance to pay tribute to one of the green movement's most high-profile campaigners.

'I am very proud to be standing next to such an inspirational leader in the fight against global warming,' he announced. 'You are a true champion for the cause, Mr Gore.'

The set piece was in danger of descending into a cringe-worthy, mutually beneficial, backslapping exercise as Gore returned the compliment by thanking the actor for being such a 'great ally on this subject.' It was saved, however, by a smoothly delivered send up of the former VP's presidential hopes. As Leo gently tried to convince Gore to use the platform to tell the American people he would stand for President, the Oscars music kicked up just as the politician seemed on the verge of announcing his intention.

An Inconvenient Truth, Al Gore's 2006 film on the perils of global warming, in a heartbeat helped change attitudes to the problem but as the science and political lobby went on the attack, dismissing the documentary as based on wrong information, there was still work to be done. It was hard to believe that Leo – so often dismissed as a party-loving playboy – could do anything to sway public opinion but with his popularity still riding high, he felt a burning passion that to do nothing was not an option.

CHAPTER 19

GOING GREEN

It certainly was an unusual setting for a first public date together – meeting the former Israeli Prime Minister and pledging to do what they could to help the country's peace process with Palestine.

Yet, that's the situation Leo and Bar Refaeli found themselves in on his first visit to her homeland, in March 2007, scotching rumours around the time of the Oscars that they'd split. The purpose of the trip was primarily to meet her parents and visit some sacred sites, but as if the ordeal of meeting the prospective in-laws wasn't daunting enough, DiCaprio combined it with a quick stop off to discuss global warming issues and world peace. No sooner had he touched down in Tel Aviv than a meeting was arranged between the Vice Premier and former PM Shimon Peres and Leo and his then girlfriend.

'The meeting was pleasant and interesting,' said an aide to the politician. 'Shimon told Leo about his Peace Valley project [a joint Israeli-Jordanian-Palestinian economic development plan] and Leo spoke about his documentary on the environment.'

Dressed casually in a sweater and reversed baseball cap, Leo looked every bit the tourist caught unawares that he'd have to do anything serious but both parties seemed to get something out of the brief summit.

Peres said: 'They called my office and asked to meet me, and I immediately agreed. Leonardo apologised for not dressing properly and in order to look fine, turned his baseball cap.'

The couple had hoped to sneak undetected into Israel on a night flight from Frankfurt, Germany, but unfortunately for them the plane was also carrying a group of Israeli entertainment reporters on their way back from a press junket in Ireland and so their cover was blown.

According to aides, Peres asked DiCaprio to help promote the stalled Middle East peace process and to further campaign for protecting the environment globally. With the environmental issues, the actor was on fairly solid ground but it remained to be seen if he could come up with a solution to the Middle East which had so far eluded the most prominent thinkers.

Bar must have had some idea what it was like to be Leonardo's girlfriend by then, but she was to get a crash course during the Israeli visit. On his second day in the country she took him to Jerusalem's Western Wall, one of the most sacred sites in Judaism. Together with members of her family, they toured a tunnel near the structure (dating back to around 19BCE). Desperate to get a close-up of the lovebirds, a scuffle broke out among the photographers. In the ensuing mêlée, bodyguards clashed with the snappers, leaving three lensmen injured. As police investigated whether to charge Leo and Bar's minders, his PR was adamant who was to blame.

Shawn Sachs said: 'Leo is horrified that anyone might have gotten hurt in this situation, but the paparazzi really made this happen.'

One of the few times that the couple were able to enjoy some peace and quiet, free from press attention, was when they took a quiet trip to Galilee in northern Israel. There, DiCaprio stayed at Bar's family home in suburban Tel Aviv, where he enjoyed hanging out and struck up a friendship with her ten-year-old brother.

When the time came for Leo to depart, the emotional send-off was again captured by a waiting media. 'They were hugging and kissing until the last minute when he had to go on the plane,' one witness said. 'It looked liked it was really hard for them to stay apart.'

Much more civilised was their next public appearance together, back in New York in April, where Leo was attending Robert De Niro's Tribeca Film Festival to help launch a movie he produced. *Gardener of Eden* (2007) was a dark comedy starring his old pal Lukas Haas as an ordinary Joe living at home with his parents, who accidentally gets transformed into a vigilante.

Leo was invited to use the festival to air his environmental documentary, *The 11th Hour* (2007), which he wrote, produced and narrated. Instead, he chose to premiere it at Cannes the following month. For years, DiCaprio had wanted to produce a film highlighting the fragility of the planet. 'Global warming is not only the No. 1 environmental challenge we face today, but one of the most important issues facing all of humanity. We all have to do our part to raise awareness about global warming and the problems we as a people face in promoting a sustainable environmental future for our planet,' he declared.

Focusing on the environmental crisis through the eyes of A-list activists such as Stephen Hawking, David Suzuki and Mikhail Gorbachev, DiCaprio produced the movie on a miniscule budget, calling in favours to make the project happen. It was an issue close to his heart since his schooldays, when he dreamt of becoming a biologist and he rejected criticism that he was jumping on the green bandwagon.

'If people don't want to listen to what I have to say on environmental issues, that's their right,' he responded. 'It's not going to stop me from using the opportunity as somebody in the public eye to highlight issues that aren't being given enough attention. The next generation – my children, my grandchildren –

are the ones who are going to feel the hardest effect of what's going on in the world today.

'Working with environmental organisations, I've seen how issues like global warming have been represented in the media, with people at one end saying it doesn't exist and at the other saying we need to make radical changes. Most of the time, it becomes an argument.'

DiCaprio went on to describe the movie as running 'the gamut of all the different environmental issues in the world: global warming, deforestation, biodiversity, the pollution of our water systems and oceans.' As with everything else he had done, he threw himself into the project. 'It was a two-year odyssey,' he said. 'And it's finally come together.'

Wary of the criticism he would receive if he didn't practise what he preached, Leo was quick to highlight his own green credentials. As well as his eco-friendly car, he installed solar panels on his villa in the Hollywood Hills and continued to eschew private jets for commercial airlines when travelling abroad. The point that he was trying to get across was that everyone has it in them to make small, but powerful changes.

'I try to live a green lifestyle,' he said. 'I've done the things that I can do in my house to make my house green – energy efficient appliances, I drive a hybrid car, I have solar panels – but I don't walk to work.'

Given 2007 was a big year, however – leading up to the next presidential elections in the US in 2008 – Leo revealed he hadn't yet found a candidate worthy of his support in the same way as he threw his backing behind John Kerry in 2004. He also firmly refuted any suggestions he was making his own bid to follow Arnold Schwarzenegger into politics.

'I have no political aspirations whatsoever,' he insisted. Regarding a suitable green candidate, he added: 'I've yet to hear a candidate that has clearly laid out their environmental policy in a way that's inspiring to me. I want to hear hardcore facts. I went to 14 different states to support Kerry in the last campaign because I thought he had an amazing environmental policy, but I've yet to hear a candidate that's compared in that regard.'

If Leonardo thought he'd be able to command headlines for all the right reasons ahead of the premiere of *11th Hour* at Cannes, he was wrong, though. In May, his publicist Ken Sunshine was forced to refute claims in a new book, *Tabloid Prodigy*, that there might have been anything more to his friendship with Tobey Maguire. DiCaprio had been plagued by gay rumours for years and insisted it was one of the worst things he'd heard about himself.

Yet, the insinuation reared its head again in 2007 in the most spurious of circumstances. Freelance writer Marlise Elizabeth Kast penned a supposed exposé on the antics of the tabloids. She claimed editors at *Globe* had asked her to probe into whether the best pals were hiding a deeper 'secret'. Kast says she got in touch with the *Spider-Man* star's mother Wendy, who unwittingly gave the editors ammunition by 'divulging details of how the two friends "shared a bed and wore ribbons in their hair."'

Wendy Maguire told Kast: 'Those two are just free-spirited guys. Most of the friends they hang around with are gay; they're comfortable with that. But I think Leo and Tobey are the crossover between men and women – they have feminine traits they are willing to accept. They aren't ashamed to have any sort of title, even if that means someone calling them gay.'

The author herself wasn't about to claim the stars were gay, but she said: 'Wendy had provided exactly what the editors wanted – insinuations.'

So even though no one was willing to claim anything substantial, the insinuation that there might have been something going on somehow made the public domain. If nothing else, it was a bizarre illustration of how the modern media operated. Almost certainly wishing he could treat the matter with the contempt it deserved, Ken Sunshine insisted that the report 'is untrue'. Maguire's spokesman Kelly Bush added: 'This is so ridiculous I don't feel the need to respond.'

Even aside from the number of women Leo had been with over the years, what made the suggestion even harder to comprehend was that Maguire at the time was planning his wedding to fiancée Jennifer Meyer, with whom he had a daughter named Ruby.

It didn't help, though, that the baseless rumours followed on from another book with the potential to cause embarrassment for Leo and his friends. His former financier, Dana Giacchetto, was attempting to find a publisher for his memoirs on the cash scandal and in a bid to ramp up interest, was peddling old photos of Leo. One showed DiCaprio and Maguire prancing about in costume as members of the kitsch 1970s band Kiss.

Video footage of the jape, which happened years before, was being touted to promote *You Will Make Money In Your Sleep*, Giacchetto's autobiography (ghostwritten by journalist Emily White). 'Leo was his constant companion,' White said of Giacchetto and the actor. 'They were living in a kind of limbo before *Titanic* hit. They had a Halloween party, where everyone was dressed up like Kiss characters. Dana made a home movie of it, and there is character actor Lukas Haas playing "Hey Jude" on the piano, while Dana and his friends danced around in their masks. Watching the film, I can't tell which one is Leo, which one is Dana or Tobey Maguire – they are in hysterics.'

Mercifully, Leo continued his focus on matters of much greater global importance and carried on his theme of promoting green issues by taking part in the American leg of Live Earth, a global live event to combat climate change. He took to the stage in the Giants Stadium, New Jersey, to help present acts including Bon Jovi, Kanye West and The Police.

The year was shaping up to be one of the busiest Leo had ever known. He had signed up for two movies, which although worlds apart in subject matter and style, were similarly enticing and demanding in equal measure. The first appealed to him because it signalled a reunion that Leo fans had been dreaming of since his frozen body slipped beneath the waves at the end of *Titanic*. Kate Winslet and Leonardo DiCaprio together again on screen – what could be better? Fans could never have imagined, however, that, after a 12-year wait, they'd catch up with each other again though this time not as hopeless, star-crossed lovers but as a bitter, stifled married couple, who slowly tear each other apart.

There were good reasons why Richard Yates' novel, *Revolutionary Road* (1961) had never made it to the big screen. Although widely considered a little-read classic, its dark and unforgiving subject matter – not to mention the mid-1950s setting, an era that until *Mad Men* came along was considered to have zero entertainment potential – meant it hardly screamed 'fun night out'.

On the positive side, like *Titanic*, both the central characters are desperately unhappy – just with each other this time – and there's an equally desperate demise. No, when Kate and Leo signed up to rekindle their on-screen partnership as April and Frank Wheeler, a married couple sinking into suburban Connecticut hell, they were not doing so with the audiences who returned to *Titanic* five and ten times in mind. Part autobiographical, *Revolutionary Road* charts the disintegration of the Wheelers' marriage in agonising detail. April, like Yates' first wife Sheila, has theatrical aspirations and believes the answer to the drudgery of their existence is to relocate to Paris. Frank is stuck in a seemingly dead-end office job. After he begins a somewhat passionless affair with a colleague, it's the beginning of the end.

Several attempts had been made to adapt the book for the big screen but for various reasons, none of them made it off the ground. Eventually BBC Film bought the rights and hired Justin Haythe to write a screenplay because, by his own admission, he was 'hugely affordable'.

Yates' biographer Blake Bailey is surprised a movie of the

Revolutionary Road plot was even made. He said: 'It has long been an ambition in Hollywood to make a movie that's the last word on postwar suburban malaise, but like any highly nuanced work of literary art, *Revolutionary Road* is awfully hard to translate onto the screen.'

That it was made at all was mostly down to the enthusiasm of Kate Winslet, who was captivated from the moment she read the script. She and Leo – who had remained close since their *Titanic* ordeal – had always harboured dreams of working together again but were waiting for the right project.

According to Winslet, *Revolutionary Road* was it – 'I loved the emotional nakedness, the brutal honesty about what can sometimes happen in a marriage. And also all the minor characters are so good.'

She gave Leo a copy of the script over a coffee and then set to work on her husband, Sam Mendes – also the Oscar-winning director of *American Beauty*. 'I just told him, "Babe, you've got to do this,"' she said.

Mendes agreed and once Leo came on board, almost immediately the movie went into production. What none of the crew appreciated when they took the project on was just how cherished the novel is by the literary community. Even Matthew Weiner, creator of *Mad Men* – the stylish series about the morally questionable ad men of the early 1960s – is a fan.

'The book is such a kind of cult classic,' remarked Sam Mendes. 'It was terrifying. The most common comment from friends of mine who had read the book was, "Don't fuck it up!" That was basically all they said, "Don't fuck it up!" And the biggest compliment I get now is, "Thank fuck you didn't fuck it up!" That's all I get. Thank God I didn't fuck it up!'

Mendes, who followed his success with *American Beauty* (1999) with *Road to Perdition* and the war movie *Jarhead*, was drawn to the intimacy of the two central characters. 'I just loved Frank and April,' he explained. 'Even though it's set in the fifties it seemed to me to be really a movie about a couple, about a relationship. And I've never made a movie that intimate before – I wanted to try.'

The story chimed with DiCaprio because it posed the big question: 'What is the American Dream supposed to be – and how similar are we now to that era in a lot of ways?' He added: 'It's about two people going crazy in that kind of environment, being stripped of their identity and feeling they are living a life of clichés. What drew me towards it was that it's very reflective of the United States' moral position in the fifties and this is where we still hinge ourselves morally, how we view our family, our fundamentals. And also, I'm a huge fan of Kate and Sam.'

DiCaprio also revealed how he and Kate Winslet had decided a long time before that if they were to work together again it had to be on something completely different to *Titanic*. 'We fundamentally knew that if we were going to do something together again, we didn't want to tread on any type of similar territory,' he explained. 'We just knew it would be a fundamental mistake to try to repeat any of those themes.'

Before filming began Mendes faced challenges in trying to recreate the claustrophobic atmosphere he desired. Period houses were too small, so instead he decided to shoot all the interior shots in an actual house in Darien, Connecticut, which was adapted to suit the 1950s. It had the desired effect. 'It was many months in this house and there was no escaping the environment,' DiCaprio recalled. 'I think it fed into the performances.'

Leonardo also relished the opportunity to once again face his old sparring partner. 'I knew that Kate and I could really get stuff out of each other, performance wise, that we could push each other's buttons. It was exciting.'

And it seems the actors' shared experience of filming *Titanic* came out during their latest project. 'Seeing her now on set as opposed to back then is very different,' explained Leo. 'I think in the past we both looked up to the director or the producer as guidance systems, wondering, "What are they going to tell us to do?" We were very young in the industry. Now it's a different dynamic: we've both produced movies on our own, both been a part of them and it's a difficult level of responsibility we have now.'

When asked how much Kate had changed in the intervening years, Leo said: 'It's more what has remained the same with Kate. She's still one of the most real individuals I've ever met, and I don't use that term lightly. She's got a real genuine soul. She's a sweetheart and she's also one of the most committed actresses I've ever met, and she's had that ever since she was young. Ever since I knew her, the girl did her homework and she's committed to what she does – and she wants to make the best movie she possibly can. That, she's retained.'

In many ways, Winslet's life and career had followed a similar trajectory to Leo's since *Titanic*. Although her performance in Cameron's epic earned her a second Oscar nomination by the age of 22 – the youngest actress ever to achieve such a feat – in contrast, her career and personal life suffered a series of stutters.

Marriage to Jim Threapleton – who she met on the set of *Hideous Kinky* (1998), her next film after *Titanic* – led to a beautiful baby daughter, Mia, but then it all started to fall apart. After breaking up from Threapleton, she divorced him in 2001. Her subsequent affair with the director Sam Mendes brought more criticism that she was somehow using him to further her career. They married in 2003 and had a son – Joe – later that year.

Like Leo, Kate had also been the victim of some unkind, and often unmerited, criticism. Always considered a champion of curvy women, Winslet soon experienced her own image coming under scrutiny after she became embroiled in a magazine airbrushing furore. In February 2003 GQ magazine printed photographs of the actress that had been digitally altered to make her appear thinner. Kate stressed the images were altered without her consent and the magazine later apologised, but it was a controversy she could have done without.

On screen, many of Winslet's roles were considered offbeat and wrong for her; although she landed her third Oscar nomination for *Iris* in 2001, many of her films were slated by the critics. Like Leo when he linked up with Martin Scorsese, Kate's career suddenly enjoyed a renaissance. *Eternal Sunshine of the Spotless Mind* (2004) and *Little Children* (2006) earned her further Oscar nominations, while she won a BAFTA for her performance in *Finding Neverland* (2004).

Although Winslet now commanded £6 million a movie by the time she was filming *Revolutionary Road*, she insisted family still came first. Before filming began, she also revealed concerns about the effect such an intense role – in the first movie they'd done together – might have on her relationship with her husband.

'Going into it, I did have several moments where I would say "Oh my God, what if we have a row? What will we do?" And Sam would say, "Oh, don't be silly, of course we won't." And I was thinking, "Oh, well, I'm sure we won't – I hope we don't."'

While Mendes shared his wife's view that the process would be challenging, he did not have the same concerns: 'It's as challenging as it ever is doing a big emotional film,' he said, before adding about the intense, sexual and emotional scenes: 'Those are tough scenes to shoot with anyone. Actually, I found them easier to shoot with Kate because I know her so well. I didn't find it difficult or awkward, particularly; it's kind of cathartic. Put it this way, you spend twelve hours a day staging an all-mighty fight: the last thing you want to do when you get home is fight. You're just relieved and thrilled you're doing it, or actually quite elated that you've done it together. So it weirdly puts you in high spirits rather than the opposite.'

The script called for a dramatic sex scene, which might have been awkward. Instead Mendes was crouched by the camera, shouting instructions to Leo. His tips included: 'Press your fingers right into her back, hard. Grab her butt, Leo!'

Even though Winslet admitted she found it off-putting to have her husband directing her on-screen lover, Leo insisted: 'I didn't think about it. I was entirely used to kissing Kate after making *Titanic*. We'd done a lot of sequences like that before so this time it was kind of easy.'

Overall, however, Leonardo found the shoot particularly draining, so much so that he delayed the start of his next project by two months to recover mentally and prepare himself for his next challenge. 'Coming from *Revolutionary Road*, where it was like a piece of theatre, talking about our feelings for months at a time, it took a while to adjust,' he explained.

Winslet also found the experience to be draining and revealed that she and Leo spent almost the entire time 'in each other's pockets. It wasn't a very big budget film so we couldn't afford to shoot in a studio and we were in this house, which was tiny, oppressive, claustrophobic, sweaty, boiling hot, with a whole crew of people. It was like a pressure cooker every single day. And so we were physically close together and able to have a constant dialogue about the scenes – running lines, sharing ideas. He knows my buttons and I know his, and we know how to push them in very specific ways.'

Decompressing after such an intense shoot, he might have hoped to take things easy for a while. As Leo should have expected by then, however, controversy is only ever a headline away.

CHAPTER 20

UNDER FIRE

At first, the reports from Tel Aviv seemed innocuous. 'From the army of the people, the Israel Defense Forces are gradually becoming the army of half the people,' Defense Minister Ehud Barak announced in August 2007. 'A soldier must not feel when he goes to battle that in the eyes of part of our society he's a sucker.'

He went on to say that a worrying trend was developing whereby celebrities in his country were dodging the draft. Leonardo's supermodel girlfriend was mentioned but it seemed only because she, along with many other now-famous Israelis were among the 43 per cent of women and 25 per cent of men who were not performing their military service (three years for men, two years for women). Under Israeli law, military service was compulsory, but increasing numbers of young people were choosing to op out by claiming to be religious or feigning mental illness.

Barak said that he intended to halt the trend: 'I will act to reduce draft dodging. As a society, we must not turn draft dodgers into heroes.'

Bar Refaeli soon found herself sucked into the controversy when it was claimed that at the age of 18, she had avoided the draft by entering into a quickie marriage with a contemporary of her parents before divorcing shortly afterwards.

She herself then stoked the flames by giving an interview in which she stated: 'I really wanted to serve in the IDF [Israel Defence Forces], but I don't regret not enlisting because it paid off, big time. That's just the way it is, celebrities have other needs. I hope my case has influenced the army.'

And she went on: 'Israel or Uganda, what difference does it make? It makes no difference to me. Why is it good to die for our country? What, isn't it better to live in New York? Why should 18-year-old kids have to die? It's dumb that people have to die so that I can live in Israel.'

As if that wasn't enough to infuriate those in her homeland, for good measure she added an attack on the paparazzi. Claiming the treatment she and Leo received when they visited Jerusalem had convinced her that she would never bring any other celebrity pals to the country, she added: 'In Israel, the photographers nudge me in the shoulder and ask me to pose. Enough already, don't touch me – I'm not your friend!'

As the controversy threatened to get out of hand, the Israeli Forum for the Promotion of Equal Share in the Burden (an organisation encouraging people to do their bit for the good of Israel) threatened to boycott the Israel fashion chain Fox if it hired Refaeli. Eventually a compromise had to be reached where the model agreed to visit injured IDF soldiers on visits to Israel and encourage enlistment in the army.

Amid the furore, Leo and Bar were not seen together in public and it appeared their relationship might not survive the year. What sparked this speculation was that Bar was spotted in Tel Aviv with the same man Gisele had turned to after her split with Leo: surfer Kelly Slater. It seemed to be the same old story – Bar's 'no celebs in Israel rule' notwithstanding, perhaps because he wasn't famous enough – because Slater did not take too kindly to being snapped in public and lashed out at photographers.

At the same time Leo appeared to be up to his old tricks in New York, hanging out with fellow actor Josh Hartnett and being accused of checking out the talent at the after-party for the new skateboarding film, *Nothing But the Truth* (2008). Happily, though, by the end of the year any talk of a split was long gone after it emerged Leo had simply been too busy to keep up their long-distance relationship. The rumours were quickly quashed in December when *Us* magazine quoted a source who claimed their period apart was solely down to DiCaprio filming *Body of Lies* (2008) in Morocco.

The film that had kept Leo away from his girlfriend was a thriller based on a theme of international terrorism and was one DiCaprio had been eager to do because it provided an opportunity to work with British director Ridley Scott, the man behind masterpieces like *Blade Runner* and *Alien*. 'Ridley's been on my list of people to work with for a long time and there are only a couple of people on there,' said Leo. 'Besides Kubrick, he's probably one of the only directors to have made a masterpiece in every genre.'

He hadn't anticipated, however, just how gruelling an experience it would turn out to be. In one scene his character, CIA man Roger Ferris, is tortured to extract information. 'I was strapped up to a wooden table for hours and hours, with my hands wired to it,' he revealed. 'There was enough stuff there to freak me out – yet it was a film, not real life.

'*Body of Lies* was probably the toughest film since *Titanic*,' he went on. 'I found the whole thing difficult to deal with. Fortunately, as an actor, I am not the type who goes home and broods about my character. I can go from playing the role on a film set to being myself in a very short space of time. I especially needed that sort of approach on *Body of Lies* because otherwise the part could have been harmful. As it was, the only mental pressure was waiting and wondering about what would go on screen.'

The movie was set mainly in the Middle East, but because the authorities in Dubai refused permission to film there because of the sensitive subject matter, it was shot mainly on location in Morocco (which doubled up as Jordan and a host of other locations). Filming also took place in Washington, DC, where it began in the September and lasted over 65 days until December 2007. DiCaprio and his co-star Russell Crowe spent months away.

'It was quite a shock to be suddenly filming in Morocco alongside Russell, being shot at from helicopters,' DiCaprio explained. 'A lot of life is put on hold when you make these movies. Everything – including personal relationships – is put on ice when being on location for five or six months.'

His character, a covert agent in Iraq trying to track down the leader of a fundamentalist cell responsible for bombings in the West, is an Arab speaker who has developed a high regard for the culture and countries where he has to work. But his boss (Crowe, who put on 50lb for the role) cares nothing for the region and will sacrifice anyone in the fight against terrorists.

Leonardo revealed: 'It was exhausting. Ridley and Russell like to keep up this frenetic sort of tension. But when you get into that pace you embrace it and it actually became exhilarating.

'For me, the film asks a good question – what do you do when you are trying to hold on to a higher moral context in an immoral world? Ferris is trying to do good by his country, while his country is slapping him in the face – I'm very anti-war.

'It's important for me to do movies that spark a debate,' he continued. 'But they're hard to find and they don't always have a director I would want to work with. I love doing movies like *Body of Lies* or *Blood Diamond* because when you are dealing with issues the world is facing, you get that much more excited.'

The movie was also the first time he had worked with Russell Crowe since they'd both appeared in *The Quick and the Dead* (1995). Since then Crowe had gone on to become a major

Hollywood player, earning three Academy Award nominations and winning one for *Gladiator* (2000), also directed by Ridley. Crowe joked that he wondered if all the *Titanic* madness had changed DiCaprio. 'Two major things have changed with Leo,' he quipped. 'Now he can drink legally and he's not a virgin.'

Leonardo laughed it off, saying: 'He's come up with that line a couple of times. He actually doesn't know what he's talking about, though for professional reasons I'm going to let him have his shtick. That's all I'm going to say.'

After an intense year, Leo must have been grateful for the chance to return to some normality that December in Los Angeles. Any talk of him and Bar splitting up was finally quashed when they were spotted holding hands at the Polo Lounge in Beverly Hills and a source was quoted, saying: 'They were never really "off" – it was always a distance thing. Leo was making a movie in Morocco and Bar had her modelling career. It's a struggle to make a relationship like theirs work, but yes, they're together.'

Yet while distance had certainly been a factor in the speculation about their status, emotionally-speaking it seemed they still had a bit of a chasm to bridge. During their time apart it was suggested that Leo had renewed contact with his old flame Gisele, by then settled in a new relationship with New England Patriots' quarterback Tom Brady. A friend told *In Touch Weekly*: 'Leo now realises what a mistake he made by not marrying Gisele. He knows she's with Tom, so if he can't have her as a girlfriend, he wants her as a friend.'

Brady wasn't exactly thrilled by the news and had allegedly been upset that DiCaprio was back in Gisele's life, despite her reassurances that the relationship was just platonic. Leo had apparently confided in Tobey Maguire that he regretted losing her back in 2005 because he was afraid of marriage. The fact that he still felt he needed to go outside the relationship with Bar for emotional support can't have pleased her either.

Nevertheless all appeared well as Leo and Bar found time to relax together in Mexico at the end of the year. She guaranteed the watching press photographers would go home happy after parading about in a tiny bikini, showing that men's mag *Arena* was justified in crowning her 'Body of the Year' for 2007.

Going into 2008, Bar must have been wondering whether her relationship with Leo would follow the same fate as her Brazilian rival's as she continued to receive mixed messages, though.

Leo had presented a ring to the woman who held a special place in his heart, yet Bar's wedding finger remained conspicuously bare. Leo had made the touching gesture to his co-star Kate Winslet after shooting wrapped on *Revolutionary Road*. The actress proudly wore the ring – that bore a personal inscription inside – next to her wedding and engagement bands.

It also emerged that Leo was still finding it hard to cut loose from Gisele when pals revealed he often dialled her number, particularly after a few drinks. 'It's like he just needs to hear her voice,' said a source. 'I think he never thought she'd walk away.'

Perhaps luckily for Leo, he was able to duck any tricky questions about his long-term commitments by throwing himself into his next project: his fourth with Martin Scorsese. In March 2008, filming for Paramount Pictures began on *Shutter Island*, an adaptation of Dennis Lehane's hit psychological thriller of the same name.

DiCaprio plays US Marshall Edward 'Teddy' Daniels, who is investigating a sinister establishment called Ashecliffe Hospital for the Criminally Insane, a psychiatric facility located on an island where he comes to question his own sanity. Set in 1954 – the same era as *Revolutionary Road* – it's a gripping journey into the dark side of the human psyche.

Accompanied by his new partner Chuck Aule (played by Mark Ruffalo), Daniels is looking into the mysterious disappearance of patient Rachel Solando (British actress Emily Mortimer), who has apparently vanished from her locked cell.

As well as solving this particular case, Daniels hopes to track down another of the Ashecliffe inmates – an arsonist responsible for the death of his wife (Michelle Williams), two years earlier. However, Daniels is a character not without his problems. Haunted by his loss, he's also plagued by crippling migraines, disturbed by his experiences in the Second World War and is seemingly thwarted at every turn in the investigation by Ashecliffe's head psychiatrist Dr John Cawley (Sir Ben Kingsley). Soon Daniels realises that there's far more going on in the madhouse than just the strange disappearance of a young woman.

Boston writer Lehane's books had an impressive track record of being adapted for the big screen. *Mystic River* (2003) produced Oscar-winning performances from Sean Penn and Tim Robbins, while *Gone Baby Gone* (2007) led to an Academy Award nomination for Amy Ryan.

What attracted Scorsese to the story was the atmosphere it conjured, reminiscent of classic psychological thrillers such as *Vertigo*, *Flatliners* and *Se7en*. 'I've always enjoyed this type of film,' the director said. 'I like it when the characters gradually learn more with the audience. It's the mystery of it all. I like seeing how the characters behave. It's very rich and it's very elemental about being a human being. There is something in this story that touches us inside. Hopefully, I've succeeded in portraying that.'

It was a film where DiCaprio felt he suffered as much mental torture as his character. 'I was intrigued by this screenplay,' he said. 'It's very much a throwback to great detective films from the past, like *Vertigo*. It's a genre thriller piece with twists, turns and lots of different layers. Once we started to unravel who this man was and what he had been through, it took us to a place where no way out was seen. It got darker and darker, and more emotionally intense than we ever expected.'

The movie was shot at various locations in Massachusetts and to make the settings as authentic as possible, Scorsese filmed the asylum scenes in the former Medfield State Hospital and what were once industrial buildings in Taunton's Whittenton Mills Complex became the Dachau Concentration Camp, the subject of Daniels' flashbacks. To capture a dramatic hurricane scene, he battered his actors with wind and rain.

'There were a few weeks there that I have to say were some of the most hardcore filming experiences I've ever had,' Leonardo recalled. 'It was like a living trauma in a way; it was pretty intense. I don't say that stuff very often because it always seems superficial when you're talking about moviemaking but it really went to places in unearthing who this man was that I didn't think it would get to. Shooting in an old mental institution on an island, every day, we were surrounded by mental illness.'

While Leo was filming *Shutter Island*, Bar set out her plans for children – 'at least three' – and for them to have a similar upbringing to hers. 'I had a very beautiful childhood,' she revealed, 'and I hope that my kids will be able to experience the same thing.'

Although she might not have been able to get Leonardo to commit to anything much longer than a basketball game, Bar was at least able to boost her career on the back of the exposure she was enjoying. Having begun her career before the age of one, starring in a TV advert aged just eight months, she was to feature in her first movie: *Session* (2011), an English language film directed by Israeli director Haim Bouzaglo. Around this time, she was also chosen as the cover model for Jewish magazine *Heeb*'s first swimsuit issue.

For Leo, however, any future plans would have to be temporarily put on hold. In the summer of 2008, he suffered a personal loss that would consume him with grief.

CHAPTER 21

BAROMETER OF TRUTH

Helene Indenbirken always spoke her mind – it was what Leonardo loved about her. He enjoys recounting a story about the time he took her to the Musée National Picasso in Paris when the DiCaprios were treated to a private tour of the great master's latest exhibition – by the artist's great-grandson.

Knowing his 'Oma' would be unimpressed by Picasso's unique style, Leonardo feared she might offend their generous host. 'I could tell she was not into these paintings whatsoever, and I was, like, "Oh boy, Oma, you just be polite! You know, this is the great-grandson,"' he told Oprah Winfrey. 'And she was sitting there, looking at the paintings. She goes, "What is this? What is this?" I said, "Well, that's a woman." She goes, "You could tell me this looks like a dog, a flower, a cat. It looks like nothing to me. If you paint a woman, paint a woman." So, of course, he came. She repeated the same thing to him – I was in total shock.'

He needn't have worried, however. 'Afterwards, he wrote me this long letter,' Leo went on, 'saying how in love he was with my grandma, that it was so refreshing to meet people of the Old World like that; that he had his butt kissed his entire life because he was

Picasso's great-grandson and it was just totally refreshing to meet people like that again. So that really touched me.'

Fond memories like this came flooding back in August 2008 when the sad news emerged from Germany that Helene had passed away, aged 93. She'd led a remarkable life and remained an indomitable spirit to the end. Her passing was publicly marked by a brief statement from the Mayor of her hometown, Oer-Erkenschwick, who simply stated that she had died in hospital in nearby Recklinghausen. But when Leonardo finally spoke of his loss, some months later, it was clear that the loss had hit him hard.

Describing her as his 'barometer of truth', he said Helene, who accompanied him to the German premiere of *The Aviator* when she was 89, helped him keep his feet on the ground. 'I feel very sad that Oma is gone,' he told *Parade* magazine. 'I always loved being with Oma. She was completely pure, honest, unaffected – so unlike anything else that I was ever used to. She was my barometer of truth.

'Sometimes I'd ask Oma, "Isn't it great now, all this stuff happening in my life?" She'd say, "Don't you worry about that. Take a break – be a bricklayer, work with your hands. You'll love it. Step back and reflect on what's going on in your life. Appreciate it."'

His grandmother's passing also made him question whether there was more to life than simply having a successful career. 'I definitely feel a need to make my life about more than just my career,' he said later. 'I was thinking to myself how little of it has been lived normally as opposed to being spent on some far-off movie location. Family is something I'm starting to think about more and more, especially now that my grandmother is no longer around. It makes you think about the impermanence of things and how important it is to be part of a family – to have some meaning apart from your work.'

It wasn't clear what effect this introspection would have on his relationship with Bar Refaeli and the frustrations of being a film-star's girlfriend were all too evident when, at the start of October, she had to endure conflicting reports about Leonardo's long-term plans – all on the same day!

First, he was quoted by the Press Association as being fairly certain he had no immediate plans to settle down. 'Ah, how do you answer something like that? So, um, I am being asked to look in the future, I suppose, quickly. No, I don't have any plan,' he said when quizzed.

Yet the same agency also quoted him as saying that he would one day like to tie the knot. 'What I definitely feel a need for is to make my life about more than just my career,' he stated. 'Just last night I was thinking to myself how little of my life has been lived normally and not spent on some far-off movie location. I want to get married and have children. In saying that, I realise I am contradicting everything I've said before. I absolutely believe in marriage.'

What might have given his young model girlfriend hope that one day she might be Mrs DiCaprio, was when he added: 'I hope I never get cynical – I think you need youthful energy, excitement and optimism in life. There is a lot I want to do, and the more cynical you become, the more you sit on your butt and do nothing. The one thing that I would love is to never become cynical about the things I think are really important, like family, like the environment. What I want is to be known as someone who stood for something.'

Bar did, however, find an unexpected cheerleader in the shape of British celebrity interviewer Chrissy Iley who, after chatting to Leo to promote *Body of Lies*, wrote that he seemed much more content than he'd done the last time they'd met – when he'd still been with Gisele.

Giving a fascinating insight into Leo's homelife, in an article for the *Observer*, Iley wrote: 'The last time I was in a room with Leonardo DiCaprio was in 2001. It was his kitchen, and I was interviewing his then girlfriend, Brazilian gorgeousness Gisele Bündchen. Her Yorkshire terrier was yapping and she was talking non-stop in a dizzying way, with demanding eyes, lavish hair. She was warm, volatile and had a sense of entitlement. Leo was withdrawn, quiet and perhaps a little lost, chopping vegetables meticulously in the kitchen. He was making food to take over to a friend's house and he kept saying, "Baby, we're late." But Baby carried on talking and demanding empanadas. Gisele and the Yorkie were going crazy for the tasty meaty morsels. Leo just kept chopping vegetables. Eventually, Gisele drove me home. Joni Mitchell's "California" was playing, and we sang along. She told me Leo didn't do karaoke, but apart from that, life with him was great. But it didn't surprise me when they split up. It seemed as if they had nothing in common.'

Iley went on to wonder if his relationship with the Israeli model was less complicated. Certainly Leo seemed to recognise the cosmic forces at work – he is a Scorpio with Libra rising – and revealed he was getting better at balancing the more passionate elements of his personality. 'That means I'm trying to balance the passionate, dark, insane parts of Scorpio the best I can, and I think I'm doing a pretty good job,' he said.

Indeed his newfound calmness was something Russell Crowe had recognised during the filming of *Body of Lies*. Crowe was quick to point out that his co-star had remained essentially the same 'likeable guy' he'd encountered all those years ago on *The Quick and the Dead* but was now 'older and wiser'. But DiCaprio responded: 'Who knows if I'm down to earth? I think we all go through an obnoxious phase in our teenage years. There's a perception of people in the arts, and sometimes people live up to the image of the egomaniacal actor who's a prick to everyone.'

Certainly, at this stage in his career, though DiCaprio appeared more settled, more comfortable in his own skin and more willing to give an insight into what made him tick. He acknowledged that in some respects he was putting his partying behind him and slowing down somewhat. 'I celebrated my birthday over a quiet dinner with family and friends,' he revealed. 'Ten years ago, it would have been a giant party.'

And, rather than checking out the nightlife in Los Angeles, he revealed that he would rather be scoping out the wildlife for real in Africa and South America: 'I am regularly able to escape to watch wildlife in Africa and South America. Looking at lions, elephants and zebras in the wild is a passion. When watching whales, it brings it home what a wonderful world it is out there. I've had pet dogs, frogs and even a lizard. Animals have always been a big passion for me and I remember, at one stage, wanting to be a travel agent so I could get out in the world.'

On his other passions, he added: 'I collect art and I have a good movie-poster collection. Everything I dreamt about as a kid. I am a fan of hip-hop, the band A Tribe Called Quest, in particular, and my friend, Q-Tip. I have been trying to persuade him to put out another solo album and he's finally about to do so – it's called *The Renaissance*.'

Film-wise, he remained a huge fan of anything by Nicholson, De Niro and Scorsese, but also old movies such as *The Third Man*, *Lawrence of Arabia*, *Sunset Boulevard* and *East of Eden* were personal favourites. 'One of my favourites is *The Bicycle Thief*, made in 1948 by the Italian director Vittorio De Sica,' he added.

The one subject he remained coy about was romance, declining invitations to say if he had any plans to settle down with Refaeli. 'Do I want to settle down and marry? Sure,' he said, rather unconvincingly. 'But I don't have a crystal ball and so I can't tell you when that will happen.'

Body of Lies was eventually released in October 2008 and while it took over $115 million at the box office, it opened to mixed critical response. It merely served as a warm-up, however, for Leo's main cinematic event of the year and his keenly anticipated reunion on screen with Kate Winslet in *Revolutionary Road*.

Although Richard Yates died in 1992 and was unable to see his work adapted for cinema, his daughters were delighted with the treatment and assisted at some screenings, providing introductions. 'They've been wonderful cheerleaders for the movie because they obviously loved it and are proud of it, and feel like their father is getting some of the praise that he deserved during his lifetime,' said director Sam Mendes. 'It's as close to getting a thumbs up from the man himself as you can get and that matters a lot to us.'

The movie was released just time for the awards season, appearing in only three theatres in December 2008 before a general release the following month. It quickly earned glowing reviews – particularly for Winslet and DiCaprio's stunningly authentic performances – and for Mendes' ability to capture the oppressive atmosphere of the novel. Despite its late arrival, it featured in a number of the lists of top ten films of 2008.

Angie Errigo, of *Empire* magazine, warned fans of Kate and Leo from *Titanic* days that those 'keen to reaffirm the transforming power of love may experience the desire to slash their wrists after this bleak drama in which love turns to loathing, defiance to tragedy'. Kenneth Turan of *The Los Angeles Times*, who famously panned director James Cameron at the time of *Titanic*, was kinder this time out, remarking that it 'takes the skill of stars Kate Winslet and Leonardo DiCaprio and director Sam Mendes to get this film to a place where it involves and moves us, which it finally does – but it is a near thing.'

But Roger Ebert in the *Chicago Sun-Times*, gushed: 'Frank and April are played by DiCaprio and Winslet as the sad ending to the romance in *Titanic*, and all other romances that are founded on nothing more than romance. They are so good they stop being actors and become the people I grew up around. This film is so good it is devastating. A lot of people believe their parents didn't understand them. What if they didn't understand themselves?'

The Foreign Press Association shared the opinion of its American counterparts and swiftly nominated *Revolutionary Road* for four

Golden Globes. Kate and Leo were recognised in the Best Actor categories, Mendes was nominated for Best Director and the film was up for Best Picture.

For Winslet, it set up an exciting awards season as she was also nominated for a Globe for her supporting role as a former Auschwitz guard in *The Reader* (2008), an adaptation of Bernhard Schlink's parable about post-war Germany. She had originally been first choice for the part but had pulled out because of a scheduling clash with *Revolutionary Road* and the role had subsequently gone to Nicole Kidman. When Kidman fell pregnant, however, the part became Kate's again.

Incredibly, she'd been nominated five times previously for an Oscar and a Golden Globe but never won. Before the ceremony she spoke of how much she wanted to win – 'Do I want it? You bet your fucking ass I do! I think that people assume that I don't care or don't want it, or don't need it or something. It's hard to be there five times, and I'm only human, you know?'

Perhaps she should have known what happens when you wait a long time for something – two come along at once. In the event, she triumphed in both the Best Actress and Best Supporting Actress categories – a feat never before achieved.

Having already been named Best Supporting Actress for her role in *The Reader*, Winslet took to the stage to deliver a breathless speech inundated with exasperated remarks like 'I'm so sorry' and 'Oh God!' – and in her excitement, even managed to forget the name of one of her fellow nominees.

'I'm so sorry, Anne Hathaway, Meryl Streep, Kristin Scott Thomas – and who's the other one? Angelina Jolie,' she panted. 'Now forgive me, is this really happening?' she added, refusing to 'wrap things up' as instructed by the autocue and instead spending a further three minutes acknowledging people, including co-star – for whom she declared her love and described as a 'special person in her world'.

'Leo, I'm so happy I can stand here and tell you how much I love you and how much I've loved you for 13 years, and your performance in this film is nothing short of spectacular. I love you with all my heart, I really do,' she said, as the actor blew her kisses from the audience.

The speech brought to mind Gwyneth Paltrow's tearful display at the Oscars in 1999. Paltrow won Best Actress for Shakespeare in Love and said afterwards that she got emotional because she realised it would be the last outing for her grandfather, who was in the audience and who died not long after the award ceremony.

Amid all the melodrama of Kate's speech it was almost overlooked that Leonardo lost out on the chance to make it a memorable double as Mickey Rourke collected the Best Actor award for *The Wrestler*. But Leo was more than delighted for his good friend and co-star: 'It was an unbelievable achievement. Not one, but two in one night – I don't know what the records are, but it seems to me that has never happened. Certainly not for Supporting and Best Actress.'

When it came to the Oscars, *Revolutionary Road* was cruelly overlooked – only nominated in minor categories – although Michael Shannon received a Best Supporting Actor nomination for his powerful performance as the neighbours' troubled son, John. According to Academy rules, an actor or actress may receive only one nomination per category and due to the difference in rules between the Golden Globes and the Academy Awards, Winslet's role in *The Reader* was considered a leading one by the Academy, so her performance in *Revolutionary Road* could not be nominated.

Against tough opposition, including two previous Oscar winners in Meryl Streep and Angelina Jolie, Winslet finally triumphed. Although her achievement wasn't for *Revolutionary Road*, she never passed up an opportunity to gush about how much Leo meant to her, though. 'He feels more like my husband than my real husband,' she said. 'I'm talking about him so much!'

For Leo, his Oscar wait would have to continue but he was

determined to put on a brave face despite the continued snub from the Academy. 'I have a theory,' he said. 'We all have our personal choices of who we think should win, but there are certain times you look back at the movie that won that year and you think, "How was that humanly possible?"

'But I am not feverishly hunting one down. I am trying to do the best work I possibly can and making movies that will have resonance for years to come. I think if you try for an Oscar or a goal like that, the more people are going to see it as transparent. It's not on my radar. If it happens, great, but I'm happy to continue working as I am, really.'

For Leo it was business as usual, but for his ambitious girlfriend, it was high time to remind the commitment-phobe what she had to offer.

CHAPTER 22

ARE THEY,
AREN'T THEY ?

Big things were certainly on the horizon for Bar Refaeli, who was proving she had the front to be one of the world's most famous models. First, Marks & Spencer unveiled her as its latest lingerie model and then it was revealed the 23-year-old would be the cover girl for the coveted *Sports Illustrated* swimsuit edition – the first Israeli to do so.

In a provocative image, she was photographed wearing a stunningly skimpy Missoni bikini, teasingly tugging the strings on her bottoms southward. That one cover can make or break a career and Bar was fully aware of its importance, especially after narrowly missing out the year before. 'As soon as I found out I'd got the cover this time, I called 30 people,' she said, 'all my friends in Israel, all my friends in LA, my grandma and my grandpa.'

She added: 'I don't know if Leo will like the cover, but I really, really love it. I'm sure other people will, too.'

SI group editor Terry McDonell explained the thinking behind choosing Bar for the cover – other than the fact that using Leonardo DiCaprio's girlfriend would guarantee acres of coverage.

'This photo is modern, her hair and swimsuit look natural. You see her freckles. Her body is amazing and she looks intelligent,' McDonell said.

Of all the shots SI could have used, Bar was delighted with the one chosen, mostly because it showed her with her bikini top on. 'This is the one I felt the most comfortable with,' Refaeli said. 'You have the beach, blue water and a body. That's it.'

Bar also found herself in the limelight when she chose to front a 'Save the Beach' protest – an environmental campaign that must surely have been appreciated by her other half. Closely flanked by her over-bearing manager and ever-present dad Rafael, she remained tight-lipped about Leo as she gave the *Irish Sunday Independent* a little insight into her life. Strangely, for someone who stripped down to her underwear for a living, she revealed she was remarkably shy and didn't like attention.

'You know what?' she said, 'I was a very shy girl growing up. And I never liked the attention – you can tell today, I don't like attention. I wanna be left alone. And I don't like – even when people pay me compliments, I'm very shy about it. I feel more comfortable in front of the camera. I wear things that I wouldn't feel comfortable in normally, and I just take on a different character that is way more open and way more confident.'

She continued: 'And then I go home and I don't feel comfortable wearing too big of a cleavage and things like that – I'm just embarrassed. So I try to dress simple and keep simple. But when I do take photos, I like the attention.'

Warming to a theme championed by her boyfriend, she added: 'I think there are a lot of things in our world that need our attention. This is very dear to my heart, because I had a great childhood growing up at the beach. And if we're not going to create action, the contamination of the oceans and the water is going to lead to no beaches. It's not going to be safe anymore to go into the water. Eventually, we're not going to have sand, because we are destroying the coral reefs. It's going to be a problem for my kids, or for me to be OK with my kids to go swim in the ocean.'

Bar also spoke of her annoyance over the constant attention she and Leo received. 'I don't think you can ever get used to it,' she explained. 'It's not a normal thing to be followed or photographed, or [to] be aware of who is around you, looking at you. You can never feel so comfortable with it. But I try to live a very simple lifestyle, so I don't go to the places where I can be shot or followed, or seen. It's the way you want to live, basically. Don't go to the high-profile places. I wouldn't go to the main mall in Israel and I would not go to The Ivy in LA.'

And, although she refused to say how much influence Leonardo was having on her career choices, when the supermodel girlfriend came to talk about the future, she might have been reading from a script prepared by her actor boyfriend. Revealing plans to design a line for beachwear label Hurley, she said: 'I wanna grow and try new things. And it's also the things that I am passionate about. For instance, I love to do things that make me feel like I'm doing a good thing at the same time. You know, it's not just about money and career, it's also about contributing and helping to change something for the better.'

Meanwhile Leonardo was honoured at the eighth annual Cinema for Peace Gala in Berlin by former Russian president Mikhail Gorbachev, when the Nobel Prize winner presented him with an International Green Award. The pair collaborated on the *11th Hour* movie and the actor was clearly honoured by the recognition.

Although stricken with a virus at the time, DiCaprio recalled: 'My mother and grandparents are all from Germany and I will never forget that moment of joy as we sat around the television and celebrated with the rest of the world, watching as the Wall fell.'

'Years before [at age 12], I visited my grandparents in a divided Berlin and even then I was able to see how a simple wall threatened people's freedoms; my "Oma" took a picture of me in front of the

Wall, the moment we came back from the East side, and I immediately pretended to push the Wall down.'

It was a proud moment for Leo, who for years had been practising what he preached – setting up The Leonardo DiCaprio Foundation in 1998 to support environmental projects and collaborating with organisations such as the Natural Resources Defense Council and Global Green USA to foster awareness of environmental issues.

Leo had also bought an island in Belize, where he had grand plans for an eco-hotel. He had originally discovered Blackadore Caye island, just west of Ambergris Caye, while on holiday in 2004 at the nearby luxury Cayo Espanto resort. A year later he bought the private island with Cayo Espanto owner Jeff Gram for a reported $1.75 million and was working with Four Seasons to create a five-star luxury resort based on sustainable design and environmental conservation. Although this was yet to materialise, Leonardo was no hypocrite.

'People talk about personal action,' he said. 'I believe in personal action. It's great to recycle, it's great to do all these things but we should have some leadership here. It's now up to the powers that be to really do something and we're waiting on that, waiting on them.'

The actor then turned his speech to President Obama. 'In America,' he continued, 'we finally have an administration in Washington that wants to fight alongside you. I sincerely believe that President Obama will be proactive in combating some of the most complex environmental issues facing us. Realising the opportunities of a green revolution for our country will hopefully make America an environmental leader.'

The fight to save the planet was an on-going struggle, yet Leo must have wondered if a campaign wasn't being waged against him at home either. On his return to the US, he was further reminded of his obligations – should he ever intend to take his relationship with Bar to the next level. He was greeted by the news that if he did have plans to marry her, he would have to convert to Judaism first. According to boxing promoter Aaron Braunstein in the *New York Daily News*, Bar's father had told him: 'If Leo doesn't convert to Judaism, there will be no marriage.'

Such an ultimatum might not have been made to Leo personally but it seemed evident that as he prepared to film his next movie – Christopher Nolan's *Inception* – he had much to think about. Meanwhile, the controversy that looked to have died down surrounding Bar's draft dodging reared its head again. This time Israeli army officer Major General Elazar Stern was calling on Jews to boycott all products endorsed by the model because of her ruse to escape National Service. 'I called the companies and the managers of those companies, and they told me, "That's what the youths like,"' explained Major Stern in June 2009. 'I told them our job is to stress what the youths should like, not what they like now.'

It's highly unlikely this attempt to sabotage a young woman's career would have had any bearing on Leonardo's feelings but the ensuing controversy, plus the strength of feeling from Refaeli's family about the type of man she should marry, may well have been weighing on his mind. Just one month after the outburst from the Major, it emerged Leo and Bar had split up. The end of their three-and-a-half-year romance was as understated as it began. 'They're taking time off for the time being, they've split,' a source told *People* magazine. 'It could just end up as a break, but for now they're doing their own thing.'

The break-up came about after a weekend in June that saw the supermodel walk the red carpet at *Hollywood Life*'s Young Hollywood Awards solo, refusing to speak about DiCaprio. Meanwhile, Leo hit the hot Manhattan club Avenue, where he was seen chatting with another woman.

Although some reports claiming the couple had been spotted shopping in New York on the Monday after these events seemed contradictory, the *Sun* newspaper claimed the end had come following months of arguments over Leonardo's refusal to commit.

That he'd been spotted up to his old tricks in nightclubs, chatting to a series of beautiful women – including Hollywood car crash figure Lindsay Lohan – only added to their fractured relations.

The *Sun* quoted one source as saying: 'Leo was out partying in the city last week. He had a girl sitting on his knee and the two of them were drinking from the same glass. He was behaving very much like a single guy and Bar is now fed up with his behaviour. She wanted to see any sign of commitment from him but he just wasn't prepared to change his ways for her.'

On a second night out in the Big Apple, another witness revealed: 'He was getting hit on by a few girls and wasn't doing anything to discourage them. At one point he had his arms draped around a couple of them and later he had his hand on a girl's knee.'

And on a third night, a fellow reveller revealed: 'He slipped into a nightclub on Tenth Avenue with some of his male friends, trying to keep a low profile hidden under a baseball cap. A sexy blonde very quickly caught his attention and she attached herself to him for much of the night.

'He left without any female company at the end of the night, but the blonde headed for the exit shortly after he did.

And it didn't take long for Leonardo to be linked to another woman – surprisingly an attractive model – as it was claimed he'd been cosying up to British beauty Emma Miller, a former squeeze of *Desperate Housewives* star Jesse Metcalfe, while in London filming the sci-fi thriller.

He was then linked to his *Gangs of New York* co-star Cameron Diaz, recently single after splitting from her British boyfriend, Paul Sculfor. A source told the *Sun*: 'Leo is back on the pull after he split from his long term girlfriend Bar Refaeli. Cameron has been showing a lot of interest while he is in London filming. She was back at his rented apartment in Knightsbridge, West London, a couple of times last week after a series of secret dates. They were joking with friends that they played chess together.'

Bar could at least take consolation from the move by Rampage clothing brand to replace a certain Gisele with the Israeli, a clear indication her blossoming career was unlikely to be affected by the split with Leo, certainly in the short-term. Bündchen, incidentally, wasn't likely to be too disheartened either. She was expecting her first baby with New England Patriots quarterback Tom Brady, who she'd recently married in a small, private ceremony in Santa Monica, California.

But the Gisele connection was never far away as Bar was then bizarrely linked to one of the Brazilian's former lovers. Bündchen had famously turned to compatriot Ricardo Mansur, the polo-playing nightclub owner, while on the rebound from Leo and then appeared to unceremoniously dump him when DiCaprio renewed his interest.

Perhaps Bar was hoping for a similar outcome when allegedly spotted in a St Tropez hotel, according to a Brazilian showbiz website. 'On Saturday, they were all over each other at Hotel Byblos at the swimming pool bar, and then in a club later that night,' a source reported in the July. Incredibly, history seemed to repeat itself when just weeks later, the Ricardo effect did its trick and Bar was back with Leo.

Never mind that in the intervening period he had notched up links to Pussycat Doll Ashley Roberts and Refaeli's fellow *Sports Illustrated* swimsuit model, Anne Vyalitsyna. Although their reunion didn't come together in time for his birthday in November, by the end of that month they were on a secret break in the Bahamas at the Baker's Bay resort.

By the Golden Globes in January 2010 they joined George Clooney and others at the Paramount pre-awards party at the Chateau Marmont. However, Leonardo attended the ceremony – where he presented a Lifetime Achievement award to Scorsese – alone. Now reunited, their relationship seemed to be gathering momentum and Leo once again dropped hints about future plans when he said the idea of having children didn't seem 'too far-fetched'.

He also suggested life on location was lonely, describing how he had looked in his hotel room mirror and realised, 'how lonely you are, and how far you are from leading a normal life – that is quite a punch in the gut.' During such moments, however, he could at least console himself that he was trying to make a difference in the world. In addition to his environmental work and orphanage aid in Africa, he generously donated $1 million through his Leonardo DiCaprio Foundation to the fund to rebuild Haiti after the poverty-stricken nation was devastated by a massive quake in January 2010.

His 'extraordinary generosity' was hailed by Bill Clinton and President George Bush: 'This donation sends a clear message to the people of Haiti,' said President Bush, 'that America's commitment to helping rebuild their country is strong. I thank Leo for setting a wonderful example for all Americans of helping a neighbour in need.'

Meanwhile, the media believed it had still more positive DiCaprio news to report when Bar Refaeli returned from a luxury break she'd enjoyed with Leo on board a yacht off the coast of Cabo, Mexico, flashing a new ring on her left hand. Gossip columns were alight in the hope that Hollywood's most eligible bachelor was finally settling down.

Alas, it was a false alarm. Refaeli revealed the gold ring had been made by a pal and there was no truth to the rumours that DiCaprio had proposed over a romantic Valentine's dinner. 'No, there wasn't [a proposal],' she told E! Online. 'Let me explain: These rings – which are beautiful and made by a friend of mine – won't fit any other finger except this one. I'm 24 and there's still time [for marriage]. I'm in no hurry. I'm happy with where I am.'

Sometimes having a big movie about to be released could prove a combined blessing and curse. It allowed Leonardo to focus on what he did best, but also put him in the firing line when it came to questions about his private life. Thankfully, though, when *Shutter Island* was finally released – somewhat controversially, in February 2010 – he was able to concentrate on the business of moviemaking.

For DiCaprio and his director Scorsese, the lengthy delay in the movie's release was frustrating, especially as it prevented their latest work from benefiting from what would have been deserved hype. A trailer released in summer 2009 generated an early buzz and test screenings reported a healthy response, sparking speculation that *Shutter Island* could be a contender for awards, come Oscar season. However, Paramount surprised the industry in shelving plans for release in the October and instead put it back to February – too late for the Academy Awards. Theories put forward to explain the shock move were that Paramount didn't have the requisite budget to adequately promote the $80 million movie and that Leonardo's schedule meant that he wouldn't be able to give the film the support he desired.

Paramount Chief Brad Grey was forced to issue a statement reflecting the studio's stance in the midst of an economic downturn that was affecting the whole industry. 'Like every business, we must make difficult choices to maximise our overall success,' he explained. 'Leonardo DiCaprio is among the most talented actors working today and Martin Scorsese is not just one of the world's most significant filmmakers, but also a personal friend. Following a highly successful 2009, we have every confidence that *Shutter Island* is a great anchor to lead off our 2010 slate and the shift in date is the best decision for the film.'

Paramount settled on a date of 19 February 2010 because 'that's when *Silence of the Lambs* came out' back in 1991 and went on to win the Oscar. With the Academy expanding the Best Picture nominations to 10, the studio believed it was in with a chance. However, despite storming to No. 1 on its opening weekend, with takings of $41 million – DiCaprio and Scorsese's best box-office opening yet – and going on to make $295 million worldwide, it failed to make a dent in any of the award lists.

Even though it missed out on major awards, *Shutter Island* was Scorsese's highest-grossing film ever and further cemented the remarkable bond between himself and Leo. Already they were mulling over their fifth collaboration: a Frank Sinatra biopic, with DiCaprio in the lead. Despite this successful partnership, Leo continued to refuse to be drawn on comparisons to De Niro's relationship with the great director.

'That to me is the greatest cinema duo of all time,' he insisted, 'so I wouldn't dare even have that conversation.'

A conversation he also appeared to be ducking was his long-term plans with Bar. Over the next year, a depressingly familiar pattern emerged: every time Leo made a comment about his future plans to settle down, it was said he was ready to walk up the aisle and every time he was spotted in a nightclub talking to attractive girls, it was reported he and Bar were on the rocks.

It was all strangely reminiscent of the last months of his relationship with Gisele, which may perhaps not have been coincidental. Sources close to the star hinted that while he was very fond of Bar and loved her company, he continued to hold out for that spark – the feeling that told him he'd met the right person.

Occasionally he had to deal with situations not normally encountered by an ordinary couple. For instance, in March 2010, an Israeli nationalist group urged Bar to dump her American boyfriend and instead find herself a Jewish husband. Baruch Marzel, an Israeli politician, sent a letter to Bar on behalf of the Lehava organisation, saying: 'It is not by chance that you were born Jewish. Your grandmother and her grandmother did not dream that one of their descendants would one day remove the family's future generations from the Jewish people. Assimilation has forever been one of the enemies of the Jewish people.' Marzel added that he had 'nothing against Mr DiCaprio, who I have no doubt is a talented actor,' but added: 'Come to your senses, look forward and back too and not only the present. Don't marry Leonardo DiCaprio, don't harm the future generations.'

Such interference would have tested anyone but it was to Leo and Bar's credit they refused to rise to the bait, instead maintaining a dignified silence. And while they might have tried to go about their business quietly, that wasn't always as easy as it sounds.

CHAPTER 23

DREAM MAN

I t's one of the most annoying things that can happen on a trip to the cinema: you pay your money, choose your seat but when you get in the theatre you find there's some guy sitting in it.

At a showing of *Iron Man 2* at Century City, Los Angeles, one weekend in May 2010, three couples had the irksome task of shifting a baseball-capped man and his blonde girlfriend from their seats.

'Clearly they didn't realise you could reserve seats,' said one on-looker. Mercifully, the man took it all in good humour and, even by the third time, didn't cause a fuss about being asked to move. Thankfully the disruption was during the previews and, incredibly, no one seemed to recognise anything unusual about him. Even when a trailer started for a mysterious new sci-fi thriller called *Inception*, no one twigged that the man shuffling around the darkened cinema was none other than Leo DiCaprio, star of the cryptic new Christopher Nolan blockbuster being advertised on screen. He'd snuck in to catch a movie with Bar, hoping to quietly blend in – until he realised he'd made a mistake in not selecting their seats.

Only one eagle-eyed star-spotter was alert enough to tip off the *New York Post*, telling the paper that Leo and Bar were asked to move three times – 'Then, as the trailer for his new movie, *Inception*, began playing, they were asked to move again. They were gracious, Leo was smiling at the irony of it. They finally sat in the front row.'

Leo was used to being hassled in public but this was one of the few times it came about because he was inadvertently making a nuisance of himself. What was more remarkable is that just two months from then, cinema-goers would flock in their thousands to see his new movie, in what was to be his most popular on screen appearance since *Titanic*. No one would have asked him to move then.

Staggering in its scope, *Inception* was a science-fiction action heist movie conceived and directed by *The Dark Knight*'s Christopher Nolan, which had been nearly 10 years in the making. The director, who had made a name for himself with intelligent movies such as *Memento* that played tricks with the mind, first devised an outline about dream-stealers in 2001 but felt he needed more experience first. After the critically acclaimed *Batman Begins* (2005) and *The Dark Knight* (2008), he returned to his original idea and this time convinced Warner Bros to buy it. During the same period, Nolan had been courting DiCaprio about a variety of projects but couldn't quite convince him to work on any of them. When he approached the star about *Inception*, however, he had Leo's attention.

Nolan revealed: 'Leo is someone I had been trying to work with for years. I'd met him many times and nothing had come together, but I finally managed to convince him with this one.'

For Leo, the project had the three elements he always looked for – a great script, a great director and the chance to work with some great people. 'I want it to be special and really original,' he said. 'That's what I want, and I guess it would sum up the dream for any actor.'

Nolan's script focused on the idea of what would happen if we could share the same dream. Expanding that concept, he had devised the notion of dream extractors, those who are able to participate in and shape the dreams of others. With these skills, extractors can teach clients how to safeguard secrets locked away in their subconscious, or how to steal them from unfortified minds.

Leo was suitably intrigued and attempted to research in his usual diligent manner by reading philosopher Sigmund Freud's *The Interpretation of Dreams* and studying dream analysis but soon found the only way he'd get his head around what the film was really about was by sitting down with Nolan himself.

Although Leo's character Dom Cobb – the leader of the dream thieves, who agrees to take on one last job – was very much the foundation on which the movie would be built, Nolan wanted to assemble a cracking cast around him.

'I really wanted to put together a really great ensemble for this movie,' the director explained. 'Cobb is very firmly the emotional centre of the story but around him, we put together an incredible cast on screen. My ambition was to create a story and a world that embraced all different types of human experience, all the very different types of grand scale Hollywood entertainment that I like to imagine is going to come on screen when I sit in a movie theatre.'

From day one, he had kept the plot a closely guarded secret and actors under consideration had to read the script in his office or have it hand-delivered to their homes, where someone stood guard while they perused it. Eventually the supporting cast included Oscar winners Marion Cotillard and Michael Caine (making his fourth appearance in a Nolan film), Cillian Murphy, Ellen Page and Pete Postlethwaite.

The plot revolves around Cobb and his business partner Arthur (Joseph Gordon-Levitt), who use 'dream within a dream' strategies to perform illegal corporate espionage by entering the subconscious of their targets to extract valuable information. Dreamers are awakened either by a sudden shock or 'kick', or by dying in the dream. Each extractor carries a totem, a personalised small object to determine whether they are in another person's dream. Cobb's is a spinning top that perpetually spins in his dreams but these are plagued by memories of his dead wife, Mal (Cotillard), who frequently appears and tries to sabotage his efforts.

Cobb is wanted for questioning about his wife's death but wealthy businessman Saito offers his influence to clear him of charges in return for 'Inception' – the planting of an idea into the subconscious of a rival (Postlethwaite) so that he decides to break up his conglomerate. If successful, Cobb will be able to return to the US and be reunited with his children.

Although Arthur insists the job is impossible, Cobb assembles his dream heist team. In order for his ambitious plan to work, he needs an identity forger, a chemist and a young architect (Page) to build the dream sequences. While the team are able to infiltrate their target's mind, they must combat the defence mechanisms he has put in place to stop such an attack occurring. This leads to attacks within the dreams. Anyone who dies in a dream state will be locked in limbo, where they can lose their grip on reality and be forever trapped.

In a series of increasingly elaborate dream sequences, Cobb tries to achieve his objective, while also ridding himself of the guilt he feels over his wife's death. Eventually seemingly back in the real world, he is reunited with his children but as he uses his spinning top totem to test he is not dreaming, he becomes distracted by his kids before he can see the result.

In June 2009, filming started in Tokyo and altogether would stretch to over five months in six countries. From Japan, the action moved to England and to a converted hanger in Bedfordshire, where a set that could tilt 30 degrees was built. Nolan's designers also constructed a massive 100ft hotel corridor that could rotate a full 360 degrees. Joseph Gordon-Levitt (Arthur) spent weeks trying to fight as the corridor spun like 'a giant hamster wheel'.

Filming then moved to France, where some of *Inception*'s most iconic scenes were set and shot. Paris authorities blocked plans to use explosives for the bistro blast so instead Nolan used high-pressure nitrogen. The movie's most famous scene – where a Parisian street folds on top of itself – was one of the few shot using a CGI green screen, yet even with computer assistance the challenge was to accurately demonstrate what would happen if reality could flip on a hinge.

Leo found himself back in Morocco – where he'd filmed *Body of Lies* – as Tangier passed for Mombasa, where a dramatic foot chase takes place. The shoot then relocated to Los Angeles, where a Warner Brothers sound stage was used for interior shots and the city formed the backdrop for the car chase involving a freight train. Los Angeles was also the site of the climactic scene where a van falls off the Schuyler Heim Bridge in slow motion. For this, the actors were underwater for four to five minutes while drawing air from scuba tanks. Finally the crew moved to Alberta, Canada, where a deserted ski resort was transformed into a mountain top fortress. Production had to wait for a severe snowstorm to give Nolan the shots he wanted.

Nolan defended the scale of the production that ate up the majority of the $160 million budget: '*Inception* is a project that demanded this very large scale approach. As soon as you enter into the idea of what the human mind can conceive of; what world could it create, you want to see this on a grand scale.

'We shot in six countries and I think we experienced all the extremes from heavy rain to burning sun, to incredible snowfall. I really wanted to test ourselves by photographing things in real places. People actually being in the place – that adds a massive amount of credibility. Taking the actors up to the top of mountains, taking them underwater and just all over the place.'

He went on to praise the 'incredible amount of emotional focus' that Leonardo brought to his character and for the actor's part, although he relished the opportunity to work with 'an extremely talented director and so many different, unique talents', this proved to be another physically punishing shoot.

'Every week there was some new spectacle on set so there was a constant state of surprise for all of us,' said Leo.

For a movie that relied so much on its incredible special effects, Leo was proud to say there had been 'very little green screen' on it. 'If we were doing a scene that was tipping or upside down or floating in the air,' he explained, 'he would really do that.'

He added: 'I knew very early on that Chris was going to push all of us physically and it really became the norm. We expected the unexpected constantly. He had such a great stunt team and they really planned most of this out beforehand, so many of these insane action sequences, and you really felt comfortable and completely safe most of the time. There were no close calls but you read the script and you worry how you are going to do fight sequences in zero gravity or tumbling in an avalanche. You think, how is this guy going to pull it off? But he seems to make it seem easy. It's about trying to envelope yourself in the jigsaw puzzle of what *Inception* is, and our emotional journeys amidst this giant canvas of the dream world.'

For Ellen Page (who shot to fame on *Juno*) working with DiCaprio was 'an incredible experience'. 'He's someone I've watched since I was a little kid and have been inspired by,' she said. 'I think he makes wonderful choices and at one point in his career they were attempting to pigeon-hole him as a very attractive young man but he just always moved forward as an artist. He clearly is an actor because he loves to act and doesn't get involved in the circus of everything. To work with someone like that, who is also kind and very generous – and also funny – is a great experience.'

As someone who had a poster of Leo in her locker when she was just a school kid, Page appreciated the level of stardom he inhabits, but still admitted to being shocked to see how far his fame had reached.

'Leo is a f****** movie star,' she told the *Sunday Telegraph*. 'It was really insane to be in a place like Morocco in an area that seems semi-abandoned and have people yelling, "Leo, Leo!" I was maybe 10 or 11 when I saw *Titanic*. And, yes, I was a fan. I loved it.'

She also revealed how she and DiCaprio 'had great conversations about the ecological situation' on the set of *Inception* and his affiliation with the Natural Resources Defense Council, among other environmental groups in America prompted the actress to become a 'humble crusader' for renewable energy back home in Nova Scotia.

In July 2010, *Inception* premiered in London and aired to largely rave reviews. One of the major talking points was the ending, which prompted speculation that Leo's Cobb was trapped in a dream state as the top remained spinning. Nolan insisted the ambiguity was deliberate, imposing an ambiguity from outside the film. 'I've been asked the question more times than I've ever been asked any other question about any other film I've made,' the director said. 'What's funny is that people really do expect me to answer it.'

But he added: 'The real point of the scene – and this is what I tell people – is that Cobb isn't looking at the top, he's looking at his kids. He's left it behind. That's the emotional significance of the thing.'

Interestingly some comment was made by critics about Leo's preference for damaged or flawed characters but he stoutly defended his movie choices, where *Inception* and *Shutter Island* were concerned. 'There's nothing more boring than to show up on set and say a line and know that your character means exactly what they say,' DiCaprio declared during a news conference at the Beverly Hilton. 'It's interesting to have an unreliable narrator in a film, and that's what both of those films have been. Both of these characters are unreliable to themselves and the characters around them.'

Inception hit the top spot on its opening weekend in North America, earning a whopping $63 million – the second-highest grossing for an original sci-fi movie behind James Cameron's *Avatar*

(2009), which earned $77 million on its opening weekend a year earlier. It held the No. 1 spot for three weeks.

However, while Leo was earning plaudits for his acting ability, talk of his acting was put to one side when the public was once again reminded of the downside to fame. DiCaprio had to go court to seek a restraining order against a woman who believed she was his wife and was carrying his child – called Jesus.

According to papers filed with the Los Angeles Superior Court in August, he said he was frightened of the 'delusional' female and felt his personal safety was in jeopardy. Accompanying the documents were a number of hand-written letters to Leo from the woman, named as Livia Bistriceanu.

'Do you want to be with me for real and to be the father of Jesus? I've explained [to] you I can't be with nobody virtually. I have to have a father in reality for Jesus not like this,' read one of the letters obtained by celebrity website TMZ.com.

Eventually the court ordered Bistriceanu to stay at least 100 yards away from DiCaprio, but the restraining order was granted in the same week that another woman was ordered to stand trial in Los Angeles on charges of striking the star with a wine glass – the incident of 2005, as previously described, when he required stitches to his face and neck. The accused, 40-year-old Aretha Wilson, was extradited from Canada to face the charge and eventually jailed for two years.

Those unsavoury incidents aside, 2010 had been a productive year for Leo and *Inception* continued to exceed expectations, raking in a staggering $823 million worldwide, making it the 29th highest-grossing film of all time. It featured prominently in Best of Year listings and was among the most heavily nominated movies for awards in 2010. However, while it picked up four Oscars for technical achievements, it lost out on artistic merit to *The Social Network* and *The King's Speech*.

Bar Refaeli wasn't always visible on Leo's arm at awards

ceremonies, which led to still more speculation about their status, but she explained why this was. 'I am there for him and I am at all the events. I just don't walk in hand-in-hand with him,' she said. 'I don't see any reason. I don't need to strike poses with him in front of the cameras.'

Indeed the Israeli model was speaking with new maturity about her feelings, saying that in the six-month break from Leo, she'd become a lot stronger. 'It was half a year, for which I am very grateful,' she told Israel's *L'Isha* magazine. 'I needed it. I came to understand a lot of things about myself. I worked on myself [and] I grew up. I didn't know what "alone" was like. Today I know that a relationship can work only if you know you can be alone and you are not afraid. Today I'm not afraid of being alone.'

In a candid interview, she even spoke about how she'd tried to see other men during the time spent apart from DiCaprio but couldn't 'stomach' any of them. 'It was fun,' she revealed. 'I tried going out with this one and I tried going out with that one. I met men of the world. I told people, "Just so you know, I don't have much to give right now."

'But at the same time I felt a little bad because I thought, "When will this end?" I hoped that one day I would be able to give myself again to someone.'

Such maturity almost certainly deserved a statement of intent from her partner who, on and off, she had been with for five years. There was talk that Leo was on the verge of proposing, even getting Irmelin to help him choose a ring. Out of the blue he did make a very long commitment indeed – but it wasn't with supermodel Bar, it was with a 10-year-old tortoise.

While Leo continued to make up his mind whether he wanted to spend the rest of his days with beautiful Bar, he bought a reptile to keep him company. DiCaprio stopped off at the North American Reptile Breeders Conference and Trade Show in Anaheim, California in November 2010 to pick up the Sulcata tortoise, which cost him $400, *TMZ* reported. It was a big commitment from the actor as this creature can live up to 80 years old, weighing up to 200 pounds.

To the outside world, he appeared to be taking his girlfriend for granted but Leo continued to display great generosity in other ways. In November, he travelled to Russia to join a summit aimed at saving the tiger. He donated $1 million to the effort and arrived in St Petersburg despite horrendous flights. One plane was forced into an emergency landing after losing an engine; the other had to make an unscheduled stop after encountering strong headwinds. His dedication to the cause prompted Russian Prime Minister Vladimir Putin to describe him as a 'muzhik' – real man.

His interest in the plight of tigers might have generated a lot of coverage but it was the on-going saga with Bar constantly intriguing the media. When Leo and Irmelin arrived in Israel in the November to meet her parents, Bar had to be patient as sources insisted this was simply a vacation. The following month, it was suggested Leo was even considering conversion to Judaism so that he could fulfill her father's wishes and pave the way to a marriage but still there was no proposal.

They spent New Year's Eve at a private villa he'd recently acquired in Cabo, Mexico, and attended a star-studded party that included Naomi Campbell and her boyfriend, Russian billionaire and property mogul Vladimir Doronin, Kid Rock, Nicky Hilton and fiancé David Katzenberg, Paris Hilton and boyfriend Cy Waits, top art dealer Tony Shafrazi, Jessica Alba, Dori Cooperman and Jennifer Worthington.

Perhaps the final straw came when Leo and Bar surprised actress Penelope Cruz at her baby shower. Girl friends of the actress, who was expecting a baby with *No Country for Old Men* star Javier Bardem, threw a party at a Hollywood mansion, but a source revealed that, 'Leo wanted to show up to surprise her.' Most girls know that a good way to tell if their man is thinking about one day having children of his own is if he gets excited around other new parents but if Leonardo was feeling broody, he wasn't letting on.

Inevitably, the news broke in May 2011 that DiCaprio and Refaeli had split up. Once again, there was no formal announcement but this time it looked permanent. Like Gisele before her, Bar must have realised she was in danger of becoming an old woman before Leo decided to propose.

A source told the *New York Post*: 'It was amicable, they're still friends and they are still talking. They just grew apart and went their separate ways. Neither are ready to settle down, and both have busy careers that have been taking them in different directions.'

Much was made of comments Leo had made about the uncertainty of marriage, after he'd witnessed other friends tying the knot, only for the unions to fail.

He explained: 'I don't know whether I'll ever get married. I've seen too many supposedly happy marriages go down; I've been as shocked as anyone. No one can look at the marriages of other people and make a judgement. I don't know the private lives of the actors I work with, I just know if they are good actors or good directors.'

Whatever the reasons, the facts were simple – one of the world's most eligible bachelors was available once more… but not for long.

CHAPTER 24

LOOKING LIVELY

B lake Lively might not have known it then but although her meeting with Baz Luhrmann did not result in a starring role in his lavish adaptation of *The Great Gatsby*, she had successfully auditioned for another key role – that of Leonardo DiCaprio's girlfriend. And the *Gossip Girl* star was about to discover what it was like to be in the midst of real-life speculation.

That dinner in Manhattan's The Lion restaurant in November 2010 did much to propel the talented blonde into the big league. Nothing might have happened until Leo had finally extricated himself from his five-year on-off affair with Bar Refaeli, but that night the groundwork was laid for a second screen test with the actor.

The 24-year-old actress – Serena van der Woodsen in the teen TV drama series – had just come out of her own relationship with fellow *Gossip Girl* star Penn Badgley, who played Dan Humphrey. However, the dinner with Leo was hardly romantic – six other people joined them, including director Luhrmann, who had already cast DiCaprio as Jay Gatsby in his keenly-anticipated 3D version of F. Scott Fitzgerald's classic examination of America's idle rich during the Roaring Twenties.

Luhrmann's 'whole crew was there,' said source for *Us Weekly*. Lively was in the running for the role of tragic heroine Daisy Buchanan, a part coveted also by, among others, Scarlett Johansson and Keira Knightley. Eventually the role went to British actress Carey Mulligan, suggesting that Luhrmann was perhaps influenced by the performance of the similarly elfin Mia Farrow in Jack Clayton's 1974 film version, which also starred Robert Redford.

It was a setback for Blake but Leo had an almost immediate opportunity to commiserate with her when they both attended the 40th birthday party of *Hurt Locker* actor Jeremy Renner at his house in The Hills, just two months later. The two spent a long time on the balcony flirting, with Bar nowhere to be seen (she was believed to be working). Again, there was no suggestion that anything between them began that night, but friends weren't completely surprised when Blake and Leo met up again at the Cannes Film Festival in May, just one week after his split with Refaeli.

What was surprising was how relaxed Leo was about being seen in public with a new girl. DiCaprio and Lively were seen roaming around the Hotel du Cap Eden Roc on the Friday night, looking very much together. Rumours were further fuelled that they were an item after they enjoyed an intimate trip on Steven Spielberg's luxury yacht in the French Riviera.

As someone who was normally reticent about being seen with a new love interest, especially so early in a courtship, this was a dramatic departure for Leo – and indeed his behaviour had friends wondering what had hit him.

A source told the *Sun*: 'Leo and Blake are getting on brilliantly. They're definitely at the early flirty stage, although Leo does seem more smitten than her. He got pretty drunk and proposed to her but she laughed it off, saying it was the worst proposal she'd ever had. Before she arrived on the yacht, Leo was chewing Steven's ear off about being in love.'

From Cannes, the couple moved on to Portofino, that much-loved romantic destination of the jet set, on the Italian Riviera before taking in the delights of Monte Carlo.

Yet, while the pair were getting to know each other better in some of Europe's most romantic hotspots, Blake was, like many of DiCaprio's women before her, getting a taste of what it means to be Leo's love interest.

A series of pictures emerged apparently showing her posed naked. Five photos of a naked busty blonde taking snapshots of herself with an iPhone in front of a bathroom mirror spread among major gossip websites, prompting celebrity blogger Perez Hilton to predict: 'Blake Lively won't be happy about this.'

In four of the pictures, the woman's face was partially concealed by her phone. A fifth was too blurry to be sure. The early-generation iPhone seen in the pictures and a different shaped nose suggest the pictures were several years old and cast doubt on whether it was indeed Blake. A spokeswoman moved quickly to deny her client being in the pictures, branding the images '100 percent fake' before insisting, 'Blake has never taken nude photos of herself.'

If the furore was upsetting for Blake, she wasn't showing it as she joined Leo at a party for the Monaco Grand Prix. One on-looker told *Us Weekly*: 'He looked very in love. Her face lit up when Leo was talking. He had introduced Blake as his girlfriend. I would say they're totally smitten!'

Evidence certainly seemed to suggest so. Leo, in particular, seemed to be on a mission to impress as his tour continued to Venice, where they took a trip around the famous canals in a water taxi. DiCaprio also treated the actress to a helicopter ride to Saint-Paul de Vence for a stay at the $5,000-a-night suite at Hotel de Paris and a trip on a $52 million yacht in a display of opulence that left stunned friends.

'I've never seen him like this with a girl,' said one. 'Being charmed by him isn't the worst thing in the world!'

For Blake – who, like Leo, was raised in Los Angeles around people in the entertainment industry – it must have seemed like a dream come true. She had held a torch for her new boyfriend ever since *Titanic*. Blake had posters of the heartthrob on her bedroom wall and said in an interview back in 2008: 'I had a premonition when I was nine that I would marry Leonardo DiCaprio'. And her fairytale romance continued when DiCaprio agreed to join her as she attended the MTV Movie Awards in June 2011. Afterwards the couple and a group of friends enjoyed a late-night trip to Disneyland.

As love blossomed, the tabloids and celebrity websites pored over former interviews with Blake for indications that Leo was 'the one'. 'I like someone who makes me laugh. I enjoy someone that's really fun,' femalefirst.co.uk quoted Lively as saying in an indication that she and DiCaprio were perfectly suited. 'I'm very domestic. I love art, painting, interior decorating, baking,' readers learned about the girl who had seemingly captured Leo's heart. 'There are so many things I want to do in my life. I'd love to open restaurants and have an interior decorating business,' she said.

But Blake had her own movie to promote – the blockbuster *Green Lantern* (2011) based on the DC Comic books – and she told US NBC's *Today* show that she believed she was equipped to deal with the extra stuff that comes with having a celebrity boyfriend. 'You know getting into this business what comes into it,' she explained. 'You do it for the art, for the wonderful work that we get to do. Otherwise you keep your head down, you keep to yourself.'

In another interview she added: 'I don't comment on my relationships. My anonymity is something I treasure. Wanting to be an actor and wanting to be famous are different.'

But, aside from the constant coverage in the gossip columns, her relationship had its upside. Just weeks after she started dating DiCaprio, Blake was revealed as the brand ambassador for British designer Stella McCartney. A source revealed that McCartney believed Lively, who was an animal lover like Leo, would be the perfect ambassador for her company in America. 'Like Leonardo,

Blake is an animal lover and believes in cruelty-free fashion so when she met Stella at the Met Ball last month, she found they shared many of the same ideals,' a source told the *Daily Mail*.

As the relationship progressed, the honeymoon period showed no sign of ending. Although some unkind reports surfaced claiming Blake had apparently bombed during a meeting with Leo's mum, the actress seemed to be a permanent fixture at his Malibu home, with the pair barely setting foot off the property for two weeks. And, when Blake had to be back in New York (where she was spending nine months of the year filming *Gossip Girl*) Leo went with her, meeting her for dinners after she finished shooting.

As interest in the couple only intensified, one of the more bizarre claims was that Blake had employed the advice given in the cult manual *The Rules* by dating coaches Ellen Fein and Sherrie Schneider to win DiCaprio's heart. According to *Now* magazine, Lively following the rules of attraction to the letter, keeping him keen by not calling him, making him jealous and acting 'busy'. 'Blake knew Leo could have any girl he wanted and she figured she had to stand out from the crowd,' a 'friend' was quoted as saying. 'Blake told him he had to break up with Bar before she'd even go on a date with him, so he did. She's making him work for it – and he's fallen hard for her.'

He had the incredible career, but did he finally have the girl? Only time would tell, but Leo certainly seemed to be having more fun than in recent years. There was an air of contentment about him, too as he prepared to face the press about another movie role, one that had already caused controversy before anyone had even seen it.

CHAPTER 25

THE MOST POWERFUL MAN IN AMERICA

A close relationship with his mother, a desperate need to escape his surroundings, the power to do what he wanted from a young age and a desire to safeguard his privacy in the face of unbearable scrutiny – if someone was planning a movie on Leonardo DiCaprio's life, these are all themes that would be ripe to explore.

Yet it was Leo who found himself examining these particular issues to understand the character of a man whose public profile was much more ambiguous than the Hollywood superstar's.

After *Inception*, he had waited a year and a half for the right project to come along. Though he was offered plenty of scripts, nothing caught the imagination or was tied to the right director. Manager Rick Yorn then drew his attention to a script on the first director of the FBI – J. Edgar Hoover. Clint Eastwood was directing a potentially controversial biopic on the man considered to be more powerful than any of the eight US presidents he served under.

Hoover rose to power shortly after the First World War and remained in office until his death in 1972. Yet, while he revolutionised crime fighting, pioneering the use of forensics and centralising fingerprint databases, he abused his power and was eventually accused of using the FBI to harass opponents and serve his own ends.

After his death, there was much speculation about Hoover's private life but given his position, the era in which he lived and the presence of a disapproving mother, he could never have admitted to an alternative lifestyle. Yet, while Leonardo could acknowledge the ever-so-slight similarities in character he shared with Hoover, he was quick to point out significant differences. 'The difference is that Hoover's mother told him what to do, and my mother listened to me,' he said. 'My mother was incredibly supportive.'

Hoover lost himself in his own ego and his need to be the centre of attention. But something Leo had learned, albeit the hard way in some regards, was that success could be temporary. 'It's not something that I actively worry about,' he insisted. 'I'm fully aware that every career is fleeting in some respects.'

One thing he was sure about was the appeal of the script. 'There aren't a lot of great scripts out there,' he continued, defending a hiatus almost as long as his time off after *Titanic*. 'After *Inception*, I waited a year and a half to find this movie and I pounced on it. Because the types of film that are getting financed are not dramas, like J. Edgar.'

Credit for the screenplay that had so attracted the actor went to Dustin Lance Black, the Oscar-winning writer on gay activist Harvey Milk. It was 2008 when he first had the idea of writing a warts-and-all biopic on the life of the FBI chief. He'd immersed himself in research, speaking to as many people who knew the man as possible but while he was left staggered by some of the personal revelations, he was also somewhat surprised by how much Hoover polarised opinion.

'A lot was written when it was just hip to vilify J. Edgar,' said Black. 'And the books contradicted each other so often. Some would come out and tell you he wore dresses to parties; others would say that's impossible and he was so dedicated to his work, he was married to the FBI.'

Over the years, many had speculated about Hoover's sexual preference and whether he was a cross-dresser. After his research, Black was convinced the FBI chief was a closet gay – 'Reading his mother's journal entries made it quite clear you were not allowed to be a gay kid in that household.'

Although Eastwood – who had already picked up two directing Oscars for *Unforgiven* (1992) and *Million Dollar Baby* (2004) – had his own ideas about the script, originally titled *Hoover*, DiCaprio was kept informed throughout the process and when Eastwood was happy, quickly jumped aboard. He immediately threw himself into research, travelling to Washington, DC, to see where Hoover had lived and worked. 'I went on a little tour of his life – his childhood home, his bedroom, his workplace,' Leonardo said. 'I walked through his daily routine, saw his office, met the historian at the FBI – they have an incredible amount of respect for him and rightfully so. He did a lot of wonderful things for our country, and also some pretty heinous things.

'He's always been somebody I never could quite put my finger on,' he noted, before adding, 'one of the most incredibly ambitious human beings I've ever heard of. The more I researched him, the more intrigued I became.'

'He's intensely curious,' said screenwriter Black of the actor. 'He had a team looking for video of Hoover and found things I'd never seen. He'd pull me aside and say, "Listen to this speech! Can we get that in there?"'

One example was the frequent animal metaphors that DiCaprio discovered Hoover had loved. On one occasion, during a speech on criminals, he told a Congressional committee: 'We must not for a moment forget that their squirming, their twisting and slimy wriggling is no less than an assault on every honest citizen.' Black said: 'We put a lot of slithering, slimy, snaky words in those speeches.'

Even with superstar talent like Eastwood and DiCaprio attached, the financing for such a movie wasn't forthcoming. Warner Brothers were keen but only for a specific budget, eventually capped at $35 million. To make the film possible, Leonardo generously agreed to a pay cut, from his usual $20 million to just $2 million.

For that – and his brave career choices – he earned his director's respect. 'He could have made a lot of money just doing spectacle movies with all kinds of CGI,' Eastwood noted. 'But he wants to vary his career, like I've always looked to vary mine as a director.'

The 39-day shoot began on 7 February 2011 in downtown LA. By that time seasoned hands Dame Judi Dench (Hoover's overbearing mother) and Naomi Watts (secretary Helen Gandy) were hired, along with *Social Network* star Arnie Hammer (as the loyal protégé and perhaps love interest, Clyde Tolson).

A tight time schedule and small crew meant the shoot was a challenging one. For example, when a house was bombed in one scene, the whole set had to be transformed within an hour from an unscathed building into a bombed-out version during the dinner break.

To replicate the Department of Justice where Hoover had his office, a set was built in Warners' stage 6. Everything had to be meticulously planned beforehand because there was little margin for error.

'With Clint,' explained Leo, 'you prepare, you prepare, you do an incredible amount of research and it's like getting ready for a stage production because you move at an unbelievably fast pace and it keeps you on your toes. But then you get this instant adrenaline rush.'

The role demanded that DiCaprio age from 24 to 77 years old and to transform himself into the aging Hoover, he had to sit for up to seven hours a day in make-up. Leo said: 'The physical transformation with the make-up becomes incredibly claustrophobic. I wanted to take it off as soon as possible.'

Fangs FX – a company that made teeth for the Harry Potter films

– produced upper and lower dental implants for the actor using ceramic pieces to plump out his mouth to mirror Hoover's famous bulldog jaw. DiCaprio asked for the lower set of jaw implants even when he was playing the younger man because it helped him mimic his voice.

Sian Grigg, who has worked with Leo since his starring role in *Titanic*, said J. Edgar was his most challenging transformation to date. She revealed to *Hollywood Reporter* how to mirror Hoover's hair loss, DiCaprio wore a full silicone bald cap with individual hair strands punched through. A toupee was then glued on top of that cap before both layers were blended together.

DiCaprio also wore two pairs of coloured contact lenses – one on top of the other. One set was brown, the other set were yellowed lenses, which aged the whites of his eyes. Hoover's nose also protruded as a result of an infected boil from his youth, so Grigg inserted a circular augmenter in one of DiCaprio's nostrils to make his nose look slightly off-centre.

All over the actor's face were placed super-soft silicone appliances, which Grigg said were so soft they were hard to apply. 'They are like pieces of Jello,' she explained, 'but they enable the face to move like real skin.'

To portray the older, more rounded Hoover, the usually slim Leo had to wear moulded latex on his body so that it felt like his own flesh. And as his character aged, so too did the fat suit expand. Despite being overweight, Hoover was very fashion conscious and during production, DiCaprio wore 80 suits, several custom-made from vintage fabrics for authenticity.

Grigg revealed she had a real battle on her hands because DiCaprio looked so very different from Hoover, but she added: 'We wanted him to look like Hoover, but not in a way that was distracting.' Yet, for all her hard and ingenious work, she paid tribute to Leo's performance in bringing the make-up to life: 'Layers of prosthetics are like acting with a paper bag on your face and Leo had to learn to exaggerate his expressions so they would show through the appliances. I really believed he was old, and I stuck it on his face.'

Leo might have been spared hours in the make-up chair because producer Robert Lorenz offered to use CGI for the aging process. 'We discussed the idea of relying on visual effects, to make it easier for the actors,' said Lorenz. 'But Leo was insistent – he wanted to be sure it was going to look right.'

DiCaprio had actually wanted to bulk up for the role but time wouldn't allow it. However, so he wouldn't overheat under all the prosthetics, the set was chilled like an ice hockey arena. Co-star Miles Fisher (who plays Agent Garrison in the movie) said: 'It's so much make-up. I think Leo was there for six hours each time and they had to keep the set really cold.'

The part also meant Leonardo had to memorise endless monologues that needed to be delivered with Hoover's own breakneck cadence. Additionally, DiCaprio once again had to pucker up with a man – *and* wear a dress.

Before the crucial scenes with Hoover and Olson were filmed, Arnie Hammer spoke of his anticipation about locking lips with Leo. He said: 'It's not a kissing scene, it's a ton of kissing scenes. I actually just met him for the first time at the DGA Awards. He's a talented actor. I'm not nervous or afraid of it being awkward. The script is great – the scenes are in there for a reason.'

For those working with Leo for the first time, it was a revelation to see the star – now approaching legendary status for his performances in *Titanic*, *The Aviator* and *Blood Diamond* – in action. Indeed Eric Matheny (who plays Doc Ferguson) was amazed by the generosity he showed to lesser names.

'He's a great actor, that's sort of a given,' Matheny said. 'We all know that from his movies as well. I have some friends who are friends of his. I didn't know him before the shoot, but I'd heard he's a really great guy and man, it's really true.

'The way I like to work is, when the scene starts, I'm another person. I'm in a different time, and I'm just going to live and see what happens and deal with the moments that are thrown me. And when you're working with someone like Leonardo DiCaprio, he really throws you some beautiful moments – looks and gestures and intensity that really gives you something to play off of. He's a very giving actor in that way.

'He and Clint and I, in one of the scenes, we were talking, along with Dustin Lance Black. And Leo says, "Oh, there's a line in here, maybe Doc Ferguson should say something to me." And Clint's like, "Oh, what would he say exactly?"

'Then we start talking and I improvise a couple of lines. Then Clint improvises a couple of lines. Then we find the right line and Clint's happy with it and is like, "OK, let's do it." And it was just really collaborative.'

By the time filming had switched to Washington, DC, and then to Virginia, the scenes that would cause the most controversy were in the can and Hammer reported the same-sex smooch 'wasn't that weird.'

Sounding a little like DiCaprio way back when he had to kiss Thewlis in *Total Eclipse*, Hammer told ET Canada: 'It's the same kind of thing as if you walk onto a set and they hand you a machine gun and [say], "Shoot this like you know what you're doing" – you can't grab that thing and go, "uhaEUR" – you kind of have to go, "OK, I know what I'm doing," and you've just got to go for it. It wasn't that weird – I have never kissed a guy – it's not something I'm going to do in my private life, but at the end of it I was, like, man, there is a lot of weird hype.'

With production ending on 30 March, Eastwood then embarked on an unusually long editing phase as he brought the picture down from a rough cut of three hours to two hours and 15 minutes. He never shied away from Hoover's more controversial aspects, though – to the relief of his scriptwriter.

'I'd wondered how Clint would treat [the homosexuality],' pondered Black. 'But when we were shooting and I saw the tenderness with which he approached some of those scenes, I felt I was in very safe hands.'

The cross-dressing scenes would prove the most contentious, with Hoover supporters claiming the rumours were malicious. But Eastwood said: 'All along the way, people accused him of being a cross-dresser, but nobody knows how accurate it was. Evidently the woman who accused him of that, her husband had been sent to the slammer by Hoover. So you don't know how much was vengeance.'

The claims first surfaced in Anthony Summers' 1993 biography, *The Secret Life of J. Edgar Hoover*, and then US President Bill Clinton once joked when trying to choose a new FBI director that it would be 'hard to fill J. Edgar Hoover's pumps.' Eastwood himself believes 'there is a certain amount of truth' in all the allegations, but wanted to retain some ambiguity. While there is just one passionate kiss between DiCaprio and Hammer, Hoover's relationship with Tolson is a central theme. In real life, all Washington knew was that the pair dined daily together, vacationed together, did everything but move in together, and so the whispers flew. In the movie, however, Hoover is depicted donning one of his mother's dresses after her death.

Eastwood tried to move attention away from Hoover's private life, claiming the movie's main focus was how a young man (Hoover was just 29 when he became director of the Bureau of Investigation in 1924) survived to become the 'most powerful guy in the country at a time when America was by far the most powerful country' in the world.

As Leo concurred: 'I think that's the essence of this story – absolute power corrupts absolutely. Here's a man who created the most advanced police force and investigation system the world has ever known. But then as time went on, his obsession with Communism took over. No one else has had such a position of power for that long – to blackmail presidents, to wiretap political leaders, to be able to manipulate the world around him. It was scary.'

While the movie was still being edited, the jungle drums in Hollywood started beating that this could be the year when Leonardo DiCaprio would finally win an Oscar. Previously having been three times nominated, he was in danger of stealing Marty Scorsese's crown as the 'nearly man', but the buzz from the studio was that Leo's performance was so compelling, he would get the Academy's vote in 2012.

After a period of relative calm in his career came a flurry of activity. Leo was being linked to every major project in Tinseltown. That he would link up with Scorsese again was practically a given, but the identity of their next collaboration ranged from *The Wolf of Wall Street* – a film of the life of Jordan Belfort, a former trader who ended up in jail in the 1990s for defrauding investors out of millions of dollars – to a biopic on the life of Frank Sinatra.

Leonardo was then linked to a remake of *A Star is Born* – the movie that Judy Garland made her own in 1954 – also directed by Eastwood and featuring Beyoncé in the lead role. It was also confirmed that he would star as Calvin Candie, the evil villain in Quentin Tarantino's controversial Western about slave trading, *Django Unchained*. His production company, Appian Way, was said to be behind a move to bring Don Winslow's best-selling novel, *Satori*, to the big screen. DiCaprio was considering the role of protagonist Nicholai Hel in the Warner Bros project, which follows the post World War II tale of a Westerner trained in Japanese assassination skills.

Leo was also understood to be interested in playing Enigma code-breaker Alan Turing in a biopic of the British mathematician called *The Imitation Game*. Turing was prosecuted by British authorities after the war for having a sexual relationship with another man and forced to undergo 'chemical castration' instead of being sent to prison for his sexuality. The genius computer scientist committed suicide by eating an apple laced with cyanide – a tragedy that inspired Steve Jobs to name his company Apple in tribute.

Given the way his career had been propelled in recent years, it was little wonder that Leo was confirmed as Hollywood's highest earning star in 2011, earning a staggering £75 million and remarkable given he'd only released two movies in a year – *Inception* and *Shutter Island* – though both were monster hits. He replaced Johnny Depp at the top of the earners' list and the two heartthrobs would also be going head to head in the race for honours, it seemed.

With that news, it came as no surprise that DiCaprio was being linked to every worthwhile project – in many ways he was now the most powerful actor in Hollywood.

Following the announcement that the Hoover movie – by now called *J. Edgar* to remove any confusion with the former president or the vacuum cleaner – would premiere at the American Film Institute's annual AFI Festival in LA on 3 November 2011. Leo was now a serious contender for an Oscar nomination. Also in the running was Depp for *The Rum Diary*, Brad Pitt (*Moneyball*, the basement underdog story), Ryan Gosling (for either *Drive* or the George Clooney-directed *Ides of March*) and Gary Oldman in the latest adaptation of *Tinker Tailor Soldier Spy*.

It wasn't long before controversy was surrounding the release of *J. Edgar*, however. Just weeks before the premiere, the FBI came out to refute any suggestion the film might make about Hoover's sexuality.

Assistant FBI Director Mike Kortan said he'd met with Eastwood and DiCaprio and assured them there was 'no evidence in the historical record' that Hoover was gay. Denying the Bureau had been trying to influence the tone of the movie, Kortan said it had provided the information so the film was 'accurate'.

In fact, groups of former agents have campaigned forcefully against any depiction of the long-rumoured sexual relationship between Hoover and former top aide, Clyde Tolson.

'There is no basis in fact for such a portrayal of Mr. Hoover,' William Branon, chairman of The J. Edgar Hoover Foundation, wrote to Eastwood. 'It would be a grave injustice and monumental distortion to proceed with such a depiction based on a completely unfounded and spurious assertion.'

The Society of Former Special Agents of the FBI fired off a similar missive, saying a 'rumored kissing scene' reported in early media accounts involving the actors portraying Hoover and Tolson, 'caused us to reassess our tacit approval of your film.'

After the premiere, Leo responded by insisting it was obvious that Hoover was more than just friends with Olson. 'You talk to the FBI, they'll tell you, "Absolutely not. These men were of service to their country,"' he told *The LA Times*, 'and you talk to another crew of people, and they say, "Absolutely, without question. These men vacationed together, they lived together. Hoover left Mr. Tolson everything he had when he passed away." You know, come on! These two men spent almost every minute together for decades.'

Although the reviews were mixed, with critics divided between those who considered the movie a triumph and others who thought it lacked cohesion, one thing many were united on was in praise for DiCaprio.

'A roaring wonder as J. Edgar Hoover,' was how *Rolling Stone* rated Leonardo's performance, while reliable cheerleader Roger Ebert in *The LA Times*, praised his 'fully-realized, subtle and persuasive performance, hinting at more than Hoover ever revealed, perhaps even to himself.' Elsewhere, *OK! Magazine* raved that DiCaprio again, 'proves to be a chameleon capable of tackling any task set before him,' while the *Hollywood Reporter* saluted a 'vigorous, capable performance, one that carries the film.'

The buzz around Leo's performance appeared justified – but did it mean that his 19-year wait for an Oscar might soon be over?

CHAPTER 26

THE MODELISER

While *J. Edgar* was sparking controversy back in the United States, on the other side of the world, Leo and Blake were about to face the biggest test of their short romance.

In August 2011, he travelled to Australia to begin filming *The Great Gatsby* after Luhrmann chose to shoot the $150 million epic in his native homeland rather than the US. The Australian government had offered a 40% tax rebate if Luhrmann moved the operation Down Under and also provided funding from its enhanced film fund that made it cost-effective to switch from the US. In return, it was estimated the movie would make $120 million for the New South Wales economy.

The Great Gatsby stands as one of the great American classics and many take the view that the 1974 adaptation starring Robert Redford and Mia Farrow cannot be bettered. However, Luhrmann – whose *Romeo + Juliet* defied expectations – felt the current economic climate made it the perfect time for a story whose central theme is a critical look at the lifestyles of the wealthy. Indeed it was a view shared by DiCaprio, who was instantly cast as the enigmatic lead, Jay Gatsby.

'I thought it was poignant. Gatsby is an idealistic man trying to embody the American Dream and become wealthy fast,' he said, 'all for the love of Daisy, of course. But it's very interesting to see what's going on now. We've been living in the Roaring Twenties and it's all starting to come crashing down.'

The film gave Leonardo the chance to work with Luhrmann again for the first time since their radical interpretation of Shakespeare's tragic love story. They had attempted to collaborate on an epic on Alexander the Great but that project had fallen by the wayside when a rival movie from Oliver Stone (starring Colin Farrell) went into production first. In keeping with Luhrmann's innovative streak, his latest film was to be produced in 3D – a concept usually reserved for sci-fi blockbusters and animation – but Leonardo defended the use of 3D on this project.

'*The Great Gatsby* is a voyeuristic novel where you feel like you're a fly on the wall with these incredibly intimate moments – all these people in a room,' he explained. 'Baz comes from theatre, and he knows what has more dramatic intensity as far as who is in front of the stage and who is in back. He's simultaneously able to put three different characters in focus; it is like watching theatre.'

The movie also gave Leo the chance to work with his closest buddy, Tobey Maguire (who takes on the role of Nick Carraway, the narrator). The two leads were joined in filming by Indian superstar Amitabh Bachchan, Isla Fisher, Jason Clarke and newcomer Elizabeth Debicki.

British actress Carey Mulligan, who surprised many in the industry by winning the role of Daisy, showered praise on DiCaprio for helping her land the part. 'Leonardo is the most incredible actor on the planet, with a couple of people alongside him,' she declared. 'I walked away from my audition for that and I couldn't believe that I'd been acting with him.

'We did 15 takes of one scene. He didn't really have much dialogue as Gatsby, and the camera was never on him, but he played three other characters. He'd say a line as Gatsby, and then he'd jump up and play Tom Buchanan.

'We were doing the scene with the cameras over my shoulder, and he was lighting a cigarette for me and looking at me. It was all me, and he didn't have any words, and he was improvising stuff to say, just to help me. I was like, "Leonardo DiCaprio doesn't need to be helping me in this audition." He was auditioning girls all day. I was so blown away by how generous he was, let alone being amazing to act with.'

Although Luhrmann initially chose to film in New York – and even relocated to the Big Apple ahead of production, enrolling his family in a local school, he switched to Australia. To recreate the glittering Long Island and New York of the Jazz Age, sound stages at Fox Studios Australia were transformed. In addition, a fleet of vintage cars, including a pair of 1929 Duesenbergs and a 1929 Packard to be used by DiCaprio's character and rumoured to be worth up to $3 million each, were shipped in from a museum in Illinois.

Lurhmann wrote the screenplay from Fitzgerald's novel, with longtime writing partner Craig Pearce, while his collaborator (and wife), Catherine Martin, was doing production and costume design. Filming was to take place over 17 weeks and would feature over 400 cast and crew.

DiCaprio settled into a $10,000-a-week mansion in the eastern suburb of Vaucluse, Sydney, for his four-month stay and at the first opportunity, Blake flew out to join him and celebrate her birthday. Between visits to an ice-cream parlour, the couple appeared to make good use of his five-bedroom, five-bathroom waterfront home, which came complete with an infinity edge pool and a private jetty to park a super yacht.

They also stunned staff at the city's Featherdale Wildlife Park by turning up and asking for a tour. 'We only knew when they arrived,' Featherdale marketing manager Kellie Ames said. 'I made sure I was the one who escorted them when I saw it was Leo – I'm a big fan of his movies. They were both so nice and down-to-earth. There was certainly no diva behaviour. Leo was asking about the endangered animals, Blake was absolutely beautiful.'

Clearly Leo and Blake were enjoying each other's company and seemed to revel in behaving like any other normal couple – if 'normal' means being able to fly to any destination in the world at a moment's notice. Which was why it was all the more surprising when, just as quickly as it had begun, the romance was all over. Representatives for both confirmed they'd split up and said the pair would 'remain friends' but no further indication as to why the five-month fling had fizzled out was forthcoming.

If Leonardo was left with a broken heart, he set about mending it in the only way he knew how: by enjoying the company of another beautiful woman. No sooner had the news ink dried on reports that he and Blake were no longer an item than he was said to be dating Australian model, Alyce Crawford.

A 21-year-old former contestant on *Australia's Next Top Model*, Crawford had met Leo at a local hotspot, Beach Haus, which had become one of DiCaprio's favoured hangouts since arriving in Sydney. She denied there was anything going on between them when asked but described him as 'a lovely, lovely guy.' 'We have a lot of mutual friends and he seems really nice. We're just friends,' she said. Alyce was to discover she'd be the first in a line of beautiful, and quite similar-looking, models that Leo would attach himself to during the remainder of his time in Oz as he seemed to live up to his reputation as a serial dater.

Just as Leo fans were getting their heads around that development, it was said he had the hots for another model, this time 20-year-old Kendal Schuler. A dead ringer for Bar Refaeli, Schuler was a runway girl who had apparently first met the actor in Los Angeles but got reacquainted in Beach Haus.

Blake also seemed to have shaken off the effects of her sudden split by hooking up with her *Green Lantern* co-star Ryan Reynolds, who for a brief time could say he was the husband of Scarlett Johansson before their split in December 2010.

Leo responded by inviting one of Italy's hottest underwear models – a woman considered to be one of the most beautiful in the world – to hang out at his Australian mansion. Romanian-born Madalina Ghenea even sampled some paddle boarding at the actor's digs but like his other recent companions, it didn't seem as if she would become a permanent fixture.

Back in New York, DiCaprio was delighted to learn his hard work on *J. Edgar* had been rewarded with a Golden Globe nomination – his eighth in total. As predicted his rivals were Ryan Gosling (*The Ides of March*) and Brad Pitt (*Moneyball*), they were joined by George Clooney (*The Descendants*) and Michael Fassbender (for his critically acclaimed performance in *Shame*). The nominees gave an indication as to who DiCaprio could be up against when it was the time for the Academy to announce its contenders, with French actor Jean Dujardin (nominated in the Musical/Comedy category for his role in the feel-good silent movie *The Artist*) also a good bet for the Oscar.

While back in the Big Apple, Leonardo returned to form and flanked by old pal Lukas Haas and *Inception* co-star Joseph Gordon-Levitt, he attended a Victoria's Secret party, where willowy ballet dancer and model Karlie Kloss caught his eye. His undoubted charms might not have worked on Karlie but he did seem to strike it lucky at the event. Just a few days later her fellow Victoria's Secret Angel, Erin Heatherton, jetted in to Sydney from New York to join him as he returned to Australia to continue filming shortly before Christmas.

Just 22, the graceful fashion model – born Erin Bubley – who hailed from Skokie, Illinois, stands at 5ft 11in, just half an inch shorter than DiCaprio. And she gave an indication that she was certainly about to add some cheer to Leo's festive celebrations after diving into an upmarket underwear store in the city, where she snapped up almost £1,100 worth of lingerie.

It was Carrie Bradshaw in the cult TV series *Sex and the City* who coined the phrase 'modeliser' to describe those men who only date models and watching DiCaprio's antics in Australia caused many to wonder if she might have had the actor in mind.

Although it seemed like he was having a lot of rebound fun after his split from Blake, blonde Erin appeared to be sticking around – for the short-term, at least. Leonardo felt sure enough to make plans to introduce her to his mother over the Christmas period when he was back in Los Angeles, with brunch booked at the Four Seasons hotel on New Year's Eve, just the three of them. He would be bidding goodbye to a year of change, but ultimately one of success.

After filming wrapped, Erin joined her actor boyfriend when he finally flew home to America. After four months of hard work Down Under, Leo was jetting out of Australia, having left a lasting impression on the country's modelling community.

And as 2012 dawned, he had a lot to look forward to. With *Titanic* hitting the big screen again and a model girlfriend on his arm, it was easy to look at the life of Leonardo DiCaprio and reflect that somehow the more things changed, the more they stayed the same.

EPILOGUE

WHEN the nominations for the 2012 Academy Awards were announced early one January morning, one name stood out – but it was noticeable only by its absence.

Leonardo DiCaprio, who only 10 days previously had narrowly lost out on a Golden Globe to George Clooney, was mysteriously overlooked in the Best Actor category. Commentators had predicted that his convincing portrayal of J. Edgar Hoover was a safe bet for a nod but his omission stunned moviegoers. *The New York Times* labelled it a 'snub', while social networking site Twitter was ablaze with condemnation for the Academy for once again ignoring one of the world's most popular actors.

Instead the nominations went to Clooney for his performance in *The Descendants*, Jean Dujardin (who also picked up a Golden Globe for *The Artist*), Brad Pitt (*Moneyball*), surprise package Demián Bechir (who played an illegal immigrant gardener in *A Better Life*) and Gary Oldman for *Tinker Tailor Soldier Spy*.

Shortly before the nominations were announced, Leonardo admitted that he'd love to bag an Oscar, though perhaps sensing the writing was on the wall for another year, added that it wasn't what motivated him. Hollywood's highest paid actor might have been nominated for an Academy Award three times previously, but he simply stated: 'I don't think anyone would say that they wouldn't want one – I think they would be lying. I don't think I ever expected anything like an Oscar ever, to tell you the truth. That is not my motivation when I do these roles.'

Despite the snub, the future was already looking bright for the star who'd made his showbiz debut aged two and had grown up to be one of the most powerful men in Hollywood.

By Valentine's Day he was back on our screens, going through 'torture' once again as Jack Dawson in *Titanic*, revamped in a 3D format that Leonardo described as 'fantastic.' Ahead of the movie's re-release, which had its full launch in April, producer John Landau gave him a sneak preview. And, just as he had 12 years before, he was knocked out by the presence of his leading lady, Kate Winslet.

'He watched the scene where Kate arrives at the dock and steps out the car, and he said to me, "She's so beautiful,"' Landau revealed. Leo would be reunited with Kate for the premieres of the new version. Indeed theirs is an on-screen partnership that has endured like few others since the golden age of Fred and Ginger, Katharine Hepburn and Spencer Tracy, as well as Lauren Bacall and Humphrey Bogart.

With a budget of $18 million for the 3D element alone, the re-issue will cost more to release than many new independent films but there is little doubt it will make millions again at the box office, earning the stars another healthy pay-check through their original contracts and introducing Leo to a whole army of new fans.

Yet, although another bumper payday loomed, money was also not a motivating factor. 'Throughout my career, I never knew which movies of mine made money and which didn't,' DiCaprio explained. 'When *Titanic* came out, people would say, "Do you realise what a success this is?" And I'd say, "Yeah, yeah, it's a hit."

The money stuff never mattered to me until I was into my thirties and got interested in producing.

'But even now I say that unless you want to prove that you can carry a film with your name, continuously trying to achieve box-office success is a dead end.'

That said, it seemed box-office success was something Leonardo looked set to achieve for the foreseeable future. And, as he looked forward to another incredible year in his acting career with *The Great Gatsby* and *Django Unchained* due for release on Christmas Day and productions of *A Star is Born* and a biopic on Frank Sinatra in the offing, it was a good time for the talented actor to take stock of what still drove him to make great movies.

'I really am motivated by being able to work with great people and create a body of work that I can look back on and be proud of,' he said. 'I grew up when I was 15, when I had my first opportunity in movies. I watched every great movie for a year and a half, and since then I've asked myself how I can emulate such artistry. That's really my motivation – I want to do something as good as my heroes have done.'

And he has revealed, Leonardo harbours dreams of emulating his heroes, among them Martin Scorsese and Clint Eastwood, by following in their footsteps to make the transition into directing. He said: 'If I did direct, I would try to have the same straightforward approach to it as Eastwood and his crew have. There are no frills on his set, it's a small, tight-knit crew.'

For the leading ladies in his personal life, Leo appears almost as unattainable and enigmatic as ever. At the recent Golden Globes he showed once more that it would take someone truly special to dislodge his devoted mother Irmelin from his side, as she accompanied him to the Awards.

But, as he looks to a future filled with promise, Leonardo had a message that will gladden the hearts of his millions of fans. 'If I have anything to complain about, I should really pack up and set up shop in some other state in the middle of the forest and disappear,' he declared. 'I'm getting to live my dream. I hit the lottery in the sense that I get to do what I love, choose the projects that I want to work on and try to be the actor that I always dreamed of being. All the other stuff that goes with it – the loss of autonomy, the intrusion into your private life – is a small price to pay at the end of the day and I feel I have been able to handle it pretty well and hopefully I'll continue to do that. As far as quitting anytime soon is concerned, that is just not on my agenda. I love doing this too much.'

One thing is for sure: Leonardo DiCaprio looks like being King of the World for some time to come.

FILMOGRAPHY

Django Unchained (2012) as Calvin Candie
Directed by Quentin Tarantino
Screenplay by Quentin Tarantino
Released by The Weinstein Company/Columbia Pictures
Cast Jamie Foxx, Christoph Waltz, Joseph Gordon-Levitt,
Samuel L. Jackson

The Great Gatsby (2012) as Jay Gatsby
Directed by Baz Luhrmann
Screenplay by Baz Luhrmann and Craig Pearce
Released by Warner Bros
Cast Carey Mulligan, Tobey Maguire, Isla Fisher,
Amitabh Bachchan

J. Edgar (2011) as J. Edgar Hoover
Directed by Clint Eastwood
Screenplay by Dustin Lance Black
Released by Warner Bros
Cast Armie Hammer, Naomi Watts, Josh Lucas, Judi Dench

FILMOGRAPHY

Inception (2010) as Cobb
Directed by Christopher Nolan
Screenplay by Christopher Nolan
Released by Warner Bros
Cast Ken Watanabe, Joseph Gordon-Levitt, Marion Cotillard,
Ellen Page

Hubble 3D (2010) Narrator
Directed by Toni Myers
Written by Toni Myers
Released by IMAX Filmed Entertainment

Shutter Island (2010) as Teddy Daniels
Directed by Martin Scorsese
Screenplay by Laeta Kalogridis and Steven Knight
Released by Paramount Pictures
Cast Mark Ruffalo, Ben Kingsley, Michelle Williams,
Patricia Clarkson

Revolutionary Road (2008) as Frank Wheeler
(nominated Golden Globe for Best Actor)
Directed by Sam Mendes
Screenplay by Justin Haythe
Released by Paramount Village
Cast Kate Winslet, Michael Shannon, Kathy Bates, Richard Easton

Body of Lies (2008) as Roger Ferris
Directed by Ridley Scott
Screenplay by William Monahan
Released by Warner Bros
Cast Russell Crowe, Mark Strong, Golshifteh Farahani,
Vince Colosimo

The 11th Hour (2007) as narrator and producer
Directed by Nadia Conners and Leila Conners Petersen
Screenplay by Nadia Conners, Leonardo DiCaprio and Leila
Conners Petersen
Released by Warner Independent Pictures
Featuring Stephen Hawking, Mikhail Gorbachev,
Thom Hartmann

Blood Diamond (2006) as Danny Archer (nominated Academy
Award for Best Actor/Golden Globe for Best Actor)
Directed by Edward Zwick
Screenplay by Marhsall Herskovitz, Graham King, Paula Weinstein
and Edward Zwick
Released by Warner Bros
Cast Djimon Hounsou, Jennifer Connelly, Michael Sheen,
Arnold Vosloo

The Departed (2006) as William "Billy" Costigan Jnr (nominated
BAFTA for Best Actor/Golden Globe for Best Actor)
Directed by Martin Scorsese
Screenplay by William Monahan
Released by Warner Bros
Cast Matt Damon, Jack Nicholson, Mark Wahlberg, Martin Sheen,
Ray Winstone, Vera Farmiga

The Aviator (2004) as Howard Hughes (winner Golden Globe for
Best Actor, nominated Academy Award for Best Actor, nominated
BAFTA for Best Actor)
Directed by Martin Scorsese
Screenplay by John Logan
Released by Miramax Films
Cast Cate Blanchett, Alan Alda, Alec Baldwin, Kate Beckinsale,
John C. Reilly

FILMOGRAPHY

Catch Me If You Can (2002) as Frank Abagnale Jr. (nominated Golden Globe for Best Actor)
Directed by Steven Spielberg
Screenplay by Jeff Nathanson
Released by DreamWorks
Cast Tom Hanks, Christopher Walken, Amy Adams, Martin Sheen

Gangs of New York (2002) as Amsterdam Vallon
Directed by Martin Scorsese
Screenplay by Jay Cocks, Steven Zaillian, Kenneth Lonergan
Released by Miramax Films
Cast Daniel Day-Lewis, Cameron Diaz

Don's Plum (2001 – filmed in 1995) as Derek
Directed by R.D. Robb
Screenplay by Bethany Ashton, Tawd Beckman, R.D. Robb, David Stutman, Dale Wheatley
Released by Polo Pictures
Cast Kevin Connolly, Jenny Lewis, Tobey Maguire, Amber Benson

The Beach (2000) as Richard
Directed by Danny Boyle
Screenplay by John Hodge
Released by 20th Century Fox
Cast Virginie Ledoyen, Guillaume Canet, Robert Carlyle, Tilda Swinton

Celebrity (1998) as Brandon Darrow
Directed by Woody Allen
Screenplay by Woody Allen
Released by Miramax Films
Cast Hank Azaria, Kenneth Brannagh, Judy Davis, Melanie Griffith, Famke Janssen

The Man in the Iron Mask (1998) as King Louis XIV / Philippe
Directed by Randall Wallace
Screenplay by Randall Wallace
Released by United Artists/Metro-Goldwyn-Mayer
Cast Jeremy Irons, John Malkovich, Gabriel Byrne,
Gerard Depardieu

Titanic (1997) as Jack Dawson (nominated Golden Globe
for Best Actor)
Directed by James Cameron
Screenplay by James Cameron
Released by Paramount Pictures/20th Century Fox
Cast Kate Winslet, Billy Zane, Gloria Stuart, Bill Paxton,
Frances Fisher, Kathy Bates

Marvin's Room (1996) as Hank
Directed by Jerry Zaks
Screenplay by Scott McPherson, John Guare
Released by Miramax Films
Cast Meryl Streep, Diane Keaton, Robert De Niro

William Shakespeare's Romeo + Juliet (1996) as Romeo Montague
Directed by Baz Luhrmann
Screenplay by Craig Pearce, Baz Luhrmann
Released by 20th Century Fox
Cast Claire Danes, Brian Dennehy, John Leguizamo,
Pete Posthlethwaite, Paul Sorvino

Total Eclipse (1995) as Arthur Rimbaud
Directed by Agnieszka Holland
Screenplay by Christopher Hampton
Released by New Line Cinema
Cast David Thewlis, Romane Bohringer

FILMOGRAPHY

The Basketball Diaries (1995) as Jim Carroll
Directed by Scott Kalvert
Screenplay by Bryan Goluboff
Released by New Line Cinema
Cast Lorraine Bracco, James Madio, Mark Wahlberg, Bruno Kirby

The Quick and the Dead (1995) as Fee Herod 'The Kid'
Directed by Sam Raimi
Screenplay by Simon Moore
Released by TriStar Pictures
Cast Sharon Stone, Gene Hackman, Russell Crowe

Les cent et une nuits de Simon Cinéma (1995) as a Hollywood
actor (uncredited)
Directed by Agnes Varda
Screenplay by Agnes Varda
Released by Mercure
Cast Michel Piccoli, Marcello Mastroianni

The Foot Shooting Party (1994) as Bud
Directed by Annette Haywood-Carter
Screenplay by Kenneth F. Carter
Released by Buena Vista Pictures
Cast Jake Bussey, Michael Rapaport

What's Eating Gilbert Grape? (1993) as Arnie Grape (nominated
Academy Award for Best Supporting Actor/nominated Golden
Globe for Best Supporting Actor)
Directed by Lasse Hallstrom
Screenplay by Peter Hedges
Released by Paramount Pictures
Cast Johnny Depp, Juliette Lewis, Mary Steenburgen,
John C. Reilly

This Boy's Life (1993) as Tobias 'Toby' Wolff
Directed by Michael Caton-Jones
Screenplay by Robert Getchell
Released by Warner Bros
Cast Robert De Niro, Ellen Barkin

Poison Ivy (1992) as Guy (as Leonardo Di Caprio)
Directed by Katt Shea
Screenplay by Andy Ruben, Katt Shea
Released by New Line Cinema
Cast Drew Barrymore, Sara Gilbert, Tom Skerritt, Cheryl Ladd

Critters 3 (1991) as Josh
Directed by Kristine Peterson
Screenplay by David J. Schow, Rupert Harvey, Barry Opper
Released by New Line Cinema
Cast Aimee Brooks, Don Keith Opper, John Calvin, Nina Axelrod

TELEVISION

Growing Pains (23 episodes, 1991-92) as Luke Brower
Parenthood (12 episodes, 1990-91) as Garry Buckman
Roseanne (one episode, 1991) as Darlene's classmate (uncredited)
Santa Barbara (five episodes, 1990) as Young Mason Capwell
The New Lassie (one episode, 1990) as Young Boy
The Outsiders (pilot episode, 1990) as Kid Fighting Scout

PRODUCER

Akira (2013) (producer)
The Ides of March (2011) (executive producer)
Red Riding Hood (2011) (producer)
Orphan (2009) (producer)

FILMOGRAPHY

Greensburg (2008) (TV series) (executive producer and writer)
The 11th Hour (2007) (documentary) (producer and writer)
Gardener of Eden (2007) (producer)
The Aviator (2004) (executive producer)
The Assassination of Richard Nixon (2004) (executive producer)